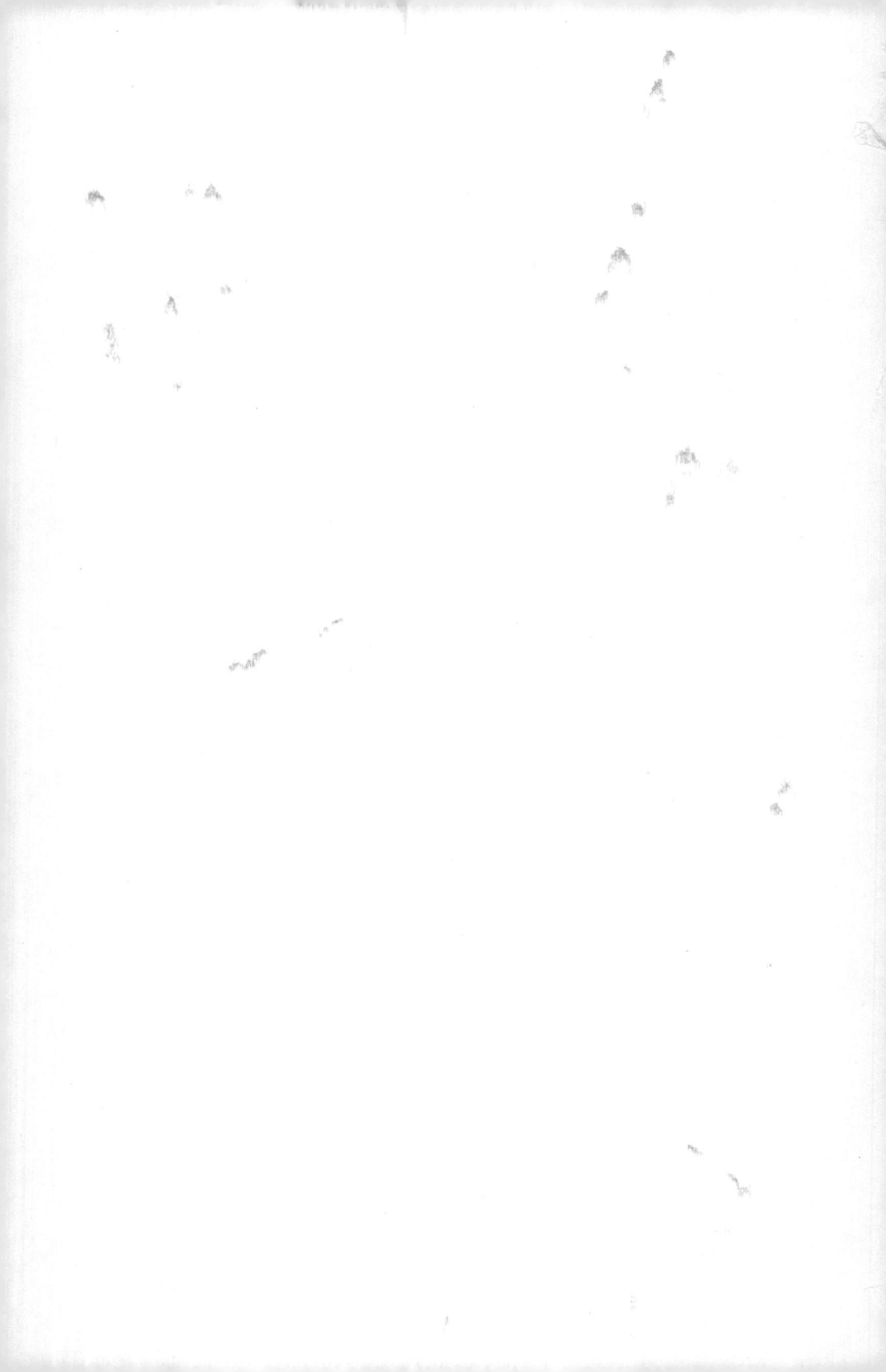

THE MERITOCRACY PARADOX

The Meritocracy Paradox

WHERE TALENT MANAGEMENT STRATEGIES GO WRONG
AND HOW TO FIX THEM

Emilio J. Castilla

Columbia University Press
New York

Columbia University Press
Publishers Since 1893
New York   Chichester, West Sussex

Library of Congress Cataloging-in-Publication Data
Names: Castilla, Emilio J. author
Title: The meritocracy paradox : where talent management systems
go wrong and how to fix them / Emilio J. Castilla.
Description: New York : Columbia University Press, [2025] |
Includes bibliographical references and index.
Identifiers: LCCN 2024061760 | ISBN 9780231208420 hardback |
ISBN 9780231557429 ebook
Subjects: LCSH: Personnel management | Organizational behavior |
Merit (Ethics) | Prejudices
Classification: LCC HF5549 .C337 2025 | DDC 658.3—dc23/eng/20250515

Cover design: Noah Arlow

GPSR Authorized Representative: Easy Access System Europe,
Mustamäe tee 50, 10621 Tallinn, Estonia, gpsr.requests@easproject.com

CONTENTS

PREFACE

In today's world, we constantly navigate selection and screening processes that shape our opportunities in life—whether securing a bank loan, gaining acceptance to a training or educational program, landing a job, or launching a business. I did too. And I am deeply grateful to institutions like the European Union educational scholarship, Lancaster University in the United Kingdom, La Caixa Foundation in Spain, Stanford University, the Wharton School (UPenn), and MIT Sloan, among many, for their opportunities to help me advance and build a successful career. Without their support, I would not be where I am today. A sequence of selection processes and outcomes ultimately led me to my current role as a faculty member at MIT.

Similarly, this book underwent its own rigorous selection process before Columbia University Press chose it for publication. Once I had a strong book prospectus and a few chapters ready, I started to carefully consider which publishers would be the best fit for a book like this. After researching their missions, editorial teams, and back catalogs, I narrowed my choices down to three leading publishers in the social sciences. To have a "fair chance," I did my homework in following their websites' submission guidelines closely when putting together the required materials.

In full disclosure, I approached all three publishers simultaneously, submitting the same materials with the same level of enthusiasm. Each of them advertises proudly that their publication review process relies on rigorous peer review. And this was an important factor for me: I wanted my manuscript to be reviewed by experts in the field who were best positioned to constructively assess and help me improve the work. I did not hire an agent or third party to represent me or my work. Nor was I even interested in having publishers "bid" for the book. I simply wanted the book to be evaluated on its merits.

Through my research, I was already familiar with the challenges organizations face today in maintaining fair, meritocratic, and effective organizational processes. Unsurprisingly, I found that the world of publishing is also vulnerable to potential inefficiencies and inconsistencies when evaluating manuscripts. My experiences with the three publishers varied greatly. One editor (editor 1) promptly expressed great interest in the book and asked for the prospectus. Upon receiving it, the editor wrote back briefly to say: "*Many thanks for sending the proposal. It's a great topic and having read the proposal just now, it looks terrific. . . . I'd love to send it out for review.*" I wrote back, "*Go for it, please.*" And I never heard back from them.

The second press never responded to my initial or follow-up email inquiries. Following the instructions on its website, I patiently waited for several weeks for an editor to consider my submission. Eventually, I received a stock response saying: "*We are grateful to receive a high volume of submissions. . . . If you do not receive a response from a member of our editorial team within this time frame, we encourage you to pursue other publishing opportunities for your work.*" After a third email attempt, one editor (editor 2) provided a more personalized rejection, writing, "*It's a great topic, for sure, and I think the structure of the book makes good sense. . . . But I'm not sure that it's quite right for my list here, so I'm going to pass.*" The editor wished me good luck "*in finding a good home,*" adding, "*I am certain there are other top presses that will be interested.*" That was encouraging.

The third press, Columbia University Press, handled the process differently. From the outset, it was clear that this press had a structured and diligent process for evaluating book prospects. Of the three publishers, Columbia University Press was the most responsive and transparent in outlining its process. The editorial director, Eric Schwartz, not only expressed interest in the book but also clearly explained the steps that he and the press would follow to determine whether or not to move forward with the project. These steps included selecting a panel of expert reviewers, gathering their detailed feedback and publication recommendations, and convening an evaluation committee to assess the external reviews and the manuscript itself before making a decision. This structured process stood in contrast to the more opaque approaches taken by the other two publishers, where decisions appeared to rely on individual discretion (this is speculation, given my limited information about the process though); such as editor 2's reasoning, "*I am not sure that it's quite right for my list.*" Two of these editors never shared any reviews they may have received of the manuscript.

I am going to leave it up to you to decide which editor made the best, most meritorious decision. You now hold this book in your hands, and I hope its insights will help you critically assess and improve how you and your organization make talent management decisions.

The core mission of *The Meritocracy Paradox* is to help readers understand why well-intentioned organizational processes and practices aimed at advancing and rewarding the best talent often fall short—and, crucially, how to fix them. This book is for leaders, researchers, and professionals who are committed to fostering truly meritocratic and equitable workplaces, where individuals are given equal opportunities to thrive, regardless of their demographics or personal backgrounds. It is for anyone dedicated to improving workplaces and organizations where all can work and succeed. And it arrives at a moment when merit, once again, is the "word of the moment."[1]

I look forward to learning how you take the warnings and the frameworks of this book to the next level—whether in research, for scholars interested in further investigating the challenges of meritocracy, equity, and diversity inside organizations, or in practice, for professionals and leaders striving to build more effective and fair talent management systems within their organizations. More than anything, I hope this book encourages organizational leaders and professionals to foster organizations that offer great educational and professional opportunities to all. That, in essence, is the true meritocratic aspiration behind my work.

***

For the past twenty years of my academic career, I have studied real-world examples of merit-driven and talent-based organizational processes, as well as related individual and social factors influencing who gets access to education, training opportunities, and ultimately good jobs with good companies. Some friends and colleagues would likely argue that I was doing so even earlier when I decided to emigrate to the United States, leaving loving parents and siblings behind in Spain with the goal of pursuing my American dream in a country that has historically cared more about intelligence, ability, and effort than about who your parents are, where they came from, or what their position in society is. Drawn to the alluring melting pot of the United States, I was excited to join Stanford University and Silicon Valley in the mid-1990s—a place often referred to as the Land of Meritocracy, even the Capital of Meritocracy. Little did I know my experiences there would become the motivation for decades of subsequent research.

I became the type of social scientist who loves getting inside real businesses and institutions to investigate how organizational processes affect employment and education outcomes in organizations and labor markets. I then produced, together with amazing collaborators, research articles for top journals in our field. Such articles take a long time to get done and published. They go through rigorous scrutiny because top peer-reviewed journals strive to publish novel and empirically rigorous work that advances our knowledge in the social sciences. Such studies are and must be purely scientific—which is why our opinions, ideologies, values, or aspects of our personal lives do not appear in them. They are erased from the review process—they are subjective and don't contribute to the scientific method. The same often applies to business leaders and professionals, who are expected to keep their personal beliefs separate from their professional lives and get work done for the benefit of their organizations and businesses.

But, just as with speeches and presentations, prefaces and acknowledgments can give academics some freedom to show a warmer and more human side. In this preface, I am going to tell you how I came to write this book, while describing the contexts in which my academic and professional adventures have taken place. My hope is that my personal story can stimulate students and professionals who are currently trying to advance not only their own careers but also the careers and lives of others.

As an economist and sociologist, I am interested in combining the two disciplines to study phenomena in business and the public interest. In general, my work aims to study the effects of social and organizational factors—such as social networks, personal relationships, demographics, hiring and performance evaluation processes—and the role of individuals in charge of making employment-related decisions within organizations and businesses. As a researcher at MIT Sloan, I dedicate myself full-time to the world of research and teaching while providing, when possible, advice on economic, business, and social issues. It is a privilege to be surrounded by bright, innovative, entrepreneurial faculty, staff, and students. This environment also comes with huge responsibilities.

However, I can't honestly claim that being a professor at MIT was a dream come true for me. I had never dreamed of such a career in my earlier life. When I started college, I had no plans other than graduating and getting a good job, like most. In fact, I was among the first in my family to complete college; that was already a huge achievement. I never expected that I would get a scholarship from the European Union to study abroad during my undergraduate education, let alone get the opportunity to pursue a PhD in a prestigious university thousands of miles away. Why would a kid born in the suburbs of Barcelona ever want to leave home to pursue a doctoral program abroad? Back then, I did not even know much about what professors do or how to become one. And once I began to understand the landscape of academia, the probability that someone like me would become a professor seemed unthinkable, unaffordable, and unattainable. I didn't even know, when I was a child, that there was a university like Stanford—where I ultimately got my PhD—or that there were business schools like Wharton or MIT Sloan, where I could be a researcher and a professor encouraging hundreds of students each year to pursue their professional dreams. The reality is that when I was growing up, dreaming was discouraged. There were too many other serious concerns affecting families, like paying the mortgage and bills, raising kids, and taking care of loved ones.

Even though my elementary and high school teachers wanted us to get a good education and have a successful career, none would have imagined that one of their students, a very shy one, would become a full professor in the social sciences or write a book such as this. I grew up in a satellite town along the Barcelona metropolitan belt, Santa Coloma de Gramanet, "Santako." Coming from a working-class family, I always attended public primary and secondary schools. I then went to a crowded public University of Barcelona with old classrooms; it was a place where there was little enthusiasm and motivation for learning and teaching in general.

My story, however, is not unique. It is similar to the story of other colleagues and friends who currently teach at the best institutions in the world. Many are also leading organizations and businesses. Many of us were born and raised in humble homes without resources to spare, without any type of social privilege. But our homes were undoubtedly rich and generous in values and principles such as respect, solidarity, honesty, loyalty, responsibility, and hope. They were homes that invested in their children's education so that they might have better lives than their ancestors and help create a better world.

I still remember the enthusiasm with which I started college at the University of Barcelona while living at my parents' apartment in Santako. How eager I was to experience learning and research at the university. I studied very hard during high school because I was determined to learn and have a good professional career. I came to believe that it was important to get excellent grades and to obtain outstanding scores in the standardized tests then (and still) used to determine who would gain access to excellent educational and employment opportunities. Studying hard was fully under my control.

I could have pursued any career I wanted because my high school grades and standardized test scores were extremely high. I could have gone into medicine, law, engineering, or any other field. I note this humbly to make the point that I was indeed highly motivated to work hard and get good grades in high school to secure a spot in a good college and get a good education. I did not want to be an *obrero* (a manual laborer) because I knew that was an extremely hard life to live.

I agonized for months over which university and major to go into. At the time (still true to a certain extent), we had to decide our university major at the age of seventeen, which felt like a humongous decision.[2] Millions of graduating high school students face similar decisions every year. Ultimately, I decided to list the School of Economics and Business at the University of Barcelona as my number one choice. This school has a long tradition of having trained many of the best economists in Spain. It has always been large; today, it has more than 9,000 students, with 500 lecturers and 100 staff members.

I decided to become an economist at a time when many other young people also wanted to be economists. The rise of professions such as economists, executives, and businesspeople in Spain was imminent, as Mauro F. Guillen argued in his 1989 book *La Profesión de Economista: El Auge de Economistas, Ejecutivos y Empresarios en España* (The Profession of Economics: The Rise of Economists, Executives, and Businesspeople in Spain).[3] As an economist, I dreamed of perhaps becoming a consultant for a major firm, traveling to help companies become more successful. Or I dreamed of working at a renowned banking institution such as La Caixa or Banco Sabadell. I simply wanted to learn in school and then get a good job in a good company that would pay me for my abilities and my work, and not for how many pieces of output I was able to manufacture on the assembly line. But things changed a lot in college.

My college experience was unlike what I had imagined. Enrollment was large and completion rates were low, with students lingering for years without completing their degrees. Many lecturers did not seem motivated to teach us, and many of my peers appeared uninterested in learning. Nobody seemed to be excited about higher education.

This all changed when, two years before graduating, I received a European Union (EU) scholarship to attend Lancaster University in northern England. At its Management School, I studied economic, sociological, and psychological theories that can help us understand how companies, markets, and public policies work. I was surrounded by highly motivated students and professors who wanted to share their research ideas. I remember thinking, "So this is what college is supposed to be."

I graduated as an economist in 1995 and moved to the United States the same year to pursue a PhD. It was not an easy transition, but thanks to mentors who saw some potential and promise in this introverted yet hardworking recent graduate, I had the opportunity to cross the ocean and be blown away by *Amerika*.[4] With this move, I understood that I was taking a real first step toward becoming an academic. But I was intimidated. I had stepped into the unknown, with my still-developing English abilities, and with no one I knew to keep an eye on me. I left my youth and my dearest family behind to learn and continue learning—in new schools, with new colleagues and friends, and new heroes to admire. It was a huge privilege to earn a PhD at Stanford University and then to secure my first academic job as a faculty member at the Wharton School. These accomplishments changed my life and shaped who I am today.

All this makes me feel very thankful. I don't feel lucky in that I don't believe it is fortune but rather tenacity, effort, and intelligence that help us succeed. However, I must acknowledge too that I did benefit from organizational and social structures that value talent and ability, that give opportunities to succeed, and that seek to reward merit. That was certainly what I found when I moved to the United States: "the land of opportunity," a society where, with talent, you can climb the rungs of the social ladder, where inequalities are more pronounced but so are the opportunities to succeed in life. I was totally sold on that message at the time. Thus, I arrived at the promised land of opportunity in 1995, whose promises soon became aspirations to achieve, aspirations that required more effort and hard work.

I am not trying to sell you on the idea (and privilege) of living in *Amerika,* or in any other developed society or region. The United States has its problems and challenges, which have become quite evident, unfortunately, recently. But the United States and its educational and corporate systems have been part of my American dream—like the dreams of many other immigrants and born citizens. It is a land where one is (and should be) valued for one's knowledge and training, professional success, ideas, work, and contributions, and where one is not *entirely* judged by country of origin, accent, skin color, or social class. We have learned, however, that this equality may not necessarily be the case for many, particularly historically disadvantaged groups.

At the time, I was drawn to the proud message that America is a melting pot, not just racially and ethnically but also of personalities, professions, and experiences. That was something I did not notice when I scanned the horizon from the other side of the Atlantic. Americans still dream and are motivated to achieve their goals in life. The United States is a country where Barack Obama, a talented, brilliant, hardworking Black politician born in Honolulu, Hawaii, could be elected twice as president of the United States. This is a country where MIT, my university, can have a former president like Rafael Reif, the son of Venezuelan immigrants. Although it is not a perfect society, American society strives for ideals such as a person's freedom, which includes the opportunity for prosperity and success and the opportunity for social mobility based on hard work and skill. The definition of the American dream implicitly includes equal opportunity for all and the rewarding of merit.

This book comes at a pivotal moment in our understanding of opportunity and merit, particularly within workplaces, educational institutions, and governments. It arrives at a time when corporate leaders once again are promoting meritocracy as the solution to organizational challenges, often in place of diversity, equity, and inclusion initiatives. The narrative of meritocracy is not new. It emerged as a progressive alternative to earlier distributive systems of status, power, and authority that favored patronage and favoritism based on class, wealth, or family ties. For decades, the practice of advancing and rewarding individuals based on their talents and efforts—on "merit"— has been widely regarded as fair across various institutions worldwide. It has shaped admissions at selective colleges and universities, guided hiring and promotion in organizations, and inspired visions of a just society where ability and hard work matter more than class background, wealth, or demographics.

Yet, meritocracy has come under increasing scrutiny. Critics have called it a "trap,"[5] a "tyranny,"[6] a form of "aristocracy of talent,"[7] even an "unfulfilled promise" or "false promise."[8] Many argue that instead of leveling the playing field, meritocratic systems often reinforce privilege, perpetuate inequities, and sustain systemic biases based on demographics and personal characteristics. Some even question whether businesses can ever operate as true meritocracies, especially at a time when concepts like merit, excellence, and intelligence have become central to business discussions about talent management and opportunity.[9]

In *The Meritocracy Paradox*, I examine these contradictions and start digging into fundamental questions like the following: How did meritocracy, once seen as a progressive solution to inherited privilege and demographic bias, gain a reputation for promoting *inequality* rather than equity and fairness? Can it still serve as a foundation for fairness in today's organizations and businesses? What often goes wrong when organizations rely on merit as their guiding principle, and how can those shortcomings be addressed?

Drawing on decades of research—my own and others'—I analyze the structures and cultures of meritocracy, exploring how talent management processes and decisions work inside today's organizations and businesses. Like executives and managers as well as HR professionals, I define talent management processes as those designed and implemented with the goal of attracting, developing, retaining, and motivating individuals who can drive organizational success and excellence. From merit-based bonus systems in large companies to admissions decisions at elite universities, my research reveals a troubling pattern: even in organizations committed to selecting and rewarding the best, personal biases and social barriers can affect hiring, promotion, and pay decisions within organizations, undermining the very ideals of a high-performing meritocracy.

The Meritocracy Paradox is not, however, a simple "takedown" of current organizational merit-driven efforts. It offers a forward-looking framework for making organizations and their talent management systems more meritocratic, fair, and effective. Grounded in real-world experiments and collaborations with organizations, the book presents concrete strategies for improving recruitment, hiring, evaluation, pay, and career development processes. So leaders who are serious about fostering excellence, fairness, and opportunity for all will find practical tools to identify *where*, *how*, and *why* their talent management strategies may fall short—and how to fix them with effective solutions, often at surprisingly low cost and with rapid returns.

I hope you enjoy reading this book, that it challenges your thinking, and that it inspires you to put meritocracy into practice in ways that truly create opportunity and fairness for all.

THE MERITOCRACY PARADOX

INTRODUCTION

For decades, the principle of advancing and rewarding individuals based on their talents and hard work—on "merit"—has been widely accepted as fair and legitimate across education, corporate settings, and government. Merit is central to selective educational institutions, which aim to admit and educate the most qualified students; to employers, who seek to hire, reward, and promote the most talented employees; and to public institutions striving for efficiency. Meritocracy also remains a popular ideal among those who envision a social system where success is determined by talent, initiative, and effort rather than class background, wealth, or demographics. Even as I finish this book, merit persists at the center of the buzz in education, business, and government circles.

Yet, many merit-driven initiatives have recently been criticized for paradoxically contributing to workplace inequities and sustaining systemic biases based on demographics and personal characteristics. How did meritocracy, once seen as a progressive solution to inherited privilege and demographic bias, gain a reputation for promoting unfairness and inequity? And why has meritocracy returned as an alternative to diversity, equity, and inclusion initiatives? What structures and processes can help organizations and businesses become *truly* meritocratic? Conversely, what biases and obstacles get in the way of fair and meritocratic decision-making when organizations seek to attract, retain, and reward the best-qualified and highest-performing employees? These questions have been at the heart of a stream of research

I have conducted for two decades. They are also the motivation behind the writing of this book.

My interest in these research questions got its start in an executive education classroom in Philadelphia in 2004 when I met a senior business executive whom I will call Janet.[1] At the time, I was a new faculty member at the Wharton School, teaching about performance-based reward systems as part of a course on strategic talent management. Top executives of well-known businesses took the class, including Janet, a C-suite executive at a large service company in the northeastern United States. At the end of class one day, I summarized what I still see as critical guidelines for designing successful performance-based reward systems while displaying a slide on the classroom screen with the following bullet points:

- Make sure your performance rating process is strategically useful to your organization (*Alignment with Strategy*).
- Strive for precision in defining and measuring the performance of your managers and employees (*Measurability and Specificity*).
- Involve the managers and employees being rated in the design and development of the performance evaluation process (*Acceptability*).
- Train the raters (typically managers) and ratees (typically workers) on how to evaluate and provide helpful feedback (*Feedback and Development*).
- Pay attention to equity and fairness principles when designing and implementing your evaluation process (*Meritocracy and Fairness*).
- Ensure that the evaluation process is related to job performance (*Validity*) and meets legal requirements (*Legal Defense*).

I had been researching workplace inequality in organizations and found that the recommendation about being meritocratic and fair was missing from many textbooks, articles, and guides to strategic talent management that I had consulted when preparing to teach the class. However, given my training in the social sciences, first as an economist and later as a sociologist, I saw such a recommendation as fundamental.

"Does anyone have any questions about these guiding principles?" I asked. Although the audience had been engaged throughout the presentation, there were no questions. Perhaps I had been so clear and convincing in presenting the research behind each guideline that there was no need for questions. Perhaps, I thought, these are obvious ways to ensure success in how organizations evaluate and reward employee performance. After a minute of silence,

I tried a different question: "Based on your own experience, how many of your businesses have considered every single one of these guidelines when designing processes to reward your top performers?"

That did it. Janet raised her hand, nodding and smiling, the only participant who did so. I smiled and asked, "Janet, can you please tell us more about what your company does when implementing all of this? I have never heard of any organization that has met all these guidelines. Your organization seems perfect!" The class giggled. Janet started to explain how, in the late 1990s, her company had hired a prominent consulting firm to help address employee motivation and performance issues. "We wanted to improve performance, and the team of consultants we worked with made us realize that we had to reward top performers for their effort. It was time for us to build a solid performance-pay process."

What Janet described was not unusual. Beginning in the early 1980s, many North American companies began implementing incentive pay and pay-for-performance schemes. These schemes quickly gained traction worldwide, attracting significant attention in the media and in academic research.[2] Since then, various studies and company reports have stressed a noteworthy positive relationship between incentive plans and organizational success.[3] By 2011, over 90 percent of US organizations were said to be tying pay increases and annual bonuses to performance.[4] One often-cited study, based on data from the Panel Study of Income Dynamics—which surveyed a nationally representative sample of over eighteen thousand individuals living in the United States—reported that the percentage of salaried employees receiving some form of variable pay based on performance (e.g., bonus, commission, or piece rate) increased from less than 45 percent in the late 1970s to nearly 60 percent in the late 1990s.[5]

It was clear that more businesses were relying on performance-related rewards to motivate their employees.[6] Consultants and other experts were recommending some merit-pay program to boost employee engagement and effort.[7] Salary.com has estimated that close to 77 percent of companies in the United States use variable pay programs as part of their total rewards package.[8] Similarly, worldwide, 77 percent of organizations are estimated to use employee performance ratings when determining pay increases or variable pay and bonuses.[9]

Janet's initial statement about implementing a performance-pay system was not that surprising at the time, and it would definitely not surprise many business leaders today. What *was* surprising is what she said next: "Yes, it was important for us to build a solid performance-pay process to attract and retain our talent. We are now a *true meritocracy*." Curious about this company and its performance-reward system, I asked: "Can you tell us more about what makes your company a *true* meritocracy?" In response, Janet proudly described how her company collected annual employee performance reviews and how these data were used to distribute "merit-based bonuses" among the employees "based on their performance *alone*, and not any other irrelevant factors." We all listened attentively; many executives in the room did not appear to be particularly struck by the discussion. Given its already widespread adoption, they all seemed familiar with the concept of pay for performance and the specifics behind its implementation.

Everyone in the class seemed to recognize and support—unquestioningly—the concept of meritocracy. Nobody asked what meritocracy was. I ended that interaction with an encouraging message for Janet and her team: "It sounds like you have figured out a successful way of implementing meritocracy in your organization. If I may, I would love to find a way to carry out research into your *meritocratic* processes." I smiled. She smiled back. After I made some concluding remarks, the class came to a close.

In retrospect, I wish I had prompted the class to define and articulate their understanding of *true* meritocracy in practice, particularly in relation to their own organizational processes. Little did I know then that Janet's in-class remarks would become one key research lead into the complexities of meritocracy, equity, and fairness in the workplace, ultimately enabling me to extensively analyze her company's performance evaluation and pay processes. Through a decade-long collaboration with the company where Janet worked, which I call ServiCo in this book, I began to investigate why merit-driven and other talent management processes seem so appealing (and even logical) to leaders, why they often fail to work the way they are supposed to, and how they can be improved to ensure fairness and equal opportunity for all individuals, regardless of their demographic characteristics and other personal qualities. The project also became the launching point of an important stream of empirical research for me, as I collaborated with colleagues to study the critical processes and key decision-makers in charge of recruiting, hiring, and making evaluation decisions across several workplaces, organizations, and colleges.

In this research, I have sought to study the concepts of merit and meritocracy inside real organizations. I have also studied talent management systems aimed at finding, rewarding, advancing, and retaining the best employees and managers. In the process, I have uncovered common pitfalls that often arise when organizations attempt to implement meritocratic processes. This knowledge has allowed me to develop forward-looking frameworks (presented and illustrated with research evidence in this book) that help leaders identify where their efforts to reward and advance the best employees might fail. These frameworks offer organizations and their leaders a systematic approach to identifying meritocratic challenges, unfairness concerns, and inefficiencies, providing actionable strategies for improvement. In particular, the key framework addressing the *paradox of meritocracy* can help leaders pinpoint interventions that mitigate biases, ultimately fostering a more equitable and inclusive workplace.

My field study research at ServiCo helped the company's top management identify relevant shortcomings when selecting and rewarding individuals from particular demographic groups. But our work together did not stop there; our continued research collaboration enabled ServiCo to address biases and inefficiencies in its merit-based processes, not only during the distribution of rewards but also in its recruiting, hiring, and promotion decisions. Over time, this work helped ServiCo become a more equitable and fair organization—that is, an organization that gives opportunities to all and advances and rewards the best for their demonstrated efforts, skills, abilities, and performance. That is an outcome close to what I would indeed call a *true meritocracy*.

The concepts of merit and meritocracy are highly relevant to organizational efforts aimed at removing structural barriers and promoting fairness, diversity, equity, and inclusion. Managers and professionals are tasked with making work decisions based on merit and talent. Whether it is deciding who gets hired or promoted, who gets a raise or reward, or who is admitted to an educational program, many organizations rely on talent management tools to assess, select, and reward top candidates and employees. They often develop training programs, performance appraisal methods, and promotion schemes to motivate, retain, and advance the best talent.

For years, many executives, managers, and business students have taken my talent management and people analytics courses to learn about successful strategies for managing and motivating people. Numerous courses and programs on these topics exist. Googling "talent management" returns millions of results, including many ads from companies eager to help organizations think strategically about managing employees. Leaders celebrate when their businesses are named on lists such as *The Best Places to Work, Top*

Workplaces, and *Great Places to Work*, potentially signaling that their companies can perform well financially while still being rewarding and enjoyable places to work. The secret to achieving this recognition is often putting people first when running organizations.

The powerful underlying assumption driving both the demand and supply sides of contemporary labor and educational markets is that the most qualified candidates not only should be encouraged to apply but should also be hired, and that the top performers should be rewarded, retained, and advanced to positions of higher authority, responsibility, and status. This notion that the best talent, regardless of demographic background and other personal traits, should be rewarded with top jobs and leadership positions has long been considered progressive and appealing. It has been accepted by leaders and their workforces in the United States and globally. In their relentless competition for the best talent, companies face ongoing pressure to improve their talent management processes.

The belief that social and economic mobility should be determined by merit and talent and that everyone should be given an opportunity to succeed remains a core value in many postindustrial societies, especially in North America. This belief is seen as a sign of progress because, in theory, it promises to replace prior class-based and demographic-based systems of opportunity and advancement.

At the center of the American dream lies the belief that the United States is a meritocracy where anyone can succeed personally and professionally as long as they are willing to put in the effort and hard work.[10] Survey research repeatedly shows that Americans endorse the meritocratic ethos. Most have believed for many decades that meritocracy is not only the way the system *should* work but also the way it *does* work.[11] Compared to citizens of other countries, Americans are more likely to believe that successful people deserve to be so and that those who fail are equally deserving of their fate.[12] That said, as awareness grows about the effects of socioeconomic inequality and structural racism, Americans have started to express more skepticism about meritocracy and related concepts.[13]

Contemporary organizations and businesses, too, have embraced meritocratic principles when designing and implementing their people management processes. In fact, strategies aimed at attracting and hiring the best talent or linking performance evaluations to employee career outcomes, such as pay-for-performance reward systems, are often depicted as concrete illustrations of meritocracy at work.[14] Merit pay, whether in the form of bonuses or pay raises, is considered a standard organizational practice today because it distributes rewards solely on the basis of performance, output, and effort rather than on other factors such as needs or tenure in the organization.[15] In my own research, as well as in the popular press, I find many examples of practitioners who stress their commitment to giving everyone an equal chance to advance professionally and to be rewarded for their individual merits, talent, and efforts. In addition, many organizations have become almost obsessed with hiring and retaining top performers.

WHY THIS BOOK?

I wrote this book with the following questions in mind:

- What is the actual evidence of meritocracy and meritocratic practices inside today's organizations and businesses?
- Do current talent management processes—especially those designed to select, reward, and advance the best talent—deliver on their meritocratic promises?
- And if not, how can organizations and businesses achieve true meritocracy in practice?

To address these questions, *The Meritocracy Paradox* draws on over two decades of research, both my own and that of others. I have focused my research and teaching on how merit-driven organizational practices, as well as individual and social processes, influence who gets access to beneficial education and training opportunities, and then good jobs with good companies. My research across multiple organizations has also helped me investigate why meritocratic work practices often fail to function as intended and how they can be improved to eliminate biases and provide career opportunities to all, particularly women, racially disadvantaged groups, immigrants, and many others whose personal characteristics often hinder them in the workplace and in society overall.

I have typically tackled my research questions by obtaining access to comprehensive internal data on candidate selection and hiring, employee performance evaluations, and promotion outcomes from real organizations, as well as through studies of the individuals who make critical employment, advancement, and pay decisions about applicants and employees. I have also recruited professionals and managers for simulation exercises to study workplace behaviors related to different aspects of the meritocratic process.

This work has revealed significant variation in how leaders and managers define merit and consequently make merit-based employment decisions, depending on the organizational context in which they work and on the characteristics of the individuals they screen and evaluate. In fact, my research has shown that under certain organizational circumstances, stressing meritocratic goals for an organization can paradoxically favor White native-born men over equally qualified women, racially disadvantaged groups, and immigrants. As a result of this paradox, my work has also explored critical questions about *where* and *why* meritocracy may inadvertently reinforce biases rather than eliminate them.

In *The Meritocracy Paradox*, I explore the widespread appeal of a *true meritocracy*—whether implicitly or explicitly stated by organizational leaders or embedded in workplace practices—while also showing how many organizations fail to achieve their meritocratic goals. Furthermore, I discuss how organizational efforts to promote meritocracy can sometimes backfire (often unintentionally), increasing workplace inequities and biases. Specifically, this book addresses questions such as these:

- Why was meritocracy once seen as a solution to patronage and favoritism linked to class, wealth, or family connections? And why is meritocracy being positioned as an alternative to diversity, equity, and inclusion principles?
- What can go wrong when organizations and businesses implement merit-driven processes and practices to hire, reward, and advance individuals?
- How can organizations and their leaders develop and implement strategies that truly promote high performance, fairness, and opportunity for all?

In this book, I synthesize and explain both my work and the work of many other researchers who have gone inside real organizations to study how employers recruit, hire, evaluate, and promote individuals from different demographic groups and with different social and cultural capital. The book also discusses research findings about the decision-makers who are responsible for implementing these talent management processes, with implications for the individuals they hire and retain as well as for those they do not. As a result, *The Meritocracy Paradox* will be especially valuable to leaders and managers seeking to attract, hire, and advance a high-performing and diverse workforce.

Beyond critique and caution, *The Meritocracy Paradox* offers practical, research-supported strategies for improving merit-based decision-making in organizations. I present frameworks to help organizations identify *where* and *when* they may be failing at being truly meritocratic and fair and *how* to effectively design and implement successful interventions to correct those failures. While I acknowledge that meritocracy in practice is hard to achieve and that many prominent organizations have failed to deliver on their promises, I nonetheless argue that leaders should aim to improve their talent management approaches to ensure fairness and equal opportunity. After all, a renewed, healthy, well-functioning meritocracy remains a far better, more effective basis for employment-related decisions than prior alternatives such as rampant favoritism, bribery, or nepotism without quality checks or accountability.

I wrote *The Meritocracy Paradox* for a broader audience, including scholars, professionals, managers, executives, policymakers, consultants, and students—anyone concerned with shaping a fair, diverse, and inclusive future of work. My fellow academics may be drawn to its theoretical arguments and supporting evidence. At the same time, practitioners will gain practical insights into implementing meritocratic systems that genuinely support fairness and high performance. I also hope this book inspires future research studies and collaborations with companies on the topic. Additionally, the book is relevant for students and employees striving to build successful careers for themselves and their loved ones and who thus need to understand the principles underpinning successful advancement within an organization.

Ultimately, I hope *The Meritocracy Paradox* encourages multiple stakeholders to work together to promote a *true* meritocracy—one that *truly* advances and rewards individuals based on their actual contributions rather than personal or demographic characteristics, while ensuring equal opportunity for all to succeed. The good news is that organizations can achieve these goals at relatively low cost and, in many cases, quite easily. By embracing the principles outlined in this book, organizations can create workplaces that are not only fair but also highly effective, benefiting both employees and employers alike.

THE THREE PARTS OF THIS BOOK

In part I of this book, "The Meritocratic Ideal," I provide some relevant historical context on the origins of merit and meritocracy, exploring how the concepts emerged and why many organizations shifted to rewarding and advancing individuals based on merit. I explain how a meritocracy is intended to work in theory while also raising potential fairness and diversity concerns stemming from different interpretations of meritocracy in the workplace. Clarifying these concepts up front will help us understand both the potential shortcomings of meritocracy and existing talent management systems, as well as why the solutions proposed in this book can effectively work in organizations and businesses that take meritocracy seriously.

Part II, "Where Meritocracy Goes Wrong," makes the case that current recruiting, screening, and selection processes may not necessarily produce the best (and most diverse) hires for organizations. I discuss key prior research, including findings from my research collaborations with real organizations, and document how demographic biases and social processes can influence employment decisions and outcomes within widely used talent management practices. Crucially, just because an organization and its key decision-makers *believe* that they are meritocratic or talent-driven does not mean that their decisions and processes reflect that ideal. In fact, my research has demonstrated the existence of what I call the *meritocracy paradox*: emphasizing meritocracy alone as the basis for hiring, promoting, and rewarding employees may paradoxically backfire on women, racially disadvantaged groups, immigrants, and many other underprivileged groups.[16] Furthermore, there is no universal agreement on what merit actually is, even among leaders and managers working for the same organization.[17] As a result, when managers embrace merit as an overarching concept, they may apply different criteria in their decisions around employee evaluations, rewards, and promotions.

The research presented in parts I and II has significant practical relevance for organizations and businesses. It suggests that truly objective evaluations of merit or talent are extremely difficult (perhaps impossible) to achieve and that many organizations that self-identify as meritocratic may be anything but. In part III, "Building Meritocratic Organizations," I provide leaders and managers with tools to start putting these research-based insights into practice by assessing whether their organizational processes are truly meritocratic and effective. I outline strategic steps to identify *where* and *how* biases and other social dynamics may interfere with hiring, evaluating, rewarding, and advancing employees. These steps can help organizations diagnose their meritocracy and fairness challenges so they can find the most effective solutions and interventions to address them. This section also provides guidance on how to redesign talent management processes to foster objectivity, fairness, and equal opportunity for all.

The good news is that measuring a company's deviation from true meritocracy is not that difficult. It is also relatively straightforward to "debias" and improve the efficiency of organizational and talent management systems by introducing clear processes and criteria for recruiting, selecting, and evaluating employees; monitoring the outcomes of these processes; and assigning individuals within the organization the responsibility of guaranteeing that the processes are fair and encourage diversity. In fact, I have successfully helped organizations and businesses take these steps easily and effectively.

THE RESEARCH AND DATA IN THIS BOOK

While I reference research from many influential academics and their studies, the key findings in this book are based on original data collected by my collaborators and myself using a range of research methods, including field studies of real organizations and experiments. My empirical approach has primarily focused on gathering and analyzing comprehensive information from organizations and businesses, with the aim of understanding why meritocracy and talent management systems may fail to attract and manage diverse top talent. This approach also offers practical guidance for such failures.

I mostly rely on research from three important organizational field studies that illustrate the *paradox of meritocracy* phenomenon in real organizations. One study investigated the implementation of a merit-based system at ServiCo, the company where Janet worked—a large service organization with more than twenty thousand employees. This company study is significant for the purpose and context of this book because it was the first in-depth study that revealed demographic biases in translating performance evaluations to rewards in a company whose processes were intended to be meritocratic. In fact, my analysis of ServiCo's personnel data uncovered some non-meritocratic outcomes. Women, Blacks, Hispanics, and non-US-born employees earned a *lower* merit-based bonus than White men despite working in the same jobs and work units, having the same supervisors, holding the same human capital, and, notably, obtaining *the same* performance score. Although the company stated that "performance is the primary basis for all salary increases" in several of its personnel documents, the reality was that women, Blacks, Hispanics, and recent immigrants had to work harder and receive better performance scores than White men to receive similar amounts of bonus pay. My later research across a variety of organizational settings confirmed the risks organizations may face even when they try to adopt variations of meritocratic processes to manage people in their workplaces.

An additional study analyzed two longitudinal datasets with information on the careers of all support staff at the same service organization. The first dataset stored the pay and performance evaluation history for almost nine thousand employees from 1996 to 2003, *before* new organizational processes were introduced that increased accountability and transparency in the company's performance-reward system so that it could solve the observed gender and racial gap in merit-based bonuses. This dataset included approximately 28,800 employee evaluations made by over 2,600 unique direct supervisors. The second dataset covered the period from 2005 to 2009, *after* the adoption of the new processes, and contained approximately 23,000 employee evaluations made by over 2,500 direct supervisors.

Another study, conducted at an elite business school in North America, included approximately four hundred participants with managerial experience, many of them MBA students and executives. The participants played the role of a senior manager in charge of a small group of consultants, for whom they had to make decisions on bonuses, promotion, and termination. One key finding in these experiments is that when a firm's core values emphasized meritocracy, participants gave a larger monetary reward to a male consultant than to an equally performing female consultant. I will also discuss the findings of additional experiments conducted in other organizational settings.

Those three key field studies are complemented with recent research evidence that the meritocracy paradox persists in other organizational settings, including other businesses, colleges, and government entities. Throughout the book, I provide an overview of the quantitative and qualitative techniques used in each study—such as reviewing organizational documents and records, observing participants, giving in-depth interviews, and conducting simulations with employees, managers, and executives. These methodologies can equip leaders and managers with practical tools to collect and analyze company data, helping them identify their people-related challenges and implement targeted solutions to build more effective, meritocratic talent management processes. Most importantly, I illustrate how simple, low-cost, and targeted solutions that apply the strategic tools and frameworks I have developed can help improve fairness and equal opportunity for *all* within organizations. In part III, I present a comprehensive plan for building effective and equitable talent management systems so that organizations can implement the meritocratic project as it was originally intended to work.

PART I

The Meritocratic Ideal

Aristocracy went wrong because so many of the people who had power simply because they inherited it from their parents were clearly unfit to exercise it. Nobody should be born with a silver spoon in his mouth, or, if he is, it should choke him.

There was nothing new in the proposition that I.Q. + effort = merit; only in the way it was formulated. Ever since the industrial revolution, and indeed even before that, "la carrière est ouverte aux talents" . . . has been one of the primary goals of social reform. . . . Nepotism should go, bribery should go, inheritance should go as a means of attaining public office. They haven't disappeared, of course, but the belief has become established that it is wrong to allow nepotism, bribery, or inheritance any sway: individual merit should be the only test that should be applied.

—MICHAEL YOUNG

Chapter One

THE ORIGINS AND EVOLUTION
OF MERITOCRACY

On September 21, 2012, Leo Rafael Reif gave his inaugural address as MIT's seventeenth president. Addressing a large crowd of students, faculty, and staff, he said: "The MIT that welcomed me thirty-two years ago was unlike any place I had ever seen. *Meritocratic in principle*, it welcomed talent from everywhere. Then as now, MIT radiated a spirit of openness, fairness, and decency, from the commitment to need-blind admissions to the practice of not favoring legacy applicants." The audience cheered enthusiastically. "MIT cherishes values and principles, so continue to pursue your commitment to meritocracy, integrity, and excellence; to be actively caring and respectful; and to always take the high road," he continued.[1]

Reif was not alone among contemporary leaders in praising such ideals. The idea of meritocracy as a "high road" for selecting and advancing individuals is not exclusive to higher education and elite educational programs; it is common in business as well. For instance, Ray Dalio, founder of Bridgewater Associates, one of the world's largest hedge funds, stated in 2017 that the company's "success occurred because we created a real *idea meritocracy*," which he defined as "a decision-making system where the best ideas win out."[2] Similarly, Red Hat, an IBM subsidiary that provides open-source software and solutions to client companies, also prides itself on being a meritocracy, "where reputation is earned by how well you help others succeed," according to the company's website.[3] In an article on *Wired*'s website, Jim Whitehurst, Red Hat's former CEO, wrote that "in many technology companies that employ a meritocracy—Red Hat being one example—people forge their own path to leadership, not simply by working hard and smart, but also by expressing unique ideas that have the ability to positively impact their team and their company."[4]

Professional service firms such as law, accounting, and management consulting firms have also long honored the meritocratic distributive principle, whether or not they explicitly state it in their mission statements. Accenture, for instance, uses the term "global meritocracy" on its website to emphasize that "all matters relating to employment with the Company are based on, and operate according to, the principle of merit."[5] McKinsey's global managing partner Bob Sernfels wrote in a memo to Bloomberg News, "Some have asked whether we will continue to prioritize diversity *in our meritocracy*. The answer is yes. We will continue to boldly pursue both, because these two things together—our *diverse meritocracy*—is what makes us distinctive and has defined who we are over our nearly 100 years."[6]

The popular policy of "up or out"—a crucial aspect of what has come to be known as the "Cravath system"[7]—sounds meritocratic. This policy, commonly used in law firms, consultancies, and investment banks worldwide, is based on the notion that (1) the best associates are hired and paid exceptionally well and that (2) only those few who demonstrate top performance and potential within a certain period of time are promoted to partnership; otherwise, they are asked to leave. Something similar occurs in the tenure process in universities and colleges, where junior faculty members on a tenure track are allowed a limited time period to achieve a record of published research, academic impact, teaching excellence, and community service before a decision is made about whether they will be granted tenure for life.

In the world of consulting, many experts argue that meritocratic cultures can enable women and disadvantaged racial groups to succeed: "A meritocracy has many benefits," wrote Candice Lu, the founding partner at OnPrem Solution Partners, in May 2021. "For example, it encourages young professionals to confidently share ideas, which will ultimately benefit the business. For women, it will accelerate their path to promotion and support flexibility. A meritocracy also supports a team environment and higher-quality work. People become less focused on titles and age and more focused on delivering the best work."[8]

In 2024, meritocracy has reemerged as the "new pitch" among business leaders and successful founders.[9] In an email to employees, startup Scale AI founder Alexandr Wang—who has championed merit, excellence, and intelligence (MEI) as an alternative to diversity, equity, and inclusion (DEI) initiatives[10]—shared a post on X that stated, "Scale is a meritocracy, and we must always remain one. . . . Hiring on merit will be a permanent policy at Scale. . . . That means we hire only the best person for the job, we seek out and demand excellence, and we unapologetically prefer people who are very smart."[11] Several prominent corporations have also lately emphasized meritocracy as core to their functioning.[12] Accenture chief Julie Sweet affirmed in a memo, "We are and always have been a meritocracy."[13] On the first page of its report, ExxonMobil declared, "We are focused on building an engaged global workforce, grounded in meritocracy." Rich Lesser, global chair of Boston Consulting Group, publicly spoke about building a "meritocracy where everyone has the opportunity to succeed."[14]

However, not everyone experiences meritocracy the same way—a point I will unpack later in this book. The response from the start-up community to Wang's post was, for instance, quite lukewarm, with many calling it a "dangerous oversimplification" or "a great example of the box many leaders and companies find themselves trapped in. . . . Can they trust that having meritocratic ideals is enough to lead to truly meritocratic outcomes, and promote diversity?"[15] Some even question whether businesses can ever be true meritocracies.

Similar tensions exist between the ideals of meritocracy and how employees actually experience it in their organizations. For instance, the global professional services EY has long sought to promote meritocracy and diversity in its workforce worldwide. An associate director who worked at EY for more than five years wrote on the website Glassdoor: "[EY is] the closest to a meritocracy I have seen so far." But later, in February 2021, a different EY professional in London wrote a starkly different view: "Good place to learn. *Zero meritocracy*. Promotion based on loyalty and brownnosing."[16] JPMorgan Chase similarly prides itself on maintaining "an open, *entrepreneurial meritocracy* for all" and further claims that the company makes "people decisions based on meritocracy." Writing on Glassdoor in 2017, an investment banking summer analyst in New York agreed that JPMorgan is "meritocratic and innovative, leading the financial services industry." But not everyone inside JPMorgan agrees. In 2019, a banker executive director in Washington, D.C., wrote in an employee review titled "Not a Meritocracy" that "bonuses are discretionary and determined by managers. . . . Many managers do not understand what a merit-based environment would mean." Another employee in Miami, Florida, who has spent more than eight years at JPMorgan, wrote a Glassdoor review in March 2023 titled "Where Meritocracy Disappears While You Are Treated with Disrespect and Unfairly."[17]

In the high-tech sector, there are reasons to question the meritocracy narrative. For a long time, many high-tech companies in the United States celebrated their cultures of meritocracy. Venture capitalists and entrepreneurs often described Silicon Valley as a bastion of meritocracy, full of opportunities regardless of who you were or where you came from. Yet, most tech companies have had low numbers of female executives or corporate officers.[18] (There has been notable progress, with the share of women as tech CEOs, for instance, almost tripling in the space of one year, from 3.9 percent in 2020 to 10.9 percent in 2021.[19]) In the case of race, a *Wired* survey in October 2019 estimated that the proportion of the Silicon Valley workforce that was Black, Hispanic, or Indigenous was only about 5 percent.[20] In September 2024, the US Equal Employment Opportunity Commission reported that female, Black, and Hispanic workers were still substantially underrepresented in the high-tech workplace and sector in the United States, with 22.6 percent of the high-tech workforce being women, 7.4 percent Black, and 9.9 percent Hispanic.[21] Are these percentages what we would expect in a truly meritocratic sector? Or would one instead expect to see women and disadvantaged racial groups equally represented across positions of status, power, and authority, with no relationship between gender or race and the probability of being hired, promoted, or fired?

Further concerns about the underrepresentation of Blacks and other disadvantaged racial groups are expressed in the science, technology, engineering, and mathematics (STEM) workforce—a particularly noteworthy issue given the public perception that STEM jobs offer higher pay, are more respected, and offer more advancement opportunities than many other fields. According to a 2018 Pew Research Center survey release, 71 percent of Americans see STEM jobs as paying better than jobs in other industries.[22] Yet, the same survey reports notable differences among STEM employees on the role of racial biases in underrepresentation. Seventy-two percent of Blacks and 43 percent of Hispanics in STEM jobs believe that discrimination in recruitment, hiring, and promotions is a major reason behind the underrepresentation of Blacks and Hispanics in these jobs. By contrast, 27 percent of Whites and 28 percent of Asians believe so.

Despite such discrepancies, the promise of meritocracy in distributing opportunities and rewards more broadly in society has been appealing for a long time, especially before scholars and practitioners started to write about its failures and false promises.[23] In particular, the idea of working for an organization that hires and rewards individuals based on their own merits and talents rather than their connections or social status remains highly attractive today. This ideal has been upheld for years and is regularly invoked in policy debates as the right thing to do, particularly in progressive organizations and societies. It is regarded as both legitimate and effective.

Today, many job applicants want to know that prospective employers have structures and processes aimed at rewarding the highest-performing workers. A meritocratic model plays to our sense of fairness and justice—it seems fair to reward and promote those employees who perform at high levels—motivating people to want to join those organizations and work hard for them. After all, who would want to work for an organization or business that encourages promotions based on someone's family ties to top management? Or who would want to work someplace where, no matter how hard you try to learn and perform well, you will never get rewarded for your efforts? The promise of a *true* meritocracy is that—regardless of our personal characteristics—we all have an equal chance at succeeding if we are talented, motivated, and hardworking. That belief explains why many people with varying political views, social classes, and demographics, especially in North America, have come to internalize meritocracy—whether implicitly or explicitly—as a fair and legitimate principle for guiding decisions about people.

The principle of meritocracy has become influential over the past century in recruiting, attracting, and retaining talent, as have the talent management processes currently in place to support meritocracy. Studies of unconscious and structural biases, however, have raised serious concerns about the operation of meritocracy and talent management systems in practice, leading many to question whether meritocracy is such a fair system after all. To understand how meritocracy became such a powerful and revolutionary idea, as well as the flaws that have led to critiques of meritocracy, it is important first to understand the origins and evolution of the concept.

THE ROOTS OF MERITOCRACY

Meritocracy describes a social system in which those who have power and authority have earned their positions through merit, as demonstrated through their ability, competence, effort, and hard work. First popularized in the 1958 dystopian satire *The Rise of the Meritocracy*, the word was the brainchild of Michael Young, who became director of research for the UK's

Labour Party in 1945. Young left the party in 1951 to enroll in a doctoral degree program in sociology at the London School of Economics. He helped found the Institute of Community Studies in 1953, a research institution that still exists today as the Institute for Community Studies.[24]

The Rise of the Meritocracy made Young world-renowned. Often misquoted, his ideas on meritocracy continue to be discussed today. Written in the voice of a fictional historical narrator in the year 2034, Young's book describes the rise of a new elite in society based on intellectual talent and achievement—as measured by standardized intelligence tests, an essential part of twentieth-century Britain's educational system—rather than on class origins or wealth. To name this new elite, Young coined the term *meritocracy* by combining the Latin word *mereo* ("I earn") and the Greek word *kratia* ("power" or "rule"). He later wrote, "A friend, a classical scholar, said I would be breaking the rules of good usage to invent a new word out of one Latin and one Greek word. I would, she said, be laughed to scorn if I did."[25] Nobody seems to laugh at the word now. On the contrary, many mistakenly believe that the ancient Greeks invented the word *meritocracy*.

In the book, Young explains the feasible consequences of a society in which merit alone, defined as "I.Q. plus effort," determines each individual's professional and social achievement. Individuals with merit are identified and chosen at an early age to receive education, training, and development in an area of study or practice, and the most meritorious will attain the highest positions of power, status, or authority. At the time it was written, this book criticized societies that rarely focused on intelligence and effort when determining who got to occupy influential positions; these positions were often allocated according to nepotistic connections among members of the same social class. Ironically, given its criticisms of nepotism, Young notes that *The Rise of the Meritocracy* was "only published because I happened to meet an old friend, Walter Neurath, on a beach in North Wales."[26]

Although we attribute the current definition of meritocracy to Young, discussions of the underlying concept of awarding individuals positions in society based on their ability and character can be found in the works of numerous earlier philosophers and writers, including Confucius, Plato, Aristotle, Tocqueville, and Jefferson. Moreover, the use of merit-based systems dates back more than two thousand years.

An often-cited illustration of a merit-based system comes from China. Starting about 200 BCE, the Han and Qin dynasties developed an administrative meritocracy that aimed to attract talented officials to maintain the expanding empire's power. Prospective candidates from anywhere in the empire were selected through arduous civil service examinations for key government positions.[27] The main approach consisted of professionally advancing and handing power and authority to individuals of high merit and virtue, following ancient Confucian principles. Later, Chinese emperors also required their citizens to learn and be tested on their knowledge of Confucianism, a philosophy that stresses ethics, morality, and proper behavior and that is often regarded as the foundation for efforts to establish a meritocracy. Ruiping Fan, an expert on Confucianism, states that Confucius "invented the notion that those who govern should do so because of merit, not of inherited status."[28] Confucius and Confucian thought stress that rulers and key decision-makers should be moral and competent.

China's merit-based systems for selecting government officials influenced not only neighboring countries in Asia but also the Western world, including France, Germany, Spain, and Italy, among many others. The French Enlightenment philosopher Voltaire supposedly admired the Chinese meritocratic system, with some scholars claiming that he proposed replacing European monarchies with meritocratic processes: "What should our European princes do when they hear such examples [referring to the Chinese meritocratic approach to selecting rulers]? Admire and blush, but above all imitate," Voltaire wrote.[29]

Prominent organizations and businesses emulated the Chinese model of merit-based systems in government bureaucracy; the British East India Company in the early seventeenth century used similar selection methods to screen candidates based on ability. Starting in the nineteenth century and becoming more widespread in the twentieth century, standardized exams designed to assess ability and competence—particularly for aspiring public officials—became prominent examples of meritocracy in many parts of the world. Today, the use of aptitude and personality tests is closely tied to the meritocratic ethos governing admissions into higher education institutions, not only in the United States but also in numerous other countries.[30]

Similarly, tests and methods aiming to measure job seekers' ability, intelligence, and personality have long appealed to those in charge of screening and selection in organizations and corporations worldwide. Human resource (HR) professionals have been tasked with formalizing screening and hiring processes in their organizations, particularly those dealing with increasing numbers of applicants and employees. In fact, some question whether meritocratic systems can even survive without standardized tests or measures of ability and competence.[31] For decades, practitioners have promoted such preemployment testing, including popular tests assessing candidates' job knowledge, honesty and integrity, aptitude, cognitive ability, personality, emotional intelligence, skills, and physical ability. Such tests have been (and still are) praised for providing hiring organizations with "an objective measure of a candidate's qualifications, skills, and suitability for a role."[32] They are also praised for helping businesses and their HR professionals "minimize hiring time and select the most qualified individual who best fits the organization."[33]

Meritocracy remains an essential component in governments around the world. Daniel A. Bell asserts that it plays a central role in the Chinese government. In his 2015 book, *The China Model: Political Meritocracy and the Limits of Democracy*, Bell introduces the term *political meritocracy* to describe how merit-based principles underpin the functioning of China's contemporary political system. The two basic premises behind this concept are that (1) everyone should have an equal opportunity to receive education and contribute to politics, and that (2) only a few will be selected for their highest ability to make morally informed political decisions. According to this model, it is key for successful political systems to identify those with the highest ability and put them in positions to contribute to the political community. In chapter 2 of his book, Bell lists the three key qualities that characterize a good leader in a political meritocracy—intellectual ability, social skills, and virtue—and then proposes a strategy to identify and select for these qualities.[34]

The concept of meritocracy has been particularly crucial in the history of the United States, a nation fundamentally focused on individual achievement, effort, and capability. In his 1899 book *Democracy in America*, Alexis de Tocqueville argued that in the United States, individuals attain success based on merit rather than heredity, highlighting "equality of opportunity" rather than "equality of outcomes."[35] Similarly, Thomas Jefferson, one of the Founding Fathers, called in 1813 for a "natural aristocracy" based on talent rather than birth.[36]

Indeed, the widespread metaphor of the "American dream" relies on a culture of meritocracy. James Truslow Adams, the wealthy Brooklyn-born son of a father from Caracas, Venezuela, coined the term *American dream* in his 1931 book *The Epic of America*, describing it as the belief that everyone, regardless of their birthplace or social class, can be successful in a society where upward mobility is not only possible but also celebrated.[37] The main idea was that in the United States, individuals could attain positions in society based on their innate capabilities and regardless of their "fortuitous circumstances of birth or positions."

THE RISE OF MERITOCRACY

In his 2021 book *The Aristocracy of Talent*, Adrian Wooldridge provides a detailed account of the historical development of meritocracy, from its conception in China and later in the West in response to corruption, patronage, and nepotism to contemporary critiques of meritocracy.[38] Wooldridge makes many important historical observations, including that Jewish people played a "prominent role in developing the meritocratic idea" by emphasizing objective measures of intellectual success as a way of combating anti-Jewish prejudice.[39] He further argues that the "great meritocratic breakthrough" took place in the Western world at a time when the West was emphasizing science, capitalism, and individualism after the Second World War.

Many social scientists have endorsed the concept of meritocracy in contemporary organizations and institutions. For example, the sociological theory of modernization proposes that, in modern societies, individuals' positions in the social hierarchy should be determined solely on their merit.[40] While in traditional societies an individual's position and status in the social hierarchy were decided by ascribed factors (e.g., family inheritance, social class, race, gender), the theory of modernization proposes that in a society, social position and status should rely exclusively on *achieved* traits such as education, skills, and experience. Most recently, in contexts where discussions have taken place around reducing dependence on meritocratic systems, such as peer evaluation in science, merit has been lauded as a "central pillar of liberal epistemology, humanism, and democracy"; in one such article, the authors defend the use of merit in science because it "has proven effective in generating scientific and technological advances, reducing suffering, narrowing social gaps, and improving the quality of life globally."[41]

The concept of meritocracy has been so popular for so long that few doubted that it was both achievable and beneficial. The main goal was to ensure that we got more of it. By the end of the twentieth century, meritocracy was the most widespread ideology for advancing and rewarding individuals in organizations and institutions across the globe.

Moreover, despite critiques of meritocracy, the belief that merit and talent should determine social and economic mobility remains central to postindustrial societies, particularly in North America. Americans tend (or at least tended) to believe that anyone can succeed in life and their career as long as they are willing to work hard. Survey after survey has shown that Americans widely support the meritocratic ethos.[42] Several studies using data from the General Social Survey, a representative survey of US adults, have repeatedly found that most Americans agree that getting ahead in society depends on meritocratic factors such as hard work, intelligence, and abilities. However, their beliefs vary in strength, and there is disagreement about the importance of non-meritocratic factors such as family wealth, race, and social relationships. For example, one study reported that young, affluent Whites are most likely to believe that meritocratic factors predominate in the United States. Older, lower-income minorities, on the other hand, are most likely to see non-meritocratic elements such as family wealth and race as important.[43]

Surveys of Americans continue to emphasize the popularity of the meritocratic ideology: Americans often believe that successful people deserve to be so, and those who are not successful deserve their fate. Furthermore, there is a generalized sense that organizations that adopt meritocratic selection and rewards—hiring, promoting, and compensating based on talent and performance—are organizations that win, that are effective. In the context of higher education, a 2022 survey found that more than nine in ten Americans see grades and standardized tests as the top factors that should be considered in college admissions, including 61 percent who say that high school grades should be key deciding factors. By contrast, almost three quarters of Americans say that gender, race, ethnicity, or whether a relative attended the school should not affect admissions decisions.[44]

In line with those survey findings, some commentators rightly remind us that meritocracy was intended to rule out nepotism and bribery and promote upward social mobility. As one *Wall Street Journal* column put it in 2021, "Whatever meritocracy's shortcomings, the cure is clearly more meritocracy, not moving back in the direction of what it replaced."[45] And Gallup surveys consistently rank the United States, often seen as the most meritocracy-oriented country in the world, as the top choice for migrants: around 158 million adults worldwide, or one in five potential migrants, name the United States as their top preferred destination in 2022.[46]

In the workplace, individuals continue to appreciate employers who offer them opportunities for professional growth and development, and rewards based on their merits and contributions, key features of current meritocratic talent management systems. In fact, the top reason why individuals quit their jobs is the lack of career opportunities in their organizations, defined as opportunities for development and rewards (a factor cited by 41 percent of 13,382 respondents from forty-four countries and territories surveyed between April 2021 and April 2022), followed by inadequate pay (36 percent).[47] Conversely, one common characteristic of companies regarded as the best to work for, in the United States and beyond, is the provision of career opportunities to all employees.[48]

MERITOCRACY TODAY: THE RISE OF TALENT MANAGEMENT SYSTEMS

The workplace is a domain in life where people are highly likely to experience the language of meritocracy, implicitly or explicitly. Inside businesses and organizations, strategies aimed at hiring the best talent or linking merit and performance to employee careers, such as pay-for-performance reward systems, are often depicted as illustrations of meritocracy in practice.[49] Merit pay and benefits are critical in today's workplaces. Such practices highlight that work is to be rewarded based solely on performance and effort, not on factors such as equality, need, or seniority.[50] In my own work, I have found many examples of practitioners who stress their commitment to guaranteeing that anyone can equally advance based on their individual merit, talent, and effort, regardless of demographics such as gender, race, class, social origin, sexual orientation, or religion.

In the last two decades, the meritocratic ethos has driven interest in designing and implementing talent management systems and in expanding them. Since its inception, human resource management (HRM)—defined as the process of recruiting and hiring people; employing, training, and compensating them; and adopting strategies and policies to manage, promote, and retain them—has emphasized the importance of merit and talent in determining whom to hire, promote, and reward. This emphasis helps explain the growing adoption of HRM systems since the beginning of the twenty-first century in the United States and abroad.[51]

While HR departments date back to the 1910s, when personnel departments first appeared, most of the work initially done in these departments, along with hiring and firing, involved administrative tasks such as processing employee payroll and benefits. HRM, as a strategic approach to managing people in the workplace, originated in the 1970s and 1980s.[52] As Frank Dobbin describes in his 2009 book *Inventing Equal Opportunity*, in the 1970s these corporate HR and personnel experts introduced important changes in how employers hire, promote, and fire employees in the United States; they started formalizing hiring, promotion, and termination practices to limit managerial discretion and potential biases, ultimately defining how equal opportunity has since operated in practice in the American workplace.[53]

In the subsequent wake of globalization, company restructurings, and technological changes, HRM experts started to focus on strategic initiatives. Particularly in the early 2010s, the focus shifted toward management of mergers and acquisitions, succession planning, and diversity and inclusion initiatives. Most recently, the field of HRM has introduced analytics to better understand, predict, and manage key talent management processes such as recruitment, hiring, performance, and retention. The meritocratic assumption behind these HR developments no doubt continues to be that workplaces can and should proactively manage people and their people processes in an efficient way. Indeed, the term *human resources* implies that people and their talents can drive organizational performance and success, much as other resources such as money, materials, connections, and information do. In today's post-COVID environment, managing employees has become even more crucial because technological and cultural changes have profoundly impacted the workforce. These shifts have reshaped how organizations need to engage, develop, and retain talent to remain competitive in a rapidly evolving landscape.

The HRM trend toward analytics was further accelerated by the emergence and proliferation of "people operations" positions and departments across the world, pioneered by Google and other tech companies in the early 2000s. These were established in clear opposition to traditional HR approaches, which were seen as less effective and more administrative. The growing focus of these operational departments is on analyzing how the organization manages its people from recruitment and hiring to performance appraisals, training and development, and career management.

Artificial intelligence (AI) and people analytics are increasingly being praised for enhancing the efficiency and efficacy of people-related decisions while potentially reducing bias in organizational processes. The current implementation of these talent management approaches remain tied to the fundamental underlying promise of meritocracy: that individuals' engagement, performance, and effort can be systematically measured and evaluated based on work-relevant criteria, "merits," or "talents."

MERITOCRACY, TALENT MANAGEMENT, AND
ACHIEVEMENT-BASED WORKPLACE INEQUALITY

The theory and practice of HRM, as well as much of the research supporting them, have fully encouraged the shift from *ascription* to *achievement*, a
key characteristic of meritocracy. *Ascription* is a sociological term that refers
to placing individuals in a hierarchical or stratified social system based on
qualities or traits beyond their control. Examples of such qualities include
parental class or socioeconomic status at birth, sex, race or ethnicity, age,
religion, nationality, and sexual orientation. *Ascribed status* is a concept first
developed by Ralph Linton to refer to the social position offered to individuals or groups based on qualities or traits beyond their control.[54] By contrast, *achieved status* refers to the social position that an individual can attain
because of merit. Unlike ascribed status, it considers an individual's skills,
abilities, and efforts when allocating those positions.

Many of the duties of managers and HR professionals indeed promote
such a meritocratic shift from ascription status to achievement status. These
professionals' goals are to ensure that the most talented and qualified are
hired; to manage compensation, professional development, and benefits programs; to train and reward their top talent; and to evaluate and encourage
high performance at work.

HRM further takes as a given that people have different talents and abilities and should be rewarded accordingly, a philosophy that runs counter to
the nineteenth- and twentieth-century ideal of socialist egalitarianism (that
all people are equal and should be rewarded according to need, as Marx
insisted, rather than talent or effort). HRM is typically used today to refer to
the policies and practices aimed at managing employees' (and often managers') behaviors, attitudes, and performance in the workplace. HRM practices
include key activities such as analyzing and designing work and the workplace, identifying and planning current and future employee needs, attracting and selecting candidates, training and developing employees for their
roles and future growth, compensating and rewarding employees, evaluating
performance, and fostering a positive and productive workplace.

In the early 2020s, following significant social movements in the United
States and worldwide, diversity, equity, and inclusion (DEI) became a central
focus in HRM, even though basic DEI principles had already influenced HR
practices through equal employment laws in the mid-twentieth century. As
a result, companies prioritized integrating DEI into their HR functions to

address systemic biases and prevent discrimination against employees based on ascribed characteristics. Additionally, these efforts aimed to improve diversity and inclusion inside organizations and businesses.[55] Several scholars have noted that HRM has not placed comparable emphasis on individuals' socioeconomic background.[56] They have also noted that socioeconomic background was rarely considered in HRM research until recently.[57]

Building on traditional HR and HRM efforts, the people operations and analytics movement represents more than a simple change in semantics. It signals a shift in the mindset of leaders and HR professionals with regard to their people-related practices. The term *people operations* often refers to a business strategy that places employees at the forefront of an organization's operations. Such an approach, therefore, recognizes the importance and value of employees to business success. It also encourages the application of "evidence-based" solutions. Data, frameworks, social science theories, and prior studies can all be leveraged to better inform people-related processes and outcomes in businesses. In this regard, this new model for talent management offers an alternative perspective to traditional HR practices. Like the ideal concept of meritocracy, it implicitly acknowledges and endorses the argument that an organization's competitive advantage lies in the quality and qualifications of its people, not just the services or products it produces. The challenge then becomes how to measure the merits and talents of individuals accurately and how to be successfully fair, equitable, and diverse when doing so.

The development of AI and people analytics to improve people-related operations and processes is a growing trend in the management of people and businesses. According to a report by Accenture, 98 percent of executives worldwide agree that AI foundation models will play an important role in their organization's strategies in the next three to five years.[58] Moreover, many HR leaders have already incorporated AI into their talent management processes. For instance, in 2021, Diane Gherson, CHRO of IBM then, spoke about IBM "reinventing HR with AI and analytics" to provide "personalization" of messages, feedback, and necessary training opportunities for employees to improve their skills and advance in the workplace. "And people love it," Gherson said. "It is the AI that they love about it. It makes managers better managers, just giving managers advice about what size of an increase to give their people based on the demand for their skills, based on their performance, and so forth, but really taking it all into account."[59] Note that behind such AI efforts is an implicit endorsement of the meritocratic ethos in the workplace: that individuals are responsible for their own success in a true meritocracy.

In HRM circles, there is also discussion about how AI and people analytics might be used to mitigate biases,[60] enhance diversity and inclusion,[61] and increase fairness in decision-making.[62] And a growing industry of technology platforms and online tools is indeed emerging to help companies address these goals. For instance, Pymetrics introduces itself as a platform "redefining hiring and talent management—using data-driven behavioral insights and audited AI to create a more efficient, effective, and fair hiring process across the talent lifecycle." The company boasts of numbers such as 198 percent longer tenure, 59 percent decrease in time to hire, and 62 percent increase in female representation.[63] Many other companies use predictive tools and methods other than AI to improve employee selection and recruitment. For instance, Applied, a technology applicant tracking and hiring platform, relies on behavioral research to help employers find and select qualified candidates for their job openings and debias their hiring processes.[64]

CRITIQUES OF MERITOCRACY

Many have critiqued the concept of meritocracy and the principle of using merit as a way of distributing and allocating opportunities and rewards. In *Capital in the Twenty-First Century*, Thomas Piketty heavily criticizes the current narrative around meritocracy and even entrepreneurship because it "often seems to serve primarily as a way for the winners in today's economy to justify any level of inequality whatsoever while peremptorily blaming the losers for lacking talent, virtue, and diligence."[65] Books by Daniel Markovits and by Michael Sandel go further to share their view that there is a link between the pursuit of meritocracy and the recent escalation of populism, the radical right, and disenchantment with both democracy and current employer practices.[66]

Such criticisms generally focus on three broad categories of problems with the operation of meritocracy. The first is the possibility that organizational leaders and other key decision-makers who are selected through meritocratic practices may be incompetent or immoral or may abuse their power and authority. The second problem is the risk that talent management strategies within an organization's meritocratic talent system—whether in businesses, nonprofits, or public entities—may perpetuate unfairness or fail to provide equal opportunities or to promote social and economic mobility for all. The third problem is one of legitimacy, in that meritocratic beliefs and ideology can help justify and legitimate existing socioeconomic disparities and the unequal distribution of opportunity within a society.

Such criticisms are consistent with empirical studies showing that individuals' social background still significantly affects professional careers, even beyond achievement-related factors such as education level or experience.[67] Thus, in contemporary societies, social class and family background continue to matter: on average, individuals from better-off families can access premier higher education and achieve better jobs and careers than those born without such wealth advantages.[68] In this regard, many scholars have long condemned societal processes that allocate individuals to different positions based on traits beyond their control, as such traits lack legitimacy and are considered antimeritocratic.[69] Scholars and practitioners writing about institutional and systemic racism have pointed out the forms of discrimination and racism that are embedded in the current norms, values, laws, regulations, practices, and structures of societies and organizations.[70] These biases create structural barriers to the economic and social advancement of disadvantaged racial and ethnic groups.

A pervasive criticism of meritocracy regards rising inequality as a by-product of meritocracy, something Markovits calls the "meritocracy trap."[71] This line of thought criticizes meritocratic approaches as "traps" that help to sustain social and economic inequalities. Others have faulted systems that advance people based on merit alone as lacking humility and solidarity because they stress personal responsibility as the anchoring driver of disparities in significant social and economic outcomes. In his book *The Tyranny of Merit*, Sandel offers an alternative approach to individual success, focusing on the role of luck and encouraging an "ethic of humility, solidarity, and dignity of work for all."[72] He traces the rise of the meritocratic ethos back to Puritan providentialism, often summarized by sayings like "God helps those who help themselves."

Many have further pointed out how meritocracy, particularly what has been called "technocratic meritocracy," has not helped Black Americans and many other racially disadvantaged groups. Ifeoma Ajunwa stressed that point in "What to the Black American Is the Meritocracy?" In this article, Ajunwa concludes that "if we are to escape the tyranny of the meritocracy, we must start with childhood interventions. . . . We must ensure access to early childhood education and to affordable childcare that could allow families to escape generations of poverty. The college admission process is merely the tip of the iceberg."[73] This observation echoes important points from Randall Kennedy's book *For Discrimination: Race, Affirmative Action, and the Law*. In particular, Kennedy reminds us that an essential condition for meritocracy to be successful is the provision of equal opportunity to everyone, particularly to historically disadvantaged groups.[74]

Certainly, many meritocratic efforts, particularly those in the workplace undertaken by organizations and businesses, have failed to ensure equal opportunity and fairness in practice. That said, it is worth noting that Young, in *The Rise of the Meritocracy*, meant the term *meritocracy* as a pejorative and as something not to be desired. Although the test-based method of advancement in postwar Britain seemed to offer greater opportunities than those offered before that, Young foresaw that this approach could become a new way for the wealthy elites to maintain their positions of power, influence, and wealth.

Young's argument, anchored in classical (and even contemporary) theories of stratification and social mobility, is that underprivileged children lacking access to critical resources such as high-quality primary and secondary schools are likely to perform poorly on some of these standardized exams used to decide which students gain access to selective colleges and universities. When such examinations and tests determine an individual's professional and personal future, those who have been disadvantaged will likely remain disadvantaged, with their low scores being used to justify why they should stay at lower levels of the social hierarchy. This line of argument from *The Rise of the Meritocracy* has been recognized for helping to limit the use of the eleven-plus exam in Britain, which was previously heavily used to allocate students ages eleven to twelve in grammar schools and other academically selective secondary schools.[75]

Other scholars and practitioners have since expressed similar concerns. Even though the test-based system appears fair and objective, it allows privileged youth to continue being privileged in primary and secondary schools and when gaining college admission.

Many have argued that similar problems can be identified in many of the existing processes used by businesses today, not only when deciding on the "right person" or who is the best to hire,[76] but also when focusing on who should be retained, rewarded, and advanced, especially in lean economic and social times.[77] Think about the particular criteria currently used when screening and hiring individuals. In many organizations, credentials like graduating from an elite higher education institution come into play when deciding whom to interview for a job opening. Later, it may turn out that the interview went well, perhaps in part because those recruiting had positive inclinations toward graduates from elite institutions to begin with, not necessarily because they were the most qualified for the position. Through such selection mechanisms, those individuals who never got a chance to get into some of the most elite programs in the world may be screened out of certain hiring processes.

Along similar lines, as current organizational efforts increasingly aim to complement and even replace human decision-making with AI and other technological solutions, many real-life examples have proven that algorithms can also be biased—in part because they still reflect the real world and can consequently be as biased as the natural-born intelligence applied to hiring in organizations. In a 2019 study of healthcare-related decisions published in *Science*, Ziad Obermeyer and colleagues found evidence of racial bias in a commercial algorithm widely employed in the United States to predict which patients would likely need extra medical care; the algorithm clearly advantaged White over Black patients. Even though the algorithm did not use the variable *race*, it used the variable *healthcare cost history* as a proxy for a person's health needs. This cost variable turned out to be highly correlated to race: on average, Black patients appeared to incur lower healthcare costs than White patients with the same medical conditions. Accordingly, the authors found that the algorithm falsely predicted that Black patients were healthier than equally sick White patients. As a result of this bias in the algorithm, the researchers estimated that the number of Black patients for whom extra care was recommended was lowered by more than half![78]

In 2018, Reuters also reported on Amazon's sexist hiring algorithm, originally designed to streamline the recruiting and hiring process by coding applicants' information from their résumés to pick the best-qualified candidates.[79] This AI tool, apparently trained using hiring data based on existing selection practices and outcomes at Amazon, strongly favored male candidates over female candidates.

To many, it is unsurprising that technological change can introduce bias. After all, AI models offer statistical representations of the world and provide answers based on what they have learned from existing data, whatever the quality or quantity of these data. Bias can come from the data that the AI tools are trained on (which can often be of low quality and biased), as well as from how such tools are designed, programmed, or implemented. Algorithms can also be subject to new hazards, such as misspecification problems and manipulation, and even when properly specified, they can still provide answers that are incorrect, inappropriate, or biased.[80] In that regard, as the use of AI continues to expand and progress, many advocate that "the best way to fight this [bias] is through education, training, and awareness."[81] Others recommend regulation.[82] I would further emphasize the need to proactively search for, collect, code, and analyze employment-relevant, high-quality data that can help organizations be more meritocratic and fair, with or without the use of new technologies.

BACK TO THE FUTURE OF MERITOCRACY

As David Civil and Joseph J. Himsworth neatly noted in 2020, "the concept of meritocracy still appeals and repels in equal measure."[83] For some, a true meritocracy represents a just, forward-looking distributive system aimed at removing nepotism, bribery, inheritance, and an individual's social and economic origins from key hiring, promotion, and compensation decisions. But to its critics, in practice, meritocracy has widened economic and social inequalities in income, wealth, and demographics.[84] They also point out how characteristics such as gender, race, and family origin continue to shape access to social and economic opportunities, ultimately determining who makes it and who does not in today's world.[85]

Because it is unclear whether a truly viable (better) alternative to meritocracy exists, I argue that our focus should be on identifying how meritocracy falls short in practice—and how it can be successfully improved. For the purposes of this book, it is therefore critical to understand *where* and *why* the meritocratic project has failed inside some organizations and businesses. Only then can we explore the practical steps leaders can take to strengthen meritocracy in their organizations, by targeting its failures and reinforcing its core principles.

This is why, in part II of the book, I outline the ways in which meritocracy has failed to live up to its promises in today's organizations and institutions. Then, in part III, I provide practical frameworks for leaders and managers seeking to improve and redesign their talent management processes to foster fairness and opportunity for all while restoring the promise of meritocracy. This is particularly relevant because, once again, we currently have no other clear, practical alternative to meritocracy for managing talent in a way that effectively recruits, selects, advances and retains the best talent—and the alternatives that *are* often proposed, as I discuss later in this book, do actually (even closely) resemble what I describe as the meritocratic ideal.

Chapter Two

MERITOCRACY IN THEORY

For several years, I have been investigating merit-driven organizational processes that aim to attract and hire top talent and then reward high performers over time. Whether implicitly or explicitly, those processes invoke the ideal of meritocracy and emphasize the importance of merit, talent, and opportunity in attaining it. Accordingly, my research collaborations with organizations have led me to identify patterns and develop predictions about what to expect if, indeed, an organization's processes and employment-related decisions are truly meritocratic.

I began this work at a time when meritocracy was widely popular, often celebrated and encouraged as a sign of progress in societies, organizations, and institutions worldwide. It continues to be so today. The ideal of meritocracy unambiguously promotes the goal of individuals getting ahead in society and organizations on the basis of their talents and encourages equal opportunity for all. It was also appealing because it is often assumed that meritocracy enhances efficiency and could even serve as a remedy for demographic discrimination and unfairness. Furthermore, meritocracy represented no doubt a significant improvement over previous distributive systems for deciding who gets ahead in life, which relied on family inheritance, nepotism, and patronage.

To evaluate meritocracy in practice, it is essential to first consider how meritocracy is supposed to work in theory, particularly in the context of working organizations and businesses. Ideally, how should organizations and their talent management systems operate to be considered fair and meritocratic? In particular, how should truly meritocratic organizations recruit and screen applicants for their positions? How should they then reward and advance the employees they hire? Who among their managers and workers should be promoted to the highest positions of power and authority? Before addressing these critical questions, I need to define meritocracy and talent management systems driven by merit, as well as to outline the key conditions that can help foster true meritocracy in today's organizations and institutions.

I define *meritocracy* as a social system that allows individuals to attain positions of power, status, or authority and to be rewarded with economic and social resources solely through their demonstrated intelligence, efforts, skills, abilities, or performance—often referred to as merits or talents relevant to employment and educational success—rather than because of their family class, wealth, origins, or demographic characteristics.[1] Since this definition of meritocracy applies to every single position and professional opportunity, especially in hiring organizations and selective institutions like public sector organizations and higher education, the successful operation of meritocracy implies that individuals should be matched to positions, jobs, and programs or degrees that best fit their merits and talents. In this regard, meritocracy has been equated with efficiency (i.e., it helps allocate individuals with the right talents to positions that align with the specific requirements and responsibilities of the job). Indeed, meritocracy is reflected in (and has inspired) many fundamental economic theories relating to labor markets and the role of education, experience, and skills in employment outcomes.

In the context of building meritocracies in practice, talent management systems are critical. By *talent management systems*, I refer to the organizational processes, practices, routines, values, norms, and beliefs—whether formalized or not—that shape the management of people within workplaces and organizations more broadly. These systems not only structure how individuals are attracted, hired, trained and developed, paid and rewarded, promoted or terminated, and retained, but also shape the underlying cultural expectations around performance, success, and fairness. They encompass a wide range of activities, including recruitment, selection, and hiring; training and professional development; performance evaluations; compensation and rewards; succession planning; leadership development; and career management, among many. To the extent that talent management systems align with an organization's strategic goals, their role in placing individuals into roles and positions where they can thrive, contribute meaningfully, and grow professionally—while also promoting long-term organizational success—makes them essential for fostering meritocracy in practice.

Equality of opportunity and *inequality of outcomes* are core principles in the design and functioning of a true meritocracy. As practiced by many contemporary organizations and businesses, meritocracy allows for, and even legitimizes, the presence of inequality in the distribution of social and economic resources and positions of power, status, and authority, as long as there are processes and procedures in place to guarantee that everyone has an equal chance to succeed. While the concepts of meritocracy, equality, fairness, and equity have been continually defined and refined over time, they are often misrepresented, used interchangeably, or conflated—leading to confusion and, at times, unintended consequences.

MERITOCRACY, INEQUALITY, AND OPPORTUNITY

According to its proponents, a meritocracy should permit inequality in the distribution of resources, as well as in positions of power, status, and authority, provided that all individuals have an opportunity to succeed based on merit.

A true meritocracy, therefore, relies on two fundamental premises. First, *meritocracy allows for and legitimizes inequality in the distribution of socially and economically desirable outcomes.*[2] It thus does not necessarily imply equality in the distribution of social goods and positions such as rewards and promotions. In other words, it is acceptable and often expected for meritocratic organizations and institutions to reward and advance certain individuals more than others, leading those with more valued merits and talents to do better economically and socially than those with less valued merits and talents. For example, certain large, middle-sized professional firms such as law firms or management consultancies often hire a cohort of excellent professionals each year, many of whom will never be promoted to higher positions within the firm.[3] In this respect, proponents of meritocracy favor unequal distribution of career outcomes, such as rewards and advancement to higher positions in the organizational hierarchy, if (and only if) societal institutions and organizational processes enable individuals to access positions and rewards based on their own merit (that is, based on meritocratic factors such as effort, skills, abilities, performance, and results). If other factors such as demographics, class, wealth, or family background do influence organizational processes relating to individuals' opportunities and career outcomes in organizations and businesses, then the distribution of social resources and positions is unlikely meritocratic because it is not based entirely on merit but instead includes non-meritocratic factors as well.

Second, *meritocracy relies on the provision of equal opportunity for all individuals in a society or social organization*, so that all individuals with merit and talent can be identified and can have an equal chance to advance to higher positions or obtain desirable social and economic resources.[4] This principle implies that the resources necessary to help individuals succeed in society are provided to all, regardless of their demographic background. In other words, meritocratic organizations must offer equal opportunities to all, irrespective of their personal characteristics and other features ascribed at birth, even if that requires correcting for circumstances that may have disproportionally disadvantaged certain individuals. To do so specifically, organizations and businesses may have to provide *unequal* resources to different groups of individuals for them all to have equal opportunity to succeed. For example, organizations may provide different types of onboarding programs to different groups of hires in order to give them all an equal opportunity to perform successfully in their jobs. Another example is when organizations may offer free and reduced-cost meals and other basic learning materials to parents of children from low-income families to ensure that children can attend school and focus on learning without being distracted by hunger or economic burden. This second premise behind ensuring equal opportunity is often conflated or confused with the first one.

As described in chapter 1, the meritocracy philosophy arose in response to prior approaches to determining the "proper" distribution of key resources in society and deciding who deserves an opportunity to reach higher levels of success and income. In aristocratic societies, it was considered legitimate to allocate the best educational opportunities and jobs based on individuals' social position at birth (that is, on hereditary family wealth and social origins).[5] Meritocracy was also a response to prior class-based and demographic-based systems that determined which people should be hired and advanced. It was about explicitly removing nepotism, bribery, patronage, inheritance, and individuals' social and economic origins from key employment and other societal decisions—all factors that were contributing to professional success in life (or lack thereof) at the time. This proposition is precisely what made meritocracy an appealing alternative to existing distributive processes; it was seen as a forward-looking and fair distributive approach.

The meritocracy principle relies on key assumptions about individualism, intelligence, hard work, family origins, wealth, and class, as well as norms regarding what is appropriate, just, and equitable when it comes to determining socioeconomic mobility. It tells, as reflected in current strategies driving talent selection and promotion inside companies, the motivational story that the merits, talents, and abilities of individuals (not their family members or their wealth or position in society) determine what they achieve and how they achieve.

In figure 2.1, I represent the two necessary conditions for an organization to operate as a true meritocracy. First, recruitment and selection should be equitable in the sense that hiring and promotion opportunities are open (and

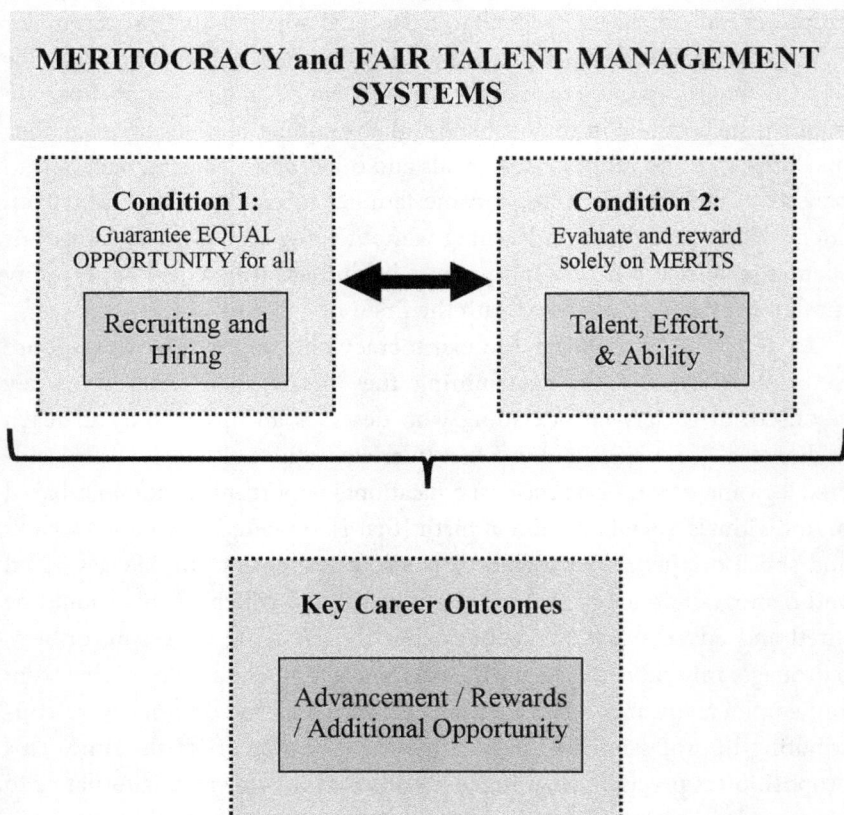

MERITOCRACY and FAIR TALENT MANAGEMENT SYSTEMS

Condition 1:
Guarantee EQUAL OPPORTUNITY for all

Recruiting and Hiring

Condition 2:
Evaluate and reward solely on MERITS

Talent, Effort, & Ability

Key Career Outcomes

Advancement / Rewards / Additional Opportunity

FIGURE 2.1. The ideal of meritocracy and opportunity in organizations.

should be proactively made available) to all. Candidates should be evaluated on their talents and accomplishments alone while ensuring that those qualifications are indeed relevant and valid for the opportunity, role, or job in question. However, as I will explain later, to accomplish equal opportunity during screening and hiring, organizations may need to provide extra resources (including relevant education, experience, and training and development) to ensure that *all* can be successful to begin with. Second, after guaranteeing equal opportunity to succeed, different career outcomes based on key and employment-relevant merits are allowed, though not always expected, in a true meritocracy. This last condition is what is often described as an equitable and fair approach to allocating rewards and career opportunities in organizations.

When met, these two key conditions can help make an organization more meritocratic in practice. Consequently, organizations that aim to be meritocratic should focus on meeting and reinforcing such conditions when designing, implementing, and monitoring their talent management processes to ensure that those processes are fair and promote equality of opportunity. Further, a truly meritocratic approach can guarantee that the most talented employees are best positioned to help the organization succeed. In this respect, meritocracy is not only an ideal way to provide equal opportunity for all; it is also effective in that it matches individuals to roles and organizations in which they can best use their talents and rewards them for their contributions to an organization's success.

In education, an example of an ideal meritocracy is offering all children free, high-quality educational opportunities irrespective of their parents' class, wealth, origins, demographics, or any other individual characteristics at birth. This approach helps ensure that all children with the relevant talents can advance in education and compete for jobs based on their achievements. This has been, in fact, the focus of many policymakers' and politicians' aspirations across the world, particularly in progressive societies. But much more could be done. For instance, consider what higher education institutions and policymakers can do, through fellowships and scholarships, to open the doors and put more students on the path to college and a degree. Such policies are helpful in providing less privileged children (of all demographics) the same opportunity for and access to higher education as the children of more privileged parents, who can afford the tuition and the opportunity cost of their children not entering the workforce right after high school.

An example in the workplace is organizations offering merit- or performance-based rewards to help achieve their performance goals. Indeed, the premise that the best performers should receive greater rewards has led to the growth of incentive pay and other merit-based benefits in organizations. It has also been part of an effort to increase motivation and effort by distributing rewards and bonuses only when employees meet their performance targets. To ensure that there is a true meritocracy in the implementation of such systems, organizations can and should allocate bonuses and other forms of incentive pay and benefits based on performance while guaranteeing that all employees, regardless of their demographics, have the same opportunities to achieve high performance. This involves employees all having access to resources like onboarding, training, mentoring, feedback, flexibility, and even, in some cases, childcare or other home care programs.

CONDITION 1: GUARANTEE EQUAL OPPORTUNITY FOR ALL

The provision of equal opportunities across the board is, therefore, a key requirement for a true meritocracy. Indeed, the lack of equal opportunity has been the most criticized aspect of the so-called meritocratic fabric of America. For example, as noted earlier, a Pew Research Center survey of STEM (science, technology, engineering, and math) US workers found that, while the majority of such workers believe their race or ethnicity has made no difference in their ability to succeed in their job, there are substantial differences in such beliefs depending on the race of the STEM worker: Blacks (40 percent), Asians (31 percent), and Hispanics (19 percent) in STEM jobs are much more likely than White STEM workers (5 percent) to say it has been harder for them to find success in their career because of their race or ethnicity. The survey further indicated how perceptions of being treated fairly or unfairly when it comes to hiring and promotions vary significantly depending on the respondent's race. For instance, 43 percent of Blacks in STEM jobs (compared to 78 percent of Whites) believe that Blacks are usually treated fairly during recruitment and hiring at work; 37 percent (compared to 75 percent of Whites) say that this is the case during promotion and advancement opportunities.[6]

From a social science perspective, *opportunities* consist of all the plausible choices an individual can make given their key constraints.[7] Such constraints can be social, economic, organizational, political, or technological. For example, a recent college graduate's opportunity to get an analyst job in a consulting firm may depend on the number of analysts that the firm can hire (that is, the supply of available jobs, often affected by broader economic conditions outside the firm), the number of other college graduates applying for the same position (the demand for jobs), the graduate's qualifications ("merits") relative to those of others (the quality of the pool of candidates), and other geographical and financial constraints. In this respect, the various opportunities available to an individual may involve many factors outside their control, even though situations exist in which new positions are created for individuals or exceptions are made to job specifications to fill a position.

In theory, equal opportunity in *choices* would imply that all individuals, regardless of their backgrounds, would have the same choices. However, the personal decision-making behind such choices does not occur in isolation; instead, it is contextual and is often affected by other conditions and the choices and actions of others. For example, the many disadvantages that mothers of young children, particularly single mothers, face in the labor market and workplace have been well documented, particularly in households where mothers are expected to do most of the childcare.[8] Such expectations (often realities) make it much harder for mothers of young children to succeed in the workplace compared to fathers. In such situations, if mothers choose paid work, their job options and the features of those jobs tend to be much more constrained than those of fathers (in terms of number of hours worked, commuting time, job travel requirements, etc.). The job options that single mothers have are likely to be even more reduced, especially if they are mothers without much support to raise their children while working.

Further, opportunities can be created, expanded, reduced, or even eliminated over time. For instance, COVID-19 clearly provided opportunities for certain groups of professionals while limiting opportunities (and even making it much harder) for others. Compare, for example, retail employees with university staff members, given the different expectations and resources provided to each group during the pandemic to perform their jobs. Changing the structure of opportunities in a given organization or institution also clearly affects employees' particular choices.

Finally, even if they face equivalent choices, individuals likely have different *preferences* regarding which opportunities they choose to pursue. Based on their preferences and constraints, some may seek specific opportunities, while others will not. Scholars have long argued, for instance, that job seekers may be steered to particular jobs based on their gender.[9] Biased expectations may additionally shape job search and application behaviors by gender, as candidates evaluate their own competencies based on how they expect others to assess them,[10] especially employers and those in charge of recruiting and hiring.[11] A classic study by Shelley Correll suggested that such gendered self-assessments shape the career choice processes differently for women and men; when participants in a lab experiment were led to believe that men, on average, are better at a particular task, men rated their abilities higher than women did and had higher aspirations for completing the task.[12]

The concept of opportunity has been extensively covered in the study of social and workplace inequality; for instance, numerous studies have looked at the effect of sex and race on access to education and employment, as well as access to healthcare, housing, and credit. That said, equality of opportunity does not necessarily ensure equality of outcomes and professional success. This may be the case because people have different merits and talents, as a true meritocracy would acknowledge, but also because they have different preferences for educational programs or jobs, or face constraints preventing them from considering some opportunities. In this respect, a study of job-seeking MBAs revealed that women are less likely than men to expect to get offers for jobs in stereotypically masculine industries such as finance, thereby reducing their likelihood of applying for such jobs.[13]

Along these lines, job seekers' expectations for their success in getting hired by an organization may vary based on factors such as the recruiter's gender. One study found, for instance, that when a woman is the key hiring decision-maker in a law firm, women make up a larger proportion of new hires compared to when the decision-maker is a man.[14] Additionally, evidence suggests that such expectations can influence application decisions for members of disadvantaged groups: for example, studies have identified a positive relationship between the presence of Black hiring managers and the number of Black job applicants.[15] They posit that Black candidates may perceive Black recruiters in positions of authority as indicators of reduced discrimination or increased preference for Black applicants in the hiring process at that firm. Furthermore, the presence of a Black recruiter could signal better advancement chances for Black employees at the firm. This research suggests that job seekers might anticipate greater success when interacting with hiring personnel from their own in-group. Similar social processes may be at play when, for example, an individual belonging to a historically disadvantaged group may prefer to work at an organization where that group is well represented; the individual may also believe that members of the same group are more likely to be interested and apply for jobs in certain occupations and industries. Such preferences play a role in decision-making. Similar arguments can be provided for many other demographics and personal qualities that can shape expectations of success and opportunity in particular occupations and firms.

Constraints also limit the set of potential opportunities. For instance, demographic segregation into geographic regions may advantage groups that live closer to better opportunities. Others may be unable to accept better jobs farther away from their homes because of constraints such as parental needs to be close to their families, poor availability of public transportation, or other factors.

All of this illustrates that promoting equal opportunity in education and the workplace is incredibly challenging. In practice, I have found that many organizations fail to meet this first critical condition when, for instance, their recruiting and selection processes do not give equal opportunities to diverse populations, especially those that have been historically disadvantaged. Additionally, organizations often fail to meet this condition when demographic biases and social barriers influence selection and hiring processes, favoring certain demographic groups over others.[16]

CONDITION 2: EVALUATE AND REWARD SOLELY ON MERIT

The second key requirement for a true meritocracy consists of distributing rewards and socially desirable outcomes based on merit. This means that there could be unequal rewards, promotions, and even developmental opportunities across demographic groups, and that is legitimate and fair when merit and performance differ. That is why the concept of equal opportunity for all is critical for the pursuit of meritocracy in the workplace. Truly meritocratic organizations need to ensure equal access to education, training, orientations, and other necessary resources that individuals need to be successful in their roles, regardless of demographic and other ascriptive (i.e., given at birth) characteristics.

Meritocracy does rely on a particular definition of *fairness*: treatment and behavior that are free of bias and other social processes that may favor or hinder certain groups of individuals based on ascriptive personal qualities that are irrelevant to employment and performance. In this regard, concerning the popular concept of "procedural justice" in the academic literature, meritocracy, too, requires fairness (defined as formal equal opportunity for all) and transparency of the organizational processes by which decisions are made regarding how to reward and advance individuals in organizations. Similar to the concept of "distributive justice," meritocracy considers it fair for the distribution of outcomes to be entirely based on merit—sometimes resulting in equal distribution and sometimes in unequal distribution—provided that equal opportunity for all is guaranteed.[17] (Unsurprisingly, research studies have shown that people cannot clearly separate their judgments about procedures from knowledge of the outcomes of such procedures.)[18]

A related concept is *equity*, broadly defined as fairness and justice. In organizational and social contexts, equity often refers to fairness and impartiality in processes, policies, and resource distribution, taking into account individual or systemic disadvantages to ultimately guarantee just outcomes. Unlike *equality*, which provides the same resources or opportunities to everyone, equity recognizes that people have different starting points and face unique challenges; it consequently seeks to address disparities by allocating resources unequally based on need. In this regard, like meritocracy, equity aims to create conditions where all individuals have a fair chance to succeed, regardless of background or circumstances.[19]

Equity and meritocracy share a common goal: fairness in opportunity and outcomes. Both emphasize that individuals should be evaluated based on their abilities, contributions, and efforts rather than factors like socioeconomic background, wealth, or demographics. They are similar in their commitment to fairness, recognizing that talent and effort should be the basis for advancement rather than inherited status or favoritism. Additionally, both principles seek to identify and remove barriers to success—while equity typically (and explicitly) addresses systemic disadvantages, a properly functioning meritocracy also requires eliminating any biases and any social processes that prevent fair evaluation and treatment. In this respect, a true meritocracy depends on equity to ensure that all individuals, regardless of their starting point, have a fair chance to compete and succeed based on their merits.[20]

Significant work in political philosophy regarding inequality has also been critical in shaping present-day discussions of meritocracy, fairness, and equity. Many theorists and philosophers have underscored that with meritocracy, one will, without question, have (and should expect) inequality. In this context, I would argue that many theorists (even scholars and practitioners) are egalitarian; the question is in which dimension they are egalitarian. Should it be in opportunity, resources, outcomes, and/or welfare?

In chapter 6 of *The Constitution of Liberty*, titled "Equality, Value and Merit," Friedrich Hayek argues that the fundamental equality required for a free society is equality before the law, "in spite of the fact that they [people] are different," which will inevitably lead to unequal outcomes.[21] In this line, American legal professional and philosopher Ronald Dworkin emphasized that governments should show equal concern for all citizens.[22] Behind this account of political equality lies a form of distributive justice—the idea that individuals should have equal resources to pursue their lives successfully, which may result in different outcomes. The real question, as Amartya Sen put it, is "Inequality of What?"[23] Sen argued that our concerns should be about people's capabilities rather than their resources or welfare. He advocated for ensuring that everyone has the same opportunities to succeed, regardless of personal characteristics, with a focus on improving access to the tools individuals can use to live the kind of life they want.

Meritocracy as a distributive principle, while relying on equality of opportunity, does not necessarily support equality of outcomes. Indeed, organizational practices that reward and promote employees without considering performance, for instance, may be regarded as not only unfair but also demotivating because they provide little incentive for employees to improve performance in their roles. This belief is widely held, even though the psychology and sociology of motivation are much more complex than that.[24]

Similarly, organizational practices that equalize monetary rewards across all employees (regardless of performance, effort, and other achievements) are often unpopular and discouraged by HR professionals and consultants. Ironically, some even label these efforts unfair, given the prevailing meritocratic ethos that employees should be rewarded for better performance. That is, even though pay-for-performance schemes have been proven to be optimal only under particular circumstances, such as when productivity can be measured accurately in terms of quantity and quality, and when high levels of productivity, while challenging, are achievable. [A note of clarification: Meritocracy does not always have to lead to inequality in the distribution of desirable outcomes. For instance, if all employees of an organization possess similar merits and perform equally in the same jobs, then the magnitude of their performance-based bonuses should, in principle, be equal.]

Fairness in the evaluation of performance, effort, and skills, as examples of key merits in today's organizations, is also critical. In fact, when certain demographic groups experience bias in their performance evaluations, for instance, with consequent unequal outcomes for rewards and promotions, an antimeritocratic ethos may also come into play because the employees experiencing systemic bias are not being offered fair and equal opportunities to succeed. This is especially problematic in situations where performance is subjective, does not include relevant information about the role, introduces irrelevant factors (especially non-meritocratic ones), or allows for personal prejudices and favoritism to affect the evaluation process.

Another worrisome problem occurs when "merit" or "talent" is defined selectively to prevent particular groups of individuals from attaining better organizational roles and positions. Consider empirical studies of the "glass ceiling," a metaphor often used to describe the invisible barriers that prevent women,[25] as well as other disadvantaged groups,[26] from reaching higher positions of power and authority in organizations. These are cases where scholars have repeatedly suggested that certain demographic traits make it more difficult for individuals to advance professionally and achieve leadership positions in organizations and society.

THREE LOGICS THAT INFLUENCE ORGANIZATIONAL DECISION-MAKING

One crucial part of achieving meritocracy in practice is clearly defining what the organization and its leaders consider fair, just, and appropriate in decision-making in their particular organizational context, mainly when distributing desirable resources and determining employment outcomes. Several common logics around this definition of fairness in decision-making are what we have called the *meritocratic, material,* and *diversity* logics.[27]

When considering how individuals are selected and rewarded within organizations, the most widespread assumption is that decision-makers in hiring organizations look for the best talent. This *meritocratic logic* refers to the reasoning by which decision-makers invoke qualifications and professional accomplishments when deciding which applicants to hire into an organization, promote, or reward.[28] They may prefer certain types of candidates if knowing an applicant's type helps them identify who is the most talented.[29] In the context of screening and hiring, for example, we could focus on three reasons or explanations why some applicants may be preferred over others when decision-makers evaluate candidates: the candidate may be "better qualified," a "better performer," or a "better citizen or better team player."

The first explanation implies that applicants will be more likely to get hired because they appear to be stronger applicants on paper in terms of their listed skills and abilities. We call this the "better qualified" explanation. Hiring managers and recruiters may also prefer candidates who are perceived to be "better performers," that is, who are expected to achieve higher levels of performance and greater professional accomplishments. In accordance with the "better citizen" explanation, hiring managers may prefer candidates who display a strong capacity for increased company involvement and support for the organization. All these explanations would reinforce the meritocratic logic: that the most qualified, best-performing, and most committed candidates should be selected and advanced in the organization.

A second key logic is the *material logic*. Often, decision-makers and their organizations have economic and financial interests or constraints when hiring and promoting individuals. Indeed, many organizations are encouraged to establish their material interests and targets when selecting candidates—especially given today's highly competitive landscape and pressure to be profitable.[30] For instance, some scholars and practitioners have warned that wealth and family connections could influence recruitment and screening, especially in elite institutions.[31] Many businesses have indeed admitted that they prefer applicants with strong ties (family and friends, for instance) to current employees because of the potential business benefits.[32] In colleges and universities, admissions officers have recently faced criticism for giving preferential admission to alumni's children or siblings, and many have begun to terminate legacy admission practices formally.[33]

A particular type of material logic, related to the meritocratic one, is the so-called business logic, which proposes that it makes "business sense" to recruit and hire certain types of individuals. The business logic usually invokes revenues, performance targets, and profitability metrics attributed to a company's leadership. It also refers to future measures of business success, such as promotability and retention. Such logic is invoked in situations where particular groups of candidates are seen as more appealing than others when making employment decisions.[34]

Finally, a third decision-making logic has to do with *diversity*. In today's organizations and businesses, particularly in North America and across other Western societies, leaders and managers are frequently prompted to recruit and retain candidates with diverse experiences and backgrounds, and to promote successful inclusion of all hires in the workplace. In the past decade, multiple reports and recommendations from HR professionals and leaders have promoted diversity in the management of people; some even make the business case for it.[35] Accordingly, certain organizations and businesses have tried to promote diversity and inclusion in response to past racial and gender injustices, among many.[36] This logic, therefore, refers to organizational goals to increase the diversity of the pools of recruits, hires, and long-term employees and professionals in contemporary organizations.

Diversity logic currently faces significant criticism, especially when individuals appear to be selected more for their demographics than for being the most qualified or talented. The backlash has primarily centered on diversity, equity, and inclusion (DEI) initiatives in higher education and corporate settings. Some critics are seen as misunderstanding or overlooking DEI's mission to address historical injustices and systemic biases that have disadvantaged certain social groups historically.[37] Others contend that DEI promotes reverse discrimination, claiming that it legitimizes practices such as hiring or promoting fewer men or fewer individuals from groups like Whites or Asians. Some believe that DEI undermines meritocracy by prioritizing diversity over qualifications or talent; this belief has contributed to the rise of anti-DEI legislation in higher education and recent efforts to eliminate DEI efforts in organizations and businesses.[38] Many have also pointed out that the tension between meritocracy and DEI may have been aggravated by DEI consultants, who "were detached from the core business, pursuing social justice rather than evidence-based initiatives."[39] Concerns have also been raised that DEI initiatives add layers of costly bureaucracy without yielding substantial results.[40]

Whether these criticisms are justified or not, any one of these competing logics alone can become problematic when or if it clashes with the other two, such as when the diversity logic seems to contradict the meritocratic one or is materially costly.

WHY MERITOCRACY IS SO DIFFICULT TO ACHIEVE

I am often asked why it is so difficult to design and implement a true meritocracy in organizations and businesses. To answer this question, I have developed a framework that illustrates the tensions among the three previously described logics when leaders and managers make employment choices such as which candidates to hire, advance, or reward in their organizations.

The framework, as summarized in figure 2.2., shows that the three logics are not mutually exclusive in practice. The best position to be in, but one that is often difficult to attain, is at the center of the figure, where the three logics overlap. In reality, achieving such a balance is challenging and requires

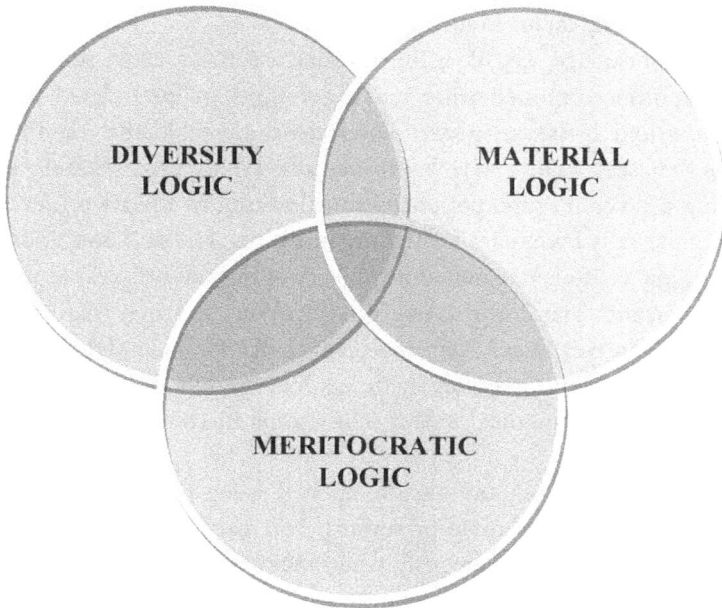

FIGURE 2.2. Three common logics in organizational decision-making.

effort and strategy. Nevertheless, it is possible to do so. For example, several businesses and organizations have effectively adopted practices to identify and hire the most talented and diverse candidates while minimizing screening and hiring costs.[41]

Often, however, organizations and their leaders end up navigating other parts of the framework, where one or two of the other logics may not necessarily be maximized. Such approaches can be counterproductive and problematic in the long run. For example, affirmative action in university admissions has long been criticized for the potential negative effect (not always empirically supported) that it may have on the meritocratic logic. The 2023 Supreme Court ruling that effectively ended this practice in the United States means that universities will need to rethink and redefine the concept of merit and assess candidates not only on current achievements but also in the broader context of their individual circumstances.[42] Similar challenges face organizations that have relied purely on material logic to select candidates for their most important roles. For instance, this is often the case in family businesses, where nepotism, regardless of the candidate's merits, may be a deciding factor in hiring decisions.

In the workplace, key decision-makers use these three sense-making strategies, often combined, when making complex people-related decisions. Recruiters and hiring managers entertain many objectives at the same time as they seek to hire new employees who (1) are professionally strong, (2) bring a diversity of experiences and thinking to their workforce, and (3) are materially beneficial for the organization. The decision to hire certain candidates often satisfies some objectives but not others. For example, some applicants may have strong qualifications but may require strong financial incentives to get them to accept their offers (implying more cost for the organization to recruit them, such as signing bonuses in the case of businesses and financial aid or fellowships in the case of educational programs).

The same framework can also be applied when managers are deciding which candidates to promote or reward. For instance, managers consider multiple objectives simultaneously when making promotion decisions that will (1) reward high-performing employees, (2) contribute to the diversity of experiences and backgrounds in the company's talent pipeline, and (3) be in line with organizational budget constraints. Again, the decision to reward certain employees often satisfies some objectives but not others. For example, a number of employees may have strong performance, but because of financial constraints, not all of them may get a bonus or could be promoted given the limited available positions.

Although the three logics are conceptually different, they are not necessarily independent or always competing in practice. They are part of what Mitchell Stevens calls "evaluative storytelling," as gatekeepers and key decision-makers pursue many goals and strategies simultaneously when making people management decisions.[43] In this regard, this tripartite decision-making framework should warn leaders that those individuals in charge of designing and implementing merit- or talent-based practices in their organizations are critical for ensuring that meritocracy works in practice. These decision-makers can have different and multiple motivations when implementing the processes and monitoring their outcomes. Consequently, when considering why organizations may fail to be truly meritocratic, we need to assess which logic(s) may be operating during organizational decision-making and act accordingly to address any fairness challenges.

MERITOCRACY AS A MOTIVATIONAL TACTIC

One compelling business aspect of meritocracy is that it motivates individuals to work hard, take training and developmental opportunities seriously, seek positions best suited to their skills, and perform well in those positions. Motivation and responsibility are often invoked as "merits" that individuals bring to their positions and lives.

According to a 2024 Gallup report, only 23 percent of employees feel engaged at work. While this level is low, it was even lower in 2009 (12 percent) before gradually improving over time until the COVID-19 pandemic disrupted that trend. The highest levels of employee engagement worldwide are found in the United States and Canada, where 33 percent of employees describe themselves as feeling engaged at work, compared with Europe (13 percent) or the Middle East and North Africa (14 percent).[44] Particularly in times of low engagement, companies seek to revamp their organizational processes to address these challenges effectively.

Meritocracy, in this respect, offers a powerful way to foster individual motivation and responsibility; it presumably leads to greater levels of performance and success in the workplace. It not only encourages employees to excel but also motivates parents to invest in their children's education, skills, and experiences so that they can maintain or even surpass their parents' social and economic achievements. In this way, meritocracy can help guarantee a steady supply of talented individuals, essential for maintaining high-functioning organizations.

Systems that promote opportunity further motivate individuals to get jobs that match their merits and do their best once on the job. Such systems make individuals responsible for whether they get jobs or are promoted, and thus create a sense of fairness and justice, equity. Conversely, a common criticism of meritocracy is that it makes individuals wholly accountable for their successes and failures while ignoring societal and structural factors that help some individuals and hinder others. An improved version of meritocracy— one I propose in this book—will also make organizations and their leaders responsible for ensuring that all job candidates and hires have equal opportunity to succeed (which may require providing *unequal* resources to different groups of individuals for them all to have equal opportunity to succeed) so that ultimately those with merit rise fairly.

Meritocracy can also be culturally pleasing and enticing, especially to individualistic, ambitious, and driven individuals. This may explain why some organizations evaluate candidates publicly as a way of fostering competition and creating incentives to excel. "Look to your right, look to your left: Only one of you will be promoted in the future," I once heard a senior partner of a well-known professional firm tell an incoming cohort of analysts in the early 2000s. The comment intended to motivate all new hires in a firm where "great rewards and great success" awaited the best. Similar statements are made in many other workplaces.

Moreover, when the sky is the limit, individuals believe that anything is possible with talent and effort. They also tend to believe that there is little luck involved. In countries like the United States, one frequently hears inspirational stories of people, especially entrepreneurs, overcoming obstacles and challenges with hard work and ability. Steve Jobs and Bill Gates dropped out of college, while Larry Page and Sergey Brin never finished their PhD programs, but the companies they founded—Apple, Microsoft, and Alphabet, respectively— are three of the world's largest, worth trillions of dollars. These founders' personal stories of intelligence, perseverance, and effort now motivate thousands of young students and entrepreneurs worldwide to pursue their dreams.

Even stories of failure can inspire people to carry on; failure is sometimes characterized as simply another opportunity to try something new. Along those lines, Henry Ford once described failure as the opportunity to begin again "more intelligently." Many believe, in fact, that failure makes us stronger and thus can be important for future career success. The implication is that, with intelligence and effort, all is possible.

While many organizations have avoided using the word *meritocracy* in the descriptions of their structures and cultures, I argue that the ideal of meritocracy remains in commonly used rhetorical expressions such as "hiring the best," "recruiting the top talent," and "promoting the right candidate," among others. Notice that "good enough for the position" is not used at all. It is less appealing and enticing not only to those doing the recruitment and hiring but also to the prospective candidates looking for a job—who are also looking for the best job. This is partly why we keep returning, over and over again, to the meritocratic rhetoric about the best talent and the best approaches to managing such talent.

THREE CRUCIAL STAGES FOR FOSTERING MERITOCRACY

How can your organization or business implement—and even foster— meritocracy in its management of people? This is the question I want you to consider now. Figure 2.3 summarizes the key stages at which your organization

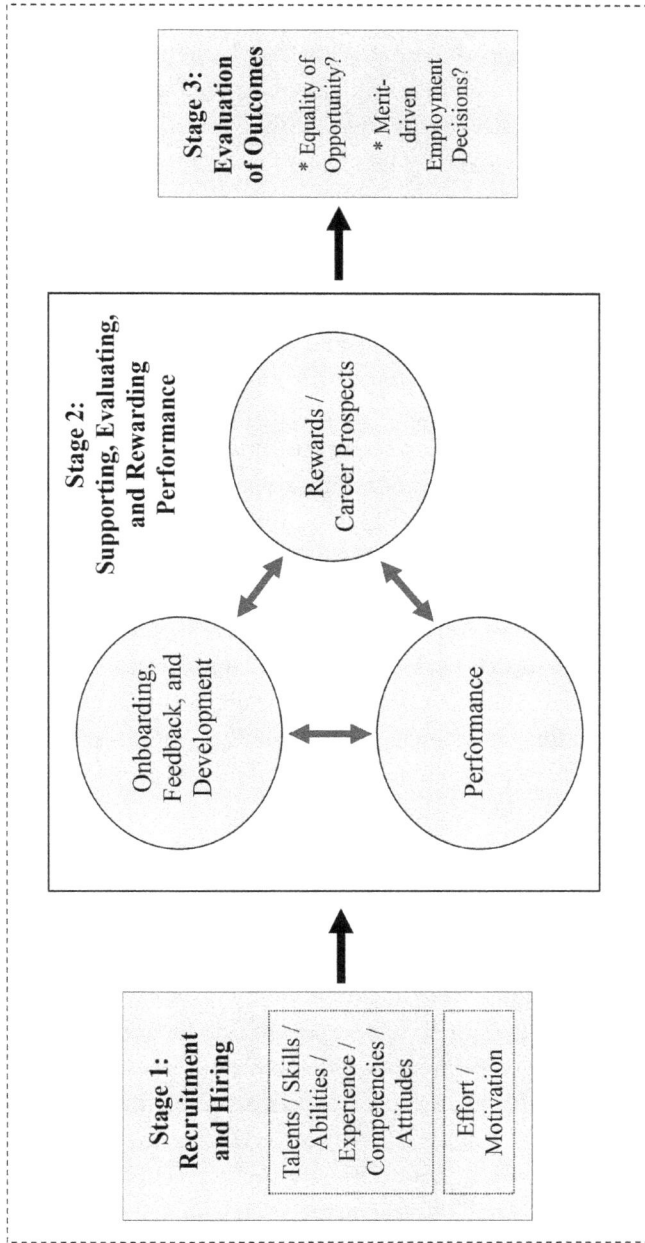

Stage 1: Recruitment and Hiring

- Talents / Skills / Abilities / Experience / Competencies / Attitudes
- Effort / Motivation

Stage 2: Supporting, Evaluating, and Rewarding Performance

- Onboarding, Feedback, and Development
- Rewards / Career Prospects
- Performance

Stage 3: Evaluation of Outcomes

- * Equality of Opportunity?
- * Merit-driven Employment Decisions?

FIGURE 2.3. The strategic management of people, meritocracy, and opportunity in organizations.

and main decision-makers (such as recruiters, hiring managers, and other managers) are likely to evaluate merit and talents and consequently make important career decisions for your employees, whether meritocratic or not.

Stage 1, *Recruiting and Hiring*, involves attracting, recruiting, and selecting applicants. At this stage, employers, either directly or through hiring managers or recruiters, advertise jobs on websites, job boards, online platforms, or through referrals. When doing so, they decide what information to include in their advertisement of the job and the organization, with the goal of maximizing the number of qualified applicants for each open position. They also describe the type of candidate (*ideal* is the word often used) they look for and the "right" attributes and competencies of the ideal hire (that is, merits). Because some employers post their jobs only on certain sites or use specific recruitment sources, they may not reach certain subpopulations of candidates, consequently limiting the organization's ability to give opportunities to all. Advertising opportunities in ways that reach everyone is crucial for successful recruitment in meritocratic organizations—that is, locating potential hires and encouraging all qualified candidates to apply.

Job seekers, in turn, learn of, inquire about, and apply for available jobs based on job descriptions, recruitment messages, and word of mouth. Consequently, any processes at work during candidate recruitment and screening that discourage or encourage particular groups of applicants to consider and apply for certain jobs should be addressed. Such processes may contribute, for example, to the maintenance of gender and racial segregation in today's organizations and businesses.[45] In addition, certain individuals may face preferences and constraints because of their personal and demographic backgrounds, something that should ideally be addressed at this stage as well.

After recruiting applicants, organizations screen and select from the applicant pool. They decide on a series of skills and competencies required for the job. Some employers look for attitude and fit. Others look for sets of skills and experiences. A few even brag about simply looking for motivated individuals who want to work for them, stating that abilities and skills can be developed after the hire. In theory, this process seems straightforward: a company knows the job it needs to fill, has a list of required criteria for the job, and has to find a person who meets those criteria well. In practice, to be successful meritocracy-wise, it is crucial to pay attention to *who* defines what is necessary for the job (and *how* they develop the definition), *what* the job really entails, and *how* criteria may be adjusted as organizations examine résumés and applications, interview candidates, and ultimately decide *whether* to offer employment and to *whom*. Similar criteria should be used equally for every-body, and the criteria should be valid and relevant for the position.

To be systematic and careful in this stage, many organizations measure and code a set of competencies for each applicant. While recognizing that not every applicant has all desired competencies, this serves as a guideline for taking a holistic approach to identifying the ideal candidate. Here, it is critical to acknowledge research suggesting that the "ideal" candidate may not really exist; rather, companies should look for good candidates and build from there. Often, I have argued for the "good enough" approach—that is, someone who is good for the position—rather than engaging in a perpetual (and often never-ending) obsession with attracting and finding the best. This is especially true for organizations that face a limited supply of employees in specific occupations and labor markets.[46]

Once offers are accepted, the process of granting equal opportunities for all should continue.[47] This is stage 2, *Supporting, Evaluating, and Rewarding Performance*. In a truly meritocratic organization, this stage presupposes that everyone has had equal opportunity to be successfully onboarded into the company and that early feedback and development have been provided to all to ensure their success in their jobs.

Many organizations offer little training after the hire, assuming that the hired candidates already have the skills and merits to succeed in their job, even though research has repeatedly shown that even "star performers" in a given organization may not perform well in a new and different organizational context.[48] In other words, a great performer in a specific role at a particular company does not necessarily perform as well in the same role at a different company or in a different role. Organizations also frequently overlook the extent to which their practices and values influence the success of candidates in their roles.

In this respect, it is crucial to examine critically how the processes behind feedback, performance, and rewards interact over time and whether they reinforce one another in productive ways. Stage 2 in figure 2.3 illustrates that performance, development, and rewards should be strategically aligned with each other, as indicated by the arrows going both ways.

This alignment is critical for the successful functioning of a true meritocracy. Once organizations hire individuals, they should provide them with the necessary onboarding and resources to help them be successful and productive in their jobs. This preparation should precede the evaluation of performance. Going forward, those who perform well in their roles should receive rewards and promotions, and those who do not should be given a chance to be trained and developed so they can learn and improve their performance. I often refer to this framework as the *Performance-Development-Reward strategic framework*: a virtuous circle of strategic development, performance assessment, and rewards for employees, whereby organizational leaders need to ensure that these three key people-related processes are aligned and reinforce one another.

I have seen many examples of misalignment at this stage. Many organizations I have worked with hire the best candidates they can identify but do not provide much onboarding or training. They then evaluate employees' performance to decide which employees to reward, which to promote, and which to fire. They presume that the smartest and the most able will survive and succeed, while those who do not probably should not have been hired in the first place. In these businesses, little attention is given to training or providing resources to give all equal chances to succeed in their jobs. Given employees' disparate backgrounds and circumstances, such organizations are consequently failing to make sure that everyone has equal opportunities to succeed professionally—condition 1 of a true meritocracy at work.

For many reasons, certain organizations and businesses also experience a problematic disconnect between performance and rewards. Often, it is because there is no proper way for managers to evaluate performance (or they are not adequately trained to do so), or they simply have limited time and resources. In such cases, though, organizations still need to reward and promote the best to remain competitive, if only to prevent top performers from taking jobs at competing organizations. As I frequently ask participants in my talent management courses to reflect: who will work for you if employees never receive proper rewards or advancement opportunities over time (that is, condition 2 of a true meritocracy)? Hence, we have seen dramatically greater emphasis on retaining and promoting top talent, but often too late, when talented employees have already applied to work for competitors. In many cases, a disconnect between performance and rewards exists, especially when employers offer rewards that employees do not value.

Stage 3, *Evaluating Outcomes*, consists of continuously assessing key employment outcomes and results at the company level and over time, especially those that relate to recruitment, development, performance, and rewards. Organizations should carefully collect, code, and analyze data to assess the extent to which their personnel management processes ensure equality of opportunity for all, and they should explore whether these selection processes unfairly advantage or disadvantage particular groups. At this stage, it is also important to investigate and ensure that specific, relevant, and valid merits are consistently employed in such talent management processes. Companies should additionally examine the extent to which key personnel decisions are driven purely by merit. Important metrics can help an organization measure and evaluate how meritocratic its key talent management practices are.

The strategic framework in figure 2.3 can therefore help organizations and businesses identify *where* they may have a problem in being truly meritocratic and find "blind spots," that is, structural places, choice points, or situations where (1) equality of opportunity may not be provided effectively (condition 1 of a true meritocracy at work) or (2) the criteria or factors considered to be meritorious fail to predict key employment outcomes, possibly leading to unfairness when giving career opportunities and rewards is not fulfilled (condition 2).

To guarantee meritocracy in their management of talent, organizations and their leaders should follow key practical steps. The following steps are meant to help them easily decide *how* to most effectively intervene to improve their talent management processes and ensure more meritocratic employment outcomes:

1. *Find and recruit diverse talented applicants in your workplace.*

   The first important step in the talent management process is to locate and recruit candidates in a way that gives equal opportunity to all, particularly those who have long been underrepresented in your organization's pools of hires and promotions. Here, you may want to be more proactive in recruiting members with different backgrounds and experiences to ensure more opportunities for them. Opportunity, at this stage, does not necessarily mean selection.

   At this step, it is often essential to investigate if the pools of candidates attracted to your organization are not talented or diverse enough (since not being diverse enough could be related to unequal opportunities). You may also want to examine why specific candidates do not apply or, when offered a position, do not accept and end up going to another organization.

2. *Rely on valid and relevant criteria that are not correlated with demographic characteristics when selecting, advancing, and rewarding candidates.*

   Taking this approach can help ensure that all individuals can be selected into your organization, regardless of demographics or personal qualities such as sex, gender, race, religion, sexual orientation, or age. It is important that the selection factors used are valid, reliable, and relevant to the role and the organization, and that the same specific criteria are used for all candidates for the job.

You should also ensure that such criteria do not have any differential impact on certain groups of individuals.[49] In other words, companies should be careful in choosing employment-related criteria that do not necessarily result in pools of preferred candidates from homogeneous backgrounds or similar experiences.

This step frequently requires being proactive and repeatedly reevaluating criteria in response to changing conditions in the labor market and other critical contextual aspects such as technology, culture and values, economic conditions, and legal changes. It also requires being alert and intentional in removing any potential biases and favoritism that might operate during selection, advancement, and rewarding decisions, as well as minimizing the impact of social processes, which are often considered antimeritocratic.

3. *Provide onboarding and training opportunities and resources for all.*

Once you have hired candidates, ensure that all new hires are successfully onboarded to maximize their future success in their positions, both in their first months and beyond. This often requires providing relevant introductory sessions and workshops, checking on new hires frequently, and matching new hires with successful employees who can help mentor and orient their new colleagues. New employees often do not excel because organizations assume they already have the knowledge and resources to succeed. A more realistic and opportunity-giving approach at this step is to make sure that all new hires have the learning opportunities needed to give them a fair chance to succeed in their new roles.

An important part of this step is ensuring that all individuals have equal access to the necessary resources and benefits that can help them focus on productively applying their merits and talents to their work. Such resources and benefits often take the form of flexibility, healthcare, paid time off, and other perks that can help employers recruit and retain high-performing employees.

At this stage, organizations need to take diversity and inclusion efforts seriously, with the goal of ensuring that *all* new hires are welcomed, supported, and feel comfortable and confident about themselves and their ability to add value to the organization. In short, this is about ensuring that once hired, everyone is an important part of the organization, feels valued and respected, is integrated into all activities and organizational processes, and therefore has an equal chance to be successful.

4. *Evaluate and develop performance fairly.*

Continuously establish targets and evaluate performance, again using methods that eliminate the potential for biases and unnecessary social processes that may introduce unfairness and favoritism. In part II, I will summarize the many existing biases and social processes that are likely to creep into performance evaluation processes in workplace settings. A continuous, careful evaluation of the criteria and the processes used to evaluate employees is an essential step.

5. *Reward "top" performers and help develop those who "underperform."*[50]

Reward, praise, and celebrate those who perform well, especially those who deliver results above your expectations. For those who do not, it is critical to help them become successful by providing resources and opportunities to succeed. At this stage, you should consider relying on your "top" performers to train and develop the rest of your hires.

If underperforming employees do not improve over time, help them land a job or position elsewhere that is a better fit for their merits and talents. The assumption is that either the individual needs more development or resources to achieve higher levels of performance or the current position is not a good fit. At this step, continue assessing whether your performance evaluation and training programs are truly meritocratic and fair.

6. *Monitor and evaluate key talent-based outcomes.*

It is crucial to continuously monitor those employment outcomes that relate to the recruitment, hiring, development and training, performance evaluation, and promotion processes in your organization. At the organizational level, carefully examine how the merits and talents of candidates and employees change over time, and establish specific talent management metrics or targets that measure employees' merit and diversity of backgrounds, experiences, and personal circumstances along the way. Stay attuned, once again, to identify whether biases and other social processes may be affecting your employment decisions.

7. *Intervene to address challenges and improve processes and outcomes.*

Based on your findings from the prior steps, you may find that you are doing a great job in ensuring meritocracy in practice in your organization. Kudos to you! If you are not, it is time to intervene. (In reality, all organizations should continuously improve how they manage their talent management processes. Great results in achieving meritocracy should not be taken for granted, and continuous learning and investigation by key organizational members is often necessary.)

Here, you should check and improve the way you recruit and select candidates, revise and develop the processes relating to onboarding and training, and revamp your performance-development-reward system. In all the previous steps, seek additional strategic considerations; also, seek legal advice to ensure that your processes and methods for strategically managing talent conform to the most current country-specific laws and regulations.

Two key points are worth emphasizing. First, steps 3, 4, and 5 are fundamental for fostering condition 1 of a true meritocracy. They rely heavily on the provision of education, experience, and developmental and performance-enhancing opportunities, as well as a climate of not only opportunity but also respect and inclusion for all. Meanwhile, steps 1, 2, and 5 are crucial for condition 2 because they recognize that not all candidates will be selected, advanced, or rewarded equally, and yet efforts should be made to guarantee the fair distribution of rewards and advancement opportunities based on relevant merits and criteria. The final two steps, 6 and 7, can help organizations and their leaders track the impact of their existing people-related processes and identify *where* and *how* to intervene most effectively. These targeted interventions also allow organizations to (re)allocate scarce resources where they matter most in achieving meritocracy.

Second, while the seven steps may seem independent, they are highly interdependent in practice. Accordingly, organizations should evaluate each step at a time and ensure that each step is aligned with the others to reinforce their effectiveness. If your goal is to successfully foster meritocracy in practice, you need to pay attention to all seven steps rather than prioritizing certain steps over others. Put differently, all seven contribute to strategically managing people, meritocracy, and opportunity, as illustrated in figure 2.3.

In theory, these strategic steps are straightforward and even common sense to many. In practice, though, few organizations and businesses do it right, particularly when it comes to hiring and retaining a diverse talent while also providing training and development throughout employees' tenure. Even fewer businesses allocate the necessary resources to ensure that all employees, regardless of their personal circumstances, have the opportunity to succeed. For example, I once worked with an organization that provided childcare and even pet care support to help parents focus on their work while managing their personal and family responsibilities. Workplace flexibility, healthcare benefits, and evaluation of employees based on results are also ways organizations can provide equality of opportunity and enable individuals to focus on putting their talents to work.

To conclude this chapter on meritocracy in theory, I want to stress that true meritocracy is an ideal—a goal, a target, an ongoing project rather than a guaranteed reality. Achieving it in practice is therefore complex and requires continuous refinement and improvement efforts to uphold its definition and its two fundamental conditions: (1) equal access to opportunities for all and (2) the advancement and rewarding of individuals solely based on their relevant merits. In this regard, the recommendations and frameworks in this book aim to help organizations move closer to a true meritocracy in practice—and, importantly, to prevent deviation from that goal.

PART II
Where Meritocracy Goes Wrong

The idea that society should allocate economic rewards and positions of responsibility according to merit is appealing for several reasons. Two of these reasons are generalized versions of the case for merit in hiring—efficiency and fairness. An economic system that rewards effort, initiative, and talent is likely to be more productive than one that pays everyone the same, regardless of contribution, or that hands out desirable social positions based on favoritism. Rewarding people strictly on their merits also has the virtue of fairness; it does not discriminate on any basis other than achievement. . . .

This is an exhilarating vision of human agency, and it goes hand in hand with a morally comforting conclusion: We get what we deserve. If my success is my own doing, something I've earned through talent and hard work, I can take pride in it, confident that I deserve the rewards my achievements bring. A meritocratic society, then, is doubly inspiring; it affirms a powerful notion of freedom, and it gives people what they have earned for themselves and therefore deserve.

—MICHAEL J. SANDEL

Chapter Three

THE ROLE OF BIASES AND SOCIAL PROCESSES

Belief in meritocracy is widespread in many contemporary societies and institutions. Indeed, most executives and managers now accept the common assumption that if their companies are to thrive in today's competitive and dynamic marketplace, they must attract, hire, and retain highly talented and capable individuals. This assumption has created a series of imperatives to attract and recruit job candidates solely on their merits and to reward and promote hires on their performance and contributions to organizational success. Adding to these competitive pressures to hire the best, organizations worldwide have found themselves at the center of significant debates about their talent management practices and have faced intense public scrutiny over workplace inequity and diversity. Pressure to improve workplace fairness and opportunity for all, especially at the higher ranks, has left many leaders grappling with the persistent challenge of eliminating biases and social processes that favor certain groups over others.

That issue raises several questions. How do the design and implementation of meritocratic strategies help guarantee equal opportunity? Do such strategies help organizations achieve efficiency while increasing fairness and reducing biases in their talent management practices? Where and why can such efforts go wrong?

My main approach when collaborating with organizations has always been structural and inquisitive: (1) identify *where* and *how* biases, prejudices, and other critical social processes may be introduced and influence key people-related decision-making and outcomes; and (2) use such information to devise targeted interventions and solutions, many of them quite simple. (The harder work is frequently to figure out where the problems may lie.) This systematic approach often requires collecting and analyzing the necessary data to precisely locate the problems affecting an organization. It also requires critical consideration and evaluation of popular practices to find the most appropriate solution for a given company's problems. Instead of mindlessly copying the practices others are using, it is vital to consider one's own existing structures and culture, as well as the potential impact of such practices on key stakeholders such as top executives, managers, employees, and customers.[1]

Successfully implementing such an approach is challenging but offers great returns, which is why I have enjoyed working with organizations whose leaders were eager to identify potential issues and barriers to becoming a successful meritocracy. In 2018, for example, I started a research collaboration with a prominent North American pharmaceutical company to investigate why the company had gender and racial gaps in employee screening, hiring, and promotion. PharmaInc (a pseudonym) offers clients a wide variety of biopharmaceutical services worldwide. The company's commitment, as articulated by its senior management team, was to attract and build a diverse and talented workforce. And an energetic and successful vice president of diversity, equity, and inclusion (DEI), whom I'll call Melinda, was appointed to implement initiatives that would accomplish this goal.

To start investigating PharmaInc's gender and racial gaps, Melinda's team and I collected information about employment applications as well as screening and selection decisions, including who had received an interview or an offer from the company since 2014. In this way, we were able to gather and code data on the education and experience of the entire population of candidates; we also received some data on performance reviews and promotion decisions for each candidate hired.

PharmaInc frequently hires clinical research associates, healthcare professionals who perform activities related to medical research. The company also recruits for clinical data analysts and many other key roles. PharmaInc was selective in its screening process: during our study period in mid- to late 2015, about 9.6 percent of applicants were invited to an interview, 6.5 percent accepted the invitation, and about 3.1 percent were ultimately hired. A preliminary analysis of hiring data revealed that female applicants were 10 percent more likely to receive an interview invitation but were 8 percent less likely to accept it. Women were 26 percent more likely to secure a job offer but also 12 percent less likely to accept the offer. One could not, therefore, conclude that the company was biased in favor of hiring men over women. Rather, it appeared that PharmaInc had a more challenging time getting women to accept its job interviews and offers. This finding prompted Melinda and her team to investigate further why. Because information about applicants' race and ethnicity was missing in 88 percent of cases, we could not estimate interview and offer acceptance probabilities based on race. As a result, we could not determine whether a similar pattern applied to race and ethnicity.

Beyond recruitment and hiring, we wanted to address management's concern about possible pay and promotion gaps between women, racially disadvantaged groups, and White men. We were also interested in exploring turnover across different demographic groups, although inconsistent performance data and poor tracking of key demographic data limited our ability to analyze post-hire outcomes. For instance, we could not investigate whether women and racially disadvantaged employees were less likely to get promoted or stay in the company compared to their White male peers after controlling for performance and professional achievement. Melinda and her team were eager to pursue this investigation because, like many business leaders in other organizations, they were making critical people management decisions primarily based on intuition, experience, advice, and guesswork, rather than relying on data-driven insights or careful analysis. Regrettably, neither could we study the extent to which top performers, regardless of gender or race, were leaving PharmaInc or where they went after their departure. Such information could greatly help an organization identify and properly address any retention challenges.

At the time we started our collaboration, PharmaInc had already implemented a DEI strategy to improve diversity at higher ranks. However, it had not systematically collected high-quality data on demographics or other personal characteristics that would have helped us identify equity challenges and start addressing them. Such data were spotty and not representative of the full population of applicants and hires—a circumstance I have often encountered when working with organizations. However, since 2018, as a result of our collaboration, PharmaInc has begun to collect data on applicants and employees. It also began gathering post-hire information about performance, training, and development opportunities to assess the effectiveness of its screening and selection practices.

Going forward, such data will greatly enhance the company's ability to identify any talent management problems. PharmaInc's goal of becoming a truly meritocratic organization was one of its main reasons for approaching me for a research collaboration. "We believe that having a diverse, equitable, and inclusive company leads to better patient and customer outcomes," Melinda repeatedly stated. At the time, however, even a quick online search uncovered complaints about the company's processes, with one former employee lamenting on social media "a lack of meritocracy in promotions." I hope to return to PharmaInc and assess its progress using the company's much-improved data-collection processes.

As PharmaInc and many other companies are learning, successfully implementing meritocracy requires having structures and procedures to help recruit, hire, evaluate, and advance employees with a diverse range of backgrounds and experiences. However, researchers have documented many biases and social processes that still affect key employment decisions, especially those related to selecting, evaluating, advancing, and rewarding employees from certain groups. In this chapter, I present research on organizational cultures and structures, individual biases, and other social processes that can affect employment outcomes. Awareness of these processes can help you design and implement talent management processes that are meritocratic, fair, and inclusive. I will particularly discuss research on cognitive biases and stereotypes and scholarship that highlights processes and obstacles that introduce bias and favoritism, affect fairness and the equal distribution of opportunity for all, or interfere with hiring, rewarding, and advancing employees purely on merit.

Rather than listing all potential barriers to true meritocracy, I chose to concentrate this chapter on the ones that, in my research experience, are most common in today's organizations and businesses.

GENDER AND RACIAL BIASES IN THE WORKPLACE

According to a 2021 Pew Research Center survey that recruited respondents from seventeen countries, including the United States, Canada, Australia, France, Germany, Italy, and Spain, people globally are concerned about racial and ethnic disparities.[2] Most survey respondents believed racial discrimination to be a serious or very serious problem in their societies. Concerning gender, across thirty-four countries surveyed by the Pew Research Center in 2020, a median of 94 percent of respondents thought it was important for women in their country to have the same rights and opportunities as men, with 74 percent saying this was *very* important. Yet, the majority of respondents in most European countries surveyed, as well as in the United States, Canada, Australia, Japan, South Korea, and Israel, believed that men in their countries had more opportunities to get high-paying jobs.[3]

Surveys such as those reflect respondents' perceptions of potential gender and racial biases. Additional work estimates the degree to which demographic inequalities persist in certain organizations, occupations, and industries. For instance, women earn an average of 85 percent of what men earn, according to a 2025 report by the Pew Research Center.[4] Even though such statistics on average earnings are heavily cited by the media and the public, they do not account for differences that arise from the jobs, workplaces, and industries in which women are more (or less) likely to work. Women, for instance, are reported to be more likely than men to work in professional and related occupations, but within this professional category alone, the percentage of men employed in higher-paying jobs is larger than that of women.[5] A potential explanation for such a wage gap is that women tend to be employed in jobs and occupations that pay less than men. Therefore, in addition to equalizing salaries within given occupations and jobs, we need to ensure greater demographic representation in jobs that historically have been dominated by one group.

Furthermore, women are more likely than men to work part-time jobs with lower hourly wages; such part-time work may also come with reduced job flexibility and limited or even no access to family- or life-friendly benefits.[6] Consequently, corporate and national-level policies that aim to increase hourly wages for women working part-time, improve their work-life balance, and ensure access to benefits such as paid leave and advanced notice of work schedules could be helpful as well.

To assist with the computation of statistics regarding key labor market outcomes, the US Department of Labor provides an online interactive tool that shows earnings by sex, race, and occupation. One can also access the US Census Bureau's Quarterly Workforce Indicators (see the Census Bureau's Longitudinal Employer-Household Dynamics [LEHD] application and survey) to compute additional statistics related to employment, job creation and elimination, pay, and hiring and retention.[7] Some of those statistics can be computed by individual characteristics (sex, race, age, and education) and also by contextual variables such as time, geography, and company characteristics (ownership, age, and size). Ideally, your organization should aim to provide comparable demographic statistics for various stages of its people management processes, from applicants to hires, promotions, transfers, and turnover. A few research centers worldwide provide many additional data resources online.

Such platforms and data may help academics and managers obtain aggregate reports about key variables relating to employment outcomes. Less comprehensive and systematic information is often available about particular people management practices implemented by employers. The analysis of employment-related outcomes by employees' demographic and personal characteristics can ultimately help locate *where* demographic disparities may exist, but it may not help identify the *reasons* for such disparities. To identify what those reasons are, more information is vital because many people-related processes may introduce, reduce, or maintain biases, stereotypes, and other social noise that affect key employment outcomes.

Among the important processes that affect the composition of a workforce, as well as other demographic differences in outcomes, are those concerning hiring and post-hire phases such as (1) attracting and recruiting candidates, (2) screening and selecting hires, (3) onboarding new hires, (4) training and developing employees, (5) assessing and rewarding employee performance, (6) compensating and promoting employees, and (7) terminating or retaining employees. Breaking down these broad people-related processes into specific phases and employer-employee choice points (that is, points at which organizational members make key employment decisions for the organization) allows leaders to locate precisely *where* their organizations may currently face challenges in implementing a meritocratic approach and *how* they might, in turn, most effectively intervene to address those challenges.

TALENT MANAGEMENT SYSTEMS ARE NOT MERITOCRATIC

Often, as was the case for PharmaInc, companies have not collected employee data or data on key employment outcomes that are necessary for identifying and targeting their fairness challenges. Collecting and analyzing such data requires significant commitment, effort, and resources. Even more challenging to study are the factors that contribute to demographic gaps in employment outcomes. That said, social scientists have made great progress in studying mechanisms that potentially account for demographic biases and inequality in employment-related decisions.

This area of study goes back to the 1970s, when scholars started to collaborate with a few companies, governments, public organizations, and foundations with the goal of getting inside the "black box" of how organizational hiring and selection practices may be creating and sustaining biases and stereotypes in occupations, organizations, and labor markets. Many organizations additionally collect survey data from job seekers and employees on some of these key hiring and work decisions. Although most of those data collection efforts are not representative of the population, and although issues may exist with the data collection processes, they can still produce findings that could generate potential hypotheses, explanations, or preliminary relevant evidence pertaining to your workforce.[8] In other words, such findings can be a starting point for identifying what your organizational challenges may be and generating solutions that can solve them.

In addition to these data and reports, a substantive body of research investigates either the demand side of the labor market (that is, how employers decide which candidates to hire or promote) or the supply side (that is, how job seekers and employees choose their education, jobs, and careers). On the demand side, scholars have studied how employers' preferences and biases may affect employees' careers.[9] On the supply side, several empirical studies have reported that job seekers' expectations and choices influence career outcomes, such as disparities in the types of jobs men and women apply for.[10] These studies often offer valuable insights into what organizations can do to locate and mitigate biases so they can operate as true meritocracies.

Certain negative effects and challenges are easier to address than others. The "supply-side problems" (those stemming from job seekers' actions and decisions), such as low demographic diversity in the pool of qualified employees for certain occupations, are hard to address. Yet, that should not be a reason not to try to address them. Ironically, believing that it is a supply-side problem can be biased in itself and should not, therefore, be given as an excuse for not effectively fostering meritocracy and fairness in the workplace.

By contrast, research also points to the "demand side" (such as employers' processes and decisions) as a potential source of biases and social processes that prevent organizations from achieving meritocracy. Classic studies of workplace inequality and organizations have documented demographic disparities, not only in North America but worldwide. In the tradition of studying particular occupations, organizations, and industries, an extensive body of research has shown that organizations play an important role in generating and sustaining workplace inequality.[11] To date, the research has largely focused on identifying and testing the various mechanisms that may contribute to gender and racial inequality in pay and career advancement within organizations.

In 2004, Trond Petersen and Ishak Saporta provided a valuable framework outlining three primary organizational processes that may result in employer biases and even discrimination in work outcomes.[12] The first of these processes, which they call *allocative discrimination*, has been extensively studied in empirical research. Allocative discrimination occurs when social groups such as women and racially disadvantaged groups are sorted into different kinds of jobs or occupations with unequal pay compared to White men, whether through hiring, career advancement, or retention.[13] In practical terms, this pattern suggests that demographic biases may shape employers' decisions about who gets hired, promoted, transferred, or terminated. A simple bivariate statistic, such as the proportion of women or racial groups being promoted across different work units, can serve as a starting point to determine if allocative discrimination is an issue in your organization. However, such an analysis is not complete enough to determine whether gender and racial biases are operating in your promotion decision-making processes. Further data collection and analysis are necessary to rule out alternative (and often, reasonable) explanations or factors that account for any such finding.

Many other studies have examined a second process, which Petersen and Saporta labeled *within-job wage discrimination*, whereby women and historically disadvantaged groups earn lower wages than White men within a given occupation and work establishment.[14] Many extensions of this work study career outcomes other than wages, such as work benefits, access to key perks, flexibility, and developmental opportunities. Here again, a basic test comparing how wages for the same job title are distributed across different demographic groups of employees in your organization can be a starting point to examine whether demographic biases are operating at this level. However, additional data collection and analysis are, once again, necessary to rule out alternative explanations for why those within-job disparities exist and to ultimately assess whether this is an actual problem that your organization faces.

Finally, some research has investigated a third process, *valuative discrimination*, whereby jobs and occupations dominated by women and racially disadvantaged groups are paid less despite having equivalent wage-relevant factors (skill, education, and ability requirements), simply because they are valued less.[15] This process is more about evaluating the work and contributions made by groups of individuals based on their demographics, with scholars raising the concern that decision-makers may devalue certain occupations because of personal biases and prejudices. This research also highlights post-hiring dynamics in which organizations assess employee performance and allocate resources and developmental opportunities to roles they consider more valuable—roles that often tend to be dominated by certain demographic groups.

Related to this prior work, a wide body of empirical studies, many experimental, has documented how demographic biases may be introduced during performance evaluations, a central component of current talent management systems.[16] Beyond performance evaluations, many scholars have argued that employers' images of the "preferred or ideal" worker are culturally inscribed in organizations and societies.[17] These preferred images guide employers to subconsciously distort judgments about the quality of job applicants.[18] This problem affects the evaluation of candidates and their success in getting jobs and promotions in the workplace.[19]

A classic study in this tradition by Monica Biernat and Diane Kobrynowicz showed that participants in a simulated evaluation of job applicants set lower minimum-competency standards but higher ability standards for women than for men and for Blacks than for Whites.[20] In the case of race, similarly, a follow-up set of experiments found that this tendency to shift standards significantly reduced the funding allocation given to a Black student organization compared to a White student organization.[21]

IT IS NOT JUST GENDER AND RACE

There have been many extensions of this type of research, whether through the study of experimental or survey data or the study of organizational data related to hiring, promotion, training, and pay. Scholars have examined other demographic and personal characteristics, such as motherhood, nationality, sexual orientation, disability, and religion, and the way that such personal characteristics have been shown to bias employment or educational decisions.

The Motherhood Penalty

For instance, researchers have found that mothers may experience additional disadvantages in the workforce compared to childless women, including a per-child wage penalty. Strong empirical evidence of this "motherhood penalty" in hiring practices, starting salaries, and perceived competence was first found in a study published in 2007 that included an experiment with students and also an audit study of real organizations in the United States.[22] Michelle Budig and Paula England introduced the phrase *motherhood penalty* in their 2001 study of data from the National Longitudinal Survey of Youth, where they showed that women experienced an hourly pay penalty of 15 percent per child under age five. For Black and Indigenous women, the pay penalty was nearly 20 percent.[23]

Since then, additional research has documented evidence of such a penalty in many countries, including the United Kingdom, Japan, and the Netherlands. Studies suggest that this penalty may account for an important proportion of the gender pay gap. In practical terms, it is, as *The Economist* put it, a "struggle to reduce the motherhood penalty."[24] Even worse, there is little evidence that the penalty has declined over time,[25] with many warning that the COVID-19 pandemic likely made it even worse.

Empirical studies have further shown that visibly pregnant women are perceived as less dependable, less committed to their jobs and organizations, and more irrational and emotional than equally qualified non-visibly-pregnant women. Other studies find, however, that men are not necessarily penalized for being fathers. Many empirically tested explanations for the motherhood penalty have to do with biased perceptions of competence and commitment to the job, as captured by participants' responses to stereotypical statements such as the following: "Mothers are devoted to their children more than their job," "Mothers will take time off from work when their children get sick," "Mothers get distracted on the job as they care for their children; as a result, mothers have lower productivity than fathers," and "Mothers need flexible schedules to take care of their children."[26]

Nationality

A long stream of research has investigated the extent to which individuals from certain countries may be favored in workplace decisions. In one research project, Ben Rissing from the ILR School at Cornell University and I studied how government agents at the US Department of Labor influence key employment outcomes for immigrants.[27] Annually, hundreds of thousands of immigrants look for legal employment in the United States. Despite US laws prohibiting nationality-based discrimination, originating with the Civil Rights Act of 1964, we found that the labor certification decisions of government agents—one crucial stage of today's US immigration review process toward the legalization of work—varied significantly depending on the nationality of the immigrants, even after controlling for employer-, individual-, and occupation-level controls. These controls in our models allowed us to compare applicants from different countries working in similar occupations and for similar employers.

In particular, we found that all Asian citizenship groups are as likely or more likely to obtain labor certification approval compared with Canadian immigrants, even when they have the same occupation and work for the same employer.[28] We chose Canada as the reference category because of its similarities with the United States, particularly in terms of geographic proximity, English fluency, GDP growth, and unemployment levels.[29] Latin American immigrants, by contrast, were less likely than Canadians to get approval. In our study, immigrants from Mexico, Brazil, Colombia, and Venezuela were 35, 22, 21, and 18 percent less likely, respectively, than Canadians to get approval.

This research, like many other studies, cautions that biases and preferences for individuals of certain nationalities may still prevail in decision-making processes, not only within government entities but also across other organizations. This issue is likely exacerbated in times when immigration faces heavy criticism from populists and the far right.[30]

Sexual Orientation

Lesbian, gay, bisexual, and transgender (LGBT) individuals are also reported to be disadvantaged in hiring, pay, and promotion decisions. A seminal audit study published in 2011 by András Tilcsik was among the first large-scale experimental investigations into employer discrimination against openly gay men in the United States.[31] This study gathered unique audit data from various states with differing levels of popular acceptance of homosexuality and varying degrees of legal protection for LGBT employees.[32] Pairs of fictitious résumés, for a total of 3,538 résumés, were sent in response to the postings of 1,769 jobs in seven different states. Within each pair, while one résumé was written to signal an applicant's involvement in a gay campus organization, the other résumé was written to signal an applicant's involvement in a control organization.

Analyses of the collected data estimated that gay applicants had a 7.2 percent probability of obtaining a positive "callback" from employers (typically an email response or phone call by someone in the hiring organization), while equally qualified heterosexual applicants had an 11.5 percent probability. The 4.3 percentage points difference was statistically significant. Furthermore, in some US states, Tilcsik found greater discrimination against gay applicants. This geographic variation, the author argues, reflects regional differences in attitudes and antidiscrimination laws, with, for instance, lower callback rates for gay applicants in southern and midwestern states such as Texas, Florida, and Ohio (3.5, 5.5, and 5.5 percent, respectively).[33]

Prior to this large-scale US audit study of sexual orientation, one correspondence audit study of 163 nearly equivalent résumés sent to law firms in Ontario had reported that for both men and women, the gay-identified résumés received a lower number of interview invitations than the unlabeled résumés.[34] A similar correspondence audit study assessed discrimination against lesbians in Austria.[35] In that study, over 1,200 applications with female names were sent out in response to 613 clerical job postings in Vienna. Résumés indicating a lesbian orientation (with the résumé listing volunteered experience in the gay and lesbian movement) were about 12 percentage points less likely to get an interview invitation than the control résumé (indicating volunteer experience in a nonprofit cultural or educational center).[36] In another study, the researcher sent pairs of applications from fictitious men to 1,714 job openings in Athens, Greece.[37] Less than 14 percent of the applications signaling gay identity (past volunteer involvement in the "Athenian Homosexual Community") received a positive callback; by contrast, 40 percent of the applications with the control signal (past involvement in an environmental group) received an employer callback.

Since then, additional studies have continued to find that gay men encounter exclusion, bullying, and poverty to a greater degree than heterosexual men.[38] One meta-analysis of twenty-four articles published between 2012 and 2020 reported that in most empirical studies, gay and bisexual men earned significantly less than comparable heterosexual men, with a few study exceptions. The same meta-analysis also reported that lesbian women earned more than heterosexual women.[39]

LGBT disadvantage has been reported to be greater within science and engineering environments. Erin Cech and Michelle Pham analyzed representative data for more than thirty thousand workers in six STEM-related federal agencies in the United States. Compared to their non-LGBT peers, LGBT employees reported significantly more negative workplace experiences, particularly in measures relating to perceived treatment and work satisfaction.[40]

Disability

Research has also shown that employees with disabilities face employment barriers and workplace disparities. Some of these findings link the disparities to attitudes about disability and its effects on productivity and other work outcomes. In the United States, the Americans with Disabilities Act (ADA)—which came into effect in July 1992, after being signed into law in 1990—requires employers to accommodate disabled employees and bans discrimination against the disabled in hiring, firing, and pay determinations. Understandably, researchers have been interested in investigating whether this policy intervention has worked to improve the employment of individuals with disabilities.

A landmark study on this topic, analyzing data from the US Current Population Surveys from 1988 until 1997, revealed a surprisingly substantial *decline* in employment among disabled male workers of all ages and female workers under forty *after* the ADA came into effect, with no significant impact on wages.[41] In such study, Daron Acemoglu and Joshua D. Angrist suggest that the sharp decline could be due to the cost of the ADA not being anticipated by employers before the law became effective. Even though the number of disabled employees receiving disability transfers (that is, payments from the disability insurance and supplemental security income) increased at the same time, the reduction in their employment did not seem to be explained by these disability transfers alone, "leaving the ADA as a likely cause."[42]

This study's findings of discrimination against workers with disabilities were corroborated by similar studies conducted in countries such as France and Belgium, where researchers sent job applications to real employers, manipulating whether the applicant disclosed a disability and, if so, what kind of disability. In the French study, fictitious job applications from highly qualified able-bodied candidates were 1.78 times more likely to receive employer callbacks than those from otherwise similar applicants with paraplegia.[43] In the Belgian study, fictitious applications disclosing a disability (blindness, deafness, or autism) had a 47 percent lower callback rate than similar applications indicating no disability.[44]

One proposed explanation for such disadvantage is "statistical discrimination": employers may think that disabled workers are, on average, less productive and more costly to employ, and this assumption may lead to a higher likelihood of statistical discrimination against the disabled. In this regard, researchers have further investigated potential biases against disabled individuals, particularly those with disabilities that are unlikely to affect productivity. After sending fictitious job applications to over six thousand accounting jobs for which the applicants' disabilities were unlikely to affect their job productivity, a team of researchers found that candidates with disabilities had 26 percent lower employer interest than applicants without disabilities.[45] These gaps were similar across types of disability: one third of the cover letters disclosed that the applicant had a spinal cord injury, one third disclosed the presence of Asperger's syndrome, and one third did not mention disability.

Many other audit studies have focused on disability.[46] Additional empirical work has explored the effect of one or more individual characteristics, such as mental health and physical appearance, on some key outcomes.[47] More research and organizational interventions are needed to help disabled job seekers find jobs in which they are more likely to be successful, particularly since many of their disabilities do not affect their ability to perform well in certain roles and positions.

Religion

Researchers have also studied how religious affiliation affects workplace outcomes. In the United States, Title VII of the Civil Rights Act explicitly prohibits discrimination based on religion regarding any aspects or conditions of employment, including hiring, pay and benefits, training, promotions, and terminations. However, a 2013 review of major workplace studies found that religious discrimination continues to be a major concern in the American workplace. This conclusion is based on the rising number of religious discrimination claims reported over time by the US Equal Employment Opportunity Commission (EEOC).[48] Some explanations for this increase include legal ambiguities, greater religious diversity in the American workforce, increased public expression of religious beliefs, and the intersection of religion with other identities such as national origin or race.

In one 2014 audit study, the researchers submitted 3,200 résumés to eight hundred jobs located near two major southern US cities.[49] For each job posting, they sent four applications with varying biographical details but equivalent job qualifications. Each résumé was randomly assigned to one of seven experimental conditions—identification as atheist, Catholic, evangelical Christian, Jewish, pagan, Muslim, a fictitious religion they called "Wallonian," or a control group with no religious identification. The findings were quite clear: compared to the control group of résumés that displayed no religious affiliation, mentioning any religious affiliation in the résumés resulted in 29 percent fewer emails and 33 percent fewer phone calls from employers. Such antireligious bias was not found only for specific religious groups but also for the fictitious religion as well—the Wallonians! Muslims were consistently reported as facing high levels of callback discrimination, with 38 percent fewer emails and 54 percent fewer phone calls from employers compared to the control group.

Religious discrimination has also been found outside the United States. A study conducted in Greece sent fictitious job applications using résumés that randomly assigned affiliation to Greece's majority religion (Greek Orthodox) or one of three minority religions (Pentecostal, evangelical, and Jehovah's Witnesses). Religious minorities received fewer interview invitations from employers, especially for more prestigious occupations (in the study, these were office jobs), compared to less prestigious jobs (industry, restaurant and café services, and retail sales).[50] They also received lower entry wages and higher wait times for a callback from employers compared to the religious majority. Another research team examined the discriminatory impact of caste and religion on employment in India. The team sent out over 3,100 fictitious résumés to 371 job positions in the information technology sector in New Delhi. They found caste discrimination for call center jobs, not software jobs.[51]

A few studies have examined the specific challenges religious minorities face in North America, Europe, and Australia, particularly Muslims during screening and selection.[52] Researchers have further reported that the applicants' sex and whether they wear religious identifiers such as the hijab may further intensify discrimination in the hiring of Muslims.[53] Other religious groups, such as Sikhs who "look Muslim," also seem to face discrimination, likely because people often incorrectly link religion with ethnicity or national origin.[54] Scholars have also looked at how employees *perceive* religious discrimination in the workplace.[55]

Additionally, personal details posted by job seekers on social media platforms could affect their recruiting and hiring experiences. In one study, researchers created profiles for job seekers on popular social network sites and manipulated their religion.[56] After creating these profiles, the researchers submitted job applications on the fictitious candidates' behalf to more than four thousand US employers. The study found no significant difference in callback rates between Muslim and Christian candidates. However, employers in Republican areas showed significantly more bias against Muslim candidates compared to Christian candidates. In these areas, about 17 percent of Christian applicants received interview invitations, whereas only 2 percent of Muslim applicants did.[57]

CONCEALING STIGMATIZED ASPECTS OF IDENTITY

An individual's identity includes many aspects beyond group affiliations, and some are clearly visible. When recruiters and hiring managers first meet a job candidate, they may assume they can clearly see certain aspects of the candidate's identity that may make them view the candidate more or less favorably. But many aspects of candidates' identities may not be visible at all.

In attempting to mitigate the negative impacts of particular identities, often those stigmatized or less favored, some candidates may choose to manage the information they convey about themselves. As far back as the 1960s, Erving Goffman observed in *Stigma: Notes on the Management of Spoiled Identity* that stigmatized individuals often conceal their stigma to "pass" as members of the dominant, nonstigmatized group. This concealing strategy aims to avoid the negative impact of stigma on their professional and personal opportunities. Another way of managing stigmatized aspects of one's identity is to actively conceal them.[58] Goffman calls this approach "covering." This strategy is commonly used to mitigate the potential negative effects of bias and prejudice, particularly in the case of sexual orientation.[59] Covering part of one's identity can also be consistent with personal values and personality traits; for instance, a private person may choose not to share personal information in a job interview.

A series of multimethod studies published in 2016 made an important contribution to this research tradition. Sonia K. Kang and colleagues examined racially disadvantaged groups' attempts to combat employment discrimination by downplaying or concealing racial cues in their job applications; this strategy has been called "résumé whitening."[60] In their first study, the researchers interviewed twenty-nine Black and thirty Asian university students who were actively looking for full-time jobs or internships to identify common "résumé whitening" techniques the students employed. The interviews uncovered two types of résumé whitening: changing their first name and modifying the description of some of their experiences. Such résumé changes could involve omitting experiences that may give racial cues and even making the applicant appear more likely to be White—by, for instance, altering the description of one listed type of experience or adding "Whiter" details to the résumé.

The same authors also conducted an audit study in which they sent fictitious résumés in response to 1,600 entry-level job vacancies in sixteen US metropolitan areas. As in their interviews, the researchers focused on Black and Asian job seekers. The study's manipulation of résumé whitening consisted of (1) no whitening, (2) whitening the first name, (3) whitening the experience, or (4) whitening both the first name and experience in the résumé. Employer callbacks were significantly higher for whitened résumés than for those that included ethnic information, despite all résumés including identical qualifications; 25 percent of Black applicants with whitened résumés received callbacks, while only 10 percent received callbacks when including their ethnic information. For Asians, 21 percent received calls when they used whitened résumés, whereas 11.5 percent received responses when their résumés included racial cues.

In this respect, the iceberg metaphor has been helpful when exploring identity and detecting and addressing potential sources of bias and favoritism.[61] You can only see a small part of an iceberg above the waterline (about 10 to 13 percent, by many estimates). Much like an iceberg, only a few aspects of someone's identity are visible. As a result, one important conclusion is that certain aspects of a person's identity, especially if visible or disclosed, can affect their careers if biases or preferences influence decision-making. This implies that organizations serious about equality of opportunity should be aware of the many cognitive biases and prejudices against certain individuals or aspects of their identity that are potentially at play in the workplace.

PEOPLE ARE NOT MERITOCRATIC

When key decision-makers choose which candidates to interview, hire, or promote, they are making decisions that are key to the operation of a true meritocracy. Decision-making in educational and labor markets has long been the foundation for many theories in the social sciences. Researchers in social psychology, for instance, have made great progress in studying how our cognitive biases affect decision-making of all kinds. One important strand of this research relates to key employment-related decisions about individuals with different demographic characteristics.

A line of research that has grown in popularity since the early 2010s investigates the implicit biases that individuals may have. The popular Implicit

Association Test (IAT), for instance, aims to help individuals discover potential gender and racial prejudices that may lie beneath their awareness. This test aims to measure implicit bias, that is, any automatic reaction that can affect our understanding, actions, and decision-making. It helps us find our "blind spots," the hidden demographic biases that "good people" may have.[62] The IAT was first introduced in 1988 by Anthony Greenwald, Debbie McGhee, and Jordan Schwartz. In the 1990s, Greenwald began developing these tests collaboratively with Mahzarin Banaji and Brian Nosek.

Implicit Association Tests were introduced to help researchers and practitioners measure and illustrate implicit biases that surveys and self-reports may not measure. These tests often consist of an online exercise that requires participants to press specific keys on a keyboard to classify words or images that appear onscreen.[63] Participants' response time to various combinations of stimuli reveals the mental associations they make, often without being fully aware of them. These tests have been used to investigate unconscious and automatic thought processes in various contexts, including among employers, police, and jurors.

Data from Project Implicit, a virtual laboratory and educational outreach organization that promotes research on implicit cognition (cofounded by Greenwald, Banaji, and Nosek), show that 75 percent of respondents who have taken an IAT about gender have associated men more closely with work roles and women more closely with family roles. While the assumption is that managers and recruiters with higher IAT gender scores (greater gender bias) would tend to favor men over women in their hiring decisions, the predictive validity of this assumption has been questioned because evidence of its real-world impact remains limited.[64] Along these lines, a 2015 doctoral dissertation presented the results of three empirical studies that suggested that even though strongly held gender attitudes were found across all three studies, such implicit associations did not "consistently translate into behavior in the manner predicted," leading the author, Jo-Anne Kandola, to conclude that "the IAT may only predict workplace gender discrimination in a very select set of circumstances."[65] In the case of race, many studies have examined the extent to which the IAT can predict ethnic and racial discrimination, with a number of them showing weak (in fact, practically negligible) associations between the observed IAT scores of the participants and their later discriminatory behaviors.[66]

The most frequently cited examples of implicit bias come from studies of race and gender across various organizational contexts. However, the IAT has also been used to study other types of implicit biases, such as those relating to age,[67] religion,[68] sexual orientation,[69] political preference,[70] disability,[71] and weight.[72] Researchers and practitioners alike continue to extend the study of implicit associations to many other aspects of individuals' identities. Some scholars have also studied to what extent specific organizational processes and routines may introduce new forms of bias or activate existing ones, such as during the evaluation of job candidates or promotion decisions.[73]

The effectiveness of Implicit Association Tests, however, has been the subject of substantial academic and popular debate, with many having identified reasonable and often significant issues regarding their validity, reliability, and usefulness in assessing (not to mention reducing) implicit biases and their impact in hiring and post-hiring work decisions.[74] Regardless of whether implicit (or explicit) biases and stereotypes affect our actions and decision-making, scholars have also been interested in understanding the rationale for discriminatory employment decisions based on gender, race, and other personal characteristics. One important conclusion of such work is that not all biases and stereotypes are necessarily "unfair," as I explain below.

Most economic explanations for labor market discrimination center around two rival theories: taste-based discrimination theory versus statistical discrimination theory. These theories are relevant for decision-making in meritocratic organizations because they implicitly consider equal opportunity and help sustain and justify unequal career outcomes.

According to *taste-based theories of discrimination* in employment, decision-makers may favor White men over women and racially disadvantaged groups when screening and hiring, even when they submit comparable applications.[75] This taste-based argument assumes that gender or racial animus on the part of the employer is the key reason for disadvantaging women and racially disadvantaged groups and, consequently, could be labeled as unfair.[76] For example, an employer might favor hiring a man over an equally qualified woman simply because of their preference for hiring men.

By contrast, *statistical theories* do not assume employers' gender or racial animus.[77] The statistical-based argument assumes that decision-makers will infer details about the prospective candidate from aggregate-level data about others in the same demographic group. For example, an employer might favor men over women in hiring for physically demanding warehouse work that involves heavy lifting based on the assumption that women, who have, on average, less muscular strength than men, are less likely to be able to do the work for a long time without sustaining an injury. Following this reasoning, even unbiased decision-makers might rely on demographic stereotypes about the average abilities and performance of candidates from different backgrounds during the hiring process.[78]

These two theories are important in the context of meritocracy and talent management systems. The "taste-based" advantage focuses on candidates of a particular demographic group being favored even when other candidates have comparable qualifications and competencies. This approach is antimeritocratic in that it ignores some candidates' relevant merits. By contrast, the "statistical-based" advantage argues that decision-makers prefer candidates from certain demographic groups because members of that group are, on average, more qualified and better performers in a particular role.

As a result of this theorizing, many scholars and commentators have concluded that taste discrimination is "bad" and inefficient, while statistical discrimination is not. Some social scientists even characterize statistical discrimination as fair and morally defensible.[79] David Autor noted in one course at MIT that economists generally believe that employers " 'should' statistically discriminate because it is profit-maximizing, it is not motivated by animus, and it is arguably 'fair' since it treats people with the same expected productivity identically (though not necessarily with the same actual productivity)."[80] Marianne Bertrand and Esther Duflo echoed this sentiment, arguing that statistical discrimination is "theoretically efficient" and "more easily defendable in ethical terms under the utilitarian argument," further suggesting that "statistical discrimination can also be argued to be 'fair'. . . . In fact, many economists would most likely support allowing statistical discrimination as a good policy, even where it is now illegal."[81]

However, András Tilcsik has pointed out that using the word *statistical* may reinforce the idea of discrimination as a "rational, calculated decision."[82] He proposes that the concept of statistical discrimination can, in fact, rationalize stereotypes and lead decision-makers to consider demographic stereotyping rational, useful, and acceptable, ultimately justifying and resulting in discriminatory decisions. Through an experimental study of over two thousand participants with managerial experience, Tilcsik found that individuals' exposure to statistical discrimination theory increased their belief in the accuracy of stereotypes, their acceptance of stereotyping, and their engagement in gender discrimination in a hiring exercise. However, when participants were exposed to a critical commentary on statistical discrimination theory, this small intervention significantly reduced gender disparities in hiring outcomes.

The research reviewed up to now has some important practical impli-cations: Organizations should design and implement organizational pro-cesses that help decision-makers base their employment-related decisions on relevant employment information about individuals rather than allow-ing implicit or explicit preferences, biases, and stereotypes to operate during such decisions. In this respect, scholars and practitioners alike have advo-cated for training individuals to be aware of their demographic biases; the most common recommendation is training that uses the IAT, even though the extent to which such trainings actually help promote unbiased and fair key decision-making remains an empirical concern.[83] Along these lines, many have warned that although IAT training is popular, it may not suc-ceed at addressing workplace disparities and unfairness issues.[84] Part of the problem may be that companies rely too heavily on implicit bias training as a panacea, neglecting to address important structural and systemic issues that contribute to bias and barriers to achieving meritocracy in practice.

Distinguishing between taste-based and statistical-based discrimination in the real world is extremely difficult. One approach, as I propose later in this book, is to use data that measure the quality of the applicant (pre-hire) as well as job performance (post-hire); such data can help validate the rel-evance of the "merits" used when screening and selecting candidates. They can help assess the extent to which individuals receive desirable opportu-nities regardless of their demographic and other personal characteristics irrelevant to the job. Such data are generally challenging to observe, collect, and analyze in real organizational settings, but they are crucial for ensuring equitable and meritocratic processes and outcomes.

SOCIAL NETWORKS HELP SOME PEOPLE BUT NOT OTHERS

Social networks and their use can also influence an organization's attempts to be meritocratic. Countless articles and blogs highlight the need to "network" because it is relevant for our careers, regardless of occupation, industry, and even demographics.[85] "If you want to be successful, you need to spend time networking," Bonnie Marcus advised in a May 2018 *Forbes* article. Numer-ous books and articles emphasize the role of networks, whom to network with, how to network successfully, what aspects of networking may be most relevant to our careers, and even "how to master non-awkward, effective in-person networking."[86] Many professionals read articles with titles such as "The Networking Advice No One Tells You," "How to Network Effectively," or even "How Leaders Create and Use Networks," a classic article by Herminia Ibarra and Mark Lee Hunter that appeared in *Harvard Business Review*.[87]

The idea that people use networks to advance their careers is not new. Mark Granovetter's classic insight—that weak (that is, less close) connections in our social networks are the most powerful source for finding employment opportunities—has long generated enormous interest, not only from academics but also from employers and professionals.[88] Granovetter proposed that within a network of strong ties (family, friends, or work colleagues), people to whom we have weak ties (that is, acquaintances or a stranger with some common trait or background) can help us bridge to other networks. In the job search and hiring context, those bridges can provide potentially more helpful information than that provided by strong ties because the weak ties may connect us to relevant, non-redundant job information and opportunities that we don't already know about.

Most empirical studies on social networks and employment trace their origins to Granovetter's classic research.[89] Scholars have further investigated why weak ties are more useful for job seekers.[90] Some researchers have analyzed the conditions under which strong ties may indeed benefit an individual's career.[91] Other research efforts have replicated the original findings on the impact of weak ties on employment outcomes by relying on more rigorous methods or unique research settings.[92] And fifty years after the seminal work by Granovetter, a large-scale study of job seekers on LinkedIn continues to find that weaker social ties are more beneficial for job seekers than stronger ties.[93]

Instead of comparing the returns of weak versus strong ties, some scholars have explored whether networking is better than common employment search methods.[94] One study reported that about half of job changers learn of their new jobs from someone in their network, and about half of job seekers use their networks to search for jobs.[95] It further claimed that job seekers who use personal ties to search for or find a job achieve higher initial wages.[96] Other classic studies have shown that job seekers who network tend to achieve higher occupational status,[97] are better matched to their jobs,[98] and experience shorter periods of unemployment.[99]

In my work, I have shown that newer informal approaches to networking, such as providing application endorsements (in quick emails or phone calls), can also significantly improve an applicant's chances of securing an interview and ultimately obtaining an offer.[100] Notably, the particular kinds of networks and network practices that are beneficial for individuals in today's labor markets are likely different from those studied in the past. For instance, technological tools (email, social media, videoconferencing, and many other online platforms) have influenced how we work and interact with one another and, consequently, have created new social norms around networking and socializing. They will likely continue to shape how we network and the effectiveness of certain networking practices.

Social networks have major relevance for attempts to achieve meritocracy and equity in organizations and businesses. Not surprisingly, scholars have been interested in investigating how such networks may advantage certain demographic groups. For instance, studies have assessed the extent to which the positive returns from using networks vary by race, gender, or prior socioeconomic status.[101] In this line of inquiry, researchers have studied whether women and racially disadvantaged groups have access to the "right networks," that is, networks that help them find good companies, jobs, and career prospects.[102] Some studies suggest that women and certain racial groups are more likely than White men to find jobs through personal networks.[103] Other studies report that women and racially disadvantaged groups are often stuck in the "wrong networks": either they are excluded from more powerful and influential White male networks,[104] or they count on networks that are less effective than those of White men.[105]

Demographic differences in the network structure seem to be explanations for why women and racially disadvantaged groups may gain different employment and career benefits from networks compared to White men.[106] An emerging area of research seeks to investigate whether White men, compared to women and the racially disadvantaged, may use their networks differently and subsequently have different outcomes.[107]

In my study of the use of endorsements in an application process at a selective business school, even though I found no difference in the selection returns of application endorsement based on the applicant's gender or race, I did find that female and racially disadvantaged professionals may have different perceptions than White men about informal networking, especially instrumental informal networking such as asking for an endorsement.[108] In that study, women and certain racial groups were less likely to ask someone to endorse their applications than were White men. From interviews, I concluded that such gendered and racial disparity is partly due to women and racially disadvantaged groups being less comfortable than White men when asking for an endorsement, expressing more equity and fairness concerns about the practice, being more concerned about societal expectations and third-party perceptions, or relying more on their qualifications and formal network methods throughout the application process.[109]

In some cases, differential returns to networking reflect conditions beyond the individual's control. For instance, certain social groups may find it more challenging than others to access and activate network resources. One classic study of high school students found that even though Black and White students had the same teachers, Black students were less likely to receive informal mentorship and "first-job" referrals from those teachers.[110]

Since networks influence the matching of individuals to jobs, they can potentially influence workplace segregation (how workers are sorted into jobs), typically along gender and racial lines.[111] Indeed, some researchers have claimed that demographic homophily in network usage may steer certain groups toward low-status jobs during the job search,[112] and some research has found that racial differences in job seeker hiring outcomes and salary negotiations disappear when the employment models control for job seekers' use of referrals.[113] Firm-level studies indicate that women are more likely to make referrals than men, and they also tend to refer other women disproportionately.[114] Moreover, women who use networks to search for jobs tend to end up in female-dominated occupations.[115] Similarly, workers who learned of their jobs from personal contacts of their same ethnicity tend to work in ethnically segregated jobs.[116]

Beyond hiring and selection, scholars have investigated how networks affect individuals' employment outcomes once inside organizations, such as socialization, on-the-job training, performance, advancement, and retention.[117] One study of low-income workers recounts how some referrers were particularly interested in helping their friends find jobs, training them, and ensuring they kept those jobs.[118]

Some scholars have also investigated how workers' use of and returns from networks vary across their careers.[119] Along similar lines, researchers suggest that various aspects of an employee's position within the organization's network structure have a significant impact on their career. Using data on the personal networks of managers in a number of single-firm studies, Ronald S. Burt has repeatedly found that employees who span more "structural holes" (that is, employees who can act as a mediator between two or more closely connected groups of individuals, in turn leading to the transfer of valuable information from one group to another) receive higher performance evaluations and bonuses, more frequent promotions, and are even more creative and innovative.[120]

All of this research highlights how important it is for organizations to pay particular attention to how networks may be affecting their most important management decisions concerning people. Leaders need to ensure that network processes do not introduce a preference for certain types of individuals; otherwise, networks could attract employees for reasons other than their talents and merits. Taken together, these studies highlight both the complexity of and the necessity for close analysis of how exactly networks may affect the operation of meritocratic practices within organizations.

While this issue is indeed complex, one should not conclude that employees' social networks are unhelpful for employers. On the contrary, some research, including mine with Roberto Fernandez, has shown that networks can be a form of social capital in which companies can invest with great social and economic returns.[121] However, under certain contextual circumstances, individuals' networks may be problematic because they may help particular groups of individuals and not others, potentially resulting in unequal opportunity. Additionally, employees' networks may not necessarily bring the best or most prepared talent into the organization, and they may advantage groups that have been historically privileged in the past, undermining the organization's meritocratic goals. Leaders should, therefore, ensure that networks and network-related activities in their workplaces augment the benefits of existing people-related processes without introducing favoritism for certain groups.

OUR PREDICTABLE PREFERENCE FOR PEOPLE LIKE US

Talk to engineers (or to nonengineers) at any tech firm, and you will probably gain an understanding of the notion that engineers, on average, tend to prefer to interact with other engineers. This phenomenon of preferring those like us is called *homophily*, or as the proverb puts it, "birds of a feather flock together." Homophily is a common sociological concept describing our tendency to associate, like, or bond with similar others. Its prevalence, in some form or another, has been found in a vast array of empirical studies involving variables such as sex, race, age, class, and occupation, among many.

In the context of people-related organizational processes, research has been done on homophily, especially as it relates to gender, race, and nationality. The main empirical queries have typically consisted of investigating whether demographically similar individuals (whether women, Whites, Blacks, or members of disadvantaged groups) help one another identify and obtain better jobs and roles, advance successfully in the workplace, and provide more help in their careers than demographically dissimilar others.[122]

In my research on how managers using merit-based reward policies shape the careers of their employees, I identified three distinct mechanisms that influence employee performance assessments: social network connections among managers, demographic similarity between managers (horizontal similarity), and demographic similarity between managers and employees (vertical similarity). Using personnel data from nearly thirty thousand employee evaluations at a large North American company, I found that socially connected managers tend to align their performance assessments of the same employee and that demographically similar managers are more likely to agree in their evaluations of the same employee. Additionally, though the evidence was weaker, employees who were demographically similar to their evaluating managers tended to receive more favorable evaluations. These findings highlight that managers' evaluations of employees do not happen in a vacuum but are influenced by the social and organizational context, potentially affecting not just performance assessments but also key decisions around hiring, promotions, and layoffs.

In the end, my study, like many others on homophily in organizational contexts, underscores the importance of seriously considering homophily and similarity when evaluating current organizational talent management processes, especially those involving decisions about rewards, training opportunities, promotions, and access to other employment benefits. The tendency to favor similar individuals can influence not only how organizations choose to recruit and attract talent but also the criteria for making interviewing and hiring decisions. Homophily can also influence who gets steered into certain jobs, who is chosen for a particular role, their subsequent performance evaluations and associated rewards or promotions, and the training and career opportunities offered.

NEPOTISM AND THE POWER OF FAMILIES

A particular form of network favoritism comes from family ties. Parents and close relatives often want their family members to do well in life. This is a natural and inbuilt desire: our limbic system governs our behavioral and emotional responses, especially those necessary for survival, including protecting and caring for our young. Like all humans, highly educated and wealthy parents have these instincts, but they also have the economic and social resources to help them protect and advance their family members. Hence, those charged with managing opportunity and meritocracy in organizations should be aware of how much family connections and friendships may interfere with talent management processes. These strong ties can cement privilege for the most influential and affluent individuals in society at the expense of those who lack comparable resources.

As Michael J. Sandel writes in *The Tyranny of Merit*, "the institution of the family can indeed compromise the meritocratic project of giving everyone an equal chance."[123] Parents who have attained privileged positions through merit, education, and hard work often use their superior resources to help their children follow a similar path and secure advantageous positions. They practice what Annette Lareau, in *Unequal Childhoods*, labeled the "concerted cultivation" of children: a parenting style frequently exhibited by middle-class and upper-class American families that emphasizes children developing skills and talents through participation in after-school activities, and organized programs and clubs.[124] Moreover, as a society grows more unequal, the level of inequality predicted by merit increases, and the "fear of falling" professionally and personally (that is, downward economic social mobility) increases.[125]

Family ties continue to play a key role in today's organizations and businesses, especially during recruitment and hiring.[126] Some organizations, such as family-owned businesses, favor applicants with familial connections to members of the organization.[127] Though the practice has been increasingly under scrutiny, many colleges and universities still give preference to applicants with certain family ties (children or siblings) or friendships with alumni of those institutions, a practice called "legacy admission."[128] In some US colleges, researchers estimate that legacy applicants are eight times more likely to gain admission than nonlegacy applicants.[129]

Ethan Poskanzer (at the University of Colorado, Boulder) and I studied this legacy practice at an elite college in the Northeast of the United States. Consistent with prior research, we found that legacy applicants were significantly favored in admissions decisions. In one of our models, legacy applicants were almost five times more likely to gain admission than professionally and academically comparable nonlegacies. This legacy advantage was predominantly given to White candidates and those from wealthy backgrounds.[130]

Our study of legacy advantage was not the first; it expanded on earlier research examining how well-connected and elite groups might receive preferential treatment in both labor markets[131] and educational settings.[132] Since legacies tend to be children of well-positioned and influential individuals, legacy preferences can be a form of class-based advantage.[133] A similar process was shown to be at play in endorsements during the application process to competitive university programs[134] and in labor markets.[135] More advantaged and privileged individuals mobilize their own educational and professional experience and their economic and cultural resources to ensure that their loved ones are successful in their personal and professional careers.[136]

That said, our study was the first to systematically illustrate how an organization can collect and analyze relevant data to identify and locate how family ties (or other forms of nepotism) may be shaping its talent management processes and outcomes. Our findings offer particularly relevant implications for organizations and businesses that aim to be meritocratic and fair.[137] Nepotistic preferences in the screening and selection process may push out applicants who have stronger academic and professional qualifications.[138] They may also benefit those who are already most likely to be successful in attaining education and a good career (i.e., have better opportunities to succeed to begin with).[139] Furthermore, any preferential allocation of high-quality higher education or job opportunities based on family ties and other class-based factors has significant consequences for guaranteeing equal opportunity, as well as possible serious opportunity costs—since not everyone would have an equal chance to access such limited (helpful) opportunities.[140]

BE AWARE OF BIASES AND SOCIAL PROCESSES AT WORK

Biases, stereotypes, and other social processes have long interfered with the functioning of people-related practices and outcomes in organizations. Biases based on gender, race, nationality, age, religion, disability, and sexual orientation, and other demographic and personal characteristics have been well-documented as influencing employment-related decisions such as employee hiring, promotion, and evaluation. These biases can lead to discrimination, unequal treatment, and an unfair, non-inclusive work environment. Additionally, social factors such as networks, nepotism, and social homophily do not always contribute to organizational efficiency or fairness. Certain organizational processes and cultures may even reinforce these biases and social factors, further compromising the achievement of meritocracy in your organization.

Consequently, my main warning is that *simply having talent management structures and procedures in place does not automatically ensure that your organization is fair, equitable, or meritocratic in practice.* I will further expand on this warning in chapter 4.

In this regard, it is imperative for organizations and their leaders to stay alert and to proactively address the challenges that biases and social dynamics may pose to the true operation of meritocracy. Left unchecked, these factors will likely continue to undermine the effectiveness of talent management systems. So leaders committed to improving meritocracy in their organizations need to carefully design, introduce, and monitor steps to ensure that their talent management systems work fairly and, most importantly, that they do not inadvertently introduce new forms of bias and favoritism that compromise their meritocratic goals. I will elaborate on these crucial steps in part III.

Chapter Four

MERITOCRACY AND
ITS PARADOXES IN PRACTICE

In 2015, the major consulting firms Accenture and Deloitte scrapped their annual performance review systems, following the example of companies such as Adobe, Dell, Microsoft, IBM, Gap, Medtronic, Lear, and Oppenheimer Funds.[1] These companies were in the vanguard of what a few called "the performance management revolution," with some estimating that over one third of US companies abandoned the traditional performance appraisal process.[2] Jim Barnett, the CEO and founder of Glint, a company selling employee engagement tools, said, "We're in the early stages of a revolution. . . . A lot of companies are doing this . . . and I think over the next two years, we are going to see a profound shift in this area."[3]

Much commentary at the time focused on how the traditional performance reviews were "deeply flawed and ineffective."[4] A Deloitte survey of executives reported that the majority of respondents (58 percent) did not think their evaluation systems improved employee performance or engagement.[5] In fact, they reported that the opposite could happen. According to Inside HR, 50 percent of employees were surprised with their performance ratings. Out of those, 87 were negatively surprised, resulting in what was estimated to be a 23 percent drop in their engagement.[6]

There was then a general sense that everyone, from managers to HR professionals to employees themselves, supported ending traditional evaluation and feedback approaches. A survey by the Society for Human Resource Management (SHRM) reported that more than nine in ten managers were not happy with the current annual review process, with almost nine in ten HR leaders stating that the process "does not yield accurate information."[7] Panelists at the SHRM Annual Conference in 2021 even claimed that the "annual review tends to promote favoritism, inconsistency, abrupt swings between leniency and severity, and recency bias (which happens when reviewers judge an employee's most recent performance and apply it to the whole year)."[8]

Others have criticized evaluation processes as not only time-consuming and expensive but also problematic and inefficient.[9] In 2019, Robert Sutton and Ben Wigert at Gallup wrote: "Are our performance reviews really helping us get the most out of our people and engage them? When organizations put their performance management system under a microscope, the answer is a resounding 'NO.' It does not equip, inspire, and improve performance. It is not the best system for determining pay and promotion." They added, "And it costs organizations a lot of money—as much as $2.4 million to $35 million a year in lost working hours for an organization of 10,000 employees to take part in performance evaluations."[10]

Performance rating systems are said to "create negative morale as anonymous peer feedback can become weaponized, turning employees against each other."[11] By one estimate, about a third of traditional performance reviews result in subsequent declines in employee performance.[12] Moreover, Gallup researchers reported that only two in ten employees strongly agree that their performance is managed in a way that encourages them to excel, and only 14 percent say that performance reviews inspire them to improve.[13] And statements to the effect that "performance reviews are broken" continue to come from consultants and executives, followed by calls for organizations to create better systems to measure and evaluate performance.[14]

If performance evaluations were not working that well, with many even arguing that they foster favoritism and inconsistency, how were organizations addressing these issues? While traditional performance reviews were facing widespread criticism, fewer discussions focused on viable, good alternatives. Some even concluded that it may be better to have no performance evaluations at all. But what about the long-standing business norm of evaluating and managing performance? What can companies do in place of ranking systems and 360-feedback models? The credo of maximizing workplace productivity—which requires *some* formal process to evaluate performance—is, after all, difficult to completely abandon, especially in organizations and societies that are driven by results and performance.

In the United States alone, a multimillion-dollar consulting and software industry promises to help companies improve their performance management systems. As dissatisfaction with traditional performance review systems grew, however, some consultants began shifting their focus from accountability to learning, promoting frequent informal check-ins between employees and their managers, for example.[15] As mentioned earlier, major companies like Accenture, Deloitte, Adobe, and Gap announced that they were discontinuing formal performance evaluations in the mid-2010s.[16] To date, companies continue to replace annual reviews with more frequent informal conversations among employees, their managers, and their teammates throughout the year.[17]

Contrary to what industry commentators thought was happening, Deloitte and Accenture were *not* really getting rid of performance evaluations—but rather redesigning or "revamping" their complex, time-consuming, and often unnecessary processes to make evaluations more effective. This revamping consisted of vastly simplifying evaluation processes while still collecting performance data about their employees. Ironically, some of their "revamping" recommendations could have been incorporated into the initial design of such appraisal systems—such as setting clear performance goals, focusing on priorities, soliciting feedback, and documenting discussion.[18] Other advice, however, was vague and at times borderline naïve (e.g., adopt a "more welcome approach," "be cohesive," or "set the right tone"). Such broad terms and buzzwords can mean different things to those assessing and evaluating performance and merit, introducing ambiguity that may undermine the effectiveness of a talent management system, particularly in the everyday decisions that shape employment and employee outcomes.

But many organizations did not "revamp" their evaluation processes at all. Instead, they took the criticisms to heart and as an opportunity to completely get rid of evaluations, reverting to a corporate world before formal performance evaluations existed at all—which also has its downsides. Consultants and HR practitioners recommended formal performance evaluations in the 1980s and 1990s, partly to correct past employer injustices. At that time, many organizations and businesses had a serious problem in that managers and leaders could easily rely on their sole subjective and potentially biased discretion to make hiring, promotion, and pay decisions.[19]

There are better approaches to addressing performance evaluation problems than eliminating evaluations entirely. I have been fortunate to have worked with some organizational leaders who were motivated to investigate concerns about performance evaluation and then build meritocratic data-driven systems that work how they are supposed to—closer to the *ideal meritocracy* I described in chapter 2. During that work, I became concerned that performance evaluations were not only reproducing existing biases but also potentially creating new opportunities for new biases and social issues to emerge.

In this chapter, I present a research-backed argument that helps explain why meritocracy often fails in practice. I have labeled this argument the *meritocracy paradox* because it reveals why leaders' attempts to promote meritocracy and fairness in the workplace may, in fact, backfire. A key finding from my research is that emphasizing meritocracy (and possibly related concepts like fairness, equity, and even performance) as the basis for recruitment, promotion, or compensation practices may paradoxically introduce additional bias against women, racially disadvantaged groups, immigrants, and other disadvantaged individuals, regardless of their skills, competence, or performance. I argue that similar challenges can sometimes arise when organizations promote diversity, equal opportunity, and equitable processes without carefully planning solutions and actively monitoring behaviors and outcomes. In part III, I will outline a framework that draws on these findings, which can help organizations and their leaders identify and address fairness challenges more effectively.

THE PREVALENCE OF PERFORMANCE
EVALUATION AND INCENTIVE SCHEMES

One organization I was fortunate to work with was ServiCo, the large US service organization mentioned in the introduction to this book. In 2004, I started a research collaboration with ServiCo's top management to evaluate how effectively the company's performance evaluation system was motivating its employees. The performance reward system in place had been designed a decade before by a prominent management consulting firm that top management had hired to help them retain and engage talent—the same problem they seemed to be facing when we started collaborating.

I was interested in studying the demographic implications of performance management systems in the workplace. I wanted to understand why Janet, my former student, had referred to ServiCo as truly "meritocratic," a term that I had used myself that day to describe an organizational set of practices and procedures aimed at rewarding the best performers regardless of demographic and personal characteristics not relevant to the job and role.

At the time we started our collaboration, a substantial amount of serious research, particularly lab and field studies conducted by social and industrial psychologists, had documented the extent to which performance evaluations may be biased based on the demographics of the individual being evaluated as well as on those of the evaluator.[20]

A parallel research tradition, often disconnected from this literature and mostly in the sociology of work and labor markets (and later further investigated by behavioral economists), had also documented the association between demographics and career outcomes. However, all this work presumed the existence of a positive and significant relationship between performance, on the one hand, and pay, promotion, and rewards, on the other—meaning, for instance, that those who excel in performance are more likely to earn higher rewards. Proponents of meritocratic practices (as well as many other modern talent management processes) further assume that, in a truly meritocratic system, adding employee performance to any model that predicts compensation should explain away the effect of any demographic or performance-irrelevant personal qualities.

Given the current beliefs regarding what motivates people in the workplace, it is important to assess how true it is that pay, promotion, and rewards have a positive relationship with performance and merit. What high achiever or performer wants to work for an organization or business that says it hires and promotes average or simply good people? Instead, high performers aspire to work for organizations that aim to attract, select, develop, and advance the most talented and motivated employees. If you ask faculty who teach courses on strategic human resources and people analytics, they will likely say that the most popular session—among undergraduates, MBAs, and executives—is the one on performance evaluation and reward systems. (The second most popular topic is motivation, followed by screening and selecting the best talent.) This is not surprising given how rapidly companies adopted performance evaluations, especially at the beginning of the 2000s, to determine key career outcomes for employees and managers.

Performance appraisal systems have become a prevalent (often even expected) tool for evaluating and rewarding the efforts of employees and managers in today's organizations; these systems are indeed core to the meritocratic ethos in the workplace.[21] According to a series of 2021 reports by WorldatWork, the large majority of US publicly traded companies offer short-term incentives (99 percent) and long-term incentives (94 percent) to their employees, compared with 93 percent of privately held companies,

82 percent of nonprofits, and 58 percent of government organizations offering short-term incentives.[22] In the case of public companies, about 97 percent of CEOs, 98 percent of executives, 97 percent of managers and supervisors, 85 percent of exempt employees, and 55 percent of nonexempt employees were eligible for annual incentives.[23]

In business education, sessions on managing performance and rewards are popular because leaders and professionals who manage people understand the practical relevance of this topic for employee motivation, effort, and even perceptions of fairness in the workplace. Every good manager wants to be motivating and inspiring and wants to reward their employees properly (*fairly*, many would add). Further, I have yet to find any participant in any of my classes who does not agree that top performers should be rewarded for superior performance. Some even obsess about what the "best practices" are for managing the underperformers. In fact, the centrality of the meritocratic ethos to this mindset and to current talent management systems is one of the reasons that motivated me to do this research.

Unfortunately, examples from my research provide evidence that the ideal of meritocracy, while deeply appealing in theory, is challenging for organizations to achieve in practice. There are many pitfalls: every time a company's leadership team changes its talent management approach or introduces a creative new way of managing people at work, it may potentially create opportunities for bias and other social processes to operate as well.

THE PARADOX OF MERITOCRACY

To remain competitive, dynamic, and strategic, many organizations and businesses have spent significant time and resources on their formal evaluation and feedback systems, with the goal of ensuring that employees are judged by their performance and rewarded accordingly. Since the mid-2010s, many companies have striven to improve the effectiveness of their performance appraisals, with 81 percent of HR professionals reporting that they are making changes to their performance management processes[24] and 70 percent saying that they are either evaluating them (31 percent) or have recently reviewed and updated them (39 percent).[25] Many organizations are also taking steps to eliminate recurrent bias in performance reward systems, such as formally separating performance reviews from bonus and pay decisions and introducing additional measures to prevent unconscious biases from creeping into the evaluation process. But have these approaches led to the achievement of true meritocracy in the workplace, or do disparities and biases still persist despite these efforts?

Certain performance-reward practices provide little or no protection against bias. In fact, the more managers and executives *believe* their organization is a meritocracy, for instance, because it has processes and values relating to performance, equity, and fairness, the more likely they may be to display the very biases those processes and values aim to prevent. According to the results of my studies, the belief that an organization is meritocratic may actually foster biased, non-merit-based behavior. In other words, demographic-based disparities and unfairness might persist in today's organizations *despite* management's efforts to eliminate them or even *because* of such efforts.

We call this effect "the paradox of meritocracy."

The Paradox of Meritocracy Experiment

Steven Benard at Indiana University and I conducted a series of experiments with more than four hundred experienced professionals to study the paradox of meritocracy effect.[26] Participants were asked to play the role of managers in ServiceOne, a large fictitious US service-sector employer. After we described ServiceOne and its core values to the participants, they were tasked to assess three fictional employees and make recommendations for bonuses, promotions, and terminations. We encouraged study participants to base their employment decisions on the yearly employee performance reviews they read. Participants did not know that they were randomly assigned to receive one of two different sets of organizational core values for ServiceOne: one set emphasized meritocracy (the "meritocratic" condition), while the second (neutral) set did not emphasize meritocracy (the "non-meritocratic" condition).

For the meritocratic version of ServiceOne, we described the core values with statements such as "Raises and bonuses are based entirely on the performance of the employee" and "ServiceOne's goal is to reward all employees equitably every year." For the non-meritocratic version, the core values instead stressed managerial autonomy and the regularity of evaluation, using statements such as "Raises and bonuses are to be given based on the discretion of the manager" and "ServiceOne's goal is to evaluate all employees every year."

Study participants were then exposed to three employee profiles. Two were "test profiles" and included one male employee (Michael) and one female employee (Patricia) with identical performance evaluation scores. We also included one "filler" profile, an employee with a lower performance evaluation score, to minimize suspicion that gender bias was the study's main focus (in one run of the experiment, the filler profile was a man, Robert; in a second run, to ensure the robustness of our results, the filler profile was a woman, Linda). Participants then decided on the size of the monetary bonus, if any, that each employee should receive. They also evaluated the three employees on other measures, including their hiring, potential, promotion, and retention assessments.

The data for our first experimental study were collected in three sessions at a private business school in the United States.[27] The sessions were advertised as an opportunity for students attending an MBA or a similar business degree program to learn about performance-reward systems in the workplace. The final sample in our first study included 229 MBAs or business professionals (163 men and 64 women, 2 no gender indicated) with substantial work and managerial experience. Although the limited supply of these participants restricts the number of experimental permutations, this approach offers more realism in assessing how managers evaluate and reward their workers. Additionally, business school graduate programs aim to prepare students for supervisory and managerial roles, including active participation in employee appraisals. Participants in the first study were, on average, nearly thirty years old, with about six years of work experience.[28]

The data collection procedure was identical across sessions. Participants were invited to participate in a "Management Personnel Decision-Making Simulation Exercise." (Since then, in workshops I have conducted with various groups of participants, I have replicated this simulation and continue to find evidence of the paradox of meritocracy effect.)

Participants who volunteered for the study were first given a verbal overview and then provided with a study packet to read and complete. They were instructed to assume the role of a manager at ServiceOne and make personnel decisions similar to those made in real organizations. The study packet included several components: instructions, a company description for ServiceOne, and details on how performance evaluations and pay decisions are made at ServiceOne. Participants were told that the description was based on a real company that one of the authors had collaborated with, with some details changed to protect the company's identity.

Following the company description was a statement about ServiceOne's core company values that either did or did not emphasize meritocracy when describing its performance–reward system to the participants. To ensure that study participants carefully read and considered each core value statement, we asked them to checkmark whether they agreed with each company value.[29] They then examined three employee profiles: two performance-equivalent "test profiles" that varied by gender and one filler profile. After reviewing the profiles, participants evaluated each employee on various employment-related measures, including our key dependent variable—the bonus amount decision. They also completed a section on "final reflections." After the experiment, the exercise was discussed in class, followed by a lesson on the unintended consequences of performance-reward systems.

The company description for ServiceOne provided general information about the company and details about its performance evaluation process. ServiceOne was described as a large private company in the service sector, located in an urban area in North America, with a focus on research and information technology. The description included information about the types of available jobs and employees' age, tenure, and demographics. Participants were asked to act as managers overseeing a small team of consultants.

The evaluation process was described to the participants as a two-step performance evaluation process, common in large companies.[30] First, an immediate supervisor evaluates an employee's performance, and second, a different manager determines the potential bonus based on the supervisor's evaluation. Participants played the role of the second manager, making decisions about the bonuses, promotions, and terminations for these employees based on their performance evaluations.

Once again, participants assessed three employee profiles, including two equivalent test profiles that varied in gender and one low-performing filler profile. All employees were "Consultants," worked in "Product Development," and had the same supervisor. We manipulated gender by using male- and female-typical names. Each profile was presented using a "Performance and Staff Development Evaluation Form," with a quantitative 1–5 score and qualitative comments for each employee from their immediate supervisor.

To test our hypothesis concerning the paradox of meritocracy, it was crucial that the test profiles had equal merit (performance score in our study) but were not identical to avoid the suspicion that this study was about gender bias. To this end, we gave each test profile, Michael and Patricia, the same quantitative performance scores and similar qualitative comments, counterbalancing these comments across profiles. The 5-point scale, labeled

"Summary of Performance," had descriptive phrases for each level, with 5 being the highest. The two test profiles received a score of 4, described as "Staff member's performance consistently meets and frequently exceeds all established goals/expectations for the position."[31]

We included a third filler profile, named "Robert Miller," in one version of our study to further reduce suspicion that gender bias was the study's focus. With three profiles, gender differences were less noticeable than with just two. The filler profile performed lower than the two test profiles, receiving a 3 out of 5 on the quantitative evaluation. This rating indicated that "staff member's performance consistently meets established goals/expectations for the position." The praise for the filler profile was lukewarm: "Robert does a good job of listening to the clients and meeting their expectations. His work has been consistently solid but not spectacular." The criticism noted: "Robert has a tendency to miss minor deadlines when things get busy. He needs to do a better job of staying on top of his projects." (Once again, to ensure our results were robust, we repeated the experiment with a female filler profile named Linda, and our key findings remained the same.)

Study participants were asked to allocate a yearly bonus to each employee from a limited pool of $1,000. To study if perceptions of meritocracy influenced other employee outcomes, participants also rated each employee on four additional items using 7-point Likert-type scales. The first question asked, "Do you think hiring this employee was the right decision?" with options ranging from "definitely wrong decision" to "definitely right decision." Similar questions were asked about whether the employee should be considered for promotion or termination, and whether they would be successful in the future.

When analyzing the data, we first checked that the meritocratic manipulation worked; we indeed found that participants rated ServiceOne as more meritocratic and fairer in the meritocratic condition than in the non-meritocratic condition.[32]

We also found that participants' reward decisions differed depending on our manipulation of their perceptions of meritocracy, as summarized in figure 4.1. In the non-meritocratic condition, equally high-performing men and women earned similar bonuses. Women earned, on average, $2 more than men, but this bonus difference was not statistically significant. In contrast, in the meritocratic condition, men earned, on average, a bonus $46 higher than equally performing women, a difference statistically significant at the 0.01 level. This is evidence of the *paradox of meritocracy*.[33]

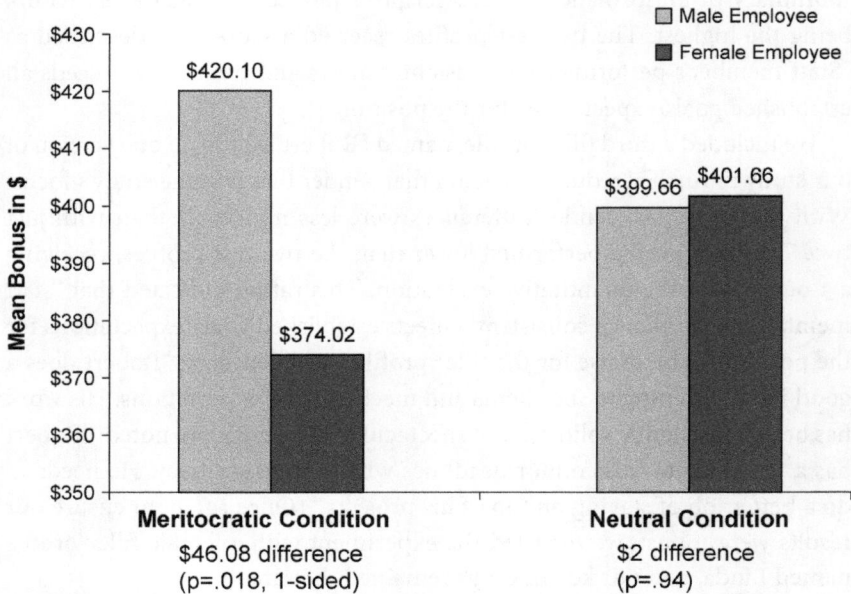

FIGURE 4.1. The paradox of meritocracy. *Source*: Study 3 (N=101) in Emilio J. Castilla and Stephen Benard, "The Paradox of Meritocracy in Organizations," *Administrative Science Quarterly* 55, no. 4 (2010), 563–6.

WHY THE PARADOX OF MERITOCRACY?

The paradox of meritocracy may help explain the persistence of pay disparities related to demographics and other personal qualities in many organizations. (An empirical question remains, though, as to whether it accounts for career disparities for employees from other demographic groups or with specific personal qualities.) But what accounts for the paradox of meritocracy effect? One potential answer is that when managers believe their company is meritocratic, they may be less vigilant about their actions and (un)intentionally make biased decisions. This could happen because they feel their decisions are unlikely to be perceived as prejudiced, making them less careful about avoiding stereotypes. They may further have a false sense of confidence in their impartiality, leading to little self-examination to uncover any hidden biases in their decisions.

Prior research has suggested many other factors contributing to "disinhibiting" biases in organizational contexts. For instance, one study showed that priming one's sense of personal objectivity prior to making hiring evaluations increased gender bias in favor of men over women, particularly among participants who endorsed stereotypic beliefs or had such thoughts activated through implicit priming. In one such study, Eric L. Uhlmann and Geoffrey L. Cohen primed such a sense of objectivity by asking participants to complete a subtle manipulation that included four self-perceived objectivity questionnaire items, including statements like the following: "In most situations, I try to do what seems reasonable and logical," "When forming an opinion, I try to objectively consider all of the facts I have access to," "My judgments are based on a logical analysis of the facts," and "My decision-making is rational and objective."[34]

In their laboratory experiment, 65 men were primed with such self-perceived objectivity questionnaire items and then asked to evaluate equivalent male and female candidates. Assuming that most people hold some stereotypic beliefs,[35] the researchers hypothesized that individuals would evaluate women less favorably than men after being primed to view themselves as objective.

As predicted, unlike participants in the control condition (who were not primed with self-perceived objectivity), participants primed to feel objective favored the male applicant over the female one. This finding aligns with the paradox of meritocracy, suggesting that organizational efforts to make us feel more objective may backfire against candidates with certain identities.

MORAL CREDENTIALING: THE TROUBLE WITH APPEARING FAIR

While these findings may seem surprising or even counterintuitive, they are consistent with prior research on rationalization, misconduct, and what scholars have called *moral credentialing*. Moral credentialing is the act of establishing oneself as moral and virtuous, which research has shown can lead to subsequent selfish or ethically questionable behavior.[36] For instance, one study found that participants who imagined volunteering or donating to charity were more likely to make a self-indulgent purchase of a luxury item afterward than those who had not just affirmed their moral integrity.[37] As Anna C. Merritt, Daniel A. Effron, and Benoît Monin stated in their article, past good deeds "can liberate individuals to engage in behaviors that are immoral, unethical, or otherwise problematic, behaviors that they would otherwise avoid for fear of feeling or appearing immoral."[38]

Much research on the so-called moral self-licensing effect has been done in areas of political correctness, prosocial behavior, and consumer choice. For instance, individuals who are given an opportunity to prove their kindness or generosity are less worried about behaving in ways that violate prosocial norms afterward.[39] Another study reported that expressing support for a Black presidential candidate presumably freed study participants from the need to prove their lack of prejudice afterward, licensing them to favor Whites over Blacks.[40]

Studies have also shown that people are more likely to express prejudiced attitudes when their past behavior has proven they are non-prejudiced. A classic study in this field by Benoît Monin and Dale T. Miller found evidence of moral credentialing in hiring decisions.[41] Men who were given the opportunity to disagree with blatantly sexist statements were more likely to rate a male candidate as better suited for a stereotypically masculine job than a woman. Similarly, White participants tended to favor a White man over a Black man or a woman for a job after first being given the opportunity to hire a highly qualified woman or Black man for a fictitious consulting firm. These results suggest that individuals are more prone to express prejudiced attitudes when their past behavior has demonstrated their moral integrity.

You can likely find anecdotal evidence of this phenomenon. Have you ever been, say, at a dinner party with colleagues or friends, when someone started their contribution to the discussion with statements like "I am not racist . . . but" or "I am not sexist at all . . . but"? Quite likely, as predicted and supported by this line of research, a racist or sexist statement is likely to follow the "but" statement.

Since those results were reported, further research has replicated and extended them to other situations and contexts,[42] particularly situations that involve the hiring and selection of candidates.[43] Researchers have even found that the expectation of behaving morally in the future can change behavior in the present. In one study, participants who anticipated taking part in a fundraiser or donating blood (as examples of performing a future moral action) subsequently made more racially biased decisions or displayed more racially biased attitudes than the control group across four experiments.[44]

Such effects may extend to other demographic groups as well as personal characteristics besides sex and race. One study of 318 elementary school teachers examined the moral credentialing effect concerning attitudes toward individuals with disabilities.[45] Alexandra Maftei and colleagues found that participants were more likely to rate a nondisabled candidate as better suited for both a teaching job and a private school manager position compared to a disabled candidate if they had previously had the opportunity to disagree with discriminatory statements about people with disabilities. Once again, giving individuals the chance to disagree with discriminatory statements makes them feel they have already proven their lack of prejudice, thereby liberating them to be more prejudiced.

All these studies, including my own with Steven Benard on the paradox of meritocracy effect, suggest that subtle manipulations that make people feel objective or remind them that they are part of a meritocratic and equitable organization may actually license them to act on biases they would otherwise suppress due to personal, organizational, and social pressures or obstacles. In other words, a sense of belonging to a fair and equitable organization or participating in fair and equitable processes may unleash individuals' stereotypic thoughts and beliefs, ultimately leading to more demographic bias and disparities in key employment-related decisions.[46]

There are additional reasons to suspect that a belief in meritocracy may hamper the achievement of true meritocracy. Core to the definition of meritocracy is the condition that meritocracy does allow for inequality in the distribution of socially and economically desired resources and positions in organizations, which has the consequence of reinforcing attitudes and beliefs that introduce or sustain inequality. Along these lines, researchers analyzed data from four studies[47] (one correlational study with 198 respondents,[48] one experiment with 198 participants, and two surveys of approximately 88,000 participants in more than forty countries) and concluded that "belief in school meritocracy"—that is, belief that success in school depends solely on willpower and hard work[49]—reduces respondents' perception that social class inequality in society is unfair. This belief also reduces their support for affirmative action policies in colleges and universities and for policies to ameliorate income inequality.

This "school meritocracy" research joined a body of scholarly work that primarily showed how priming meritocracy helps legitimate income inequality[50] and can even encourage the use of stereotypes against low-status demographic groups and negatively impact decisions involving their members.[51]

EQUAL OPPORTUNITY FOR ALL IN SELECTION AND HIRING?

So far, I have primarily discussed the evaluation of employees' performance in the workplace. However, many leaders strongly believe that to build a successful organization, they must attract and retain top talent. And to do so, the theory goes, they need to be meritocracies, hiring, rewarding, and promoting the best individuals based on their merit. But have such talent management approaches helped achieve true meritocracy and helped recruit the "best talent" to organizations regardless of their demographics? To what extent are key hiring decision-makers and gatekeepers giving equal opportunity to all? Could they be favoring certain groups of applicants on factors other than merit or talent? These have been major questions for me to tackle empirically across a variety of organizations and using a multitude of research methodologies.

For several years, I have studied organizations' screening and selection processes and how certain non-merit factors can indeed shape these important decisions. I have also embarked on fascinating collaborations with colleges and business schools to study their admissions procedures. Educational institutions are usually clear about the criteria used to admit students into their academic programs. Yet, many have documented that certain organizations and institutions do not necessarily admit the best, especially selective colleges that are known for opening doors to professional success.[52]

In my research project with Ethan Poskanzer at the University of Colorado, Boulder, we examined the admissions process at an elite US college by analyzing its records for over 235,000 applications and nearly 35,000 admissions to its undergraduate program over a span of sixteen years.[53] Our data included demographics, standardized test scores, high school grades and ranks, and the high schools attended. We also reviewed student records for academic performance, meritorious recognitions and awards, and the courses taken by over 5,400 matriculated applicants. The College—as we referred to it to protect its identity—is one of the top 25 ranked colleges in the United States and has a highly selective admissions process.

In our empirical models, we found that standardized test scores, and high school grades and ranks were highly significant predictors of admissions decisions into The College. We also found that legacies influenced admissions: the children or siblings of alumni were twice as likely to be admitted as comparable nonlegacies.

In analyzing our data to understand why admissions officers may favor legacy applicants, we found strong support for a *material logic*. Compared to their nonlegacy peers, legacies tended to be better alumni, were less likely to need financial aid, and had wealthier parents who could contribute more generously to The College. However, contrary to a *meritocratic logic*, legacy candidates were not meaningfully more qualified. Admissions officers did assess legacies as having better personal (not intellectual) qualities than nonlegacies. Still, our analyses showed that once admitted, legacies were not more involved in the student community or more active in on-campus activities than nonlegacies. Moreover, legacy applicants were not better qualified for admission in terms of test scores or high school achievements, and they did not perform better academically or secure better jobs after graduation. Based on these results, the decision by a growing number of schools to end the practice of legacy admissions appears to be a step in the right direction.

In a different research project, as briefly explained in the prior chapter, Ben Rissing of Cornell University and I investigated screening and selection in the context of foreign nationals' employment. We specifically studied how US Department of Labor agents decide on the labor certification approval, a crucial employment outcome for immigrants that grants legal authorization to work in the United States.[54]

Like other advanced nations in the world, the United States has immigration laws and policies to guard the employment of its citizens. We analyzed employment-based applications for US work and residence permits (known as Permanent Resident Cards) for almost 200,000 immigrant workers from all over the world; government agents reviewed these applicants between June 2008 and September 2011. We were particularly interested in assessing whether citizens of certain countries experienced any disparities in their labor certification outcomes. This certification process is presumed to be citizenship blind, but a basic bivariate descriptive analysis revealed that Asian immigrants were more likely, and Latin American immigrants were less likely, to obtain labor certification compared to Canadians.[55] Table 4.1 displays the approval percentages for labor certification among selected citizenship groups in our dataset.

But table 4.1 simply presents bivariate statistics; it does not necessarily account for many other factors, including merit-based factors—such as skill-level requirements for the job, occupation, type of employer, and salary—that could explain such stark nationality differences in work authorization outcomes. We estimated models that control for such factors and still found that immigrant workers from India, South Korea, and Taiwan were 18, 21, and 21 percent more likely, respectively, to receive labor certification than Canadians with similar professional backgrounds and working in similar jobs. In contrast, all Latin American citizenship groups were less likely to be approved than Canadians. Mexicans were the most disadvantaged, being 35 percent less likely to receive certification. Immigrants from Brazil, Colombia, and Venezuela were 22, 21, and 18 percent less likely, respectively, to

TABLE 4.1
Percentage of labor certifications approved for selected citizenship groups

Citizenship (select groups)	Approval, %
Asia: India	92.1
Asia: China	90.5
Asia: South Korea	88.8
Asia: Taiwan	91.6
North America: Canada	89.8
Latin America: Brazil	77.3
Latin America: Caribbean and Central America	68.2
Latin America: Mexico	60.0
Latin America: Other regions of South America	82.0
All citizenship groups	86.0

Source: Data from Ben A. Rissing and Emilio J. Castilla, "House of Green Cards: Statistical or Preference-Based Inequality in the Employment of Foreign Nationals," American Sociological Review 79, no. 6 (2014): 1226–55.
Note: We chose Canada as the reference category because of Canada's similarities with the United States, particularly with regard to GDP growth, unemployment levels, English fluency, and geographic proximity.

be approved.[56] These findings suggest that nationality does affect the work authorization process in non-meritocratic ways.

In a third research project on screening and selecting top talent, Ben Rissing and I investigated the admissions process at a major US business school.[57] In particular, we analyzed data from the population of over 21,000 applications to the school's MBA program over a seven-year period. The program aimed to "bring together the best class of exceptional professionals with a range of personal and professional backgrounds."[58] Our data included assessment scores for all applicants from both application readers and interviewers (standardized test scores, undergraduate grades, and additional competencies like professional accomplishment, creativity, and social affinity) as well as post-admissions information for the MBAs, including grades, job placement, salary at graduation, and monetary donations to the school.

We found evidence that application endorsements—a common (formal and informal) networking practice in which certain individuals advocate for certain applicants at the time of screening—influence who is selected for interviews and receives offers. Endorsed candidates were approximately twice as likely to be offered admission as nonendorsed applicants, even after controlling for key candidate qualifications and competencies.[59] Yet, endorsed candidates did not achieve better academic performance or better jobs upon graduation than nonendorsed ones.

Together, these three projects illustrate how organizations and their key decision-makers, whether admissions officers, government agents, or hiring managers and recruiters, may still introduce, whether intentionally or not, non-merit-based factors such as family ties, country of citizenship, or connections to influential people when recruiting and selecting candidates into organizations. Moreover, this bias occurs even in organizational contexts where meritocracy and the rubric of the best talent approach dominate.

MORE ON EQUAL OPPORTUNITY FOR DIVERSE CANDIDATES

Similar biases and non-merit-based factors could come into play in organizations seeking to promote equity, opportunity for all, and diversity. For instance, many organizations have featured statements on their websites and in their job advertisements highlighting that they are "equal opportunity employers." Statements like these may go even further to highlight that the organization is committed to giving equal employment and advancement opportunities regardless of the candidate's gender, race, ethnicity, religion, national origin, sexual orientation, age, marital status, disability, or veteran status. Such statements have been popular in the United States, Canada, and many European countries.

These statements, like many other employer actions and recruitment efforts, are easy ways to represent employers as good and fair, increasing their appeal to job seekers. Moreover, they are indeed cheap. Once the statements have been developed and approved, it takes only minutes to add them to a website or job posting. A similar motive could be attributed to companies' common practice of publishing their diversity reports on their websites and having their key professionals brag about the wide variety of initiatives and efforts that the organization is pursuing to achieve meritocracy and diversity.

A 2022 report by iHire, based on survey responses from 4,207 US job seekers and 539 employers from fifty-seven different industries, showed that almost a third (29.75 percent) of employers said that they "always" include an equal opportunity statement or DEI information in their online job ads.[60] Although this is less than the top three items that employers say they always include in an advertisement—benefits (70 percent), salary range (57 percent), and contact information for the hiring manager (57 percent)[61]—it raises the immediate practical question as to what extent those diversity statements actually help increase diversity in recruitment and hiring. Another related (but practically relevant) question is how to measure the effectiveness of such diversity statements.

Even more crucial is the extent to which such statements may backfire. Could such approaches potentially liberate key decision-makers from responsibility for truly achieving meritocracy and fairness in practice? Building on the research on objectivity, moral credentialing, and the meritocracy paradox, there is always the risk that managers at such organizations may feel that their organizations are truly objective, fair, and meritocratic, a belief that may unleash many of the persistent cognitive biases the managers may already have toward certain groups of individuals. Equity, opportunity for all, and diversity statements and many other *soft* organizational efforts or interventions can too create a false sense or illusion of meritocracy and fairness, making managers and recruiters believe that their organizations (and they themselves) are prodiversity, a belief that can lead them to engage in *more* biased and *less* diverse decision-making.

There are reasons to suspect that this is a real possibility. In a study entitled "Presumed Fair: Ironic Effects of Organizational Diversity Structures," Cheryl Kaiser and colleagues conducted a series of experiments involving White participants.[62] In one experiment, a group of participants was randomly assigned to read a company description *with* a diversity statement, while the other group read a description *without* it. When shown racial disparities in each company's promotion rates (28 percent of White versus 10 percent of racially disadvantaged employees getting promotions), participants who read the diversity statement rated the company as acting more fairly toward racially disadvantaged workers than those who did not read such a diversity statement.

In a second experiment, participants read a scenario in which a Black employee sued the company for discriminatory promotion practices. Those participants randomly assigned to read the company description *with* a diversity statement were less sympathetic to the Black employee and less likely to view the lawsuit as valid than those assigned to read a company description *without* a diversity statement. Both experiments, therefore, warn about the potential negative unintended consequences of diversity statements and potentially many other diversity practices: by presumably creating the illusion that equality and fairness have already been achieved or are easily achievable, organizations can lead people to downplay or ignore existing demographic disparities in employment outcomes.

What happens if organizations merely add diversity statements to their job postings and company statements without making any other structural changes to increase diversity? To answer that question, Sonia K. Kang and colleagues recruited 119 undergraduate business students of different genders and races (41 men and 78 women; 87 East Asian, 18 South Asian, and 14 Black participants) to participate in a "résumé workshop" lab study.[63] At the lab, each student received an envelope with a hard copy of their résumé and a job ad for a position that matched their field interests. Students were then asked to type a tailored résumé for the job posting.

The findings were clear-cut: Asian and Black candidates were half as likely to "whiten" their résumé (that is, remove racial and ethnic cues) when the job posting included a statement and an image describing the employer as an organization that valued diversity (diversity condition) than when the posting included a generic image and did not mention diversity (control condition). But the research team also found, in a second experiment, that Blacks and Asians with "whitened" résumés were more likely to get employer callbacks than those with unwhitened résumés, regardless of whether the job posting included a diversity statement.

Considered together, the findings from these two studies suggest that including diversity statements in job ads could negatively affect a company's hiring of candidates from racially diverse backgrounds: a diversity statement may make such candidates less likely to whiten their résumés, which in turn may make them less likely to receive a callback from employers.

The truth is that diversity statements, like many other isolated, nonstructural, or soft attempts at reducing bias, can only do so much. They should not be used in lieu of substantive structural changes to the organization's recruitment and hiring procedures to ensure equal opportunity and fairness. Furthermore, they should not be used as replacements for serious organizational efforts to ensure that new hires are successfully integrated into the organization and have equal access to training and growth opportunities, as well as to evaluate the employment outcomes relating to those efforts. Because biases are likely ingrained in our thinking and actions, organizations should take careful steps to ensure that undesirable biases do not creep into their key people-based management processes. These steps will be covered in part III of this book.

REWARDING THE TOP PERFORMERS EQUALLY?

All these prior findings are relevant for organizations and businesses that are implementing talent management systems, especially those that increase a sense of belonging to a fair, meritocratic, talent-driven organization.

To further learn about these systems, I conducted a longitudinal study of gender and racial disparities at ServiCo, the organization I mentioned earlier. As in many prior research projects, I collected, coded, and analyzed a longitudinal dataset tracking the career progression of 8,900 employees over time, including information about their demographics, education, and professional background, as well as promotions, transfers, developmental opportunities, and other work accomplishments. Some of this information was coded from the résumés employees submitted to ServiCo, while other data were collected post-hire, focusing on key employee career decisions, the job titles employees had held, and the units and supervisors they had worked for.[64]

Each year, supervisors entered employee performance ratings into an online platform, HR professionals reviewed them, and unit heads ultimately used them to allocate merit-based annual bonuses. Employees received an evaluation score from 1 "poor performance" to 5 "outstanding performance." I also collected and studied salary adjustments and rewards offered to employees over time as a result of promotions, transfers, and performance evaluations. Of particular interest were merit-based bonuses—once again, a critical element of meritocracy at work in today's organizations.

In studies like these, once the data are coded, cleaned, and ready to be analyzed, the first step is to run some basic descriptive statistics and relevant bivariate tests to identify relevant patterns for the organization. An important one in the case of ServiCo was to plot employees' level of performance each year for a particular job title and the average magnitude of the merit-based monetary reward; this information can give us an average monetary bonus for employees at a given level of performance. Then, one can easily compute the same table for different groups of employees, depending on their demographic information, and even estimate the extent to which any bonus differences are large and significant. ServiCo had collected information about its employees' gender, race, and nationality for several years before we started our collaboration. We, therefore, used those three key demographic variables to compare average merit-based bonus decisions across groups of employees.

For instance, for job grade 21 in 2001, coded as "assistant manager," I found that the average merit-based bonus was zero for both men and women whose performance was "poor" (a performance rating of 1 on the scale of 1 to 5) in the same job for the same unit. This discovery was not surprising given ServiCo's goal of offering bonuses based on employee performance. (To give more context to the relationship between the bonus and the base salary, the average salary for the assistant manager position in 2001 was $23,147 at the beginning of the research collaboration, with a minimum of $19,968 and a maximum of $26,325 observed in the sample.)

At higher levels of performance, a puzzling finding emerged: when the performance was average (that is, 3 on a scale of 1 to 5), men received a bonus $286 higher than women doing the same job in the same unit and with the same level of performance. The difference was even higher among those assistant managers who were ranked as "outstanding" (5 on a scale of 1 to 5). Within that group, women received a bonus $758 lower than that of identically performing men. The results of this preliminary analysis of average bonuses by level of performance evaluation and by gender are reported in table 4.2.

I found a similar pattern when comparing the magnitudes of the average performance-based bonus by race and national origin, two demographic characteristics collected and coded by the HR staff at ServiCo. Blacks, Hispanics, and non-US-born employees obtained a lower bonus amount than White US-born men, even when they were doing the same job at the same level of performance.

We should not immediately conclude that there is bias or discrimination against certain groups just because there are demographic differences in performance or rewards. One plausible explanation is that members of one demographic group outperform another. That said, the differences may also arise from biases in the evaluation process. I have seen evidence of such biases in certain organizations, and there is plenty of research about how hiring decisions and performance evaluations can be prone to bias and other social processes that can affect such an evaluation process. Demonstrating the existence of demographic bias is not easy; it requires us

TABLE 4.2

Average annual bonus for assistant managers by gender and level of performance evaluation

Performance evaluation	Average bonus		
	Women		Men
1. Unacceptable	$0	=	$0
2. Improvement	$281	<	$522
3. Average	$751	<	$1,037
4. Good	$1,051	<	$1,520
5. Outstanding	$1,798	<	$2,556

Source: Data from Emilio J. Castilla, "Gender, Race, and Organizational Careers," *American Journal of Sociology* 113, no. 6 (2008): 1479–526.

to rule out *real* performance differences across certain groups of individuals. In the above example, however, different levels of performance do not seem to explain the pattern observed because employees in the same job with the same level of performance received a different bonus depending on their gender.

Nevertheless, many complicating factors unaccounted for in the simple bivariate statistics reported in table 4.2 could potentially explain those gender (or any other demographic) differences away. First, such a table ignores any individual-level, often longitudinal, aspects of the employment process, that is, differences in education, experience, and tenure in the organization that could potentially affect pay. Second, relatedly, the table assumes that men and women working in this organization are "observationally equivalent"; that is, on their résumés, they look similar on average (they have the same education and professional accomplishments). The table also ignores promotions, turnover rates, and many other structural factors that can vary significantly depending on demographics (for instance, employees of certain demographic and professional backgrounds may be more likely to be promoted into that position and/or more likely to leave it). This is why additional data—not only about the characteristics of the employees themselves (particularly information relevant to doing the job well) but also about how the key evaluation, reward, and career processes are designed and implemented—become essential to fully assess what may be happening in this company.

In such cases, I recommend collecting additional longitudinal data, including information that could be coded from employees' résumés and applications (e.g., years of education, type of education, relevant skills, experience, and abilities) as well as records of employees' work history before and during their tenure in the organization.

And, if you are a researcher or consultant working within a company (rather than an executive already part of the organization), I strongly advise getting *really inside the organization* to gain a deep understanding of the organizational context and better understand the employment-related phenomena you are studying and aiming to improve. This task often requires connecting with *multiple key stakeholders* to interview them and learn about their processes and outcomes, as well as observing talent management practices in action. In this paragraph, I use italics to highlight key aspects of the analysis: I have seen many experts overlook the importance of understanding the business context they are studying or rely on information from just one stakeholder. It is crucial to assess how consistent that information is across various relevant groups, including applicants, hires, recruiters and hiring professionals, managers, executives, and even customers.

In the case of ServiCo, I was present during the three months when both the annual performance evaluation process and then the distribution of merit-based rewards took place. I thus had a great opportunity *before* collecting and analyzing any data to understand how employees, managers, and HR professionals at ServiCo approached the company's processes of performance appraisal and bonus decisions. Later in the study, after analyzing the collected data, I returned to interview many managers, HR professionals, and other employees to ensure that my understanding of the organization's talent management processes was accurate and that my research findings were robust.

The most important part of the study was the quantitative analyses of ServiCo's data, for which I ran regression models estimating who receives performance-based bonuses or pay increases and the monetary magnitude of such rewards. The goal of such analyses was to assess whether the significant demographic gap reported earlier (in table 4.2) remained once we accounted for alternative potential reasons. Specifically, I was able to estimate whether employees' gender, race, and nationality influenced the initial salary allocated at the time of hire, as well as subsequent salary increases, bonus decisions, and promotions after controlling for performance over time. Such models controlled for job title, work unit, supervisor, and year of hire fixed effects, which can potentially explain differences in the allocation and magnitude of rewards.

Even after controlling for such factors, I continued to find similar demographic effects on bonus amounts. I termed this *performance-reward bias*, which I define as a form of bias against certain demographic groups that can potentially be introduced while using performance data to make merit-based employment decisions like salary increases, bonuses, or promotions. Women, racially disadvantaged groups, and non-US-born employees working in the same job and unit, for the same supervisor, and with the same human capital earned a smaller merit-based bonus than White men, even after receiving the same performance scores that year.

To be clear, I still found that higher levels of performance translated into higher merit-based rewards, and performance was indeed the most important predictor of the magnitude of the bonuses. However, adding performance to the models did not eliminate the significance or the magnitude of the demographic effects on the bonus amount. This performance-reward bias was thus introduced when performance data were used to make employee pay decisions at ServiCo.

In my models, I also looked at pay growth. In the long run, women and certain racial groups obtained lower salary increases than White men in the same job and work unit, with the same supervisor, and even with the same performance evaluation scores. In particular, salary growth for women was 0.4 percent lower than for men, while Blacks and Hispanics received salary increases 0.5 percent lower than those of equally performing White employees. Non-US-born workers had salary increases 0.6 percent lower than native-born employees. These figures might seem trivial, but the differences can compound over the longer term. For example, if "Alice" and "Bob" both start at an annual base salary of $50,000 and he gets a 10 percent salary increase each year while she gets 9.96 percent for the same performance, then after 20 years, her annual base salary will be almost $2,500 less.[65]

The empirical evidence of performance-reward bias in ServiCo, as well as in other companies I have studied (with less data available to rule out plausible explanations for such demographic effects), was surprising to me and to ServiCo's top management when presented with my findings. This bias was especially unexpected given ServiCo's clear message about the importance of performance evaluations in justifying merit-based increases, which was often emphasized when training the unit heads in charge of distributing rewards. For instance, the HR policy manual used in training ServiCo supervisors read: "Performance is the primary basis for all employee salary increases. Performance appraisals must be completed for all employees receiving a merit increase in order to substantiate the level of merit increase awarded."[66] It said, "If performance is unacceptable, no increase will be awarded."

It is worth stressing that I discovered some aspects of ServiCo by "getting inside" the company. I found that ServiCo's top management chose to separate performance appraisals from pay decisions, following the advice of a renowned management consulting firm. One reason for doing so was to facilitate supervisor feedback and to encourage employees' future development. At ServiCo, employees were recommended for a merit-based bonus not by their supervisors but by higher-level managers, "unit heads." Many other organizations have similarly decoupled performance appraisals from pay and rewards. As my study revealed, this separation can introduce opportunities for biases and other irrelevant judgments to enter. Because subjectivity is often inevitable, the performance evaluation process is vulnerable to implicit and even explicit demographic biases. These biases can also influence decisions about pay raises, promotions, or terminations. Additionally, biases can arise when using performance evaluations to make employment decisions that impact employees' careers.

In subsequent work, I have continued to take a comprehensive approach to identify the stages in talent management processes at which merit-based practices may be associated with racial and gender disparities in key employment outcomes. The purpose of that work has mostly consisted of assessing whether there are demographic divergences in the performance evaluation, salary determination, or career trajectory decision stages, even after using these merit-based reward systems. This is why I have provided some detail as to which data were collected, how such data were analyzed at ServiCo, and which reports I could generate with such data; my goal is to enable you and your organization to follow a similar analytical approach to investigating and monitoring the functioning of your performance-reward processes. Importantly, this kind of analytical approach can help your organization identify and correct *where* and *how* your own work practices may introduce or sustain non-merit-driven disparities (as well as other career gaps based on performance-irrelevant personal qualities) in key employment outcomes for employees and managers. I will further develop this analytical approach in part III of the book.

THE PARADOX OF MERITOCRACY
BEYOND GENDER, RACE, AND NATIONALITY

One conclusion of the empirical research on merit-based practices and their outcomes is that meritocracy cannot be taken for granted. Indeed, the pursuit of meritocracy in practice is more difficult than it first appears. As I have shown, under certain conditions, being committed to meritocratic principles may make key decision-makers think they are making the right evaluations and behaving fairly when they are actually being less meritocratic in the distribution of rewards and decisions concerning promotions. I consequently have proposed that organizational practices intended to increase meritocracy (as well as many other related talent management approaches) need to be carefully designed, implemented, and continually reevaluated for their effectiveness, especially when it comes to avoiding potential bias and other factors not related to merit to enter employment decision-making.[67]

In later collaborations with a few organizations, I have expanded my focus to examine the influence of not only sex, race, and nationality but also other aspects of individuals' identities, such as religion, sexual orientation, and age, on employment outcomes—when such information was voluntarily provided by employees. For example, in a short-lived research collaboration with a large American e-commerce company, OnlineSell Inc., I started to examine information about OnlineSell's applicants, employees, and managers. One primary goal of this collaboration was to use their data and existing science to improve diversity and inclusion as well as the experience of OnlineSell's employees. This was a trend among many employers, particularly in the United States in the early 2020s, in response to the debates on systemic and structural barriers in the workplace. For me, it was a research opportunity to examine the extent to which OnlineSell had become a true meritocracy.

My contacts at OnlineSell were interested in working with me because of my prior academic work on meritocracy and potential biases during hiring and reward decisions. In one early meeting with the analytics team, I learned that the company's CEO would often say, "We're a meritocracy" in company meetings. I also found anecdotal evidence that not everyone in the company felt the same way. One anonymous employee rated OnlineSell as average online, sharing that although top management promoted meritocracy, the managers in charge of promotions and rewards did not seem to be upholding this value. The employee felt that "decisions were made arbitrarily and seemed to be based on favoritism rather than merit."

My preliminary research with OnlineSell's personnel data, however, did not empirically support at least part of the claim that "decisions were made arbitrarily," particularly in relation to who got promoted and rewarded. On the contrary, my initial preliminary analysis revealed that performance and experience were strong predictors of promotions and rewards. To help assess which factors predict performance and success, many professionals I worked with had carefully collected detailed information about their employees and managers over the years, and this information allowed for in-depth analyses of whether and how individuals' demographics and personal characteristics were significantly associated with key career outcomes such as pay, rewards, turnover, and promotion. Such information collection efforts then continued to obtain data about the characteristics of applicants and employees worldwide, including gender, race, and nationality, as well as characteristics such as religion, sexual orientation, and disability.

One discouraging finding from some preliminary examination of the collected data is that, for career outcomes such as salary and bonuses, it appeared to be disadvantageous to openly disclose one's religion or sexual orientation in the workplace if one belongs to a marginalized group (in this particular case, identifying as LGBT or being a member of any religious group other than Christian). These results align with prior experimental research, as discussed in chapter 3, and suggest that the paradox of meritocracy may extend to various demographic and personal characteristics of the individuals being evaluated.

WELL-INTENTIONED PRACTICES AND VALUES ARE NOT ENOUGH

One key takeaway from the research I have described so far is the need for caution, especially as leaders strive to be meritocratic and excellent in their talent management processes. This takeaway comes with two critical warnings for organizations, particularly those that promote, implicitly or explicitly, a meritocratic ethos.

First, leaders and managers should be aware that *simply designing and implementing talent management practices to recruit, select, evaluate, and promote the best talent does not necessarily guarantee meritocracy, fairness, equity, and diversity in practice*. These practices do not ensure that decision-makers acting on behalf of their organizations will select and reward the best individuals effectively and fairly. My own research has shown that formalized hiring, performance evaluations, and promotion criteria and processes, intended to advance and reward the best, did not always eliminate demographic biases—and, in some cases, even exacerbated them. A key practical implication is that organizations need to continuously evaluate and monitor the impact of their talent management practices on employment outcomes for different groups of individuals.

Second, *emphasizing meritocracy as the basis of hiring, promotion, and rewarding practices can paradoxically backfire on women, racially underrepresented groups, immigrants, and many other disadvantaged groups* based on their demographic and personal characteristics. A strong belief in the "objectivity" or "fairness" of meritocracy can lead decision-makers to become less aware of personal biases, ultimately reinforcing rather than reducing biases in their employment-related decisions. This finding illustrates the *paradox of meritocracy effect*. It highlights how bias can be triggered by the very attempt to address it, showing that achieving genuine meritocracy may be more difficult than it first appears. A key practical implication here is that broad, meritocratic-sounding statements from corporate leadership or websites should not give leaders and decision-makers a false sense of fairness or equal opportunity. True meritocracy cannot be attained through corporate window dressing.

In this regard, for leaders who are genuinely serious about fostering meritocracy, it is essential to ensure that their talent management processes function as intended—without backfiring or introducing new biases and inefficiencies. Unfortunately, many leaders simply adopt "best practices" to improve their talent management systems, often creating the appearance of doing "the right thing." Moving closer to the ideal of meritocracy, though, requires systematic investigation, serious leadership commitment, and sustained organizational efforts. I will elaborate on these requirements in part III.

Chapter Five

IS MERIT IN THE EYE OF THE BEHOLDER?

Expressions like "attracting the best," "selecting the most talented," and "searching for the star performers" are frequently used by corporate leaders to signal their commitment to driving organizational excellence and maintaining a competitive edge. Many businesses indeed invest significant time and resources in trying to do so, fearing serious repercussions—such as poor performance, high turnover, and low motivation in the workplace—if hiring decisions are not made carefully. These expressions reflect how our society and institutions have become deeply obsessed with strategies to attract and hire top talent. It once was sufficient to hire candidates who were simply good or great at their jobs. Now organizations feel compelled to find the smartest, most productive, and most engaged, fueled by countless statements and reports warning of dire unintended consequences if they fail to do so.

These beliefs are reinforced by commentators who advocate for "new," "better" approaches to recruitment and selection. Consider titles like *Finding the Best and the Brightest* by Peg Thoms, marketed as "the guide" to recruiting, selecting, and retaining "effective leaders."[1] Thoms's book is just one of many that promise to help businesses optimize their hiring procedures. Similarly, in a 2017 *New York Times* hiring guide, Adam Bryant shared insights gained from interviews with nearly five hundred leaders in the United States. He outlined three principles to "help you hire the right person": when interviewing job candidates, be creative, be challenging, and allow your employees to help.[2]

Certain professionals also offer advice on topics such as "the key to land-ing top talent," "how to hire the right person the first time," or how to "hire the best person fast." While such recommendations are meant to provide guidance, they can sometimes have the opposite effect—causing employers to procrastinate, overanalyze, and delay their hiring decisions in pursuit of a "game-changing talent strategy."[3] Perhaps that is why there is also a ready audience for advice that urges employers to abandon the quest for the perfect candidate and instead take chances on an "imperfect job candidate."[4] The conversation then shifts toward guidance like "the five ways you can ensure you hire the right person, not the best person," or why "hiring the right per-son is more crucial *than ever.*"

In my research, I have been interested in understanding what leaders and managers actually mean when they use phrases like "the best," "top talent," "the right individual," or "the ones with the most potential" to describe the ideal job candidate. Given the central role of "merit" and "talent" in today's talent management processes, I have specifically examined how managers and professionals define and apply these concepts when making people management decisions in their organizations.

In this chapter, I present key findings from this research, highlighting that "merit" and "talent" are often broad, ambiguous, and subjective—that is, in the eye of the beholder. Recruiters, managers, and professionals differ in their definitions of merit, leading to varying views on which qualities or traits matter most and how to assess them best. Without a shared under-standing of these concepts, decision-makers within the same organization may adopt vastly different approaches to recruiting, selecting, and advancing talented individuals. The concern is that this lack of consensus can lead to inconsistent decision-making, unfair outcomes, personal biases, and favorit-ism. This clearly poses a significant challenge for the efficient functioning of talent management systems, particularly in organizations striving to foster meritocracy and excellence.

THE FUZZY CONCEPTS OF MERIT AND TALENT

To the central question of who deserves to get hired, promoted, or rewarded in organizations, the answer in a true meritocracy involves merit or talent. These concepts are regularly invoked by those who use today's talent man-agement systems—whether human resource (HR) professionals, recruiters, managers, executives, or founders of start-ups—when screening applicants or rewarding and promoting them in the workplace. In fact, if you are serious about building processes to hire the most talented candidates and later advance and reward your top talent, you probably have your own working definition of what merit and talent mean for you and your organization.

But what *is* merit or talent? Definitions often start off sounding objective: the right skills and experience for the particular position we are hiring for. That makes sense and sounds straightforward, particularly if such skills and abilities are clearly relevant and have successfully been validated for the position. Soon, though, the definitions become a bit more subjective: candidates should be reliable, productive, and *hmmm* . . . perfect. We quickly revert to buzzwords—vague terms to define which characteristics will make candidates and employees successful. And when reflecting on what makes a great candidate ideal, we can quickly create an extensive list of desired attributes, including descriptions like "self-motivated," "emotionally connected," "goes the extra mile," and "committed to achieving results."

"If you have doubts about a candidate, figure out why," Bryant wrote in his 2017 *New York Times* article,[5] "Trust your instinct." The problem behind such general and quite subjective guidance is that, as scholars have documented, biases and prejudices can quickly be introduced in hiring managers' assessments—often adversely affecting the achievement of meritocracy, fairness, and diversity within organizations. Obviously, the complexity of the definition of merit increases as we move to roles and positions for which skills, experience, and other individual work-related competencies become less objective or difficult to measure.

Scholars have identified the potential problems that can emerge from broad, vague definitions of talent in the workplace. After studying hiring and selection practices in elite professional firms, Lauren Rivera reported that professionals heavily relied on the general term "cultural fit." Although résumés and connections initially shaped who got an interview, Rivera claims, perceptions of "fit" strongly influenced who got a second interview or an offer. "Fit" was not so much about selecting candidates who matched with organizational values as about personal compatibility: professionals wanted to hire people whom they enjoyed being with and with whom they could develop close working relationships.[6] Along similar lines, a former chief talent officer at Netflix stated that "what most people mean by culture fit is hiring people they'd like to have a beer with. . . . You end up with this big, homogenous culture where everybody looks alike, everybody thinks alike, and everybody likes drinking beer at 3 o'clock in the afternoon with the bros."[7]

Imprecise, general terms are often used in advice given to recruiters and hiring managers on how to screen candidates effectively, particularly during the interview process. Find the "right stuff" in the job candidate. Look for "red flags" during the interview. Do your homework to reduce the "unknowns." The list goes on. Such advice remains despite scholars having long raised concerns about the reliability, validity, and even utility of many kinds of job interviews. As James N. Baron and David M. Kreps, authors of the textbook *Strategic Human Resources*, write, the conclusions of such research about job interviews are "somewhat devastating."[8] In general, job interviews, as well as many other organizational processes currently used to screen candidates, are neither reliable nor valid. They can easily be subject to biases, including in-group bias or homophily, as well as improper discounting of relevant skills and experience; some interviewers even anchor on initial impressions—that is, give first impressions of job candidates too much weight in subsequent decisions.

Much research has already warned us that leaders' biases and preferences about the nature of the job, the organization's culture, and the attributes of an ideal candidate influence their later evaluations and recommendations about job candidates. This is all the more so when there is no adequate structure or process to guide hiring managers and hold them accountable to others in the organization for their decisions. Nonetheless, organizations still rely on managers' impressions of interviews and in-person interactions when making employment decisions. Such an approach, Rivera argues, can easily lead managers and professionals to depend on "chemistry," consequently preferring candidates with backgrounds and interests like their own.[9] Along the same lines, when discussing job interviews, Carol Smith, the publisher of *Harper's Bazaar*, stressed the benefits of having a meal with a job candidate. "You learn so much in a meal," she said. "It's like a little microcosm of life."[10] Some hiring advice even directly compares hiring to dating.[11]

For years, I have been concerned with how businesses, universities, and government agencies define and apply concepts like "talent" and "merit." I have also questioned the effectiveness of the strategies employers adopt to assess talent and merit in applicants and employees. Strategic talent management began with the premise that talent can be hired, developed, and managed to boost organizational success and excellence.[12] However, while "talent" may initially sound like a neutral and efficient term, it can also be problematic in practice, even harmful, potentially undermining efforts to achieve meritocracy. One concern is that the concept of talent may emphasize the value of innate traits, which are hard to change, when screening, developing, and advancing individuals. This focus may lead to definitions of talent and merit that inadvertently favor or disadvantage candidates based on aspects of their identities and circumstances.

HOW MANAGERS AND EXECUTIVES DEFINE
MERIT IN THE WORKPLACE

What is *your* definition of merit or talent? And how do you think others in your organization define it? These are the questions I often ask participants in my class. In fact, next time you have a chance, I invite you to ask the same questions to managers and professionals in your own organization. You may be surprised at their answers. They may help you reflect on why the definition of merit may be in the eye of the beholder. And the potential variation in their answers could have enormous practical implications for addressing people-related problems and for building meritocratic and fair talent management processes in your organization.

In a few workshops I have taught, I have repeatedly asked professionals to recall a recent situation in which they identified a talented job candidate worth hiring or a talented employee who deserved a promotion or a merit-based bonus. I then ask them, "In your opinion, what were the most important factors in determining their *merit*?"[13] When studying the answers I have received, I found a wide variety of responses about what factors are most important to managers in determining why an applicant is *worth* hiring or why an employee *deserves* a merit-based bonus.

Figure 5.1 presents a word cloud showing the most common responses from over 250 executives who took part in my executive education course titled "Leading People at Work." These professionals were interested in gaining a deeper understanding of how talent management systems and people analytics can help address people management challenges and opportunities during recruiting and hiring, performance evaluation, pay, and promotion and training.

The bigger the size of the word, the more frequently that word was cited by the executives. *Performance* is clearly the most cited factor, followed by *skill, initiative, attitude, leadership,* and *experience.* A few additional buzzwords were often mentioned: *passionate, mindset,* and *commitment.* In a subsequent group of 129 additional executives whom I surveyed, 78 percent chose performance as the most important factor in determining an

expertise
honest productivity
experience
level work attitude mindset
performance
motivation fit skill leadership
competent initiative proactive
qualification knowledge
passionate
commitment

FIGURE 5.1. Word cloud of most important factors in determining merit.

individual employee's merit, but 59 percent also cited effort, 58 percent mentioned initiative, and 45 percent chose ability.

When I asked executives about the qualities they look for when recruiting and hiring candidates, I again heard a diverse array of answers. Some definitions were specific: "the ability to get tasks done," "demonstrated capabilities or skills," "capability to do and learn more," "competency in their job and the results they achieve," "proven experience," "ability to produce results with minimal supervision," "ability to apply past wins to the new role," and "past experience and life lessons; this includes education, work experience, and presentation skills." Not surprisingly, the responses often referred to performance and potential performance in the job or role.

Many respondents also provided lists of desired attributes, such as "able to solve problems," "have the skills," "understand the company's processes," "reach goals and consistently have good performance," "be supportive to the team, deliver quality results on time, communicate results and insights," "takes ownership and responsibility in their work and displays commitment," and "uniqueness in combination [with] seniority, tech abilities, business abilities, experience, connection to customers, communication abilities, working abilities/skills." Other definitions of merit included factors beyond the current role: "the combination of strong outcomes and demonstrated ability to think beyond the existing role," "being worthy of raise, promotion, praise for doing great work," "consistent performance plus potential plus drive," and "going above and beyond what is expected and greater."

Other responses included concepts challenging to measure objectively or precisely, particularly when screening applications: "someone who has [a] good work ethic, leadership traits, communication skills, and can work with others," "quality and good attitude," "being worthy of joining our team," "deserving of the opportunity, based on work, grit, character," "ability to blend into the culture of the organization," and "a combination of performance, teamwork, culture, leadership."

Interesting responses included merit as "a tool utilized to encourage performance" and a "way to encourage employees and make them feel valued." Their definitions reflected how managers and professionals often use merit to engage and motivate their workforce. Merit was often defined as the "reward" itself: "pay for their performance," "monthly payroll," and "some form of incentive that employees find valuable." Merit arose when "someone is deemed worthy of praise/reward due to their performance" or seen as a "reward/recognition related to actions/accomplishment [for which] you had responsibilities."

The motivation for asking participants in my courses about their understanding of the factors that constitute merit was both academic and practical. If you aim to improve recruitment and hiring in your organization to hire the most talented, or revamp your performance evaluation program to encourage and reward top performance, you first need to consider what you and your peers—particularly those in charge of recruiting, hiring, and promotions—mean by merit, talent, and performance.

By clearly defining what it means to "select the most qualified," "hire and advance the best talent," or "reward the top performers," those responsible for selection, hiring, promotions, and rewards will be more likely to execute such guidelines carefully and consistently. In other words, articulating specific definitions of merit, talent, and performance allows your organization to establish well-defined factors and criteria to guide decision-making in your key talent management processes. Once these definitions are established and shared among key stakeholders, your organization will be well-positioned to apply them consistently in crucial decisions such as hiring, promotions, and reward distribution. Finally, continuously assessing the validity and utility of your organization's definitions of merit, talent, and performance will further enhance the fairness and efficiency of your talent management strategies.

WHAT *IS* MERIT?

In my research, as described in chapter 4, I have found considerable varia-tion in how managers make merit-based employment decisions. These deci-sions are often shaped by both the organizational context in which managers operate and the characteristics of the individuals they evaluate.

That awareness led me to a research project with Aruna Ranganathan of the University of California, Berkeley, aimed at investigating how managers and leaders understand and apply the concept of merit in the workplace.[14] We specifically sought to explore how managers create and develop their understandings of merit during the early stages of their careers, as well as how their formative work experiences influence their decisions on hiring, promoting, and rewards once they advance into management roles. We believed that this approach could provide valuable insights for organizations looking to implement or improve merit-based processes—as we suspected that a lack of agreement on the basic definition of merit may be a key chal-lenge, especially for organizations striving to be meritocratic and fair.

The main part of our study drew on 56 in-depth interviews of profes-sionals with wide-ranging managerial experience.[15] We recruited them in two stages. The first stage involved interviewing professionals enrolled in a graduate program at an elite North American business school (n = 45). The second stage involved interviewing working managers who were recruited from a large US company (n = 11). We used the first set of 45 interviews to start investigating individuals' understandings of merit across a diverse set of managers enrolled in a graduate business program. Choosing such pro-fessionals was appropriate because these individuals could freely reflect on their recent experiences in managing workers. We found that the interview-ees were keen to talk about decision-making relating to talent management.

Armed with our findings from this first stage, we then used our sec-ond set of 11 interviews—those with managers in a single company, a large e-commerce company in northern California, which we refer to as West-TechCo—to investigate whether our findings remained consistent when we studied one well-defined organizational context: managers working in the same company and location, with similar work responsibilities, and super-vising professionals with similar educational backgrounds.

In our combined sample of 56 interviewees, 32 percent were women, 5 percent were Black, 35 percent were Asian, and about 13 percent were Hispanic. Our interviewees averaged thirty-one years old, with almost eight years of work experience and three years of managerial experience. On average, they supervised twelve employees.

In-depth interviews were essential for this project because they facilitate open expression of interviewees' viewpoints.[16] Furthermore, such interviews often reveal interviewees' implicit knowledge and opinions, allowing future interpretation and analysis. Our interviews lasted, on average, 62 minutes. We used a semi-structured interview format that involved an interview protocol containing some predetermined questions and topics, using language familiar to the people being interviewed. We asked questions from the interview protocol in a conversational style, letting the discussion evolve according to the interviewees' responses.[17] The interviews centered on strategies and practices that the managers experienced at the organizations where they were currently or most recently employed and, in particular, whether they perceived these organizational practices to be "fair," "equitable," "appropriate," and/or "right." We asked our interviewees to discuss who deserved to advance in the workplace and encouraged specific examples from their experiences.

The interviews also probed participants to share their definitions and applications of merit in the workplace. We did not mention the word *merit* until the participant mentioned the word or, if they did not mention the word, until close to the end of the interview. The purpose was to uncover the managers' preconceived understandings and interpretations of merit rather than to make them invoke standard definitions used in today's corporate world. Interviewees expressed their individual understandings of merit through their stories and arguments.[18]

The Semiotic Space of Merit

We drew on the tradition of semiotics—that is, the study of signs and symbols—to analyze the interview data inductively and uncover the sometimes-hidden meaning of merit by deconstructing our interviews in context. Semiotic analysis distinguishes between surface manifestations and the underlying structure that gives meaning to those manifestations.[19] It allows us to analyze how meaning is constructed and understood in particular social systems, and we used it to examine the meaning of merit in the workplace.[20]

Our approach involved first identifying the domains in which managers make sense of merit.[21] We clearly found evidence that our interviewed managers differed widely in their understanding of merit. (This evidence was consistent with our finding that academics also use different definitions and operationalizations of merit in their scholarly work.) Second, we observed that managers' understanding of merit repeatedly emerged as varying along three main dimensions—*how* merit is assessed, *who* the unit of analysis for merit is, and *what* affects merit.

To collectively represent the varied understandings of merit, we further integrated these three dimensions to compose what scholars call a semiotic space,[22] defined in this case by three axes: the objectivity/subjectivity, individual/group, and achievement/ascription axes shown in figure 5.2. The conclusion is that when making any employment decision, a manager needs to decide (1) *how* to evaluate merit, (2) *who* to evaluate and who to rely on when evaluating merit, and (3) *what* factors to consider in the evaluation of merit.

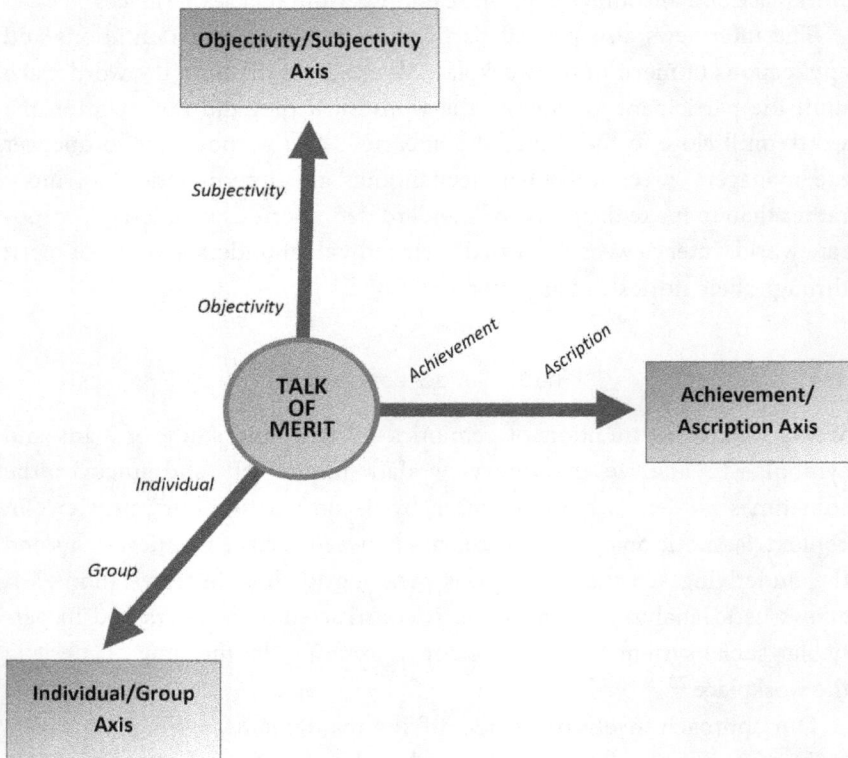

FIGURE 5.2. Three-dimensional understanding of merit.

Objectivity/Subjectivity Axis: How Merit Is Assessed

Back in 1997, in a *Los Angeles Times* article, Judy Rosener at the University of California–Irvine warned that "the word suggests that merit can, and should, be based on accomplishment that can be measured in objective terms," but "in reality, determining merit solely on objective grounds is rare."[23] Rosener's article sparked several responses, including one calling her argument "ridiculously simple"[24] and another criticizing the "subjective standards" that she proposed as likely to fall prey to "prejudice, favoritism, and cronyism"—the very dynamics that the concept of merit was supposed to replace.[25] This debate exemplified individuals' quite differing views on whether they see merit as a subjective or objective concept.

Our interviewees also illustrated these differing perspectives. On one end, some believed that merit should be evaluated entirely objectively. They often emphasized organizational rules—specific and well-known practices, procedures, and routines—designed to recognize and reward merit. They argued that the best way to assess merit is through these rules, which are often measurable in quantitative terms. One manager said that merit is "the business brought [by employees measured through] very quantifiable numbers." Another manager agreed that "people who come from a management background love to have a single metric or ratio to drive [the evaluation of employees]."

Managers who believed that merit should be measured objectively referred to three specific kinds of objective rules governing how merit is evaluated: metrics, formal reviews, and corporate policies. For example, some interviewees mentioned specific metrics like "GPA" for evaluating job applicants or emphasized the need to condense "20 different things" into "one metric" when deciding which candidate to promote. Many others spoke about the implementation of formal evaluation procedures and how those work appraisals depended on the position occupied in the organizational hierarchy, especially when determining who is promoted: "They did a biannual review process. They had a whole . . . very good form that you filled out, and you knew the specific areas you were going to be rated on; they made time to do the performance review. So that process was very good."

Some managers described evaluating merit with a formal review process that allowed them to assess their subordinates through "calibration discussions" at regular intervals, such as "twice a year," and to provide valuable feedback to their subordinates. They also detailed various organizational policies outlining how merit is assessed within their companies. Such policies clearly articulated the rules for advancement, including factors like time spent at work and seniority. They also established distinct "career tracks," such as the managerial track, the individual contributor track, and the technologist track, each with its own specific policies for evaluating merit. This particular group of managers saw comfort in the notion that objectivity in the definition of merit, together with objective rules, helped organizations successfully manage people-related processes.

Many managers stressed that merit should be narrowly defined based on an employee's performance as measured in particular organization-related, job-specific, or functional ways. This belief is often associated with the idea of how critical pay-for-performance schemes motivate employees to work hard. The relevance of narrowly defining merit in terms of objective performance metrics to determine pay and promotion is reflected in this quote from a manager: "So, the particular division I worked in was Private Wealth Management, where we really worked with people who have assets above $10 million. And there, it was designed, [it was] just more natural to be merit-based. So, whatever clients you got, you got the revenue from managing those relationships. . . . You were just paid based upon how much [*sic*] assets you have under management. So, if you are really good at that and worked really hard and built like a larger pool, you got paid more."

Furthermore, it appeared to be central for many managers that these performance metrics could be measured easily, at a low cost, and yet with a high degree of precision. While recognizing that "soft" factors may be important in evaluating employee performance, these managers stressed that their core focus was on precisely measured metrics that were understood as contributing to fairness: "We don't care about anything but the bottom line. So they [employees] just make it happen. And if . . . you don't make it happen, then you're out. So again, it's extremely fair. It's extremely meritocratic." Similarly, another manager noted that pay structure is easy to determine in certain jobs where it is based on "what you bring in" in terms of more clients or assets or even time at work (in other words, not taking too much time off): "I'm not sure how it was in the other divisions, but in Private Wealth, a lot of it . . . is just based upon purely how much you bring in. . . . At the end of the day, your salary after two years' time is based upon what you have brought to your management. If you took time off, and so now you don't have as much for the management, just structurally, you're not going to get as much pay. . . . It's just a function of you haven't built enough clients or assets to have a higher salary."

Many managers discussed the importance of transparent steps and straightforward rules when evaluating and rewarding employees. One manager stressed how these policies were clearly understood in their prior employing organization: "It's very transparent. You can see to it when you pitch it in, you give the calculations on how you will earn. So, eventually, like now, I know what bonus I expect next year if I am working. I can do the math, and it can be exactly that." Some policies were about mobility and opportunities inside the company, including procedures aimed at hiring candidates and promoting opportunities for employees to move up: "Their policy was . . . they only hired one senior consultant in the history of the firm. So . . . the highest level you could come in at would be consultant, which is a post-MBA position. . . . Then you rise up."

Other policies were clear about specific rules for advancement, sometimes relating to career paths and the clear expectations of having to work long hours to be promoted: "You have to work a lot for a long period of time. Ten years, Sundays and Saturdays, and you will reach the partner's level. So that means being the best in terms of client relationships or maybe having different capabilities and working." Other times, interviewees referred to policies relating to seniority as another factor that led to advancement.

Although many managers expressed that merit needs to be based on narrowly defined and precisely measured objective rules, others recognized that such performance measures might not fully capture all aspects of an employee's contribution to the company's success. Along these lines, HR textbooks claim that certain employers acknowledge the limitations of objective performance measures and supplement them with subjective assessments, especially for major career outcomes like job assignments, developmental opportunities, salary increases, and promotions.[26] For example, investment bankers in corporate finance are measured by objective metrics such as fees generated and overall revenues. However, investment banks and many other professional firms also devote substantial resources to subjectively evaluating other factors, such as the "quality of the deals, the bankers' contributions to customer satisfaction, training of younger associates, and marketing."[27] Even in sales and trading, where an individual's performance can be easily tracked daily, a large portion of a trader's compensation is determined through a subjectively awarded bonus.[28]

Moreover, there was a recognition that defining and evaluating merit are often at the manager's discretion (with some managers stressing that they should always be). As one respondent stated, "It's completely at the discretion of the boss . . . like 100 percent." Along these lines, many of our respondents spoke about how managers exercised their authority in the workplace and "defended" their employees at critical junctures in the talent management process: "So your boss not only gives you the evaluation but also has to defend you in the evaluation committee. He wasn't there; he was in Brazil, and he really didn't care about me. . . . I worked a lot. Everyone was very happy except for my boss. And everyone can notice, but no one will defend me. Because if your boss doesn't defend you, why me, who has ten other fellow employees, why would I defend you? I have my own priorities."

In our interviews, managers described five arenas in which managerial discretion could influence how merit is assessed: (1) managers' personal assessment of subordinates; (2) their willingness to make accommodations; (3) their power to influence project assignments; (4) their setting of work expectations; and (5) their ability to exercise favoritism. Many respondents spoke about managers making their positive personal assessment of employees known by "defending" and "recommending" them in the larger organization. Similarly, interviewees described how managers can make accommodations in their assessment of employees or offer flexibility options such as part-time work or telecommuting that can allow employees to perform better. Another way managerial discretion impacts the success of subordinates is by setting work expectations and targets/goals. According to many interviewees, expectations are included in managers' approaches to evaluating and rewarding their subordinates' merit.

Finally, many spoke about how often managers' discretion allows for favoritism despite how hard all employees work. Several interviewees reflected on their own experiences as young employees witnessing nepotism in the workplace, such as when, for example, "a dad would want to promote his sons," as well as other managerial biases when determining performance and pay; such biases have been well documented in workplace research.[29]

On the other extreme, we found subjectivity in the definition of merit. As one manager said, "Why does meritocracy have to equal objectively defined variables? Why can't meritocracy also pertain to subjectively defined variables?" Within this realm of subjective understandings of merit, managers acknowledged that merit is open to interpretation and only becomes concrete when defined and applied by key decision-makers in an organization. This is where we heard managers using buzzwords—fashionable but vague, broad, and ambiguous terms—to describe what merit means in their workplaces. These buzzwords are frequently difficult to measure, allowing for various interpretations.

Some managers appreciated the subjective nature of these buzzwords because they allowed for flexibility when evaluating merit: "I can't see any way to make [merit] more objective because all people in the investment banking industry don't have the same function. They have different functions. . . . So I think to put a harsh rule or a harsh benchmark is not fair." One interviewee praised their organization's community spirit for having a broad definition of merit: "What makes . . . the company [really good] is that it's very 'community centric.' It has done a lot to help different sections of [the] community out here and internationally. . . . Within the company, we kind of use that same kind of community-centric, collaborative approach, . . . [so] what you would do is you would try to map your shared commitments . . . within your own group to [this] overall purpose in evaluating [merit]."

In particular, our interviewees often referred to three buzzwords used in evaluating merit: *equality*, *client/customer satisfaction*, and *company values*. Some managers spoke about using equality in evaluating merit so that "all parties' interests are kept in mind" and no wrong is done to anyone. Many managers discussed the importance of client satisfaction in evaluations of merit—that is, employees should be rewarded when the client, often external to the company, is satisfied with the output. A number of managers reflected on the subjectivity of this *client/customer satisfaction* buzzword and related their experiences with situations in which tensions and conflict existed between the goal of satisfying clients and other, more instrumental goals. Our interviewees also frequently mentioned linking merit to specific company values—the core operating principles often stressed by top management and reinforced by organizational processes and activities such as company orientations, training programs, and informal events. Again, interviewees described the subjective nature of evaluating merit in line with corporate values because "there isn't a lot of process" to it.

Beyond subjective understandings of merit, some managers described merit as opaque and ambiguous. One manager stated, "Merit was definitely something that they would not put on the board. It would be a bullet point on their presentation for campus recruitments, and they would talk about transparency, but I don't think it was practiced. And the reason partly for that was there was one owner of the firm who was powerful. So having that single founder who's 100 percent of the company, it's hard to really be a transparent organization because he would want to maintain control over things."

Many managers also questioned whether the subjective definition of merit is useful: "If you say you do a subjective performance evaluation, and someone is third out of 15 consultants, what does that really mean, right? So, they call it merit-based. Is it? Does that make a better consultant? No. So, it's called merit, and a lot of attention gets paid to it in those industries, but I don't know that it's necessarily right."

In sum, managers' notions about how merit is assessed appear to be shaped by different levels of objectivity and subjectivity. In some contexts, merit is defined by objective rules, while in others, managers stress subjective buzzwords when describing merit. In between rules and buzzwords lies the importance of managerial discretion in hiring and evaluating employees.

Individual/Group Axis: Who the Unit of Analysis for Merit Is

The second axis of merit that we identified in our study ranges from individual- to group-based understandings of merit. In the scholarly literature, great progress has been made toward a better understanding of individual versus group processes in work organizations.[30] Researchers have been particularly interested in studying social influence by looking at how social groups shape individual thoughts and actions.[31] Our interviews also revealed that managers' understanding of merit in the workplace depends on the distinction between individual and group processes. When evaluating merit, managers' responses varied, with some focusing on the individual as the appropriate unit of analysis and others considering the team or the larger group that the individual belongs to. In the middle of this axis, we observed that managers sometimes saw networks—that is, an individual's extended relationships—as the main unit of analysis.

On one end, managers thought that the process of evaluating employees' merit is essentially individualistic, with each person being evaluated on their own performance and talents, one at a time. Some scholars, like certain managers we spoke with, argued that such individualistic notions of merit have advantages in that free riders cannot exploit them.[32] Some interviewees emphasized each individual's opportunities to advance within the company.

Managers further distinguished three ways in which merit could be assessed at the individual level: evaluating an individual vis-à-vis peers, evaluating an individual over time, or paying attention to individual presentation. For example, some managers spoke about merit as a competitive process in which one employee doing well necessarily implies that another (typically a peer) is doing less well. Interviewees often conveyed this view when describing a bell curve system of appraisal (that is, a forced ranking system of employees imposed by top management), with managers having to "fit the curve" and "stack rank" their employees every performance cycle. Within the realm of individual definitions of merit, others also brought up the notion that because people are different and have differences in human capital, it is more appropriate to assess an individual's progress over time, such as whether an individual takes advantage of opportunities to gain new skills or learn from colleagues. Managers also evaluate merit through individuals' presentation of themselves, especially to superiors. For example, some managers stressed the importance of "face time" and "visibility."[33]

On the other end, some managers spoke about the importance of teamwork in today's organizations and argued for a more broad-based and collective approach to analyzing merit. Indeed, some studies suggest that incentives to contribute to group and public interest might be intricately linked to the size of teams or groups inside organizations.[34] Along these lines, many managers believed that performance measures should include contributions to the group. As one manager said, "At least at [name of the consulting firm], there was a high score given to your firm participation." Indeed, some believe that evaluation of merit should consider assisting and caring about team members. One manager told us how his managers repeatedly stressed the concept of a "caring meritocracy": "They [didn't] want it to be like a cutthroat environment where people are stabbing each other in the back to get ahead. . . . They wanted to promote a culture where people are cooperating, I would say . . . [where] people will collaborate, and people will help each other out, and that defines merit."

Many managers spoke about different types of prosocial behavior, including working well with others and helping others, as important aspects of merit. As one manager said, "The employees that everyone liked the best, who [were] considered the best, were the ones who are also willing to help out other people when they needed it." Managers also emphasized the importance of communication inside organizations.

It is worth noting that managers identified three different kinds of teams that could be appropriate bases for evaluating merit—horizontal teams, vertical teams, and virtual teams—and discussed how merit would vary across these different team structures. First, many managers spoke about flat, horizontal teams as several individuals with similar training and roles working together like a "soccer team." In such structures, managers evaluated not only whether the "team delivers" but also the team's "level of interconnectedness and . . . level of understanding." Second, managers spoke about vertical teams that cross functional and hierarchical boundaries. They described how they look for synergies that come from collaboration and building on one another's work, with an understanding that a single individual's idea may "not always [be] the best idea, . . . but diverse teams can collaborate and come up with the best idea." Third, some managers spoke about virtual teams that cross organizational boundaries, often with overseas team members who are either part of the same organization or part of client teams. Managers cautioned that one key to success in such teams is overcoming "culturally different approaches to the way of getting work done or collaborating."

In the middle of our individual/group axis, some managers believed that the relevant unit of analysis for merit is an individual's network because networks often shape career and employment experiences.[35] These interviewees found it difficult to separate an individual from their immediate social connections, and they believed that an individual's social capital is a critical source of advantage. Therefore, they argued that by using the network as the unit of analysis for merit, individuals who had worked hard to build strong networks would be rewarded. As one manager put it, "In a large corporate environment, you tend to develop a network of either friends or comrades, peers. Friends with a lot of influence, I would assume, might open doors, might be able to champion you for opportunities, might be able to highlight opportunities. So, if you're involved with the right crowd, you might excel quicker than otherwise."

Indeed, many managers admitted that merit was inherently a political and social process because individuals have differences in authority and power inside companies. In such settings, the evaluation of merit is not based solely on the work performed but also on the influence exerted by powerful members of the organization. A manager explained this aspect of evaluations as follows: "Definitely knowing the right people, making sure you had good face time with them, interacting was important. It was no different from probably any other job in those respects."

Many considered the network as an important measure of one's merit or talent: "I think like anything else, [merit is] part of your network. And if you want to network and get in front of people, you certainly can. . . . I wouldn't consider it sucking up, and I think it's always a wise thing to do to get in front of your superiors, and it's part of that visibility thing, too. . . . You might have developed mentorship relationships, which then can help you." Along these lines, managers referred to important kinds of relationships that could be part of one's network and that were "fair game" in evaluations of merit—namely, personal connections, peer relationships, executive ties, and affinity groups.

Most managers expressed views about the relevance of personal connections in demonstrating individual merit. For example, regarding the significance of relationships outside of work to one's career success (including mobility across organizations), some managers mentioned "family" and "friends from school." Many managers also spoke about effective peer relationships or ties with coworkers and how those were frequently helpful in explaining variation in career outcomes. Great value was placed on recommendations from influential figures at key career stages. As one manager explained: "I think there's also a lot of weight put on . . . who's recommending you. I think they need recommendations either from your boss or whoever else [is] in your field as well."

While some managers stressed personal ties with peers as critical for career success, others talked about the importance (and even the art) of networking with a key individual in the organization who could then become a "godfather" or "advocate." In the academic literature, this idea has generally been referred to as "high-status" personal contacts,[36] which can include network ties to executives in an organization. In this respect, merit could be evaluated not solely on the work performed but also on the influence exerted by powerful members of the organization.

Finally, some managers described how common interests or experiences made it easier to expand one's network by building affinity groups. These affinity processes, such as "engineers wanted to sit with other engineers at the cafeteria during lunch," were stressed as key to influencing the definition of merit among managers. However, some managers (especially women) highlighted how they struggled to build affinity-based ties or even establish peer relationships with their colleagues, thus suggesting how using networks as the unit of analysis for measuring merit might disadvantage or advantage certain populations.

In sum, managers' notions about the unit of analysis for merit varied dramatically. In some organizations and businesses, merit was clearly treated as inherently individual, with managers viewing it either as a directly competitive process or as one based on politicking. In other organizational settings, managers evaluated merit at the team level, stressing the collective and collaborative aspects of merit based on roles and cooperation within teams of employees. In between individual and collective notions of merit, we found the perspective that networks were also a potential unit of analysis when thinking about allocative and evaluative processes inside certain companies.

Achievement/Ascription Axis: What Affects Merit

The third dimension in which we found that managers' definition of merit varied was along the achievement/ascription spectrum. For decades, social scientists have studied the importance of "ascription" and "achievement."[37] Ralph Linton first introduced the concepts in his 1936 book *The Study of Man*,[38] using the terms *ascribed status* versus *achieved status*. Typically, achievement has been used to refer to the socioeconomic position or success that an individual attains based on personal abilities, skills, talents, or efforts. Ascription, the opposite of achievement, refers to a position assigned to an individual at birth—an assignment based on traits beyond the individual's control. Examples of such traits in the academic literature have been gender, race, and parental socioeconomic class. Thus, achieved status differs from ascribed status by virtue of being earned. The tension between achievement and ascription has long been at the core of sociological research, especially in the areas of social stratification and social mobility.[39] Researchers have also focused on understanding why and how ascriptive inequality occurs in labor markets and organizations.[40]

In our interview data, we, too, found evidence of the tension between ascription and achievement in managers' understandings of merit. We found that interviewees ranged from outlining specific work actions that define merit to understanding merit as a manifestation of some innate capabilities (ability) to notions that perceptions of merit in a given organizational context are affected by personal and social qualities ascribed at birth.

On one end, interviewees stressed the importance of achievement in the workplace when defining merit. Only individuals' work actions and performance should affect evaluations of their merit in the workplace, regardless of individuals' demographics or innate traits. One manager said: "Merit would be more about effort . . . [and] applying those talents. So, you might have those talents, but then decide not to apply them because maybe you are not motivated by your manager or the organization; therefore, you are not putting merit to work." Similarly, another manager explained, "I think there's merit in you doing your job and doing it well, or doing it moderately well, . . . And then there's that above and beyond and exemplifying that . . . merits a promotion or a future project."

Managers often referred to five kinds of work actions that affect merit: *effort, performance, initiative, work experience,* and *education*. In the case of effort, many managers indicated that if individuals "put in a little bit of work, [they] get a little bit of merit," and if they "put in a lot of work, [they] get a lot of merit," so that effort has an essentially one-to-one relationship with merit. Similarly, many interviewees highlighted that job performance is and should be the key factor in determining merit: the meritorious worker is the product manager who launches a successful new product, the salesperson who achieves the highest sales, or the programmer who delivers the most straightforward working code. In talking about one of her subordinates earlier in her career, an interviewee reflected, "A good programmer usually writes ten lines of code; there will be two good lines. We test it. We want it precise and simple, and you do cut the 80 percent. For him [her subordinate], in 50 lines of code, probably only one line can survive. So that's really bad performance and lack of merit." Individual potential, effort, and drive are harder to measure, according to many managers, but are still key for decision-making. Such features fall under the umbrella of workplace achievement. One interviewee explained, "I think merit is the proportional reward for the effort provided."

Many interviewees also reflected on the role of initiative and on being "proactive or going outside one's comfort zone" when defining merit. Some focused on educational attainment by describing why companies hire individuals with specific degrees or from specific schools or educational programs.

While some talked about work actions that affect merit, our interviews revealed another key aspect that lies between achievement and ascription: individual ability, which some managers viewed as necessary for successful performance in the workplace. Here, managers referred not only to innate, "God-given" capabilities that one was born with, but also to acquired abilities that one could learn through practice. Many mentioned the words intelligence, IQ, or charisma. As one interviewee put it, "In some ways, I would almost say that . . . intelligence or charisma is a form of merit in and of itself, right? There's huge value in being well-connected and knowing what's going on in an organization and outside the organization. Quite frankly, being like a pleasant person to be around, like those are merits in and of themselves. And I say that because I think that not everybody has it, and that's something that you can develop. It's not just something you're born with."

One manager characterized merit as being "smart" and able to think "out of the box." Another defined merit as being "smart and self-motivated . . . like you could manage yourself, you could go out and say, 'Okay. I see a problem; I'm going to come up with a solution and enact it; get my colleagues to come along with me.'" One interviewee summed up this perspective: "I think there's certainly brilliance in terms of God's gift. . . . Some people are born brilliant, and some people are not so brilliant. . . . When that brilliance is coupled with a drive, intense drive, I think it's merit."

Managers additionally delineated a few types of ability that affect merit: talent, intelligence, personality qualities, cultural knowledge, and skills. In explaining how he saw the role of one's specific ability in understanding merit, one interviewee referred to individual talent in software engineering as having "a flair for programming." Other managers emphasized intelligence, specifically "being smart" or "working smart," as the most important facet of merit. Some managers referred to other individual qualities, citing "ability to work independently," "great personality," and "enthusiasm for learning."

Other managers highlighted interpersonal skills, self-awareness, organizational commitment, and even willingness to sacrifice one's personal life for work-related matters as important qualities underlying the definition of merit and success inside certain organizations. One manager opined that "in any consulting firm, the guy that decides he wants to have no life and will take whatever . . . anyone gives him will succeed. So, the manager on my project in Ghana was like that, where this guy would sleep maybe three or four hours a night for months on end every single day. He had a girlfriend in Jordan. We were in Ghana, so it's on the other side of Africa. And he would literally like to cancel to not see her; they ended up breaking up at the end of the project. . . . But he is promoted as a principal now, and he started off as a . . . post-MBA senior associate. And within three and a half years, he made it to principal which is . . . difficult to happen."

In interview data, we also found that cultural knowledge was highlighted as an ability that affects merit by influencing whether individuals can "establish a comfort level" with colleagues through "common background" and "cultural familiarity." Cultural capital, a concept first introduced by Pierre Bourdieu, refers to the accumulation of knowledge, behaviors, and skills that individuals can leverage to demonstrate their cultural competence and social status; such cultural capital directly influences an individual's access to opportunities.[41] Finally, managers mentioned the role of skills—that is, specific expertise or knowledge that relates to high-skilled jobs, such as "programming skills" and "data skills"—in affecting merit.

In describing her lack of cultural capital during a summer internship in Ohio, one manager noted that her education at an elite university and lack of knowledge of Big Ten football were liabilities in that setting: "All they do is talk about Big Ten football. I don't know if you are plugged into that, I'm not at all. . . . You do feel . . . left out. . . . I don't think it's something that cannot be overcome, but I think it's something that gives you an edge if . . . you do have the same kind of cultural familiarity."

On the other end, our interview data identified ascription as an important mechanism that affects merit in some settings. This concept of ascription, involving differential treatment according to birth characteristics, is consistent with classical research on social status and mobility.[42] Sometimes, ascription-based decision-making is intentional. As one manager explained to us when she was reflecting on the use of gender when making hiring decisions: "When I look at hiring people, I'll think at the back of my mind like 'Hey, this is a woman. Like she's not going to stay; she's going to leave because she's about 30. She's going to have kids and take off.' . . . It's terrible. It shouldn't happen, but it's just reality because being a woman is actually . . . factually more correlated with taking extended absences from the workplace. It's just the fact that more women are going to do that."

For a few managers, it was almost inevitable that demographics and other personal characteristics would somehow influence perceptions of merit. As one manager put it, "Oh, I'm sure merit gets conflated with other characteristics that people might have. Everyone has biases. You would hope not. But it would be ridiculous to assume it doesn't." A male Mexican interviewee with significant work experience in the United States said concerning nationality and ethnicity, "I think that history is very much alive today, and I think the racial and ethnic distinctions between Europeans and Indians are still very palpable in society. And I think the elite that is still, to a larger extent,

European is very closed off to people who are not from that background or not from certain families or didn't attend certain schools. . . . So, that just makes it very difficult for somebody who doesn't have that background to be able to penetrate into those organizations. Well, I think for Blacks in the United States, I think to some extent, Indigenous people in Mexico and Blacks in the United States are in a similar situation, historical situation."

Many managers referred to characteristics such as gender, ethnicity, nationality, age, and economic means as recurring examples of the ascriptive aspects of merit in the workplace. In speaking about gender, some highlighted how prevailing occupational gender sorting and work expectations appear to drive what is considered to be merit in the workplace. For example, some managers reported that social expectations that women are "supposed to be cute" or "dexterous" affect evaluations of women in the workplace.

Regarding age, many interviewees said that merit evaluations were affected by differences in perceptions of older workers' dynamism, attitude, and "willingness to bust themselves." Many managers we interviewed indicated how they came to realize that demographic features and efforts to increase diversity influence how individuals are hired, promoted, and rewarded in North American companies. As one of our Asian interviewees put it when reflecting on the racial diversity inside a US manufacturing company he had worked at in the past: "You know I would see an African American male. I would see an Indian American. I would see [a] Chinese American. I would see a . . . Caucasian. . . . Working hand in hand. And it was very unusual for me to see a different business unit that lacked . . . any one race or ethnicity. And I began to really, sort of, research that and try to understand why that's the case. And it struck me later on what that was . . . they needed to fulfill those quotas."

Other managers stressed the importance of socioeconomic class and wealth, especially how they potentially affect career outcomes by shaping individuals' expectations and behaviors. One manager said that people who "come from a wealthy, sort of a traditional all-American background that plays golf in the evenings and on the weekends" are "closer to management" and are thus treated favorably in career decisions. Concerning ethnicity and nationality, a few managers stressed how certain people gravitate toward similar others in the workplace and why they evaluate those who are similar to them more highly.[43] As one Japanese interviewee stated, "the top management would hang out, including me, because it was basically Japanese people."

Along these lines, many managers recognized how similarity in demographic traits could help individuals be successful in certain industries and national contexts. According to one manager, "In Asia, more often than not, you know, if you have the same [racial] background with the clients, it is that much easier to get the business done." In the case of gender, one professional commented about their firm's initiatives to promote diversity: "They definitely as a firm were making a lot of conscious efforts to promote more women and make sure they retain more women because the reality was with the rest of the world kind of changing, you were seeing a lot more women having the ten million dollars [to invest]. . . . There are situations where it seems we need a female because we can't keep going to client meetings and only just being four guys on a team. It looks really bad when our prospective client is female. So, I think they were making an attempt to kind of have a little bit more balanced workplace."

From our interviewees, we learned that ascription does not always involve malicious intent. Neither is it always about companies or their decision-makers keeping up appearances. Impulses toward ascription may originate as a result of organizational inertia, shared cultural understandings and expectations, intergroup dynamics, or even organizations' attempts at being rational.[44] Ascription can also occur when beliefs and traditional values shape employers' management practices or when decision-makers use ascription as a proxy for productivity or employment costs.[45]

Because obtaining pre-hire employment data on a potential employee (such as their productivity) can be expensive or difficult, decision-makers might infer a candidate's suitability based on the characteristics or performance of an average worker from the same (typically demographic) group. For example, they might assume that a thirty-year-old woman is more likely to take a leave from the workplace in the next coming years than a man of the same age.

Some interviewees highlighted how prevalent expectations of gender sorting into different occupations and jobs appear to drive perceptions of merit in the workplace. One manager claimed, "Different jobs were pretty sort of gendered. The transportation [department] . . . was mostly all male. . . . Certain kinds of jobs, especially ones that have a lot of heavy lifting, those will be men. But then the ones that were part of more, like dexterity or like moving really fast, those are usually women. So, they were gendered." Some female managers commented on different social expectations or even different qualifications required for men and women doing the same jobs. Others expressed how women are often excluded from certain aspects of work: "They see women as something that is supposed to be cute, supposed to be weak, and they need to protect them. So, when they feel like that—and especially for me, I'm small, I look young—it's really hard to prove yourself, that you're equivalent."

In the case of age, many interviewers made references to differences in status, dynamism, attitude, and even lifestyle that seniority confers. As one manager said, "Seniority . . . was like currency. It is like most manufacturing operations, the young ones, the younger, newer, or whatever people with maybe bachelor's degrees, weren't necessarily seen as these valuable entities." Age seems to be a critical factor in some organizations. As one interviewee put it, "Because you would get younger individuals, people that were of my age, coming in that were very computer-savvy, eager to learn, great employees, I mean the kind of people where you say, 'Wow, I wish everybody was like you.' Because even though you're young and you're someone inexperienced, they're willing to learn. They don't have this jaded attitude, they're really happy to be there."

Advocates of meritocracy stress that ascribed characteristics should not matter in truly meritocratic organizations and institutions; instead, emphasis should be placed on achieved characteristics, such as educational qualifications, experience, and effort.[46] However, our interviews reveal that, in practice, such factors vary. In one extreme, the only factors affecting merit are an individual's work actions, such as performance and effort. In the middle, merit is also influenced by an individual's ability, including intelligence and talent. In the other extreme, merit is affected by individuals' birth characteristics.

Putting the Axes Together

So far, I have described three dimensions along which managers' perceptions vary. I have presented each separately: *how* merit is assessed, *who* is the unit of analysis for merit, and *what* affects merit and its evaluation. These dimensions are captured, respectively, by the objectivity/subjectivity, individual/group, and achievement/ascription axes shown in figure 5.2. Yet, in practice, these axes overlap as managers and professionals navigate across them to make merit-related decisions, requiring them to determine not only how to evaluate merit but also whom to include in the evaluation and which factors to consider.

In this respect, the three-dimensional semiotic space in figure 5.2 illustrates the possible perceptions of merit along all three dimensions. At times, managers' positions along each of the semiotic axes reinforce each other; at other times, they create tension. Indeed, our interviewees differed in the extent to which they considered merit decisions to be "easy" or "tricky."

Managers in our sample navigated the semiotic space of merit in different ways. The simplest navigation of the three dimensions was at the intersection of the three axes in the center of the semiotic space, where merit is assessed objectively at the individual level with a focus on achievement. We put this understanding of merit close to the center because it is the "textbook" *ideal* definition of merit.[47] The data reveal that some managers did identify with and subscribe to this "textbook" understanding.

However, many interviewees understood merit in ways that diverged from the center. Some managers believed that merit was assessed in their organization subjectively, at the team level, while carefully considering ascriptive characteristics; this view is diametrically opposed to the "textbook definition." As one manager at a start-up firm put it, "Since some of the top management people come from Japan and they were in their fifties or sixties . . . there were like double standards. . . . Merit was different if you were Japanese or not . . . and if you were in Japan or not. . . . [Another fact is that the manager] doesn't set goals. . . . He just sits and waits for the subordinates to do things. When the team doesn't meet his silent expectations, he just doesn't talk to them. . . . But we also had a biotech culture. . . . So the focus [was] really on science. . . . The junior people were all organized in scientist teams."

Although these quotes illustrate two extreme views of merit, most managers in the sample were somewhere in the middle. Several managers stressed that merit should be evaluated subjectively, at the individual level, and with a moderate focus on achievement. As one manager working for an information technology firm said, "I used my assessment of the individual merit where I thought so-and-so really put the effort in, did the best they could, maybe they didn't quite get everything, but they really worked. It's hard to, I don't know how to describe it otherwise, like merit as an intangible quality of an individual, is more about their engagement and their personal commitment, rather than actually being able to do the work. They tried, they tried really hard. It seems like merit to me. . . . Yeah, predominantly, I think there are individuals making subjective decisions based on how they feel about that individual."

Our interview data, therefore, revealed that managers subscribe to a variety of definitions of merit. Importantly, Aruna Ranganathan and I also found that definitions of merit even vary among managers with similar professional backgrounds working for the same company.[48] As part of our research, we examined how the definition of merit varied within a subsample of eleven managers at a large e-commerce company, West-TechCo. Over a three-month period, we identified these professionals, who were all working at the *same* location and holding *similar* job titles and professional backgrounds. We then conducted interviews with them following an identical approach to that used with our broader sample. Upon analyzing this supplementary interview data, we found results consistent with those from the full sample— variation in the understanding of merit across the same three dimensions. This additional analysis reinforced the finding that a wide range of interpretations of merit can exist even within a relatively homogeneous group of decision-makers.

THE IMPACT OF DIFFERING DEFINITIONS OF MERIT

Varying definitions of merit could be a key reason why achieving meritocracy in practice has proven so challenging. Intrigued by the diversity in managers' perceptions of merit, I became determined to gather additional survey data soon after we completed the interviews. To date, I have collected over 3,500 survey responses from managers and executives across businesses of all sizes, as well as from some nonprofit and governmental institutions. All respondents are professionals with experience managing individuals in the workplace. The preliminary analysis of such responses is striking (see table 5.1).

Consistent with my work with Aruna Ranganathan, I found that managers and executives incorporate a multiplicity of factors when making people-management decisions, regardless of what the organization is looking for and what the organization values culturally. These professionals were asked a specific question: "When identifying and selecting the best, how important is each of the following factors in determining their merit?" Values ranged from 1 ("Not an important factor") to 7 ("A very important factor").

Table 5.1 shows three critical patterns. First, when selecting the best, *performance*, *ability*, and *effort* are the top three factors, each with mean values above 6. Performance is the top factor, with an average of 6.5 and the lowest variation among all the factors listed. These three highest factors are followed by five other factors that are often discussed: initiative, specific skills,

TABLE 5.1
Importance of factors affecting managers' assessments of individuals' merit

Factor	Observed minimum	Observed maximum	Mean	Standard deviation
Performance	1	7	6.50	0.89
Ability	1	7	6.17	1.04
Effort	1	7	6.06	1.10
Initiative	1	7	5.92	1.14
Specific skills	1	7	5.59	1.23
Talent	1	7	5.54	1.23
Intelligence	1	7	5.18	1.26
Experience	1	7	5.00	1.49
Training	1	7	4.80	1.50
Personality	1	7	4.50	1.53
Social origins	1	7	2.43	1.71
Age	1	7	1.99	1.41
Gender	1	7	1.65	1.32
Ethnicity	1	7	1.62	1.35
Nationality	1	7	1.61	1.32

Note: Professionals were asked a specific question: "When identifying and selecting the best, how important is each of the following factors in determining their merit?" Values ranged from 1 ("Not an important factor") to 7 ("A very important factor"). (N=3,556)

talent, intelligence, and experience, which all have average values between 5 and 6.

Second, social origins, age, gender, ethnicity, and nationality are the five factors in the list with the lowest means. Nevertheless, some respondents revealed that they think such demographics are important to consider in hiring and promotion decisions. In the sample, 6 percent of respondents thought it was important to consider gender (as measured by a value of 5 or higher in the Likert scale I used to code answers). Also, 6 percent thought it was important to consider ethnicity, and 5.6 percent thought it was important to consider nationality.

Third, notice that the observed values for all factors in table 5.1 ranged between 1 and 7. This means that some respondents considered social origins, age, gender, ethnicity, and nationality to be very important (and responded 7), while others thought they were not important at all (and responded 1). Strikingly, some participants rated performance, ability, or effort as not important, contrary to the large majority. About 2 percent thought effort was not an important factor and thus responded 1, 2, or 3 to the question. Similar percentages were found for performance and ability.

One limitation of this descriptive analysis is that the sample includes individuals working in a wide variety of industries, companies, and locations within the United States. To account for the variation in responses due to these different contexts, I computed the same descriptive statistics for a subsample of 65 engineers, participants in one of my workshops, who all were working in the *same* high-tech company. Interestingly, this more homogeneous sample of managers produced results similar to those of the entire sample. In this subsample, the two top factors were effort and performance, and yet the observed values for every factor ranged from 1 to 7. Many engineers in this company saw gender, ethnicity, and nationality as "very important factors" in their people management decisions, while others did not consider such factors at all.

With the larger sample of over 3,500 managers from a variety of companies, I also ran a vignette experiment in which participants were presented with three fictional employees working in product development projects in one unit of a large service organization. Two employees, the "test profiles," obtained the same performance score, and the third employee, the "filler profile," was always a low-performing employee.[49] After reviewing all three employees' performance evaluations, participants were asked a few questions regarding hiring, promotion, and reward decisions. One key question was to decide how much bonus each employee deserved, with a $1,000 budget to distribute among the three employees.[50] They were also asked to rate how much they agreed that (1) hiring the employee was the right decision (on a scale from 1, "Definitely wrong decision," to 7, "Definitely right decision"); (2) the employee should be considered for promotion (on a scale from 1, "Definitely do not promote," to 7, "Definitely do promote"); and (3) the employee is likely to be successful in the future (on a scale from 1, "Will not be successful," to 7, "Will be highly successful").

Participants were unaware that, while the two "test profiles" were identical in their performance scores, only their gender had been manipulated through gendered first names, Michael and Patricia, on their evaluation forms. All participants were encouraged to follow the meritocratic core values of the company, which were described as (1) all employees are rewarded fairly, (2) whether an employee deserves a raise is determined by their performance, (3) raises and bonuses are entirely based on the performance of the employee, (4) promotions are given to employees when their performance shows that they deserve it, and (5) the company's goal is to reward all employees equitably every year. The results of my analyses were striking and are summarized in table 5.2.

On average, Michael was assigned a bonus of $400 while Patricia's was $376, a statistically significant $24 difference. In the case of Michael, 40.88

TABLE 5.2
Decisions about hiring, rewards, and advancement

Key question	Response to question ( )		
	Michael	Patricia	Difference[d]
How much of a merit-based bonus should they receive?			
Average	$400.25 (3.909)	$375.95 (3.896)	$24.30*** (4.40)
Do you think that hiring this employee was the right decision?			
Average[a]	6.116 (0.023)	5.97 (0.025)	0.146*** (4.32)
Definitely WRONG decision	0.23%	0.40%	
Definitely RIGHT decision	40.88%	34.60%	
Do you think this employee should be considered for promotion?			
Average[b]	5.383 (0.028)	5.232 (0.029)	0.151*** (3.77)
Definitely DO NOT promote	0.96%	1.36%	
Definitely DO promote	17.78%	14.41%	
How likely is this employee to be successful in the future?			
Average[c]	5.884 (0.024)	5.839 (0.024)	0.044 (1.30)
Will NOT be successful	0.28%	0.23%	
Will BE HIGHLY successful	29.29%	27.09%	
Recruiters/Participants (Observations)	1,777	1,770	

Note: Michael and Patricia are equally performing employees. Standard errors in parentheses.

[a] Reponses were on a scale from 1, "Definitely wrong decision," to 7, "Definitely right decision."

[b] Reponses were on a scale from 1, "Definitely do not promote," to 7, "Definitely do promote."

[c] Reponses were on a scale from 1, "Will not be successful," to 7, "Will be highly successful."

[d] T-tests were computed to test whether the differences are significant. *** $p<0.001$, ** $p<0.01$, * $p<0.05$.

percent of the respondents answered that it was the right decision to hire this consultant, versus 34.60 percent who said that in the case of Patricia. When it came to promotion, 17.78 percent said that Michael should be considered for promotion, versus 14.41 percent who said that about Patricia. Regarding who was extremely likely to succeed at the company, 29.29 percent of the respondents chose Michael, and 27.09 percent chose Patricia. (This last difference was not statistically significant, though.)

Given the additional data collected from this subset of experiments, I was able to run several regression models predicting how large the bonus difference was between the equally performing male and female consultants. After controlling for the study participants' own gender, race, level of education, and experience in the models, there was still a significant gender gap, consistent with the paradox of meritocracy effect (described in chapter 4). Furthermore, gender, race, level of education, and experience of the study participant were not significant factors predicting the merit-based bonus gap between the two equally performing employees, Michael and Patricia.

Notably, I also found that the managers' conceptions of merit played a significant role in explaining the gender gap in the bonus. Professionals who considered performance "an extremely important factor" in merit (as measured earlier in the survey, before they had to make their decision) reduced the gender bonus gap by 64 percent. However, those who said that gender was "an extremely important factor" increased the gender bonus gap by 10 percent in favor of the male consultant. When it came to evaluating the decision to hire the two employees, those participants who said gender was "an extremely important factor" were more likely, by a statistically significant margin, to support the decision to hire Michael over Patricia.

Although this was an experiment with professionals familiar with hiring and rewarding employees, it illustrates the potential implications of a priori different conceptions of merit when making hiring decisions and allocating rewards within organizations.

THE PROCESS OF UNDERSTANDING AND APPLYING MERIT IN PEOPLE-RELATED DECISIONS

In our research, Aruna Ranganathan and I further proposed a process model outlining how managers come to define and approach evaluating merit in the workplace.[51] Figure 5.3 illustrates this model, showing key steps (represented by boxes) and the mechanisms that connect them (represented by

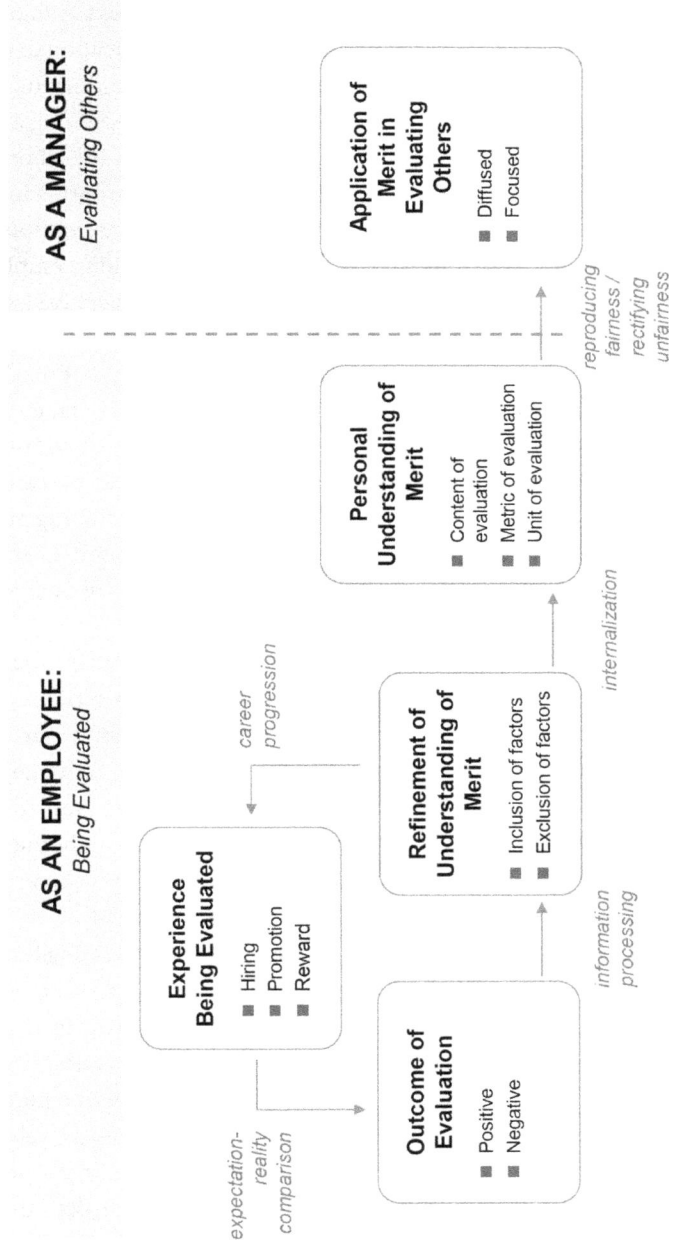

AS AN EMPLOYEE:
Being Evaluated

AS A MANAGER:
Evaluating Others

Experience Being Evaluated
- Hiring
- Promotion
- Reward

Outcome of Evaluation
- Positive
- Negative

Refinement of Understanding of Merit
- Inclusion of factors
- Exclusion of factors

Personal Understanding of Merit
- Content of evaluation
- Metric of evaluation
- Unit of evaluation

Application of Merit in Evaluating Others
- Diffused
- Focused

expectation-reality comparison

career progression

information processing

internalization

reproducing fairness / rectifying unfairness

FIGURE 5.3. The process of defining and applying merit in the workplace. *Source:* Adapted from Emilio J. Castilla and Aruna Ranganathan, "The Production of Merit: How Managers Understand and Apply Merit in the Workplace," *Organization Science* 31, no. 4 (2020): 915.

arrows). The model considers two main career stages: (1) being evaluated as an employee and (2) evaluating others as a manager. It explores the main factors influencing a manager's personal understanding and application of merit.

The process model shows how an individual's understanding of merit evolves through their experiences of being evaluated before becoming a manager.[52] Each evaluation an employee undergoes after entering the labor market iteratively shapes their understanding of merit. As they progress in their careers, employees undergo various evaluations for hiring, promotion, and rewards. By comparing these outcomes to their own expectations, employees come to perceive each career outcome as either positive or negative and the process of achieving it as fair or unfair. These perceptions then influence what factors they consider relevant to their own understanding of merit.

Our interview data revealed that individuals tend to *include* factors they believe were decisive in their own past evaluations if those evaluations were perceived as positive and fair. Conversely, if an evaluation was perceived as negative and unfair, they tend to *exclude* those factors. This recurring process refines their personal understanding of merit, which we found to include three main dimensions—*how* merit is assessed, *who* the unit of analysis for merit is, and *what* affects merit.

Then, our model shows that when individuals become managers, they often replicate the fairness or avoid the unfairness they experienced. We identified two distinct approaches to evaluating merit among our interviewees. The first, the "focused" approach, involves assessing only the work actions of employees, quantitatively and at the individual level. According to the interviewees, this approach helps reduce bias and favoritism because the evaluation is clearly specified and leaves little room for subjective interpretation or discretion.

The second approach, the "diffuse" approach, involves evaluating both the work actions and the personal qualities of employees using quantitative *and* qualitative criteria. This approach considers the individual within the context of their broader team. The advantage of this approach, as described by the interviewees, is that it allows for a more holistic evaluation of employees, accounting for factors difficult to measure quantitatively or objectively.

Figure 5.4 provides a detailed example of how one manager in our sample navigated through the process model to develop a personal definition of merit and an approach to evaluating it. (Our analysis is limited to the experiences and evaluations this individual chose to discuss.) Before entering the workforce (see "Pre Labor-Market Entry" inside "Personal Understanding

AS A MANAGER:
Evaluating Others

Application of Merit in Evaluating Others

- **Diffuse:** "I measure people's value to the company and contribution in a multifaceted way ... In a large part, what I think about as I'm going through reviews, whether these are formal or not, is about what I have asked from someone, what I have expected from the position, and whether similar people or whatever—how they're achieving against those expectations, and what they're contributing beyond or above those."

AS AN EMPLOYEE:
Being Evaluated

Experience Being Evaluated

- **Evaluation 1 – Hiring:** "I got connected with a customer of [my parents' company] who was building websites. Actually, we were a customer of theirs and they were a customer of ours; we exchanged goods for that. And in that interaction, I ended up working with the owner and he invited me to join their team."
- **Evaluation 2 – Promotion:** "I started work over at [a new company] ... and that was six years ago. ... I [wanted to] work my way up there, from coming in [from] engineering in the operations team, of all places, to building out a team, stabilizing the environment there."
- **Evaluation 3 – Hiring:** "Someone I had worked with before said, 'You know what, I'm starting this new startup e-team.' ... You get to play around with technology.' ... I signed up."

Outcome of Evaluation

- **Outcome 1 – Positive:** "Got the job ... so I moved over to the startup at that point."
- **Outcome 2 – Negative:** "We had a new CTO come in ... and we did not see eye-to-eye as to where the problems were in the Technology Department ... It was quite clear that she was not going to see the light and [evaluate me positively] ... It wasn't worth more of my life to continue to try to explain it."
- **Outcome 3 – Positive:** "Yeah, those are the kinds of opportunities that you look at and go, 'Okay, sounds like the right time.' So yes, it [worked out] great."

Personal Understanding of Merit

- **Pre- Labor-Market Entry:** "When I was young, I used to think of merit as 'Are you being rewarded for using your skills to the highest and best ability that you can?' ... Now, I'm not sure that's something we really want to reward."
- **Post Employee Evaluations:** "So, to me, merit is more about recognizing that what they're achieving is important to the company and relevant and returning that value. It's not exceptional in and of itself, but [it is] when you see beyond that."

Refinement of Understanding of Merit

- **Refinement 1 – Inclusion of Subjectivity:** "I figured ... it's all about getting projects staffed and funded, right? ... Merit is about how you can do what's best for the company, and there is a measured amount of subjectivity in that."
- **Refinement 2 – Exclusion of Personal Interaction:** "People overvalue the personal interaction piece in merit, which is part of the expectations of each role and things like that, and sometimes can significantly contribute to success or failure. And I don't mean to over-generalize on this, ... but that same kind of. 'You have to be able to work with your peers.'"
- **Refinement 3 – Inclusion of Insight:** "The flashes of insight or the moments of beyond the day-to-day work ... inspiration? ... That's merit ... I work in a more creative side of the world where it's a lot harder to evaluate ... but sometimes those inspirations are just the thing that is the most valuable to the business ... you've got moments where a casual, offhand comment changes the way you're building.... and all of a sudden everybody's twice as effective because of that insight.... You cannot say, 'And have one inspiration every three months,' but you have to take that into account as well in evaluation."

FIGURE 5.4. Illustration of a manager's definition and application of merit. *Source:* Adapted from Emilio J. Castilla and Aruna Ranganathan, "The Production of Merit: How Managers Understand and Apply Merit in the Workplace," *Organization Science* 31, no. 4 (2020): 916.

of Merit" box in figure 5.4), this professional—through his choice of a career in computer science—initially viewed merit as "being rewarded for using your skills to the highest and best ability." After entering the labor market as an employee, he experienced three important instances of evaluation (see "Experience Being Evaluated" box): two evaluations he considered positive and fair and one he viewed as negative and unfair (see "Outcome of Evaluation" box). The fair evaluations, both hiring related, led him to include "subjectivity" and "insight" as components of merit (see "Refinement of Understanding of Merit" box). The unfair evaluation, related to a promotion decision, led him to exclude "personal interactions" from his criteria for evaluating merit. Consequently, he came to understand merit as "recognizing what . . . is important to the company " (see "Post Employee Evaluations" inside "Personal Understanding of Merit" box), reflecting a shift from his original focus on "skills" and "best ability." As a result, this manager adopted a diffuse approach to evaluating merit "in a multifaceted way" (see "Application of Merit in Evaluating Others" box in figure 5.4).

Our process model, therefore, illustrates how individuals form their own personal understanding of merit, shedding light on why managers may have widely different interpretations of what merit means. It also identifies two primary approaches to evaluating merit. While we did not collect data on employment outcomes for employees assessed by these managers, we speculate that focused and diffuse approaches to evaluating merit could impact employees' careers differently, especially in organizations, occupations, and industries that already favor one approach over the other when determining who should be rewarded and professionally advanced.

GENDER AND RACIAL PATTERNS IN THE UNDERSTANDING OF MERIT

In the final stage of our analysis, we looked for demographic patterns in how managers evaluate merit. Prior studies on gender and leadership,[53] as well as on race and leadership,[54] suggest that women and racially disadvantaged groups often adopt different managerial practices and leadership styles than their White male counterparts. For example, women have been shown to adopt leadership styles that are more democratic and transformational than those of their male counterparts.[55] Similarly, leaders from racially disadvantaged groups are less likely to support "harsh discipline"[56] and more likely to exhibit considerate behavior[57] than their racial-majority counterparts. We therefore expected the White male managers in our sample to approach the evaluation of merit differently than managers who were non-White and/or female.

To explore this question, we returned to our company sample consisting of eleven interviews of managers at West-TechCo. The company sample was our most homogeneous sample of managers: they all worked within the same company and location, had similar professional backgrounds, and had all begun as engineers. We found that six of the eleven managers used a focused approach to evaluating merit. In contrast, the four managers who applied a diffuse approach were all White men (with only one White man using a focused approach). Although the numbers were small, the pattern was clear.

Next, we wanted to determine whether demographically different managers arrive at their understandings of merit differently. Relying on the labor market and workplace inequality literature, we focused on the personal experiences of being evaluated that were discussed in the interviews and the outcomes of those evaluations.[58] We wanted to determine whether the women and racially disadvantaged groups at West-TechCo. had described their evaluation experiences as having been unfair and, if so, how they had subsequently refined their understanding of merit. To do so, we coded all the evaluations mentioned in the interviews, deidentified them, and had an independent research assistant (who had not previously been involved in the project and was unaware of its objective) code whether each evaluation was perceived as fair or unfair by the interviewee. Independently, we also coded the evaluations ourselves; we found consistency between the research assistant's coding and our own.

In total, fourteen evaluations were discussed across the eleven interviews. White male managers reported six fair evaluations and one unfair evaluation, whereas women and racially disadvantaged interviewees reported one fair and six unfair evaluations. Consistent with prior research on workplace inequality, we found that White men generally perceived more of their evaluation experiences as fair than women and individuals from racially disadvantaged groups.

The process model in figure 5.3 posits that, as a result of experiencing what they saw as fair or unfair evaluations, managers refine their understandings of merit by either ruling in or ruling out particular factors leading to their merit approach. We predicted that subjectively fair evaluation outcomes would lead to a diffuse approach to evaluating merit and that unfair outcomes would lead to a focused approach. As a final step, we coded how individual managers' understandings of merit changed after having experienced a particular evaluation. Again, we found that, on average, White men experienced more subjectively fair outcomes and adopted a broad approach. By contrast, women and racially disadvantaged members experienced more subjectively unfair outcomes and adopted a focused approach.

To illustrate such a process, consider a White male manager from California who took part in our study.[59] He described a hiring evaluation that he perceived as fair. He was offered the job because of his connections and likability, and he described it as a legitimate and productive way to find jobs. He said, "I will claim, yes, that I am fantastic at identifying those hiring opportunities [through networks]. . . . I have very few complaints. . . . It looks like I have perfect timing." When describing how this hiring outcome had influenced his understanding of merit, he said, "[In] doing hiring and promotions . . . who actually has the best skills? . . . I'm not sure there's ever an awareness of who has the best skills for things. . . . Instead merit, for me, is . . . so, it values the subjectivity. . . . In my opinion, [it's] a balance between 'I understand the numbers' and 'I understand the feelings.'" As a result of this hiring experience, he incorporated subjectivity into his understanding of merit. This experience, combined with two similar evaluation experiences, ultimately led this manager to his *diffuse approach* to evaluating merit.

In contrast, consider an Asian American female manager who lived in Massachusetts before moving to California for work. She described a promotion evaluation that she had perceived as unfair: "People make different decisions based on the gender of the individual. . . . [It's] an impacting factor because women tend to be gentler and not that outspoken, and then that's a disadvantage. . . . They may seem like you are not driving things. . . . Because then you just follow instructions and don't really make a change, but . . . for men, most of them are more outspoken, I would say. So, then they get a better chance. . . . Women like me have less chances to get promoted precisely because of this." This manager attributed the unfair outcome to her gentle nature. When describing how this evaluation had affected her, she said, "I . . . don't think the promotion should be based on . . . if your voice is louder. . . . It should just be based on what you have delivered." Thus, this manager ruled out "assertiveness" as a factor that should be considered in assessing merit, and she ultimately adopted a *focused approach* to evaluating merit.

MERIT IS IN THE EYE OF THE BEHOLDER

Merit and the ideal of meritocracy are central to organizational life, as our interviews revealed. In my research, I have examined how managers and professionals define and apply the concepts of merit and talent when making employment decisions. A key finding—one with an important warning for the success of meritocratic talent management systems—is that *there is no universal consensus about what merit actually is.* Even managers and executives with similar training and experiences, working in the same organization, often hold different views. Yet, organizations rarely acknowledge that definitions of "merit" and "talent" can be broad, vague, and highly subjective—essentially, in the eye of the beholder.

As I have discussed in this chapter, decision-makers responsible for recruitment, selection, and evaluation do not always operate under the same assumptions about what constitutes merit and which qualities or traits should be rewarded and promoted in their organizations. Our research reveals that individuals' understandings of merit vary across three dimensions: *how* it is assessed (objectivity vs. subjectivity), *who* is evaluated (individual vs. group), and *what* influences it (achievement vs. ascription). This variation becomes even more problematic as individuals increasingly move across organizations, industries, locations, and roles—each with different views on what makes applicants and employees the most talented. As a result, merit cannot be taken for granted as a universally accepted principle; rather, it reflects individuals' own experiences, biases, and contextual influences.

A key practical implication of this lack of consensus—particularly among recruiters, managers, and leaders within the same organization—is that it can introduce inconsistencies and inefficiencies in hiring, promotion, and evaluation processes. Moreover, it can reinforce personal biases and favoritism in the design, operation, and outcomes of talent management systems, ultimately undermining organizational efforts to achieve meritocracy in practice.

In the following part III, I will elaborate on the actions leaders and organizations should take to address—and avoid—the key warnings discussed in part II and effectively foster meritocracy and excellence in their talent management processes.

PART III
Building Meritocratic Organizations

Building an equitable organization is a journey, not a destination. It requires ongoing self-reflection, a willingness to learn, and a commitment to taking action on what you learn.

—MELINDA FRENCH GATES, AMERICAN PHILANTHROPIST

Building equitable organizations is not a one-time initiative or a quick fix, but rather a continuous process that requires ongoing commitment, accountability, and action from all members of the organization.

—TRACIE POWELL, JOURNALIST AND FOUNDER OF THE IDA B. WELLS SOCIETY FOR INVESTIGATIVE REPORTING

Building equitable organizations requires intentional and sustained efforts to identify and remove systemic barriers, biases, and inequities. It means creating a culture of belonging where every individual feels valued and respected, and where diversity is celebrated as a strength.

—DARREN WALKER, PRESIDENT OF THE FORD FOUNDATION

Chapter Six

A DATA-DRIVEN APPROACH TO
ACHIEVING MERITOCRACY

Building meritocratic and equitable organizations is a complex yet critical endeavor, as many corporate leaders recognize. It requires effective talent management systems to attract, develop, and retain qualified and motivated individuals—key drivers of organizational success. Up to this point, I have presented research with important warnings for today's organizations, suggesting that achieving truly objective and fair evaluations of merit is a significant challenge in practice. Moreover, the research suggests that many organizations that self-identify as meritocratic or talent-driven may be anything but.

Specifically, I have cautioned that certain organizational efforts to foster meritocracy and excellence in organizations may paradoxically deepen inequities and unfairness. And I have presented evidence of three key findings—along with their related warnings—that highlight what I call the *meritocracy paradox*, the central theme of this book.

The first warning is that simply having organizational processes in place to hire, evaluate, and promote the best does not automatically guarantee fairness, equity, or diversity in practice. In fact, any talent management process can be subject to bias, and there is a risk that people-based management systems—rather than fostering excellence and opportunity for all—may actually reinforce or create advantages for certain groups over others.

The second warning is that emphasizing meritocracy—whether implicitly or explicitly—as the foundation of hiring, promotion, and reward practices may backfire on women, racial minorities, immigrants, and other histori-cally disadvantaged groups. When individuals believe a system is merito-cratic, they may be less likely to recognize and correct for biases in their decision-making. This can lead to unfair treatment of certain individuals or groups and limit the potential for equity, diversity, and inclusion in your workplace.

The third warning is that there is no universal agreement on what merit actually is. Even managers and executives with similar training and experi-ence within the same organization often hold differing views. This lack of consensus on what constitutes merit or talent can ultimately derail efforts to build a truly meritocratic system.

The encouraging news is that fostering true meritocracy in the workplace does not entail an extravagant amount of time or resources, but rather a stra-tegic and intentional focus on debiasing talent management processes. As highlighted in the opening quotes of this part, achieving meritocracy—like equity—requires "ongoing self-reflection, a willingness to learn, and a com-mitment to taking action" (French Gates); it is not "a one-time initiative or a quick fix, but rather a continuous process" (Powell); and it requires "inten-tional and sustained efforts to identify and remove systemic barriers, biases, and inequities" (Walker).

Taking action is essential. But, when doing so, organizational leaders should critically assess the effectiveness of widely promoted "best practices" not only for advancing equity and opportunity for all but also for foster-ing excellence in the management of people. Not all "best practices" or popular initiatives work for every organization and business. I frequently hear from leaders who are skeptical about the effectiveness of specific prac-tices, and many are unsurprised when certain so-called best practices fail to yield results for their organizations. Why would they when each organiza-tion faces unique challenges? Still, pressure to act—whether due to public expectations, internal demand, or good intentions—often leads companies to implement generic solutions without first diagnosing their specific needs.

In this chapter, I propose a more effective approach—*a data-driven talent management strategy that actively addresses bias and inequity while ensuring efficient, fair, and meritocratic decision-making.* To illustrate, a metaphor may be helpful. If you own a car, you know that you have to maintain it regularly and that it needs periodic checks and repairs. A car is a complex system that is constantly affected by external forces—such as rain and snow, heat, friction, and gravity—under which parts of the vehicle periodically break down. A car is also affected by contextual and even social factors, such as the quality of the roads and how other drivers operate their vehicles around us. Car manufacturers know this, so they provide dashboards that alert us to problems (e.g., low tire pressure, high engine temperature, battery issues) or the need to take the vehicle in for service.

People management systems in a meritocratic organization are also complex. Over time, all kinds of forces (including different types of biases and social processes) work on these systems. You need to monitor them and continually adjust, repair, or replace parts of the system accordingly. However, no one would decide to get their tires or catalytic converter replaced simply because they knew their neighbors recently did or because they read an article about how many vehicle owners were replacing their catalytic converters. Maintaining a car involves monitoring, diagnosing, and addressing specific problems—not just looking for popular repair solutions. Yet, many organizations take precisely this kind of "best practice" approach to talent management, imitating their competitors when instead, they should focus on monitoring and diagnosing their own system's specific challenges.

The "best practice" approach often falls short because it fails to account for the specific context of an organization. In the following sections, I will illustrate why generic and popular solutions do not work equally well for all organizations and businesses. Later, I will present and develop a more promising alternative: an ongoing data-driven strategy to continuously assess and refine meritocratic practices. By systematically monitoring and adjusting talent management processes, organizations can cultivate a fairer and more effective system—one that genuinely rewards talent and fosters an inclusive and high-performing workplace.

THE "BEST PRACTICE" APPROACH DOES NOT ALWAYS WORK

To date, many organizations interested in reducing biases and unfairness have gravitated toward popular tactics that they see other organizations use or commentators praise—for example, holding certain types of diversity and other management training sessions, blinding specific parts of the selection processes, or adding a statement about equal opportunity to their website. Given societal pressure to demonstrate that they promote fairness and opportunity for all, many employers have even treated such practices as a way of "checking the box."

However, such "window-dressing" tactics often do not achieve the desired results.[1] Empirical evidence suggests that many commonly used and widespread workplace practices are not effective for all organizations. Consider, for example, five popular practices that many companies have adopted: (1) running general diversity training programs for recruiters, hiring managers, and other key decision-makers; (2) training about implicit bias using the Implicit Association Test; (3) using "blind" screening in the recruitment and selection process; (4) removing gendered language from job postings and other recruitment messages; and (5) introducing artificial intelligence (AI) into screening and selection processes. This list is not comprehensive—there are many additional ways organizations attempt to improve equity and fairness in their people-related processes—but it illustrates how unlikely some companies are to achieve true meritocracy by adopting any particular popular tactic alone.

1. Diversity Training Is Not Always Effective

To address potential biases, many organizations have turned to training those who screen, hire, evaluate, and reward candidates and employees. Such training has become a profitable industry over the past decades. According to a 2017 blog entry on McKinsey & Company's website, about $8 billion is spent annually on diversity and inclusion training in the United States alone.[2] Some training sessions are mandatory, with the purpose of correcting past discriminatory behaviors in the workplace; judges have been mandating training on diversity, equity, and inclusion for managers and professionals as part of court rulings. These programs, despite their limited efficacy in removing decision-making biases over the long term, tended to be the ones most supported by leaders and policymakers. Further, they often help maintain good optics and can also provide a legal defense against potential discrimination claims.[3]

Unfortunately, scholars have long advised that certain diversity training programs may not achieve the intended change in the workplace.[4] By analyzing data from hundreds of US employers over time to assess how different equity measures work, Alexandra Kalev and Frank Dobbin showed that typical diversity training programs, particularly the mandatory ones, could actually lead to *declines* in management diversity.[5] In businesses that implemented mandatory diversity training for managers, the researchers found no increase in the percentage of White women, Black men, and Hispanics in management positions five years after the training. During that period, the percentage of Black women in management *dropped* by 9 percent, while the share of Asian Americans decreased by 4 percent.

This result is not surprising given that HR specialists and consultants repeatedly report that managers and professionals often dislike mandatory diversity courses and respond to them "with anger and resistance," as Dobbin and Kalev write.[6] Part of the problem may be the training material used in such courses. Many firms used to include threats and "negative incentives" in their diversity training, such as "discriminate, and the company will pay the price," which is an approach that tends to make managers defensive and resistant to change. Some diversity training programs include dated (even irrelevant) content or materials that do not necessarily encourage participants to support diversity in productive ways. Some have suggested that antibias material that articulates various stereotypes may emphasize the salience of such stereotypes, call for their suppression, and, ironically, reinforce them in the participants' minds.[7] Sometimes, training efforts to improve the views of a particular target group can unintentionally increase the negative views of others.[8] Whatever the reason, many participants in mandatory diversity training programs "report more animosity toward other groups afterward."[9]

However, Dobbin and Kalev also found that *voluntary* diversity training resulted in greater results over time: Black men, Hispanic men, and Asian American men and women saw increases of 9 percent to 13 percent in management five years after the training, with no decline among White or Black women. In their book *Getting to Diversity: What Works and What Doesn't*,[10] Dobbin and Kalev continue to show that companies benefit little from requiring their managers to participate in diversity training or from introducing hiring and promotion policies and sanctions to influence managers' behavior. Ultimately, part of the problem may be the lack of top management support for diversity or the lack of managerial rewards for increasing diversity.[11]

Even when diversity training programs yield positive effects, the returns can be modest. Edward Chang and colleagues conducted a field experiment at a global organization to test whether a brief online diversity training program could improve attitudes and behaviors toward women.[12] The study involved over three thousand employees and a control group that did not receive the training. Twenty weeks out, the researchers assessed participants' attitudes and their actual workplace decisions. The key finding of the field experiment was that employees in the receiving training condition appeared to be significantly more supportive of women than employees in the control condition after the intervention. Such a positive effect of the diversity intervention was even larger for employees located outside the United States, suggesting how the national context and other contextual factors potentially moderate the impact of such interventions.

The news was less promising when measuring actual behaviors pertaining to women compared to men. Chang and colleagues reported that their diversity training intervention "successfully generated some behavior change among groups whose average untreated attitudes were already strongly supportive of women before training." Regarding informal mentoring of women, however, the researchers found no significant differences between the treatment and control groups regarding the average number of women selected for informal mentorship per consented participant at the studied organization. Approximately six weeks after recruitment to the training, they found no differences in the number of women recognized for excellence.[13] Overall, the authors conclude, like many other prior empirical studies: "Although we find evidence of attitude change and some limited behavior change as a result of our training, our results suggest that the one-off diversity trainings that are commonplace in organizations are not panaceas for remedying bias in the workplace."[14]

A note of caution is warranted here. While some scholars and practitioners have critiqued the effectiveness of certain diversity training programs, their intent has not necessarily been to oppose diversity initiatives altogether. Instead, many advocate for organizational leaders to develop and implement targeted, structural solutions that improve diversity, fairness, and inclusion.[15] Indeed, to achieve true meritocracy, certain organizations and businesses do need to ensure that their efforts effectively promote opportunity for all, fostering diversity and inclusion at every level.

2. Raising Awareness About Implicit Biases May Not Bring About Change

One prevalent intervention, promoted by HR professionals and consultants for several years worldwide, consists of running workshops to raise awareness of implicit biases, particularly those related to gender and race. Professionals and employees often request and appreciate such initiatives. These workshops are relatively easy to implement and help inform individuals of potential demographic biases affecting the workplace. Not surprisingly, many researchers became interested in measuring the effectiveness of these interventions by examining the extent to which participants in such work-shops (typically, individuals who self-select into them) are more aware of implicit biases, express fewer biases, and become more willing to engage in action to reduce biases after participating in the workshop.[16] However, such studies often measure reported positive effects in the short term, that is, soon after the workshops take place. Additionally, some of the observed changes are potentially attributable to other factors and events that may have occurred over the same period.

A standard tool in these trainings is the Implicit Association Test (IAT), which measures associations between concepts (e.g., women, Blacks, gays) and evaluations (e.g., good, bad) or stereotypes (e.g., competent, warm, lazy). The IAT assumes that by making individuals aware of their implicit biases, we can encourage them to make less biased decisions. According to a Project Implicit blog post, since its founding, more than 20 million people have completed IAT studies through its websites.[17] In addition, many organizations and businesses use some form of the IAT to raise awareness of biases.

As I wrote earlier in this book, academic and popular debate has focused on the IAT's effectiveness or lack thereof. In 2019, Chloë FitzGerald and colleagues did a review of thirty studies conducted between May 2005 and April 2017 and tested interventions aimed at reducing implicit bias and its effects. They concluded that the impact of the kind of training that organizations favor the most, such as "short, one-shot sessions that can be completed and the requisite diversity boxes ticked," is unlikely to last long or influence participants' long-term habits and behavior in people management decisions.[18] Furthermore, many scholars have identified reasonable and often significant issues regarding the test's validity, reliability, and usefulness in assessing (not to mention reducing) implicit biases.[19]

Arguably, one potential reason for the lack of documented effectiveness could be that the concept of implicit bias and the many commercial applications to address it have been "developed by non-psychologists" and may not be "appropriately guided by the existing body of research findings."[20] Some say that the jury is still out, even though several academic studies have found evidence that the test does *not* help address biases in actual employment decisions.[21] However, while I agree with many criticisms of IAT methodology, the idea of helping leaders and professionals do some exercise or test that shows them how we can all be affected by biases and stereotypes can still be of great value for certain organizations. Moreover, it is also fair to note that *no* practice has proven to be a panacea in addressing biases or improving equity. It is, therefore, unsurprising that the IAT is not a remedy for all prejudices we may have.

Despite the criticisms, the IAT remains a popular and relatively inexpensive intervention for organizations to adopt, if only to signal their commitment to educating employees about diversity, equity, and inclusion. Some businesses may provide IAT workshops to preempt lawsuits alleging discrimination. Others have adopted implicit bias training because they believed it to be among the "best practices," when it may simply be the best guess at the time.[22]

IAT workshops may be doing little besides making leaders and professionals aware that we all have mental biases. This is not surprising, given that research indicates it is not easy to change implicit biases with short-term training interventions.[23] Common sense also helps us realize that quick training programs (online, for instance, or a couple of hours in person) will unlikely change long-term behaviors and biases. In fact, given the research reviewed earlier in the book, there are reasons to fear that poorly designed training programs could make those biases and stereotypes even more salient and justifiable in people's minds, thus ironically reinforcing the very biases they are intended to address.

3. Blind Hiring Is Not a Panacea

Many employers have *blindly* (pun intended) adopted the practice of blind hiring, that is, removing or masking applicants' gender, ethnicity, age, and educational background during screening and selection. The practice often consists of selectively hiding any information—such as name, ZIP code, or headshots—that could be used to identify a candidate's likely demographic group. Other efforts have focused on obscuring words, questions, expressions, or other information that could bias recruiters and hiring managers.[24] Some efforts at masking a job seeker's identity have consisted of simply collecting employment-relevant data about candidates' skills and showing them to key decision-makers or having the candidates complete assessments and exercises directly related to the job performance. Proponents of this approach often recommend avoiding social media prescreenings because online presence can provide information about job seekers that could bias hiring decisions.

The primary motivation behind these blind hiring practices relies on the reasonable assumption that by masking such information, recruiters and hiring managers will not allow their demographic biases to influence their processes and will instead evaluate candidates solely on their qualifications and skills. This can result in a more objective and fair hiring process, which could help improve opportunities for all.

This motivation is not new. In the 1970s and 1980s, symphony orchestras started to implement blind auditions to overcome the sex-biased hiring of musicians. As reported in a classic study by Claudia Goldin and Cecilia Rouse, none of the five highest-ranked orchestras in the United States had more than 12 percent women until about 1980.[25] As part of these "blind" auditions, musicians were asked to play their instruments behind a screen so that judges could not see what they looked like; they would even be asked to walk on carpeted floors so judges could not detect female musicians from the sound of their heels. Goldin and Rouse reported in the 1997 working version of the paper, ultimately published in the *American Economic Review*, that blind auditions improved the chances of women advancing from preliminary rounds by 50 percent. They further estimated that these auditions accounted for 30 to 55 percent of the increase in the proportion of women among new hires from 1970 until 1995.

Important field experiments in the social sciences also recommend eliminating names from résumé screening to avoid gender and racial bias. Marianne Bertrand and Sendhil Mullainathan found substantial differences in how employers responded to otherwise identical résumés that manipulated the perception of the applicant's race via the name on the résumé.[26] In this now-classic audit study, the authors sent nearly 5,000 résumés in response to over 1,300 ads of jobs in sales, administrative support, clerical, and customer service in Boston and Chicago. In those résumés, they randomly assigned White-sounding names (Emily Walsh or Greg Baker) to half the résumés and Black-sounding names (Lakisha Washington or Jamal Jones) to the other half. They reported a 50 percent gap in employer callback rates: on average, applicants with White-sounding names had to submit ten résumés to receive one positive callback from an employer, whereas applicants with Black-sounding names had to submit fifteen for the same result. Two decades later, a similar audit study was conducted in which 83,000 fictitious job applications were sent to 108 of the largest US employers. In that study, applicants with Black-sounding names received 10 percent fewer callbacks, despite having applications comparable to those with White-sounding names.[27]

Findings like these have prompted many companies to experiment with blind selection (e.g., Deloitte, Ernst & Young, and Google). Some software companies offer tools designed to help employers better integrate blind selection into application screening—for example, by allowing key decision-makers to turn off the display of some information about the candidate to boost diversity hiring (see, e.g., Toggl Hire, Blendoor, or Recruiteze, among many). Pinpoint, for instance, promises to allow users to "anonymize applicant data on a job-by-job basis with a single click."[28] Most of these efforts aim to eliminate information about the job candidates' demographics. Some mask other aspects of résumés, assuming that when unnecessary details about a person's background are blocked out, screeners will be less likely to favor candidates with degrees from specific educational institutions and employment at prestigious organizations and, therefore, more likely to focus on job-relevant skills and accomplishments.

Although these efforts are motivated by good intentions, employers may eventually want to interview the candidate before extending an offer. At these later stages, potential problems could still be reintroduced. First, since a candidate's personal data can only be concealed during the initial screening, blind hiring is not really blind hiring. It is typically more about blind selection and pre-hire screening. Once candidates have been blindly pre-screened, employers like to conduct face-to-face interviews to learn more about a candidate; there's no more masking at this point, and biases and other social dynamics can reenter the selection process.

Furthermore, research findings on the effectiveness of job interviews, in fact, are "somewhat devastating."[29] Job interviews are generally neither reliable nor valid and have limited value for predicting job performance. They are subject to biases, including in-group bias, improper discounting, anchoring on initial impressions, and so on.[30] Additionally, the interviewer's bias about the nature of the job or the "ideal candidate" may influence evaluations.[31] But employers and their screeners and hiring managers are often hesitant to eliminate interviews and cannot imagine extending an offer without somehow "seeing the candidate" first. There have been efforts to conduct anonymous interviews through chat rooms or voice-masking technology, but the results of such efforts are mixed.

In addition, blind selection is not practical or even feasible when it comes to post-hire employee decisions such as promotions or bonuses. It would be conceivable to use blind selection only if you have many employees being considered for career advancement and rewards, and a careful way to mask their identity during performance evaluations and subsequent bonus and promotion decisions. In practice, it has been challenging for employers to mask employees' demographic information when making such post-hire employment evaluations.

Another issue is the difficulty of evaluating certain types of work experiences and professional accomplishments when selecting for specific positions and roles, especially those requiring a variety of skills and competencies. Blind selection can be effective in evaluating particular technical skills and objectively measured abilities, but it may be challenging to assess "soft" skills like communication, initiative, teamwork, and leadership competencies, which are often important aspects of many jobs. Removing identifying information from résumés can further create a lack of context, making it difficult for recruiters and hiring managers to assess a candidate's professional background and work experience, particularly when previous experience is essential and cultural fit is important.

Blind selection also may not fully address bias because some demographic information can be inferred from other information included in a résumé, such as a candidate's experience, hobbies, or personal statements. Blind selection is also not suitable for all industries, organizations, or roles. In fields like sales, marketing, or customer service, it may be necessary to have personal skills and the ability to build connections, which can be hard to assess through blind evaluation of résumés and cover letters. Furthermore, while more straightforward to implement these days given the advancement of software and hiring platforms, blind hiring still requires significant effort and resources, including updating recruitment systems and training hiring managers, which may not be feasible for all organizations, especially small ones. In many cases, the problem companies face is a pool of candidates that is not very diverse, and, in such cases, masking candidates' demographic information may not help address the actual problem.

Finally, perhaps most importantly, there is limited empirical evidence to support the effectiveness of blind hiring,[32] with a few studies even discussing potential unintended effects.[33] Some argue that blind selection can increase the diversity of candidates invited for interviews, but it does not automatically result in more diverse final hires. In fact, some studies show the opposite results. A trial initiative—by the Behavioral Economics Team of the Australian government aimed at improving the share of women hired for senior roles by removing gender information from job applications—found that when a candidate's application included a male name, the candidate was about 3 percent *less* likely to get a job offer.[34] Conversely, when the application added a female name, the candidate was nearly 3 percent *more* likely to get an offer. Even the classic study by Goldin and Rouse on orchestra auditions showed evidence that blind selection does not always work: while the authors attribute about 30 percent of the increase in female orchestra members to blind selection practices, they do stress that some of their "estimates have large standard errors and there is one persistent effect in the opposite direction."[35]

It is important to note that while some studies report small effects or even unintended results, they do not suggest, and one should not, therefore, conclude that the practice of blind hiring is ineffective in reducing bias and prejudice in the screening and hiring process. Instead, the takeaway for leaders is that they should not adopt blind selection practices simply because other organizations have. Instead, leaders should identify their organization's own meritocratic challenges and then analyze whether blind hiring is the most effective response for them.

4. Tweaking the Language in Job Postings Has Little Effect

Tweaking the language used when crafting job advertisements and other recruitment messages is another quite popular recommendation given to businesses that aim to attract diverse applicants, particularly women, into not-so-diverse positions and organizations. This is a form of a broader type of "best practice"—using augmented writing platforms not only to boost recruitment but also to prevent biases when writing job descriptions. Along these lines, several software companies, such as Textio, Workable, and Grammarly, have claimed that by removing gendered language from job descriptions, their platforms help hiring organizations improve gender diversity among applicants, especially in male-dominated fields. This process frequently consists of replacing words that are considered to have masculine or feminine connotations with neutral wording.

The widespread belief in HR circles about the effectiveness of this tactic may originate from previous claims by researchers and practitioners. Academics have long warned that gendered wording prevails in job ads despite laws prohibiting language that explicitly indicates an employer's preference for candidates of a particular gender (i.e., Title VII of the Civil Rights Act of 1964 in the case of the United States).[36] A key conclusion from a series of lab experiments, often cited by scholars and practitioners (particularly those software companies promoting their bias-free recruiting platforms), is that the more masculine the wording of job advertisements, the less appealing women found such jobs.[37]

Hye Jin Rho at Michigan State University and I examined whether tweaking the language of online job ads has any positive effect on attracting diverse candidates, particularly women.[38] To investigate whether "degendering" language in job postings works, we conducted two studies: an observational field study of a recruitment company's job search platform (study 1) and a field experiment study of a real job ad posted online to actual job seekers (study 2). In study 1, we analyzed data from TopRecruit, a North American–based global company that offers web-based recruiting services. We examined nearly 300,000 job postings on TopRecruit's online platform over two years, posted by about 32,000 recruiters and reaching nearly half a million unique job seekers in the United States. On this platform, recruiters post jobs along with self-descriptions. Job seekers can view these postings and inquire about specific jobs through an internal forum. This forum allowed us to directly measure the femininity or masculinity of the language recruiters used when describing jobs and introducing themselves to job seekers.

What do we mean by feminine or masculine wording in job ads? Here, we started by relying on the study by Danielle Gaucher, Justin Friesen, and Aaron C. Kay suggesting that job ads have subtle gendered wording that—intentionally or not—may differently affect men and women when considering applying for a particular job. In their exploratory analysis of real-world job postings, these researchers found that job ads in male-dominated occupations contained more language typically perceived as masculine compared to those in female-dominated occupations. Masculine language in these job descriptions included words like *determined, analytical, independent, decisive, persistent, ambitious,* and *assertive.* In contrast, feminine words included *committed, interpersonal, cooperative, compassionate, honest,* and *understanding.*[39] These findings align with the results of previous studies.[40]

Overall, our results indicated that, contrary to widespread recommendations and assumptions behind certain writing technologies, tweaking the gendering of job posting language has minimal practical impact in a country like the United States, where employers are not allowed to discriminate explicitly by gender in job postings. Our large-scale observational study 1 of TopRecruit found that gendered language in job listings had practically negligible effects on men's or women's application behavior. Furthermore, in our experimental study 2, we observed no statistically significant effects.

We, therefore, concluded that employers' efforts to alter the language in job descriptions are not enough to help certain organizations address the persistent gendered sorting of applicants into certain jobs, occupations, organizations, and industries. That "best practice" of degendering the language in job postings may be a "best guess," after all, and better interventions are needed to solve the meritocratic challenges that many employers face during recruitment.

5. Artificial Intelligence Can Reflect Human Biases

Similarly to the augmented writing technologies described in the prior point, many machine-learning specialists and scholars have collaborated with businesses to introduce automated reviews of job applications and hiring recommendations based on algorithms. Such a goal is appealing because it appears to introduce impartial science and data into the main objective of recruiting the best talent. Unfortunately, problems may emerge.

In 2018, for example, Amazon scrapped an AI recruitment algorithm over concerns that it might introduce bias against women. Amazon has been building software since 2014 to review job applicants' résumés. Given Amazon's prior success in automating many processes involving the supply and distribution of goods and products to customers, it was only a matter of time before it attempted to automate essential HR functions such as hiring and selection as well. The company's experimental AI hiring tool ranked job applicants from one to five stars.

By 2015, the company noticed that such a new tool was not gender-neutral when rating applicants for software developer jobs. Amazon's algorithms were trained to screen applicants by analyzing patterns in résumés submitted to the company during a ten-year period. Since most of these résumés came from men, reflecting the male-dominated nature of the tech sector, the tool taught itself to favor male applicants. As a result, it penalized résumés that included words like *women* or *women's* when describing applicants' interests or hobbies. It even downgraded graduates of two women's colleges.[41]

According to company insiders, the development team worked to make the software respond neutrally to these terms. However, Amazon ultimately scrapped the tool. Other tech companies, such as IBM and Facebook, were said to be developing algorithmic bias detection tools and other AI techniques, using publicly available data, to try to remove gender and racial biases from hiring. However, as the Amazon example shows, the problem is more complex than it initially seems.

The rapid growth of generative AI technologies has led to many organizations and businesses experimenting with or adopting AI-related models.

According to a 2023 report by Accenture, 98 percent of global executives agree that AI foundation models will play an important role in their organization's strategies in the next three to five years.[42] A few are already praising the benefits of technology to achieve certain goals, such as pay equity.[43]

Yet, while these technologies are being touted as an effective method of optimizing decision-making and reducing bias in screening and selection, many are already warning us about potential unintended consequences.[44] For instance, given that these technologies provide solutions based on their learning from available data (regardless of their quality and source) as well as the specific features of the underlying AI models, they can potentially introduce errors and even hazards. Such AI methodologies can also be subject to manipulation and discretion, just like human intelligence, and even institutionalized bias and other forms of favoritism or prejudice against particular groups of individuals, with experts already proposing solutions to those potentially emerging biases and errors.[45] Many also importantly emphasize the need to incorporate worker perspectives and voice into the design and implementation of these new technologies to enhance everyday organizational work processes and achieve better outcomes, including higher quality of products and services, greater innovation, and enhanced productivity.[46]

To summarize, my goal in examining five widely adopted best practices was to illustrate how achieving meritocracy and equity in practice is far more complicated than you would expect. Research on the real-world impact of those practices shows that their effectiveness varies significantly, with some yielding minimal improvements or even backfiring. This is, again, not surprising, as many of these "best practices" do not really target the root causes of bias and unfairness. Moreover, they are rarely sufficient on their own to resolve an organization's meritocracy challenges in a meaningful and sustainable way.

WHAT DOES WORK?

If these popular, often widely recommended tactics aren't particularly effective for the average organization—and if declaring a company a meritocracy can even backfire—what approaches actually *do* help organizations and businesses become more truly meritocratic?

When advising leaders and professionals, I recommend that rather than simply adopting a popular practice for its own sake, they critically identify and assess which meritocratic strategies can effectively help them address inequities and promote equal opportunity for all in their workforce. If prior efforts have fallen short, how can they be fundamentally reconsidered and tailored to the organization's unique needs and challenges? This approach acknowledges that there is no "best practice" that works for every single organization. Instead, organizations need to do the hard work of figuring out which specific practices will address their challenges and carefully evaluate them *before* adapting them into their existing structures. This task requires some serious commitment and work to improve the organization's talent management system and align potential solutions with the company's broader strategy and existing practices.

Given how far they are from implementing truly meritocratic processes, many companies should begin by introducing policies and procedures that provide more (and more equal) opportunities to all during recruitment, hiring, and promotion. They can proactively identify and evaluate which recruitment sources, which hiring tools, and which post-hire performance appraisal processes allow them to attract and retain a highly talented and diverse workforce.

Others should invest more effort in improving post-hire processes and reducing high levels of attrition among talented individuals from groups underrepresented in professional and managerial jobs in their organization. Several technology firms faced that challenge in the late 2010s and early 2020s. Their current challenge has been to ensure that employee layoffs do not inequitably affect employees from certain demographic groups.[47] Studies have shown that female and Latino workers have been hit hardest in tech layoffs (similar to what has been reported in prior studies of corporate restructurings and their effects on racial and gender segregation).[48] According to layoff data collected by Revelio Labs Inc, female and Latino workers made up 46.6 percent and 11.5 percent, respectively, of those laid off by tech companies between September and December of 2022, although such workers represented only 39 percent and almost 10 percent, respectively, of the tech company workforce. A December 2022 lawsuit accused X Corp (formerly known as Twitter until July 2023) of "disproportionally targeting female employees for layoffs."[49]

Meanwhile, companies that are more advanced in their pursuit of true meritocracy need to systematically assess (and reconsider) the benefits and costs of the practices they employ, including their potential unintended consequences. Such examinations can help them improve practices that are not working or adopt more promising ones that can bring about the meritocratic and equitable results they are seeking.

With these goals in mind, the rest of this chapter lays out a data-driven approach to make meritocracy work in practice in your organization. This approach is geared toward helping you strategically design data collection, management, and analysis to assess whether your organization is fairly advancing and rewarding the best, and whether every member of your workforce gets a fair opportunity to succeed. By so doing, you will be better positioned to find the most helpful solutions for your organization. You will also optimize your talent management processes, particularly those aimed at finding top talent and enhancing your organization's competitiveness and profitability.

AN APPROACH GROUNDED IN TALENT ANALYTICS

My strategic approach, based on talent analytics, aims to build meritocracy as defined in chapter 2 of this book—that is, organizational systems that allow individuals to be rewarded with economic and social resources solely through their demonstrated intelligence, efforts, skills, abilities, or performance. By collecting, coding, and analyzing employment-relevant data about people-related processes and outcomes, such meritocratic organizations strive to improve fairness and equal opportunity in hiring, advancing, and rewarding individuals—three key career employment outcomes, not only for the success of individuals but also for the success of organizations.

Through a talent analytics approach, the steps outlined here aim to help you and your organization diagnose the extent to which your organization is what I have been calling a "true meritocracy." This approach will help you locate your particular organizational challenges—the first step toward successfully addressing them—in a way that reveals *whether* and *where* demographic and other employment-irrelevant disparities may be occurring. This strategic approach is, in my experience, the best way for leaders to build not only an equitable and diverse organization but also a successful and excellent organization, all of which reflect the ideals of meritocracy in practice.

In the discussion of true meritocracy in chapter 2, I outlined two essential conditions for achieving meritocracy in practice. First, there should be *equal opportunity for all* individuals at crucial decision points concerning selection, advancement, and rewards. A talent analytics approach can support this first goal by identifying any people-related processes that may be restricting equal access to opportunities. Second, once equal opportunity has been established—ensuring individuals can attain positions and rewards *based solely on their merit*—inequality in outcomes may be acceptable in a meritocratic system. The main principle here is that disparities in pay, rewards, and promotions should be driven by employment-relevant factors rather than by demographics or personal characteristics. A talent analytics approach can play a crucial role in this regard, helping organizations assess whether their people-related processes are operating fairly and pinpointing any areas where bias may still be present.

A note of clarification, even caution, is warranted. Implicit in the first condition is that opportunity for all is a "win-win" type of situation, where everyone stands to benefit equally from organizational efforts aimed at creating opportunity, such as employer initiatives that provide training and employment benefits. But the second condition acknowledges that the distribution of positions and rewards, particularly in the workplace, is often a "zero-sum" game, in that organizations have a finite number of promotions to offer, as well as fixed budgets for raises and bonuses, and consequently not everyone will "win" those promotions or rewards.

This clarification is especially relevant in ongoing debates about fairness, not just in university admissions but also in hiring and advancement within elite companies and organizations. It also sheds light on the backlash and misconceptions surrounding certain employer policies, particularly those aimed at promoting diversity and inclusion.[50] Critics often argue that such policies unfairly benefit a select few rather than everyone. However, it is naïve to assume that all people-based decisions are a "win-win" game: while this may be true in particular organizational contexts or situations, one reason for the backlash against diversity initiatives is that they often are not a zero-sum game. Typically, in "zero-sum" situations, we would expect that advancement and rewards practices will not benefit all equally but some more than others (meaning that, for instance, some will get promoted while others will not). In such "zero-sum" situations, and to foster meritocracy, it is therefore fundamental that organizations guarantee that everyone has an equal chance to compete and succeed.

WHAT A SUCCESSFUL TALENT ANALYTICS APPROACH CAN DO

Not all businesses understand how talent analytics can help improve their talent management processes and outcomes. Some still think that talent analytics is just reporting statistics about people-related decisions, while others think it is collecting "big data," often useless and full of coding and data collection issues. Such businesses do not have a successful strategy to become meritocratic organizations—even though they may have competent data scientists and analytical professionals.

I return to the car metaphor. Think of a successful talent analytics approach as an effective and well-designed car dashboard that helps you locate the kinds of forces affecting the operation of your talent management system over time (biases and social processes). Such a dashboard can help you monitor the system and continually adjust, repair, or replace its crucial parts accordingly. When done right, a successful talent analytics approach lets leaders identify where their organization may be failing at ensuring meritocracy in practice. Furthermore, they can provide leaders with invaluable help on how to achieve meritocracy by improving critical talent management processes, particularly those relating to screening and hiring, performance evaluations, training, pay, and rewards. A successful talent analytics approach also allows leaders to "listen" to the perspectives and voices of their workers and the decisions made about them, an approach that helps keep the organization dynamic in a constantly changing environment.

At a broad level, I define *talent analytics* as a data-driven approach to improving people-related decisions for the purpose of advancing both individual and organizational success. When well implemented, such an approach can help leaders make people management decisions based on actual data and data analyses rather than intuition, experience, advice, guesswork, or fashionable fads—all of which are still common in many organizations. As I will explain in more detail later, talent analytics does not always require "big data"; it does require systematic collection of good and relevant information about processes and outcomes, whether such data are quantitative or qualitative (that is, data that come from interviews, focus groups, or observation).[51]

At its most basic level, a successful talent analytics approach consists of continuously applying a four-part process: (1) identifying critical challenges regarding the management of people in your organization; (2) gathering and analyzing relevant data to tackle such challenges; (3) reporting the results of your analyses to key organizational stakeholders; and (4) helping your key stakeholders use those results to decide which solutions to consider.

At first glance, that process seems straightforward, but each part requires careful thought and wise strategic execution. Notice that these parts do not rely on any best practice or set of practices. Instead, they guide the selection and adoption of potential practices to address an organization's specific people management challenges. They often require *adapting*—rather than simply *adopting* (that is, copying)—existing popular practices to make them effective for an organization and its circumstances. I have developed this approach based on the insights of my own research and on interventions I have observed at many organizations—many relatively small but quite significant in their outcomes.

This proposed analytical approach addresses the fact that many current organizations are not equally supporting all individuals in achieving their full potential. In fact, some organizations may even be depriving certain employees of the resources and opportunities necessary to compete and succeed. It is important to distinguish between *equity* and *equality*, once again, as the two terms are often confused or conflated in practice. By *equity*, I mean processes that are fair and impartial—although equity does not necessarily entail equality, which typically allocates everyone the same resources and opportunities without any other criteria influencing their distribution. Equity further acknowledges that individuals may not have equal opportunities to begin with, due to, for example, workplace biases or other social barriers that have limited their opportunities for educational and employment achievements. This understanding implies that organizations serious about implementing equity should be willing to allocate extra resources and opportunities, if needed, to individuals who are talented but disadvantaged in some significant way.

In this regard, similar to the "equity analytics" recommended by many scholars and practitioners,[52] my analytical approach starts with collecting (and cleaning and coding) relevant employment data and then analyzing that data to identify problems and issues in key employment processes and outcomes. Doing so helps you assess the extent to which your organization is systematic and consistent when making people-related decisions regarding hiring, pay, performance evaluations, and promotions. Additionally, this approach can help you explore whether disparities in the distribution of important career outcomes can be explained by factors relevant to the position or some other information completely irrelevant for employment purposes. Are you, for example, *only* considering performance- or employment-relevant criteria when deciding the magnitude of an employee's bonus? If the answer is yes, you may be operating in a meritocratic way. Do any demographics or employment-irrelevant personal characteristics explain variation in the amount of bonus an employee gets? And if so, why is that the case? Are there social processes and barriers preventing your organization from advancing and rewarding individuals for their contributions?

If this is the case, you would need to investigate further. It is like detective work in service of your organization.

This approach can also help you detect whether there is "differential treatment" of individuals (that is, unequal treatment of individuals based on personal characteristics) and/or "disparate impact" (that is, similar treatment results in different outcomes that disproportionally affect one group of individuals) in your organization.

My talent analytics approach also offers a systematic framework for continuously evaluating the effectiveness of interventions and solutions aimed at addressing not only inequities and unfairness but also organizational inefficiencies in the management of people. In some cases, the best solution may involve ensuring equality of treatment, where all individuals are subject to the same processes and standards. In other cases, an equitable approach may be necessary, one that provides certain individuals with additional resources or opportunities to help them overcome structural disadvantages or constraints (e.g., specific training programs or flexible work arrangements). Identifying the right solution requires first gathering relevant data to diagnose the problem, then carefully selecting and implementing the most promising solutions or interventions. Over time, this dynamic talent analytics approach allows organizations and their leaders to refine their talent management practices—retaining what works and improving what does not. This approach needs to be dynamic because your challenges and priorities will change as you address some of them, and new ones may emerge.

My approach emphasizes two fundamental—yet often overlooked—aspects of successful talent management: meritocracy and efficiency. In addition to promoting opportunity for all, organizations need to advance and reward the best talent (the meritocratic logic discussed earlier in this book) while ensuring that their people management practices remain cost-effective and sustainable (the material or business logic). As a result, equitable treatment may lead to unequal career outcomes, affecting who ultimately advances and gets rewarded—which can, in turn, influence workforce diversity. This potential organizational scenario is often overlooked in discussions about implementing meritocracy in practice.

GETTING TO A GREAT TALENT ANALYTICS STRATEGY

Many organizations and businesses, even large and successful ones, lack a strategic approach to talent management that identifies and solves meritocratic and fairness challenges. I present five crucial steps to help you create and develop this powerful strategic approach in your own organization.

Step 1. Identify, Develop, and Define Key Criteria

You should follow this process for each primary employment decision in your organization. For example, when recruiters and managers are screening application materials, they should be clear about what criteria—such as required qualifications, experiences, and skills—the position uses. Some use the word *competencies* to refer to these criteria and the term *competency modeling* to refer to the process of defining such criteria. Get specific (and realistic) here. Without such clarity, biases and social processes may lead screeners to look for applicants in a limited number of ways or apply different criteria depending on the candidate, potentially reinforcing biases and social barriers.

As part of this first step, it is necessary to assess whether you see significant demographic differences in the attainment of the criteria that are being used to screen and select hires. If that is the case, check to make sure those criteria should be used, especially if only some groups have had an opportunity to meet such criteria in the past. If such criteria are essential (as they often are), consider providing the necessary resources for all hires to learn about those criteria (or become better at them) so that, ultimately, all hires have an equal opportunity to succeed. In this respect, post-hire resources and training can help "level the playing field." Indeed, many organizations have put specific onboarding, training, and developmental programs in place precisely for this reason.

As an example, suppose you are hiring structural engineers, plumbers, or electricians. In this case, I recommend seeking candidates with diverse experiences and backgrounds who possess the specific skills, abilities, and credentials needed for the job (such as degrees, certifications, or licenses). All applicants with those talents should be considered, regardless of their personal circumstances.

But this first step is not always straightforward. In many jobs and occupations, there may well be demographic imbalances in the pool of qualified applicants, and you need people who have skills or credentials. Also, simply knowing the criteria for specific jobs doesn't ensure an equal opportunity to get them; many existing societal inequities are difficult for individual organizations to address alone. For example, suppose you enter a medical organization as a certified nursing assistant and are already an adult with children and family responsibilities and no college education. In that case, there is very little chance you will become a doctor, even with information about how to become a doctor. In these situations, the challenges are clearly societal and more difficult for an organization alone to overcome—meritocratic societies and institutions, for instance, could give the opportunities and resources necessary for talented professionals to go to college and medical school.

That said, sometimes this approach could work. For example, in 2023, the state of Pennsylvania ceased requiring college degrees for many jobs, and other states, such as Utah, Maryland, and Alaska, followed suit. Many are urging employers to stop requiring college and university degrees for jobs that do not actually need them.[53] Companies like AT&T, MasterCard, Microsoft, and Southwest Airlines have created alternative pathways to good, stable jobs for those without a college degree.[54]

In implementing this first step, it is often advisable to follow a holistic approach when selecting and hiring individuals, focusing on the employee as a whole rather than on specific skills and abilities, if feasible. Many large companies and undergraduate and graduate programs use this approach to ensure a talented cohort that is professionally diverse. Candidates are screened not only on a few abilities required to do a good job currently but also on their potential to do a great job in the future.

This holistic approach, therefore, takes a long-term and often strategic perspective for the management of talent in organizations. It allows leaders to experiment and figure out whether specific abilities required in the past are still necessary. It can offer an opportunity for organizations to find untapped pools of candidates where competitors are not looking yet because they rely on narrow, rigid, and often outdated hiring criteria. For instance, when recruiters and hiring managers establish selection thresholds such as a certain number of years of work experience or a particular credential or degree, they may have to revise these thresholds after examining the pool of applicants and the subsequent performance of the hires.

The same can be done when making post-hire decisions relating to bonuses, promotions, or development opportunities. Many employers, for instance, would benefit from blinding irrelevant information when making promotions or awarding bonuses. Others could follow a more holistic approach that considers the employee's current ability to do the job and how that employee could develop in the future.

Once again, however, this holistic approach may only work in certain situations—in this case, organizations and businesses that hire many individuals for relatively entry-level or mid-level professional positions or periodically consider a large number of promotions or bonuses. This approach may not work when you are hiring for high-level or senior positions or, once again, when specific skills and qualifications are an essential part of the job.

Step 2. Measure Key Individual Features and Employment Outcomes over Time

Measurement and data collection are critical to assessing whether biases and social processes are affecting the way you screen, hire, reward, and advance employees in your organization. Such measurement can further help you "debias" those employment processes and outcomes. Without first knowing where biases and barriers may exist, it is difficult to know where to focus your efforts, as well as how to monitor and evaluate later whether those efforts were successful.

First, it is important to collect employee data (often, including data on demographics or personal circumstances), not only for employees but also for candidates applying for your jobs, as well as additional information about individuals you may want to consider when giving equal opportunity to all. Getting these data is often challenging when they have not been collected previously; often, getting such data is even not recommended by lawyers in particular countries (the thinking is often that if a company does not have the data, it cannot be found legally liable in discrimination cases). That said, many institutions and a number of experts and executives have encouraged collecting and reporting demographic data, especially for midsized and large organizations, to ensure that there is no discrimination against particular groups of employees who are protected by national, regional, and local employment laws and regulations.[55] (Please be sure to carefully review the legal constraints regarding what data you are allowed to collect, as regulations and rules vary depending on the jurisdiction in which your organization is located.) Many of these recommendations, on which I will elaborate more later in chapter 7, even promote the exercise of transparency, that is, making such data and analyses publicly available in easy-to-understand formats to show how much progress organizations are making toward equity and fairness.[56]

Individuals may additionally be rightly reluctant to provide demographic data if they have experienced bias and discrimination in the workplace in the past. However, as an organization proves over time that it is serious about correcting imbalances, addressing barriers, and giving opportunities for all, individuals may feel more comfortable about sharing such information. Although it is difficult to find a comprehensive list of companies where employees feel comfortable sharing their demographic information, some companies have publicly shared their efforts to promote DEI. They may have initiatives in place to encourage employees to disclose information.[57]

Such data can also help address concerns about "reverse discrimination," where members of a dominant group might feel they are being unfairly treated in favor of historically disadvantaged groups. This is one common reason for backlashes against diversity practices: the argument that many such practices unfairly favor disadvantaged groups. The approach I am proposing here can indeed help identify situations where this could be the case and, consequently, help organizations intervene to resolve such problems. A truly meritocratic approach should help *everyone* have equal opportunity by eliminating biases and improving talent management processes. That approach requires ensuring that no groups of individuals get unfairly penalized in the pursuit of meritocracy.

In this respect, it is key to systematically collect and store data about important employment outcomes for applicants and employees (including transfers, promotions, demotions, and exits). I include some outcomes that you should consider tracking over time:

(1) *Recruiting outcomes.* These should include the number of applicants for any given position, their professional and personal background, and their relevant skills and experiences for the position.
(2) *Screening and selection outcomes.* These should include who advances in the selection process at the interview, offer, and offer acceptance stages.
(3) *Post-hiring outcomes.* These should include performance ratings, promotions, transfers, terminations, base pay, merit-based increases, bonuses, and benefits.

These are some of the most common outcomes to track. However, it is up to you and your team of professionals to identify the employment outcomes that can affect the careers of your applicants and employees. This is a critical part of this second step because it will later allow you to critically examine the extent to which your organization is meritocratic and fair in making employment decisions.

Measuring employment-related outcomes is as important as measuring and collecting information about the inputs and the processes behind the attainment of such outcomes. For instance, it is critical to measure inputs about job seekers and employees at the time of hiring and beyond to learn about their relevant skills and abilities. This task can be typically accomplished by capturing and coding information from résumés and other employment-relevant application materials. In the case of employees, such data can be complemented with training and experience within the organization that enhances their contributions. All of this information is relevant for step 3, which involves analyzing the data to identify any disparities—and, if so, the reasons behind the disparities—so that you can find the best solutions to any challenges uncovered.

It is worth noting that an interesting tension has started to emerge even in societies and institutions where it has long been legally recommended not to collect demographic data or sensitive personal data about employees. For example, in the United States, while conventional legal wisdom traditionally advised against collecting detailed demographic data about employees, significantly beyond race and gender, DEI executives and socially driven leaders proactively sought to gather such data to better understand the impact of their DEI initiatives. Indeed, some have recommended strategies to both effectively and legally collect and use demographic data for DEI purposes.[58] In many of those cases, the recommendation for collecting such sensitive data has consisted of carefully implementing surveys of employees on less sensitive topics first. These early surveys can improve employees' confidence that such information will not be used against them and that it will be used to improve the workplace.

Furthermore, while collecting this information can assist companies in identifying areas for improvement and monitoring progress over time, it is imperative to do so in a way that respects employees' privacy and ensures that the information is used responsibly and ethically. (Once again, also review the current legal constraints regarding what data you are allowed to collect given your organization's location.)

Such collection efforts also need to be prefaced by informing employees and being transparent about why the data are being collected and how the data will be used and reported. Finally, data collection processes, analyses, and results need to reinforce that privacy will always be protected.[59]

Step 3. Analyze Your Collected Data Not Only on
Outcomes but Also on Processes

Once you have collected the information over time in a database, you can start preparing that data for analysis. First, you can explore aggregate patterns in each of the measured employment outcomes by variables of interest. For example, I have seen companies calculate the percentage of applicants who get an interview by gender and race and detect significant variations. In the case of base salary, a simple approach consists of computing the average base salary by gender and then testing whether any observed base salary differences are statistically significant.

If the sample size allows, you can then estimate multivariable models that control for other important individual factors that can explain or affect a particular outcome of interest. For example, you may want to estimate a model predicting the likelihood of getting an interview based on the gender and race of the applicant after controlling for the relevant skills and experiences needed for the job, that is, "merits." If the demographic coefficients for those models remain significant or are large in magnitude after controlling for relevant employment factors, this result may indicate some evidence of bias. It is important that the control factors relevant for the job are reliable in that they help you hire well-suited employees for the position. For larger organizations that are processing significant volumes of applications, you can incorporate additional variables relating to who the interviewers or recruiters are and when and how candidates were identified. You will be surprised to find that such factors often explain a lot of the variation in who ultimately gets an interview or job offer.

This multivariate modeling strategy ultimately allows you to compare individuals with the same control variables. For instance, to analyze who gets a merit-based bonus or a promotion, you may want to compare employees with the same jobs, performing at equivalent levels, and account for all other factors that could influence the reward or promotion outcome. This is why steps 1 and 2 are essential, as they can help you consider, evaluate, and collect data to estimate such models.

As an example, a commonly cited statistic is the gender pay gap. According to a 2024 Payscale analysis of salaries of over 627,000 individuals in the United States, women earned 83 cents for every one dollar earned by men when comparing median salaries.[60] That number was reported by Payscale as the measurement of the "uncontrolled gender pay gap" because such a statistic does not control for different types of jobs or qualifications. Their reported "controlled gender pay gap" statistic reflects that such a gap is estimated to be much lower, with women earning 99 cents for every dollar a man earns when controlling for such factors. The key here is to determine which variables you need to incorporate in your analyses (i.e., to control for) to compute the demographic gap in your organization accurately. Those variables can be job title, education and professional requirements, skills, and geography, among many others. Then you can decide whether the factors you consider essential indeed determine salary and whether, on top of such factors, demographics still play a role.

While it is important to measure work-related decisions that affect managers and employees over time, I also see enormous value in measuring beliefs, experiences, and reactions concerning your existing management practices and your work environment and culture, especially relating to opportunity, fairness, diversity, and inclusion. These can easily be measured by conducting good engagement and work surveys over time, often (and wisely) carried out anonymously. You can pay attention to external platforms that are already collecting such data, albeit not always systematically (e.g., Glassdoor and information that self-selected participants provide about their experiences at companies for which they worked or for which they interviewed). Ideally, you want to collect such data from many respondents to make your sample representative of what happens in your organization and to minimize the well-known problems associated with selection bias; that is, those who are extremely happy or dissatisfied are more likely to respond to workplace surveys.

Another equally important part of this analysis is to investigate and check every single people-related process and practice in your organization. At first, you may not have enough data or information on relevant variables, but the more you do this investigation strategically, the more you will go back to steps 1 and 2 to become better at this analytical approach. Critically, these checks must take place with some regularity because processes that used to work in the past but have not been properly updated can often get distorted or become less effective over time. Like your car, your talent management system is constantly being affected by external forces, and parts of it periodically break down under those pressures. In this regard, every single decision point could potentially let biases and social processes introduce unintended and undesirable consequences that hinder your organization's progress toward becoming meritocratic, fair, and excellent.

Once again, it is important to regularly focus on the main people-related processes, as illustrated in figure 2.3:

(1) Processes used to *find and recruit diverse, talented applicants* (for example, which recruitment sources you use to attract job seekers; what kind of messages and information about your company and your jobs could influence who applies and who does not apply; what activities and processes are being used by your recruiters and hiring managers).

(2) Processes and criteria used to *select candidates for the next steps in your selection process* (for example, who gets their application reviewed, who gets interviewed, who receives an offer, and who ultimately accepts the offer and becomes a prospective hire). Here, pay close attention to each step a successful candidate follows and the extent to which all candidates alike have equal opportunity to advance to the next stage. If certain groups of candidates are not progressing, investigate which factors drive the selection process and the extent to which such factors are employment-relevant, valid, reliable, and useful.

(3) Processes aiming to maximize the number of offers accepted by applicants, typically by *improving recruitment and onboarding activities*. Many businesses ignore this part of the selection process, even though their challenge may be convincing potential employees to join the organization. When particular groups of candidates decide not to join the organization, even when given a good offer and hiring package, for example, the organization should consider the extent to which it is an appealing employer for everyone.

(4) *Onboarding efforts and other training opportunities*. These should be designed to ensure that every employee can succeed from the outset.

(5) Processes behind *measuring and evaluating performance*. These should clearly define and establish expected performance standards and targets that are achievable and relevant to the position.

(6) Performance measurement processes used for *training and developmental purposes*, especially to develop those who "underperform." These should also be clear, consistent, and relevant for the success of the job and the organization.

(7) Processes used to *reward those who meet or exceed standards*.

(8) Processes used when deciding *advancement and other employee career outcomes* (including promotions, transfers, and terminations).

When analyzing such processes, I recommend examining not only how such employment decisions are being made but also who is ultimately responsible for them and how others (including managers and employees) may respond to them. You should also carefully examine these organizational processes with the data you collect to see if they are working as intended.

Step 4. Decide Which Intervention to Employ

By monitoring people-related decisions and outcomes, organizations can learn how much they may be deviating from meritocracy and act on the basis of their findings. For instance, in one large global company I worked with, we analyzed all promotions and merit-based increases made over a decade, assisted by a team of data scientists who put in place a system to collect, clean, and prepare data for analysis. We soon identified demographic patterns in both the promotion and the merit-based pay decisions. We first calculated promotion rates and average salary increases every year and then computed those numbers by gender, race, religion, sexual orientation, and nationality to check for significant differences. We found a large difference between male and female employees in that women were not getting the same merit-based bonuses as men.

Upon further investigation of this finding, we found that the problem probably stemmed from differing asking rates. Men were more likely to ask for and ensure that they received their merit-based bonus, while women tended to trust that the bonus was already included in their paychecks. To solve this problem, one HR professional was asked to monitor and confirm that all employees would get the bonus automatically once the level of performance required for such a bonus was met, thus eliminating the need to ask for it. After this simple intervention, gender differences in merit-based bonuses disappeared.[61]

When assisting organizations in evaluating their meritocracies, I often encounter leaders who wish they had gathered better data to analyze trends and patterns so they could have a deeper understanding and diagnosis of the observed outcomes. This step-by-step framework becomes dynamic and interactive, as discovery allows you to go back to steps 1 and 2 to reassess and gather additional information to help better address your challenges.

Step 5. Stay Continually Alert and Monitor Results Regularly

Finally, you should implement processes that alert you to potential future challenges that could affect the successful implementation of meritocratic people management processes in your organization. Accordingly, regularly reassess and reevaluate each of the prior steps. Because success criteria may change over time, and because technology, practices, and labor markets are highly dynamic, step 1 continues to be relevant in that it allows you to reassess and validate additional skills, abilities, merits, or talents that are necessary for hiring and later for promotions, as well as for rewarding your top performers fairly.

The more you learn about your decision-making processes and outcomes, the more you will want to improve the collection and analysis of your data. That is the virtuous circle from which meritocratic organizations can benefit when they thoughtfully and strategically manage and evaluate their talent management processes. Steps 2 and 3 allow you to continue improving your data collection processes. As a result, when you decide which solutions to maintain or introduce in step 4, you will be better informed and likely more successful. The more often you follow these steps, the more dynamic and successful you become at systematically evaluating current people-related practices and designing and implementing effective interventions for your organization.

MOVING YOUR ORGANIZATION FORWARD

The comprehensive, forward-looking talent analytics framework I have presented can help organizations identify *where* challenges can arise and *how* to intervene to address them. Many organizations I have worked with have found effective solutions, often small and easy to implement. These "quick wins" have been instrumental in building momentum, fostering enthusiasm for monitoring issues, and tackling biases and barriers.

This framework also enhances meritocracy and overall talent management effectiveness by enabling a more strategic allocation of limited resources. If following steps 1 through 5 allows your organization to advance and reward individuals based on their employment-relevant qualifications and skills while promoting equal opportunity for all, kudos to you! However, staying vigilant and consistently applying the five-step framework is key to sustaining progress moving forward.

If biases and social distortions persist in your talent management processes, it is time to take action. Identifying specific problem areas and deviations from meritocracy is the first step. From there, (re)allocating resources to debias and improve talent management becomes easier and more manageable. This can be achieved by establishing clear processes and criteria for hiring and evaluating employees, monitoring the outcomes of these processes, and assigning someone in the organization to guarantee fairness and effectiveness. Many scholars and practitioners have successfully guided organizations and businesses through these changes, proving that meaningful improvements in talent management systems are both attainable and impactful.

Unfortunately, many leaders are not collecting employment-relevant data on their talent management practices and outcomes, making it difficult to assess whether their organizations may face challenges or issues, as multiple conversations over the past two decades have proven. In many countries, corporate lawyers advise against collecting and analyzing such data, likely to avoid litigation and legal complications. (Be aware that in some places, collecting particular types of employee data may be illegal and/or unethical and problematic.) And for many organizations, adopting "best practices" is an easier, less costly way to appear as though they are doing "the right thing." This remains true even when those so-called best practices do not work.

That said, achieving anything close to the ideal of meritocracy requires systematic investigation of the existing talent management practices, and a data-driven analytical approach like the one I describe here. True meritocracy will not be attained through corporate window dressing. Simply having organizational processes or issuing broad statements from the corporate leadership that appear, on the surface, to promote meritocracy and fairness should not lull executives and key organizational decision-makers into assuming that their companies are truly fair and are giving equal opportunity to everybody.

AN ILLUSTRATION: LOCATING PAY DISPARITIES IN YOUR ORGANIZATION

Many leaders of organizations worldwide are interested in restoring meritocracy and promoting equal opportunity in their workplaces. To accomplish this, one corporation that I briefly worked with had its HR department collect data that could be easily coded from individuals' résumés when they apply for a job, such as years of education, skills, abilities, work experience, and other professional accomplishments. It also collected data on each worker's annual performance ratings, pay, rewards, and benefits during their tenure in the company. These data collection efforts were aimed at allowing senior management not only to better understand and value their talent but also to ensure that their processes and outcomes operate in a meritocratic way.

Once data like these are properly collected and coded for analysis, you could start conducting a rough estimate of your organization's deviation from meritocracy by estimating some basic statistics. For example, you could compute the average pay bonus for each level of employee by performance and by gender, race, and nationality. Say you are interested in whether there is any deviation from meritocracy in how performance-based rewards are calculated for each specific job title. In the case of gender, for example, you could compute the average bonus for women (w) and the average bonus for men (m) with a given job title and a given level of performance (if the data collected only have two gender categories). Then, a simple measure computed as $[(w/m) - 1)] \times 100$ will give you an estimate of how far from gender equality in merit-based pay your organization is for that particular job. A negative number shows how much lower women's bonuses are, on average, than men's. The closer your number is to zero, the closer you are to gender equality in bonus pay.

You can compute similar measures for other career outcomes as well as other personal characteristics or circumstances. For example, you can compare the percentage of White hires and promotions to non-White hires and promotions using the same basic formula. Of course, you could also compute additional statistics, such as a simple t-test or ANOVA test, to further identify whether there are notable differences in bonus pay by gender, race, or nationality in your company. (The smaller your organization is, the easier it will be to compute these numbers and consequently be aware of any gaps.)

As a crucial second step, you should conduct a more detailed analysis of the pay gap in your company, especially if you can use data collected over time to find the main predictors of work outcomes. I suggest running a multivariate regression model (for example, a basic ordinary least squares model) predicting pay bonus as a function of relevant employee, job, and work unit variables such as job title, education, work experience, tenure in the job, and number of worked hours, while including demographic variables in the equation. This model should also include performance evaluation scores, particularly if those should be the primary predictors of bonus pay in your organization.

Suppose your company bases bonuses entirely on performance. In that case, your analyses should reveal that equally performing workers will be rewarded the same bonus amount regardless of their demographics once you control for job title, tenure, work unit, manager, and other human capital factors you consider relevant for the position. In other words, the demographic variables included in your model should not have any significant impact on the size of the bonus—that is, the estimated demographic effect should not be statistically different from zero. The same multivariate analyses could be performed when predicting the chances of getting hired or promoted (in those cases, logit and probit regression models would be more appropriate). Part of your analysis should also explore whether any demographic differences in the levels of performance are observed by role or job. If that is the case, it presents an opportunity for you to identify and develop particular groups of workers to continue improving their performance in the future.

In the example of ServiCo described earlier in this book, I followed a similar approach.[62] After analyzing this company's career history data for almost nine thousand employees, I found a significant demographic gap in the size of merit bonuses. Women, Blacks, Hispanics, and non-US-born workers were awarded smaller bonus amounts than US-born White men with identical performance scores and human capital, doing the same job in the same work unit, and with the same manager.[63]

After analyzing your company data, you may find yourself in a similar situation, finding demographic gaps for a particular employee career outcome over time. This finding may indicate that your company is deviating from merit-driven processes and outcomes. In the next chapter, I will provide more solutions to address your company's deviation from meritocracy—mainly, how to debias and improve the operation of talent management processes like the performance-reward one I discussed here.

ARE YOU READY TO BUILD A MERITOCRATIC ORGANIZATION?

For years, many scholars, practitioners, and consultants have proposed various "best practices" and initiatives aimed at making businesses more efficient, equitable, and diverse. However, because many of these professionals often do not deeply examine the organizations and their people management processes, their proposed solutions may fail to deliver the intended results. Some never follow up to assess the impact of their recommendations, and in some cases, their interventions target problems that the organization does not actually have.

Well-intended initiatives often respond to prevailing beliefs, trends, or widely circulated ideas on how to best achieve equity and fairness—until new research proves that they do not work. Some advocate for "equitable and inclusive organizations," others talk about "people analytics" or "equity analytics," and many recite that organizations need to "remove systemic biases." Yet, my review of the literature suggests that many talent-driven initiatives, including those labeled as diversity or equity ones, have not effectively provided equal opportunity for all.

Some solutions may even backfire. The paradox of meritocracy, for instance, tells us that organizations that stress that they are meritocratic are often less so in practice. This underscores the need to be cautious about what management believes and to rely on data-driven insights (that is, what the data tell us). I have also cautioned against the potential biases and social forces that can undermine the meritocratic operation of talent management systems inside organizations.

This is where the described five-step talent analytics framework comes in. It is designed to help you assess the extent to which your organization is successful at removing unnecessary biases and social influences from your people-related procedures while reinforcing a structure of opportunity for all. Rather than prescribing any particular "best practice," my proposed talent analytics framework encourages leaders and professionals to be intentional and strategic in finding targeted solutions for improving and debiasing their talent management processes effectively. The five steps provide a structured roadmap for building a meritocratic organization—one that relies on systematic data collection and analysis tailored to its unique challenges, opportunities, and needs over time.

The useful analogy I have used in this chapter is to think of people management systems in a meritocratic organization as a car. Just as all kinds of forces act on a vehicle over time, biases and social processes continuously work on talent management systems. To ensure smooth operation, you need to regularly monitor, periodically adjust, repair, or replace parts of the system accordingly. So, instead of introducing generic "best practices" or imitating your neighbors' steps, think of developing a talent analytics approach that is customized to help your business achieve true meritocracy. Like an effective and state-of-the-art car dashboard, a successful analytics approach will help you focus on monitoring and diagnosing specific problems affecting the operation of your own talent management system—by leveraging your carefully collected employment-relevant data over time.

This data-driven talent analytics approach should also be complemented (even augmented!) with a cultural approach that reinforces clear criteria for success and actively identifies barriers to meritocracy. In this regard, organizations can greatly benefit from systematically collecting data not only from their employees but also from their applicants. Understanding their beliefs, expectations, and experiences regarding key aspects of talent management—such as (1) the organization's people-based processes, particularly those relating to advancing and rewarding talent, (2) the outcomes of these processes, and (3) the organization's values and norms related to work, fairness, diversity, inclusion, belonging, and opportunity—can uncover areas for improvement. Engagement surveys, for example, offer a simple way to gather such attitudinal insights and identify opportunities to enhance fairness and effectiveness.

Since neither organizational structures nor cultures are ever perfect, leadership plays a crucial role in fostering meritocracy over time. Leaders and key decision-makers are responsible and should take responsibility for ensuring that both structural and cultural aspects of their organization evolve in the right meritocratic direction. This brings us to two essential mechanisms for achieving meritocracy in the workplace: what I call organizational accountability and organizational transparency—two mechanisms I will explore in the next chapter.

Chapter Seven

DEBIASING TALENT MANAGEMENT PROCESSES IN THE WORKPLACE

In his 2021 book, *The Aristocracy of Talent: How Meritocracy Made the Modern World*, Adrian Wooldridge challenged contemporary critiques of meritocracy. By tracking its history and identifying when it "became corrupted," Wooldridge called for renewing rather than abandoning meritocracy. In a similar vein, I advocate for restoring and improving organizational meritocracies—ensuring that talent management systems are truly fair and meritocratic. This recommendation is rooted in a key insight from my research: while you cannot "debias" people or eliminate social barriers easily, debiasing and improving organizational processes and outcomes are achievable. The first step is identifying where biases and social issues may exist, followed by implementing targeted improvements to ameliorate their effects.

In the previous chapter, I outlined research-based strategic steps to uncover biases, social processes, and other inefficiencies that may be hindering your organization—not only in reducing bias and promoting equal opportunity but also in maintaining competitiveness and success. These steps provide practical strategies for senior leaders at the top of organizations as well as managers at all levels, human resource professionals, and employees eager to make their workplaces fairer and more meritocratic.

Building on that foundation, in this chapter, I further emphasize that fostering a truly meritocratic organization requires organizational leaders and key stakeholders to commit to locating and addressing potential flaws in their talent management systems. Rather than taking fragmented, tactical approaches to address equity issues—often implemented inconsistently as a mere "check-the-box" exercise—organizational leaders and key stakeholders need to engage in deliberate, serious, and comprehensive efforts to fully implement meritocratic processes. This involves reinforcing two essential mechanisms inside their organizational structures governing the management of their workforce: *organizational accountability* and *organizational transparency*.

Organizational accountability requires leaders to designate and empower key members of the organization to ensure that biases and social processes do not lead to unfair treatment of certain individuals or groups in the workplace. These designated stakeholders are unequivocally responsible for upholding the two critical conditions of meritocracy in practice: first, ensuring that all individuals have equal opportunities, and second, maintaining fair processes for deciding who advances and who obtains socially and economically desirable resources in the organization. Recognizing and rewarding individuals who take ownership of these responsibilities reinforces accountability across the organization.

But organizational accountability alone is not enough; it needs to be paired with organizational transparency. Leaders, particularly those in charge of improving talent management systems, should clearly define and communicate the criteria used to advance and reward individuals within the organization. Additionally, they should gather and analyze data on the various processes that make up the organization's talent management system—recruitment, hiring, evaluation, training, promotion, and retention—to identify where biases and inefficiencies may emerge and how to address them. Organizational transparency allows organizations to diagnose challenges, devise targeted improvements, and track progress toward achieving a true meritocracy in practice.

Simply put, fostering meritocracy requires establishing clear criteria and processes for employee advancement and evaluation (or any employee career decision), closely monitoring both procedures and outcomes, and assigning responsibility to someone in the organization to ensure that these formal processes remain fair and effective. Implementing these changes is, in my experience, often challenging, as they demand high-level buy-in and sustained commitment. Yet, they are essential for the successful renewal of the meritocratic project. Discussing these critical innovations in depth is the purpose of this chapter, offering a roadmap for organizations striving to uphold true meritocratic principles.

WHY ORGANIZATIONAL ACCOUNTABILITY IS IMPORTANT

Organizational accountability has been defined in various ways across disciplines.[1] In political science, it is viewed as a mechanism for fostering good governance and avoiding corruption and other dysfunctions at the government level.[2] In the social psychology literature, accountability refers to being answerable to others by adhering to specific standards and fulfilling responsibilities and expectations.[3]

In the case of talent management, I see *organizational accountability* as the first crucial mechanism for organizations to achieve meritocracy in practice. This requires appointing at least one individual within the organization with the power, authority, and necessary resources to ensure that people management processes are in place to (1) guarantee equal opportunity for all candidates, employees, and managers to succeed professionally (condition 1 of a true meritocracy), and (2) facilitate the fair distribution of advancement, rewards, and other professional opportunities based on clear, valid, and merit-based criteria (condition 2).

Philip Tetlock defined accountability as the pressure to justify one's actions to third parties, describing it as "the implicit or explicit expectation that one be called on to justify one's beliefs, feelings, and actions to others."[4] This definition implicitly emphasizes that accountability impacts how individuals make decisions.[5] Tetlock proposed that decision-makers who feel accountable are motivated to process information and make decisions in analytical and careful ways, using complex cognitive strategies and basing their opinions on data—particularly when they are unaware of their audience's views (i.e., individuals to whom they are accountable).[6]

This narrow definition of accountability has been extensively investigated in experimental research.[7] In these studies, accountability is often manipulated by informing participants that their decisions will be evaluated or discussed by another party.[8] In some experiment variations, participants are informed that they will have to defend their decisions to someone.[9]

Scholars have also explored how organizational practices can influence the level of accountability that individuals feel for the fairness of their decisions in the workplace. For instance, Tetlock and Gregory Mitchell have highlighted some organizational procedures that are designed to hold managers accountable for implementing fair pay and bonus practices.[10]

These procedures typically combine *process accountability* (ensuring that managers make equitable pay decisions) with *outcome accountability* (monitoring for potential adverse impact in all aspects of pay decision-making).[11]

In the broader organizational and management literature, the concept of accountability is rooted in the work of sociologists like Max Weber and Arthur Stinchcombe on bureaucratic structures.[12] The central argument in this stream of scholarship is that accountability holds recruiters and managers responsible for following specific organizational procedures and applying relevant employment criteria. This alignment of managers' preferences and incentives with those of their organizations can help eliminate demographic biases and other inefficiencies when making employment decisions.

In the context of diversity management, organizational accountability often involves creating specialized positions and implementing company procedures that hold specific individuals responsible for achieving established diversity, equity, and inclusion (DEI) goals.[13] This approach is consistent with research suggesting that when accountability for these goals is not assigned to specific individuals, they are likely overlooked when business pressures arise.[14]

Despite calls from scholars and practitioners to encourage top management to promote equity within their organizations, a 2021 national study of workplace equity revealed that few organizations conduct equity audits or designate someone to monitor the fairness of their workplaces.[15] The research team at the Boston College's Center for Social Innovation collected information from 1,062 US workplaces to identify where inequities might exist across various organizational "employment systems."[16] The researchers defined employment systems as a set of formal or informal practices related to employment within organizations, encompassing areas such as job structures (that is, expectations for where, when, and how much an employee should work), recruitment and hiring, pay and benefits, orientation and onboarding, supervision and mentoring, training and development, performance assessment, employee resources and support, promotion, and separation.

The methodological approach behind this research study is similar to the approach I outlined in chapter 6, as applied at the organizational level: that is, by collecting information on these organizational processes (in this case, perceptions of inequities across ten employment systems), leaders can identify specific problems and develop targeted solutions to tackle them successfully. The researchers found that perceptions of accountability were strongest in areas like pay, benefits, and performance assessment, but weakest in job structures, supervision and mentoring, employee resources and support, and training and development. These findings are significant because employees highly value fairness: 88 percent of US workers "believe fairness is extremely important or very important in the workplace."[17] Despite this belief, a 2021 survey of 3,500 workers revealed that 82 percent felt their working environments lacked fairness.[18]

WHY ORGANIZATIONAL TRANSPARENCY ALSO MATTERS

In order for organizations to be accountable, measures of progress must be visible, with transparency in how critical processes and outcomes evolve over time. Organizational transparency is thus the second mechanism crucial for achieving meritocracy in practice.

In the context of talent management, I define *organizational transparency* as the degree to which organizations and their leaders openly disclose and provide clear information about their talent management processes, criteria, and outcomes to at least those responsible for the effective functioning of the talent management system (and, in some cases, to other key stakeholders of the organizations). Like in the cases of organizational accountability, the goal of such organizational transparency is to guarantee (1) equal opportunity for all employees, and (2) a fair distribution of advancement, rewards, and other career opportunities based on clear, valid, and merit-based criteria. In practice, organizational transparency involves clearly communicating how people-related decisions—such as recruitment, hiring, distribution of rewards, and promotions—are made, the specific merit-based criteria used, and the resulting outcomes of those decisions.

While scholars have extensively studied accountability within organizations, the role of transparency has been less researched until recently.[19] Political scientists have claimed that certain aspects of organizational accountability are closely tied to transparency.[20] Defined as access to information,[21] transparency is claimed to reduce corruption and help address various national and organizational challenges.[22] In the management and organizational literature, transparency—often referred to as observability— has been suggested to influence organizational outcomes, including firm performance.[23]

In the 2010s, the media began paying attention to pay transparency, highlighting concerns that pay secrecy may contribute to demographic-based pay disparities.[24] A common argument is that making compensation data transparent can expose existing biases against specific demographic groups, enabling organizations to address these disparities.[25] In this line, scholars have claimed that pay transparency helps reduce pay inequality related to gender[26] and race.[27] It also seems to provide benefits for organizations by promoting organizational citizenship behaviors and increasing organizational commitment and support.[28] The most common definition of pay transparency in the literature is the extent to which organizations disclose their processes for determining and managing employee pay.[29]

Since the mid-2020s, a global pay transparency movement has gained significant momentum, encouraging organizations and businesses to disclose employee salaries, with the belief that doing so could help achieve pay equity. In line with this trend, for instance, California's Pay Transparency Act mandates that employers with at least fifteen employees share their pay scales in job postings. Pay transparency laws are spreading across the United States and other countries. Some view pay transparency as one of the most prevalent and rapidly growing trends in the field of human resources.[30]

Researchers have been interested in investigating how pay secrecy versus pay transparency policies influence how managers allocate compensation.[31] Pay secrecy, for example, may allow decision-makers to use arbitrary criteria, including demographic characteristics, when determining pay because their pay-related decisions are less likely to be scrutinized by others.[32] In addition, the lack of transparency often means that managers are less accountable because they are not expected to justify how rewards are determined.

Research in social psychology further suggests that pay transparency can help reduce compensation differences linked to non-performance-related factors. For instance, experimental studies have found that individuals are less likely to perceive gender or race discrimination on a personal level than on an organizational level.[33] A classic study by Faye Crosby and colleagues suggested that this difference is partly due to information-processing bias[34]— it is harder to detect discrimination when evaluating individual cases than when looking at aggregate data.[35]

Workplace inequality scholars have long argued that transparency in the criteria and processes behind pay and career decisions is key to addressing demographic disparities.[36] In my research, I have proposed that combining organizational pay transparency with accountability can effectively close gender and racial pay gaps.[37]

My central argument is that organizational transparency around pay can bring disparities to light, making it easier for management to address them. My findings supported this argument by showing that more visible career outcomes—such as receiving a merit-based bonus or a promotion—were less affected by gender and race disparities than less visible ones in one organization setting I worked with.[38] In particular, I found that equally performing women, Blacks, Hispanics, and non-US-born employees obtained smaller merit-based bonuses than White men; because the size of these bonuses is typically unknown to other employees, these managerial decisions remain less visible. The lack of publicly available bonus data hinders direct pay comparisons among workers, thereby obscuring any potential unfairness in linking performance to pay.[39]

These findings help explain why many have long championed pay transparency as a strategy to combat workplace inequality. Gowri Ramachandran reviewed some empirical studies suggesting that greater pay transparency can help reduce demographic biases.[40] She noted that environments with higher levels of pay transparency (such as state government and unionized workplaces) tend to exhibit smaller wage disparities based on gender and race than nonunionized private companies.[41] Another example is pay-for-performance plans: consistent with Ramachandran's argument, one study reported that piecework, a form of pay for performance, was associated with smaller unexplained gender pay gaps.[42]

Along these lines, many advocate for companies to ensure salary range transparency to ameliorate demographic wage gaps. Indeed, pay transparency has gained popularity as more organizations and businesses seek to ensure fair and equitable compensation. Several tools provide some pay data across various roles and industries, including LinkedIn's Salary Tool, Buffer's Salaries and Salary Calculator, Glassdoor, Payscale, and Elpha's Salary Database.

Many have viewed pay transparency as a step toward pay equity; the idea is that by being open about the compensation range provided to current and prospective employees, companies can avoid biases and other social processes that creep into pay decisions and create unfair pay differences.[43] In line with this argument, an increasing number of US states now require publishing pay ranges to help reduce gender and racial wage gaps.[44]

Some governments, mostly in developed economies, have also acknowledged and addressed the issue of pay secrecy by creating pay transparency measures. A notable step was the European Union's (EU) 2014 recommendation urging member states to adopt various pay transparency measures. Similar initiatives have also been implemented in Canada and Australia.[45] The EU measures focus on employees' right to request information on pay levels and require companies to report on the gender pay gap in their workforces. Some studies have documented that many pay transparency laws have been effective in narrowing the gender pay gap in countries where they have been enacted.[46]

Pay transparency advocates argue that such tools can help close the gender and racial wage gaps.[47] Research, mainly in the North American context, has shown that salary secrecy disproportionally disfavors women and racially disadvantaged groups, who are less likely than equally qualified White men to negotiate higher starting salaries or raises.[48] It is unclear if these findings are universal, particularly to what extent the same results would be found in other regions of the world.[49] That said, after analyzing 1.6 million survey responses on pay collected from 2017 to 2019, Payscale claimed that the perception of any gender pay gap diminishes the more the respondents believe their organization has a transparent pay process.[50]

These research findings, while exclusively on the topic of *pay* transparency, underscore the importance of organizational transparency to achieving meritocracy in practice. Insofar as such organizational transparency allows leaders to obtain and analyze clear information about their key talent management processes, criteria, and outcomes, they will be in a better strategic position to identify and tackle their meritocratic challenges.

THREE KEY DIMENSIONS WHEN IMPLEMENTING TRANSPARENCY AND ACCOUNTABILITY IN ORGANIZATIONS

Leaders play a pivotal role in building successful and meritocratic talent management systems. To do so, they need to focus on introducing organizational accountability and transparency at every critical stage in the career progression of applicants and their hires—especially selection, advancement, and compensation and rewards.

To define and illustrate the main dimensions behind these two crucial organizational mechanisms, consider a performance reward system involving merit-based bonuses.[51] In this specific context, I define organizational accountability as the various organizational procedures that make individuals responsible for guaranteeing fair allocation of pay, rewards, and work benefits. It can be achieved as follows. First, certain organizational leaders (*audience*) will be in charge of designing and operating the procedures for determining compensation and other employee benefits (*process* accountability). Second, certain leaders (*audience*) will oversee tracking and addressing any instances of unfair pay decisions (*outcome* accountability).

Similarly, in this context, I define organizational transparency as the various organizational procedures that provide helpful, relevant, and accurate pay information to individuals. Such information can be made available in various ways to suit different *audiences* within the organization, such as executives, managers, workers, and HR professionals. It should be collected and processed so that it is current and available before, during, and after the execution of pay policies. Like organizational accountability, transparency can be achieved in two ways. First, *process* transparency ensures that the criteria and steps for pay distribution are clearly communicated to individuals (or groups of individuals) within the company. Second, *outcome* transparency involves making it possible for individuals to compare pay and benefits across the organization.[52]

These three dimensions are central when designing and operating organizational accountability and transparency in any aspect of your talent management system: (1) *process*, (2) *outcomes*, and (3) *audience(s)*. Table 7.1 illustrates the forms these three dimensions can take in the context of a performance reward system. It also provides a working framework for implementing accountability and transparency in an organization, not only for pay and rewards but also for any other talent management process.

In the case of a performance reward system, the three dimensions should be applied with the following key considerations in mind:[53]

TABLE 7.1
Key dimensions of a performance-reward system

	Organizational accountability	Organizational transparency
Processes and criteria	Responsibility for which processes, routines, and criteria are fair (*process accountability*)	Which processes, routines, and criteria are visible (*how*)
Outcomes	Responsibility for which pay decisions and results/aspects are fair (*outcome accountability*)	Which pay decisions and results/aspects are visible (*what*)
Audience(s)	*Who* is accountable for pay processes and outcomes and *to whom*	*Who* makes pay processes and outcomes visible and *to whom*

Source: Adapted from Emilio J. Castilla, "Accounting for the Gap: A Firm Study Manipulating Organizational Accountability and Transparency in Pay Decisions," *Organization Science* 26, no. 2 (2015): 315.

Process: How will performance-based pay be determined? Companies need to decide who is responsible for outlining and setting up the criteria and processes used to evaluate employee performance and contributions to the company's success, how rewards are determined and distributed among employees, and how those criteria and processes are transparent across the organization. Some businesses, for instance, may choose to explain the calculation of merit-based bonuses to both managers and workers, or even involve them in the process, while others may limit this explanation to senior managers only.

Outcomes: What rewards are offered to employees? Companies need to determine who will collect and analyze relevant data, who will be accountable for guaranteeing that decisions are based on merit, and who will have access to the results of these analyses. At a minimum, the organization should designate someone responsible for calculating and reporting key metrics to decision-makers.

Audience(s): Who oversees and understands the pay processes, criteria, and outcomes? Companies need to identify those responsible for implementing changes to reduce biases and inefficiencies, as well as to enhance fairness. They should also decide the extent of transparency they want to maintain regarding these processes, criteria, and outcomes, both within the organization and externally.

The choices companies make regarding the three dimensions will define the levels of accountability and transparency in each aspect of their performance management systems. One company, for example, might designate a single director to oversee all aspects of pay processes, criteria, and outcomes, while another could involve multiple individuals.

When it comes to transparency, a company may opt to make the processes and criteria for distributing bonuses clear to employees and supervisors. Alternatively, it might choose to have senior managers make the final decisions about bonuses, leaving workers and supervisors in the dark about how performance evaluations translate into pay (high transparency for processes and criteria, but low transparency for outcomes). Note that the level of transparency you choose will significantly reflect the organization's leadership vision and strategy. In a more extreme case (common among businesses that champion pay for performance and full transparency), all employees, including senior management, supervisors, and even rank-and-file employees, would be informed about the processes, criteria, *and* outcomes of merit pay decisions. A slightly less transparent approach could allow workers to see average compensation data, including salary distribution by quartiles, for various roles within the organization.

While I have illustrated how organizational accountability and transparency can be applied to a performance reward system, this approach can easily be extended to other stages of hiring, promotion, training, and other people-management decisions. In fact, I encourage companies to improve accountability and transparency at each critical stage of their talent management system, as summarized in figure 2.3 in chapter 2. Strengthening accountability and transparency within your talent management system can help ensure that your organization meets the two key conditions for achieving true meritocracy.

HOLDING YOUR ORGANIZATION AND LEADERS ACCOUNTABLE FOR ACHIEVING MERITOCRACY

In the early 2020s, many middle-sized and large organizations appointed decision-makers with responsibility for reducing bias and improving equity, especially in hiring and pay decisions. The introduction of roles such as chief diversity officers (CDOs) and other diversity executives underscored leaders' commitment to making their organizations diverse, equitable, and inclusive.[54] In the United States alone, the number of roles focused on DEI at large organizations reportedly quadrupled,[55] with 53 percent of Fortune 500 companies reporting having a CDO or equivalent position by 2022.[56]

The growth of DEI in such organizations took place in response to scholars, journalists, and commentators highlighting that diversity matters,[57] that there is a strong business case to be made for it,[58] and that implementing diversity and inclusion efforts is a moral imperative.[59] The momentum for DEI further accelerated after the murder of George Floyd in May 2020, which brought attention to the pervasiveness of structural racism in US society and created intense pressure on companies to address racial inequities. However, in January 2024, the *New York Times* reported that while hiring for DEI roles did indeed spike in the early 2020s, DEI job postings on the employment website ZipRecruiter fell by 63 percent in 2023—and since the beginning of 2025, many major U.S. companies have also continued to cut back on DEI efforts.[60]

In higher education, following the US Supreme Court's June 29, 2023, decision to end the use of affirmative action in college admissions[61]—ruling that race-conscious admissions policies violate the Equal Protection Clause of the Fourteenth Amendment—college and university presidents, while complying with the ruling, have nonetheless stressed their continued commitment to diversity and inclusion.[62] The Court also ruled that colleges and universities *may* consider "an applicant's discussion of how race affected his or her life, be it through discrimination, inspiration, or otherwise."[63] Furthermore, the Supreme Court's ruling against affirmative action has inspired major corporate leaders (e.g., Microsoft, HP, Apple, and other Fortune 500 companies) to reaffirm their commitment to advocating for and sustaining equitable, inclusive, and diverse workplaces.[64] Others, however, have withdrawn support for DEI.[65]

A few experts have already outlined strategies for organizations and businesses to continue promoting DEI effectively[66] while avoiding "harmful overreactions that don't reflect real legal risks."[67] However, in recent years, some commentators have reported that such a commitment has become increasingly tenuous, with many businesses reevaluating—and in some cases, entirely abandoning—their DEI efforts. This shift is largely driven by budget constraints, fears of public backlash, concerns of employee alienation, pressure from conservative activists, and emerging government and regulatory challenges.[68] Interestingly, emerging conservative movements such as "Merit, Excellence and Intelligence," while emphasizing the selection of candidates based solely on qualifications and abilities, seem to overlook the critical need for equal opportunity for all to achieve true meritocracy in practice.[69]

Some organizations continue to incentivize decision-makers to achieve fair and meritocratic results, either as part of their selection and hiring, their performance evaluations, or their distribution of monetary rewards. A few organizations have also hired specific managers and directors who work with task forces or internal committees to regularly oversee and review some of the most critical talent management decision processes—typically pay and promotion or recruitment and hiring efforts. Such employer efforts seem to be appreciated by employees, particularly those belonging to underrepresented groups. In a 2023 survey of 3,255 US workers, approximately 33 percent of Blacks, 25 percent of Latinos, and 25 percent of Asian Americans reported experiencing poor treatment, discrimination, or unfairness in their current job due to their race or ethnicity.[70]

My research experience has shown that debiasing talent management processes and ensuring a true meritocracy in the workplace often require structural changes to enhance accountability and transparency inside organizations, not just hiring a few selected individuals. Moreover, those selected individuals put in charge of improving the effectiveness of talent management systems and making them more meritocratic must be empowered (that is, given authority, power, and support within the organization) and be given the necessary organizational resources to accomplish these goals.

Furthermore, the higher the number of stakeholders companies engage to see and evaluate the results of their talent management systems (*organizational transparency*), especially those concerning fairness and opportunity, as well as the more audiences they make responsible for creating and sustaining a fair and meritocratic workplace (*organizational accountability*), the more successful the organization is likely to be. My research experience has given me plenty of examples of why that may be the case.

To increase organizational transparency, you need to be very explicit about the criteria and processes you use to select, advance, and reward your employees and managers. Research suggests that we are less likely to make biased attributions when specific merit-based criteria and processes are used.[71] Such transparency thus makes talent management systems less vulnerable to biases and social processes that could introduce noise and unnecessary discretion into employment outcomes.

To improve organizational accountability, you need to ensure that at least one individual takes full responsibility for your people management processes and their outcomes. (Often, this responsibility is given to a group of individuals representing different parts of your organization.) Once again, research has shown that accountability encourages decision-makers to process information carefully, helping to prevent biases and other social processes that might otherwise lead to unfair decisions.[72] These individuals should also systematically monitor the outcomes of employment decisions to address any plausible challenges affecting employees and managers. Finally, they have to be empowered to fix the processes and propose interventions that can help your organization "debias" and help diversify your workplace.

This kind of organizational accountability and transparency can specifically help address the key warnings that can lead to the meritocracy paradox. Specifically, accountability and transparency can help in two main ways, as presented in the following numbered sub-sections.

1. Ensure that your talent management systems are fair and meritocratic

As described earlier in this book, *simply designing and implementing people management practices to recruit, select, and evaluate the best talent does not necessarily guarantee meritocracy in practice*—that is, such practices do not guarantee that individuals acting on behalf of their organizations will select and reward the best individuals effectively and fairly. Biases and other social mechanisms can enter many of your talent management processes relating to your organization's recruitment, hiring, pay, and development. Such biases and social processes can have significant consequences, not only for individuals themselves but also for your organization. The result can be a less diverse workforce, limiting access to talent and fresh perspectives and leading to lower job satisfaction, higher turnover rates, and, ultimately, lower productivity and profitability.

A second warning from this book is that *emphasizing meritocracy as the basis of an organization's people-related decisions may paradoxically backfire on women, racially disadvantaged groups, immigrants, and many other under-represented groups.* Belief in the objective of meritocracy can lead decision-makers to become less conscious of demographic biases and consequently to exhibit gender and racial biases or particular social preferences in their decisions.

Debiasing talent management processes involves identifying and addressing any biases and social preferences that prevent you from creating and sustaining a fair and meritocratic workplace.

SOLUTION: The kind of systematic analyses of data that I discussed in chapter 6 can help you assess whether (1) there is equal opportunity for all in your organization, especially during recruitment and hiring, and advancement, and (2) post-hire employment decisions are based on merit and talent, including decisions regarding the distribution of rewards and career outcomes such as promotions, distribution of authority, autonomy, and other work and personal benefits. In doing these analyses, make sure that some individuals or groups of individuals are responsible for evaluating the processes and outcomes behind each of your talent management processes by following the main steps described in chapter 6.

2. Ensure consensus on key employment-relevant merit-based criteria across different selection and career stages

A third key warning from this book is that *there is no consensus about what merit actually is; this may be even so among managers and executives with similar training who work in the same organization.* Organizations rarely acknowledge that the definitions of "merit" and "talent" are often subjective, that is, in the eye of the beholder. As I described in chapter 5, different individuals making important people-related decisions, such as recruitment, selection, evaluation, and promotions, may not necessarily operate with the same assumptions about what constitutes merit and which types of merit or talent should be rewarded and celebrated by the organization. This has become even more challenging as professionals and employees move across organizations, industries, locations, and roles, each with different views on the definition of talent or merit.

People's understanding of merit also evolves over the course of their careers. This understanding likely starts forming long before individuals enter the workforce, when, for instance, they are evaluated by teachers, sports coaches, professors, and others well before they start their professional lives.

SOLUTION: Here, I recommend an organizational process to clarify how your talent management processes will be designed to ensure that (1) there is equal opportunity for all, and that (2) post-hire employment decisions, such as decisions regarding compensation and advancement, are based on merit and talent.

To help managers arrive at a common definition of merit when recruiting and hiring, for example, I advise clearly defining the specific criteria and factors that are employment-relevant when screening candidates and ensuring later that those criteria are (1) valid and indeed relevant for the role and (2) predictive of performance and success in the organization. Use those criteria, too, when training managers on how to evaluate candidates during screening. Also, try to make sure that, to the greatest possible extent, such criteria do not adversely impact particular demographic groups. Clearly defining and consistently applying your screening process and criteria ensures equal opportunity and enhances fairness.

Additionally, make sure that (1) the criteria you use to screen candidates are good predictors of performance—if not, why use them?—and that (2) such criteria do not prevent particular groups of individuals from being considered or hired for your positions. Because biases and social processes evolve over time, they are often a "moving target." So, stay alert and keep practices in place to ensure that decisions remain fair and meritocratic.

In the case of recruitment and selection, for instance, I advise that organizations systematically examine and answer questions like the following:

- Which factors or criteria are used consistently when screening and selecting candidates? Are exceptions being made? If so, which exceptions?

- To what extent are merit-based factors predictive of selection and hiring outcomes? Do those factors predict performance and other critical post-hire outcomes relevant to your organization and its success?
- To what extent are non-merit-based variables (for example, personal connections or popularity) introduced during the selection and hiring process?
- How do recruitment and selection practices affect the quality and diversity of the pool of applicants, the applicants to whom the organization makes offers, and the applicants the organization ultimately hires?
- Where might you need to remedy and correct for potential biases in the processes and outcomes of recruitment and selection strategies?

In the case of rewarding and advancing employees, I advise following a similar strategy, addressing questions like the following:

- Which factors or criteria are used when distributing rewards or deciding whom to promote?
- To what extent do merit-based factors predict bonus distribution, promotion decisions, and other important career outcomes? Do those factors also predict performance and other critical post-hire outcomes?
- To what extent are non-merit-based variables introduced in the performance and reward process?
- How does the distribution of merit-based rewards, training opportunities, and promotions look across diverse pools of employees?
- Where may you need to intervene to correct for potential biases and non-performance-based factors in these decisions?

ENSURING MERITOCRACY AT A LARGE ORGANIZATION: A REAL-WORLD ILLUSTRATION

How can organizations and businesses guard their talent management systems against the operation of biases and social processes that undermine equity? And consequently, how can they ensure true meritocracy in practice? To answer these questions, I studied one feasible solution for narrowing the demographic gap in performance-based rewards at ServiCo. (Details of this study are provided in chapter 4.)

ServiCo faced two main problems. First, there was a lack of organizational *accountability*—unit heads (senior managers) were not held responsible for their pay decisions, particularly regarding merit pay increases. Second, there was limited *transparency* in the process and outcomes behind their performance reward strategy.

Before addressing the two organizational issues described here, I ran several regression models to examine which factors affected merit-based bonuses at ServiCo using its longitudinal data on employee career outcomes for nearly nine thousand employees. While my analyses showed no demographic gap in highly visible employment decisions such as promotions or terminations, I found significant gender, racial, and nationality (US versus non-US-born) disparities in the size of bonuses; these sizes are frequently less visible to many managers and employees.

The proposed solution was to introduce organizational accountability and transparency into the performance reward system with three key improvements. First, a performance reward committee was established to oversee merit-based bonus decisions. This committee, consisting of HR professionals, at least one executive, and a new full-time staff member responsible for collecting and analyzing employee data, was tasked with ensuring fairness in pay and merit bonus decisions. Second, senior managers were required to follow a formal process for assigning rewards based on employee performance, including justifying the amounts awarded to each employee in their work unit. Third, the performance reward committee was given authority to adjust any pay decisions made by senior managers.

While employees and supervisors were informed about the processes and criteria behind performance evaluations, the final distribution of bonus amounts was known only to senior managers and the committee. This committee, supported by a full-time professional, was responsible for systematically monitoring and analyzing how bonuses were allocated over time, ensuring that the company adhered to its meritocratic principles. A similar approach could easily be applied to other people-related processes.

Table 7.2 outlines the three main organizational accountability and transparency procedures that ServiCo adopted as a result of our collaboration. It also details who was responsible for what and when. Table 7.3 goes further, showing how organizational accountability (column 3) and transparency (column 4) have been applied at the company, division, and work unit levels of ServiCo since then. Each cell in columns 3 and 4 summarizes how transparency and accountability were implemented at ServiCo, focusing on

TABLE 7.2

Introducing organizational accountability and transparency in the performance-reward system at ServiCo

New stages in the performance-reward system	Location	Main decision-makers	New measures as part of the performance-reward process	Features of organizational approach
Stage 1	Company	CEO	Annually, CEO decides who will be on the annual performance-reward committee. Also decides total budget (in consultation with other executives in the organization, including HR director and vice president).	High accountability in the formation of the performance-reward committee each year.
Stage 2		Performance-reward committee	Includes at least two members of the HR Division, at least one senior executive of a different company division, and a full-time staff member in HR. This committee is in charge of monitoring merit-based pay decisions and writing reports about them.	Formalized with high organizational accountability and transparency.
Stage 3	Work unit	Senior managers (work unit heads)	First, all senior managers are required to fill out a merit-pay form the company developed to justify their rewards. Second, they are given information about merit-based pay decisions made in their work units and other units in the same division.	Formalized with high organizational accountability and transparency.

Source: Adapted from Emilio J. Castilla, "Accounting for the Gap: A Firm Study Manipulating Organizational Accountability and Transparency in Pay Decisions," *Organization Science*, 26, no. 2 (2015): 317.

processes/criteria and *outcomes* dimensions (refer to table 7.1). The first column of table 7.3 lists the relevant company levels, while the second column identifies the key individuals responsible for overseeing pay accountability and transparency at ServiCo (the *audience* dimension).

The results of improving organizational accountability and transparency were noteworthy. The company observed significant reductions in the demographic gaps in merit bonuses, with any remaining differences becoming practically negligible. Follow-up interviews with ServiCo executives and managers confirmed the effectiveness of these mechanisms in closing these gaps. A key factor was the performance reward committee's provision of detailed reports and analyses of the merit-based pay decisions to senior managers; this transparency increased their accountability. As one senior manager noted, "Annually, I am able to review numbers that have to do with how my pay decisions compare with the decisions made in the aggregate by other work units within my division."[73]

TABLE 7.3

Key dimensions of organizational accountability and transparency in the performance-reward system at ServiCo

	Audience(s)		Organizational accountability	Organizational transparency
	Level	Decision-makers		
Performance-reward processes and criteria	Company	Performance-reward committee	Responsible for ensuring that senior managers make merit-based pay decisions in equitable ways by ensuring that these managers follow the process (i.e., use the Merit-Based Bonus Form) and use criteria (only consider the performance of the employee) when making merit-based pay decisions.	Compiles information and writes reports about the processes and criteria behind the merit-based pay decisions made in each work unit of ServiCo. Also makes recommendations to high-level executives on how to improve merit-based pay processes and criteria.
	Division	Top executives and key HR managers	Review the information provided by the performance-reward committee each year about the processes and criteria used for the distribution of pay in equitable ways (in annual reports and meetings).	Know about the process and criteria used to reward employees based on their performance. Participate in designing these processes and criteria together with the performance-reward committee.
	Work unit	Senior managers (unit heads)	Responsible for making merit-based pay decisions concerning employees in their work units entirely based on the performance of the employees. Have to fill out the Merit-Based Bonus Form to justify the amount rewarded to each employee in their work units (because performance evaluations are the "primary basis" for all employee merit-based pay increases each year).	Know (and are trained on) how to follow the process and use the criteria when making merit-based pay decisions.
		Evaluating managers	Only responsible for evaluating the performance of the employees in their work units.	Know about the broad processes and criteria used by senior managers to make merit-based pay decisions. Do not get to see the Merit-Based Bonus Form filled out by the senior managers to whom they submit the performance evaluations of the employees in their work units.

(continued)

TABLE 7.3
(continued)

| | Audience(s) | | Organizational accountability | Organizational transparency |
	Level	Decision-makers		
Performance-reward outcomes	Company	Performance-reward committee	Responsible for monitoring that all merit-based pay decisions made by senior managers at ServiCo are equitable, that is, entirely based on the performance of the employee.	Compiles information and writes performance-pay outcome reports about all merit-based pay decisions made in all work units and divisions of ServiCo. Such information includes merit-based pay averages, standard deviations, and ranges (these data are reported in the aggregate broken down by level of employee performance at the work unit, division, and company level).
	Division	Top executives and key HR managers	Review the information provided by the performance-reward committee each year about the distribution of rewards by employee performance in their divisions (including work units) as well as other divisions (units) at ServiCo (in pay-for-performance outcome reports).	Have easy access to information about merit-based pay decisions made in their divisions (including work units) as well as other divisions at ServiCo. Information is provided by the performance-reward committee each year in pay-for-performance outcome reports.
	Work unit	Senior managers (unit heads)	Responsible for ensuring that any merit-based pay decisions made in their units are equitable, that is, entirely based on the performance of the employee.	Receive information (from HR, which gets the information from the performance-reward committee) about merit-based pay decisions made in their work units and other work units in the same division (these data are reported in the aggregate broken down by level of performance).
		Evaluating managers	Not responsible for distributing merit-based pay among employees.	Receive information (from their senior managers, who get the info from HR) about merit-based pay decisions made for each of their employees in their work units.

Source: Adapted from Emilio J. Castilla, "Accounting for the Gap: A Firm Study Manipulating Organizational Accountability and Transparency in Pay Decisions," *Organization Science* 26, no. 2 (2015): appendix.

TOWARD ORGANIZATIONAL TRANSPARENCY AND ACCOUNTABILITY

Building a talent management system that is both accountable and transparent does not require a complex or costly bureaucracy. In fact, it can often be achieved quite simply. Many companies I have worked with have successfully enhanced organizational accountability and transparency by applying the straightforward, cost-effective framework presented in this chapter. For instance, as discussed earlier, ServiCo's top management strengthened organizational accountability and transparency by assembling and empowering a dedicated committee with clear responsibilities for ensuring fairness in the distribution of performance-based rewards among employees. They further supported these efforts by hiring a full-time professional to collect and analyze data on employee performance and rewards.

Both organizational transparency and accountability are crucial mechanisms for fostering true meritocracy inside organizations. Accountability requires appointing at least one individual with the power and authority to ensure that people management processes guarantee (1) equal opportunity for all to succeed in the organization (condition 1 of a true meritocracy) and facilitate (2) a fair distribution of advancement, rewards, and other professional opportunities based on clear, valid, and merit-based criteria (condition 2). In the same vein, transparency involves openly disclosing and clarifying organizational processes, criteria, and decision-making outcomes, particularly to those entrusted with running the talent management system effectively.

Although implementing these organizational mechanisms can be challenging—requiring strong commitment and sustained efforts from top leadership—they are fundamental to making meritocracy close to a reality. By embedding organizational accountability and transparency in their talent management systems, organizations can move beyond mere aspirations and work actively toward a fairer, more effective, and meritocratic workplace.

CONCLUSION

I hope that the insights from this book will give you a strong foundation for improving your organization's talent management processes, making them fairer and more meritocratic. If your organization is midsized or large, you likely have many formalized processes in place to manage some critical aspects of your talent management, along with data on key employment outcomes. This information can serve as a valuable starting point for you to identify where you can improve your talent management processes. If your organization is smaller or if you do not have direct control over people management practices in your organization, this book can still help you recognize common failures in existing practices and offer actionable strategies for reducing bias and inefficiencies, ultimately fostering a more meritocratic workplace.

My goal is to leave you both empowered and accountable for your efforts to achieve meritocracy in the work you do. A key practical objective is to equip you and your colleagues with a clear approach for first locating where biases and social processes may be shaping your talent management processes—potentially leading to unfairness and organizational issues—and then ensuring that targeted solutions are effectively devised to tackle any potential departures from meritocracy.

I also hope that *The Meritocracy Paradox* has given you the knowledge, strategies, and motivation to help you build a fairer, more inclusive, and meritocratic future of work, one where equal opportunity for all is not just an aspiration but a reality. There is great *merit* (pun intended) in leaders and professionals like you taking active steps to promote true meritocracy in your own organizations, divisions, units, or teams, ensuring that individuals are advanced and rewarded based on their talents and efforts rather than personal or demographic characteristics. Moreover, achieving these goals is often easier and more cost-effective than many assume. The responsibility— and the opportunity—is in your hands now.

In chapter 6 of the book, I introduced a *data-driven talent management approach designed to address bias and foster meritocratic workplaces.* This approach leverages data and analytics to identify and mitigate any (potential) occurrences of prejudice and other social processes that prevent organizations from achieving meritocracy in practice. Beyond uncovering biases, this approach also helps pinpoint talent management problems (such as poor screening of candidates, flawed selection processes, and biased appraisals of employee performance, among many others), many of which are often difficult to detect without rigorous data collection and analysis of important employment processes and outcomes in organizations. Additionally, it provides a valuable tool for evaluating the effectiveness of existing people management practices and enhancing decision-making in recruitment, hiring, selection, and performance evaluation decisions in your organization.

The first step in implementing this data-driven approach is to gather and analyze high-quality and *relevant* data[1] on key areas such as workforce demographics, professional background, performance evaluations, compensation, benefits, and employee engagement. (Please be sure to carefully review the legal constraints regarding what data you are allowed to collect, as regulations vary depending on the jurisdiction in which your organization is located.) Analyzing these data can then help identify disparities, such as demographic pay gaps, underrepresented groups in leadership positions, or patterns of inequity and unfairness in hiring, promotions, and access to significant career development opportunities.

Once issues of equal opportunity and fairness are identified, organizations can develop targeted, data-informed strategies to address them successfully. For example, some organizations may implement targeted training programs for specific parts of an organization, establish mentorship or developmental programs for employees who otherwise may not have equal opportunities for success in their current jobs, or change hiring or promotion processes to reduce biases and inefficiencies. The ultimate aim of such interventions is to improve opportunity and fairness in the organization's talent management processes and to attract and retain the most qualified and diverse talent to work for your organization.

Moreover, organizations can use data to track progress and evaluate the effectiveness of their strategies over time. By frequently (and consistently) collecting and analyzing data on key people management metrics, leaders can measure impact, refine their strategies, and ensure meaningful progress toward meritocracy. Overall, a data-driven approach can empower organizations and their leaders to make more meritocratic and evidence-based decisions. This approach can also help organizations foster a more inclusive workplace that benefits all.

In chapter 7, I encouraged leaders and key organizational decision-makers to take serious and intentional steps to foster meritocracy in practice. I argue that achieving success in these efforts requires reinforcing two fundamental mechanisms in the organizational structures governing workforce management: *accountability* and *transparency*. Building more meritocratic processes and outcomes involves establishing clear criteria and procedures for employee advancement and evaluation (or any decision affecting employees' careers), monitoring both the processes and their outcomes, and ensuring that at least someone in your organization is responsible for making these processes meritocratic and fair.

Although implementing these changes is, in my experience, extremely hard and challenging, the research examples discussed in this book highlight their critical importance. Organizations and their leaders should first be skeptical about the effectiveness of so-called best practices in addressing the unique challenges their organizations face. And second, they need to be careful when designing and implementing any new people-related practices to successfully target the organization's specific challenges while not inadvertently introducing new biases or any unintended consequences.

TOWARD GREATER MERITOCRACY AND FAIRNESS IN YOUR ORGANIZATION

My research has shown that organizations and businesses can attain greater meritocracy in the workplace by designing and implementing talent management systems that have high levels of both accountability and transparency. Importantly, accomplishing these goals doesn't have to be costly or overwhelming.

How can organizations that adopt a talent analytics approach take concrete steps toward greater meritocracy in practice? As emphasized throughout this book, simply copying practices from other companies is not necessarily a reliable strategy. Instead, the first stage in a data-driven approach to improving talent management involves rigorous data collection and analysis. This allows organizations to pinpoint their specific issues and then develop targeted interventions that address them effectively.

It is also crucial to recognize and stress that no single practice alone can fully resolve workplace problems or challenges. With that in mind, below, I outline a selection of practical steps that companies have successfully implemented to enhance meritocracy in specific parts of their talent management systems. While this list is by no means exhaustive, it illustrates a range of solutions that, when carefully implemented, can help create a fairer, more meritocratic, and even more transparent workplace.

On Hiring and Selection

To make organizations more meritocratic and fairer when screening and selecting talent, companies and their leaders can take several steps:

1. *Use objective selection criteria.* Companies should assess candidates based on specific, measurable factors such as skills, experience, and qualifications rather than subjective aspects like personal interests and connections or cultural fit. In particular, they should avoid using vague, imprecise, and overly general terms when describing the merits required for the position.

    Later, these criteria should be validated to ensure they predict performance and success in the role. Any factor that fails to predict performance should be removed from the selection criteria.

2. *Standardize the screening process.* Standardizing the hiring process can help ensure that all candidates are evaluated consistently and fairly. This process can involve using structured interviews, where all interviewees are asked similar questions; introducing specific rubrics for evaluating résumés and other application materials; and using preemployment assessments to assess skills and abilities. At this stage, it may be worthwhile to carefully consider not asking for certain kinds of personal information about the candidates (for example, cover letters or personal statements) that may open the door for biases and social processes to be introduced and affect your screening outcomes.

An important aspect of this standardization is training the individuals involved in screening and selection—typically recruiters and hiring managers—to evaluate applications accurately using employment-relevant criteria.

3. *Establish meritocratic goals to address existing disparities.* Employers can establish goals, often related to equity and fairness goals, and incorporate them into their hiring processes. This task may require ensuring that there continue to be equal opportunities for all groups of candidates and employees in the organization, including the majority. Also, it is important to consider bringing candidates with diverse backgrounds of experience and professional accomplishments. Once again, at the core of meritocracy, all candidates need to have equal opportunity.

4. *Increase transparency.* Organizations and their leaders can increase transparency in the selection by, for instance, providing candidates with information about the job opening and the hiring process in the job descriptions, including the selection criteria and evaluation methods used. This transparency can help build trust and ensure that candidates are evaluated fairly.

5. *Train hiring managers and recruiters.* Companies can train hiring managers and recruiters to identify the merit-based qualifications and talents essential for the job. Specific forms of training can also help recruiters and managers recognize and address their personal biases and other counterproductive preferences that can arise during the hiring process. This training might include, specifically, guidance on evaluating candidates strictly on the basis of their qualifications and professional experience, structuring interviews and other screening processes to prioritize job-relevant information and minimize bias, and avoiding language or requirements in job postings, presentations, and other recruitment materials that may introduce unnecessary expectations about the job and the organization.

On Performance and Rewards

Improving the performance evaluation and rewards processes can be critical in making an organization more meritocratic and fairer. Here are a few steps that companies and their leaders can take:

1. *Use objective performance metrics.* Companies can use (ideally) nonsubjective performance metrics that are clearly defined and linked to job requirements. This clarity can help ensure that all employees are evaluated based on their job performance rather than on subjective factors such as personal connections or popularity.

2. *Train managers to focus on employment-related criteria and be fair and unbiased when conducting performance evaluations.* Given findings of potential bias in performance evaluations of employees of different demographics, certain employers could, for instance, provide training to managers to help them recognize and avoid unnecessary biases in the evaluation process. This training can include how to provide objective and constructive feedback, recognize and mitigate bias in their judgments, and evaluate employees fairly and consistently.

3. *Review performance evaluations for consistency.* Organizations can develop a system to regularly review and calibrate performance evaluations to ensure they are fair and consistent across different departments and teams. This review can involve conducting regular audits to identify areas of inconsistency or bias and implementing corrective actions as needed.

4. *Connect rewards to performance.* Companies should clearly link rewards such as pay raises, bonuses, and promotions to performance metrics rather than relying on subjective factors. This practice can help ensure that rewards are based on specific criteria and distributed fairly across the organization. This step, like many others, also requires a careful evaluation of the performance appraisal process and its outcomes to prevent biases and social processes that could be detrimental to particular groups of employees.

5. *Work toward pay equity and fairness.* Organizations can conduct regular audits to identify and address disparities in pay, rewards, and other employee benefits based on non-meritocratic factors. Audits can help ensure that all employees are compensated fairly for their work and contributions to your organization.

On Promotion and Retention

Improving promotions and retention in truly meritocratic and fair organizations can be critical to creating and sustaining a workplace where all employees feel valued and supported. Here are a few steps that companies and their leaders could consider taking:

1. *Establish clear career development paths.* Career development paths provide employees with opportunities for learning, development, and career advancement based on their skills and contributions. Organizations can offer training, mentorship, and development programs that help employees build the necessary and relevant skills and experiences to advance in their careers.

2. *Foster a culture of inclusivity and belonging.* Organizations can create and maintain a culture of inclusivity, belonging, and tolerance that values opportunity and

respect for all. They can promote employee resource groups, provide optional training programs to all employees, and foster a safe and supportive workplace where *all* employees feel valued and heard.

3. *Provide opportunities for feedback and recognition.* Companies can provide opportunities for feedback and recognition to all employees, regardless of their background or position. These opportunities can include regular check-ins with managers, peer recognition programs, and ways for employees to share their ideas and contributions with leadership.

4. *Monitor and address biases and other social dynamics in the promotion process.* Employers can monitor and address biases in the promotion process by regularly reviewing promotion decisions to ensure that they are fair and meritocratic. This effort may involve implementing structured promotion processes, training managers on recognizing and mitigating bias, and collecting data on promotion decisions to identify disparities based on non-meritocratic factors.

DEVISING YOUR TALENT ANALYTICS CHANGE PLAN

To better identify your organization's specific meritocratic challenges and develop targeted solutions, consider devising a talent analytics change plan using the following eight-step framework that I have developed:

Step 1. *Identify your talent management challenge.* Begin by selecting a specific challenge, problem, or opportunity that you want to address in your talent management processes. Think of this step as an opportunity to improve your talent management system and make your organization more meritocratic. To guide your analysis, consider answering questions such as the following:

- What people-related issue, concern, or challenge are you most interested in addressing? Or what opportunity are you trying to identify and capitalize on? Examples of some key talent management processes that can continuously be improved include recruitment, hiring, satisfaction and engagement, pay and rewards, learning and development, promotions, and career advancement.

- Why is this challenge significant, especially compared to your other business priorities?

- Why is the challenge difficult to solve? Has it been addressed effectively before in your organization or elsewhere? If so, how?

Answering these questions will provide a solid foundation for identifying and ultimately resolving your talent management challenges.

Step 2. *Reflect on why your organization faces this challenge.* Consider all the potential factors that might be contributing to this challenge or problem:

- Why do you think your organization has this challenge? Do similar organizations experience the same issues?
- What other factors might be contributing to the challenge?

This reflective process is a valuable starting point for further inquiry. Once you understand the root causes of your current challenges, you can start devising more effective approaches. In other words, by identifying the *whys*, you can better assess which solutions and recommendations to incorporate into your talent management system.

Step 3. *Review existing evidence and propose solutions or hypotheses for the "whys."* Next, review existing research and frameworks from the business world and academic research to identify and develop potential solutions that address the root causes of your talent management challenges. Focus on approaches and information that directly address the reasons behind such challenges. Consider the following:

- What feasible solutions to the problem have you seen or heard about from other organizations that may apply to your situation? What assumptions underlie each potential solution?
- What insights and recommendations do scholars and experts offer for addressing similar challenges?
- Which assumed relationships or predictions seem most consequential in helping you figure out the best solution? Based on the evidence you currently have, which assumed relationships appear most dubious or questionable, and should, therefore, be further explored?

By carefully assessing available evidence and proposed interventions, you can start proposing well-founded solutions to help you address your specific talent management challenges.

Step 4. *Plan your project.* Define and plan your project to effectively address your challenge or opportunity. Clearly articulate the purpose of your plan and establish a method for evaluating its success. Rather than simply *copying* a practice used elsewhere, focus on *adapting* existing practices to fit your organization's unique needs or developing a tailored solution that directly addresses your challenge.

As part of this planning phase, determine what specific data you need to collect and how you will use these data to measure the effectiveness of your project. This step should outline the key metrics and outcomes you aim to optimize through your proposed plan of action. Key questions for you to consider at this step include the following:

- How will you test your hypotheses and evaluate the effectiveness of your proposed solutions? Make sure you consider the pros and cons of the various solutions you are considering.
- If someone in your organization ends up carrying out the analysis for you, how will you ensure the analysis is rigorous and appropriate? What additional factors should be taken into account?
- What conclusions do you expect to draw from your analysis?
- What data does your company currently have that can support your project?
- What additional data do you need to collect? And how will you go about gathering these data? (Once again, please be sure to carefully review the legal constraints regarding what data you are allowed to collect, as regulations vary depending on the jurisdiction in which your organization is located.)
- What findings or outcomes do you anticipate from implementing your project?
- What potential challenges might arise during execution, and how can they be mitigated?

By addressing these questions, you will create a well-defined data-collection plan that enhances your organization's ability to implement effective and sustainable talent management improvements.

Step 5. *Anticipate potential project outcomes, results, and benefits.* Carefully evaluate the potential outcomes of your project and how different patterns may suggest different solutions. This step requires critically assessing (and anticipating) both expected and unintended outcomes of your plan of action and making necessary adjustments to minimize any negative impacts. Additionally, plan to collect the necessary data that will allow you to measure the success of your intervention and identify any unforeseen outcomes as a result of your plan of action. Questions to consider at this stage include the following:

- What are the potential positive outcomes of your project? What are the possible negative or unintended outcomes of your project?

- How will you communicate the results of your analysis to top management? How can you effectively summarize key findings and insights from your proposed analysis?

- How will you determine which solutions are most effective?

- What actionable insights do you expect to gain from your findings?

- What criteria and metrics will you use to evaluate the benefits and impact of your project? What measures will you need to determine whether your project has achieved its desired effects and how well it has worked?

- What challenges do you anticipate when implementing changes based on your findings? How will you adjust your project if unexpected results emerge?

By thoroughly anticipating potential outcomes and preparing for various scenarios, you can ensure a more strategic, systematic approach to implementing effective talent management improvements.

Step 6. *Revise your plan accordingly based on your findings.* After carefully assessing the potential benefits and risks of your proposed project identified in step 5, make revisions and improvements to your project to maximize the benefits and positive outcomes while minimizing any risks and unintended outcomes.

Step 7. *Implement and measure the impact of your project.* Put your plan into action and track its effectiveness. Collect and evaluate valid data before and after your plan was introduced to assess both the process and the outcomes. This step ensures that your project is driving meaningful change and achieving its intended objectives.

Step 8. *Continuously improve and adapt.* Keep going. Successful talent management is an ongoing process, not a one-time initiative. Return to step 1 to address new challenges, refine existing strategies, and explore emerging opportunities. This dynamic, data-driven approach will help your organization sustain progress and continually work toward a more efficient and meritocratic system in practice.

By following these eight strategic steps (see figure C.1), you will have a structured and systematic approach for successfully implementing any talent- or people-related analytical project. This approach will help you translate the principles outlined in this book into actionable solutions and interventions, ultimately fostering true meritocracy in your organization.

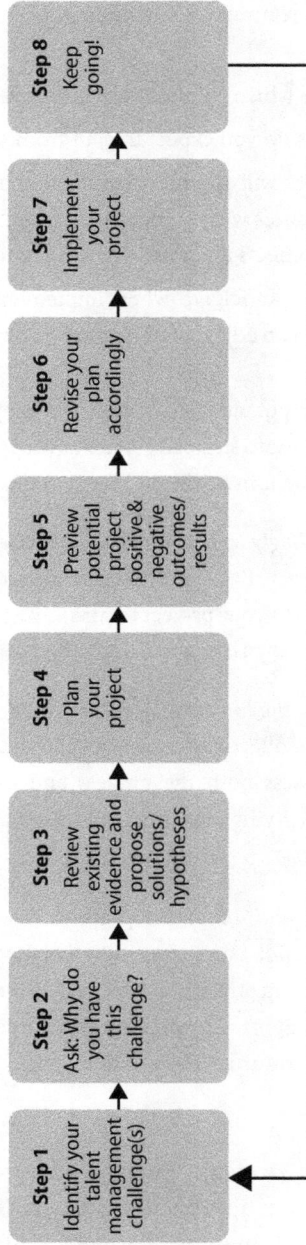

FIGURE C.1. Eight-step talent-analytics plan for fostering meritocracy in your organization.

THE END OF THE BOOK, THE BEGINNING OF YOUR JOURNEY TOWARD TRUE MERITOCRACY

As you reach the end of this book, you may feel overwhelmed, perhaps even a sense of uncertainty—especially if you are wondering where to begin or how to take your organization's transformation to the next level. If so, you are not alone. Many leaders and professionals I have worked with have shared similar feelings when first confronting the complexity of building a truly meritocratic organization.

Remind yourself that the fact that you have read this book is already a significant step forward. It demonstrates your commitment to improving your organization's talent management practices and fostering a system that promotes meritocracy in practice—not just in theory.

To move forward, I suggest you take a deep breath, revisit earlier chapters, and identify small, actionable steps that can quickly lead to small wins. Achieving meritocracy is not a one-time, easy initiative but an ongoing process that requires commitment and continuous efforts to learn, improve, and correct people-related processes. A reminder from chapter 2: true meritocracy is an ideal—a goal, a target, an ongoing project—requiring continuous refinement and improvement over time.

If you are just getting started with the building of a meritocratic talent management system, start slow, with one small step at a time that can be a win. Focus on one area—such as selection and hiring—and assess the current outcomes of your screening efforts and identify ways to improve them. Do not try to tackle everything at once.

For those of you who are further along, I suggest you proceed cautiously. Choose a specific aspect of your talent management system—perhaps recruitment sources, hiring methods, pay decisions, or promotions—and collect, code, and analyze employment-relevant data to assess how your organization is doing. Assess whether your current practices truly promote merit-based outcomes or if hidden biases, social barriers, and inefficiencies are undermining them.

I often like to stress that you do not need vast amounts of data to start benefiting from this talent-analytical approach to fostering meritocracy. Even small businesses or organizations that lack such datasets can gather meaningful insights from important qualitative methods such as interviews, focus groups, or direct observation of workplace practices and employment-related decision-making. These methods will help you collect great firsthand information about how your talent management processes are working and where your problems may lie.

No matter where you start, having a clear plan is essential. Consider the talent analytics change framework outlined in this book as you develop a data-driven strategy for embedding meritocracy into your organization's culture and systems.

This book may be ending, but your journey toward a more equitable, effective, and meritocratic organization is just beginning.

***

For decades, the principle of advancing and rewarding individuals based on their talents and hard work—on "merit"—has been widely embraced as fair and legitimate across educational, corporate, and government organizations worldwide. Meritocracy, whether explicitly or implicitly invoked, remains a powerful ideal for those who envision a society where individuals are rewarded for their talents, initiative, and effort rather than for their class background, wealth, or demographic characteristics. Yet, many merit-driven and related talent management initiatives inside real organizations and institutions have been criticized for paradoxically reinforcing workplace inequities and sustaining biases and unfairness.

I wrote *The Meritocracy Paradox* not only to address these criticisms of meritocracy but also to provide research-based strategies that can identify and tackle biases, unnecessary social dynamics, and inefficiencies within talent management systems. If meritocracies are to survive and thrive, they need to be revamped and strengthened to ensure equal opportunity for everyone participating in them.

I believe this work is essential for just, fair, successful, and stable societies and institutions. The world needs *truly* meritocratic organizations and businesses—ones that do not merely pay lip service to fairness or meritocracy but actively combat biases and social barriers that hinder equal opportunity for all. As you go about the work of building more meritocratic people management processes in your own organization through talent analytics, remember that your efforts can contribute to a larger project as well: you are helping create a fairer world where talented and hardworking individuals of all backgrounds have the opportunity to thrive and succeed. That is work well worth doing—and truly meritorious.

ACKNOWLEDGMENTS

This book would not have been written without the support of my colleagues and friends at MIT, with whom I have been grateful for numerous opportunities to present, discuss, and share the themes of this book. In the Economic Sociology Group at Sloan, I have always found colleagues eager to engage with my work and offer thoughtful reactions and suggestions for improvement. At the Institute for Work and Employment Research (IWER) seminar, which over the decades has featured scholars such as Douglas McGregor, Charles Myers, and Phyllis Wallace, I have had invaluable opportunities to present and refine my research since I arrived to MIT in 2005. The list of great colleagues and friends is long. Thank you all for your generous guidance and encouragement, and for being there for one another.

In recent years, I have taught a popular workshop, *Achieving Meritocracy in the Workplace*, to intellectually engaging groups of professionals. I have also delivered related seminars worldwide to participants with diverse personal and professional backgrounds. These participants—primarily MBAs, Sloan Fellows, EMBAs, executives, and experienced professionals—were eager to engage with the material, drive change, and tackle some of our most pressing societal challenges, including lack of opportunity for some, failure to ensure fairness in organizations, systemic racism, and many other ills in our societies. Their reactions to the material I presented (some of which became integral to this book) and their enthusiasm for figuring out ways to improve talent management systems and organizations have been truly inspiring.

I am indebted to them for enriching my understanding of these topics and for motivating me to make this book even more practical.

I have been fortunate to travel and present portions of this book around the world, engaging not only academics but also key corporate and societal stakeholders. To name a few, I am incredibly grateful to colleagues who hosted me at the University of Málaga in the south of Spain, the European University Institute (EUI) in Florence, the Imperial College Business School in London, the Fundación Rafael del Pino in Madrid, the Asian School of Business in Kuala Lumpur, the Nova and Católica University in Lisbon, and HEC in Paris. I am particularly thankful to the Otto Mønsted Foundation and colleagues at the CBS Department of Strategy and Innovation in Copenhagen for their generous hospitality and for supporting my research in the summer of 2022—special thanks to my faculty host, colleague, and friend, Mercedes Delgado.

During the most challenging months of the COVID-19 pandemic, Zoom made it possible to stay connected with intellectual communities worldwide. I am grateful for the opportunity to virtually present the research that inspired this book at institutions such as the Università della Svizzera Italiana in Lugano, Johns Hopkins University in Baltimore, and the University of California at Berkeley, among many others.

In North America, I have greatly benefited from presenting and receiving feedback on many parts of the book. I vividly recall my enriching discussions with members of the Kennedy School of Public Policy at Harvard University, the ILR School at Cornell University, the University of British Columbia, the Wharton/Columbia Management's Analytics and Data Mini-Conference, the INFORMS Winter Workshop in Seattle, and both SCANCOR Palo Alto and the Clayman Institute at Stanford University—a very dear place in my mind and heart. I am also thankful for the feedback and encouragement from colleagues and friends at the Interdisciplinary Committee on Organizational Studies (ICOS) in Ann Arbor, the Yale School of Management in New Haven, the Rotman School of Management at the University of Toronto, the Desautels Faculté de Gestion at McGill University in Montréal, the Tuck School of Business at Dartmouth College, the NYU Stern School of Business, and the Sociology Department at Boston University in the critical months leading up to the completion of this manuscript.

To end my acknowledgments, I would like to express my gratitude to all the wonderful human beings I have met along the way. It is an endless list of friends, professors, and colleagues who bet on me from the very beginning.

Special thanks to Mauro F. Guillén and Ruth V. Aguilera for supporting my career and for their friendship. I am incredibly grateful for the *Introducción a la Sociología* class I took in my first year of college with Jesus M. De Miguel— a course that profoundly transformed me as I learned about issues of social and economic inequality, structures, and cultures. With Jesus, I took my very first steps into the world of research. It was he who encouraged me to pursue research and to study in the United States.

My deepest thanks go to my academic mentors and friends, Mark Granovetter and Roberto Fernandez. You were a key part of my growth as an academic and scholar. Attending Stanford gave me the honor not only of learning from you but also of working with you to conduct research in the fields of economic sociology, organizational theory, and social stratification. Your guidance and support helped shape me into the researcher and professor I am today. It has been a privilege to have you in my life.

I, too, would like to thank my coauthors, especially those with whom I collaborated on the research that is central to this book. I owe special thanks to Steve Benard at Indiana University, Ben Rissing at Cornell University, Aruna Ranganathan at the University of California at Berkeley, Hye Jin Rho at Michigan State University, and Ethan Poskanzer at the University of Colorado.

Writing a book requires effort, attention to detail, and good communication skills. Special thanks go to Maurice Black and Martha Mangelsdorf for carefully reading early (as well as later) drafts of the manuscript and suggesting ways to strengthen the impact of my writing and ideas. Thank you, Susan Spilecki and Robin Kietlinski, for your feedback too. Many colleagues also generously offered to read draft passages and chapters, offering great ideas, examples, and critical comments. Eric Schwartz, then editor at Columbia University Press, offered wise advice and great suggestions at crucial points along the way. I thank you all for your encouragement during the difficult times and for your never-failing vision and excitement. The responsibility for all the remaining errors is mine alone.

To conclude, I will be eternally filled with gratitude for the sacrifice, efforts, and love of my parents, Isabel and Emilio. They are Andalusian, from a small village called Busquistar in the beautiful and still-peaceful Alpujarra Granadina. In the late 1960s, they immigrated to Barcelona in search of job opportunities, carrying their own dreams, and found refuge in the city of Santako, where they raised three children: Sergio, a civil engineer, Yolanda, a doctor (a real doctor, as I am often reminded!), and a third child, who went into studying economics. Although circumstances were never the best (or the worst), our parents raised us with love, honesty, and pride, instilling in us the value of hard work and education. They believed in the ideal of meritocracy even in the most challenging times. Thank you, Sergio and Yolanda, for growing up with me and helping shape who I am today. Since then, the family has expanded, so I also thank Pablo and my two amazing nieces, Aitana and Mar. Above all, I am deeply grateful to Joseph and Winnie, who have stood by my side throughout my writing of this book—before it began, during its creation, and beyond.

I dedicate this book to my dear family and dear friends. You give meaning to my life. You inspire me to be my best. You support me and energize me. And you augment my dreams. Thank you.

NOTES

PREFACE

1. Emma Jacobs, "Can Business Ever Run a True Meritocracy?," *Financial Times*, February 27, 2025, https://www.ft.com/content/87cdf51c-c8e6-439c-aef6-91cb8faed78a.

2. At the time, each high school student was ranked by their high school grades and their score in the "selectividad" exam. "Examenes de selectividad," or simply "selectividad" (in English, selectivity), is the common name for the Spanish University Admission Tests ("Evaluación de Acceso a la Universidad"). Similar admissions tests for colleges and universities—like the SAT or GMAT in the United States—are used throughout the world. This standardized exam is voluntarily taken by students after secondary school, even though it is required to be considered by the majority of universities (all public universities) in the country. Typically, over a few days in June or September, graduating high school students must take several written exams on common and specific subjects taken in "Bachillerato" (the last two noncompulsory years of secondary education). Selectividad exams are set by the public universities of each autonomous community and allow students access to the Spanish university system. Each university then sets the necessary scores to qualify for admission into its campus. The highest-scoring students can choose the schools and degrees with the highest score recommendations.

3. Mauro F. Guillen, *La Profesión de Economista: El Auge de Economistas, Ejecutivos y Empresarios en España* (Ariel, 1989). As an undergrad at the University of Barcelona, I so admired this book that I ended up writing a book review that ultimately got published in one of the top sociology journals in Spain, *Revista Española de Investigaciones Sociológicas* (*REIS*): Emilio J. Castilla, "Book Review: La Profesión de Economista: El Auge de Economistas, Ejecutivos y Empresarios en España by Mauro F. Guillen," REIS 59 (July–September, 1992), 379–95.

4. This is a reference to the American television miniseries broadcast in 1987 by ABC. This show depicts life in the United States after a bloodless takeover engineered by

the Soviet Union. The description is taken from the novelization of the miniseries, *Amerika: The Triumph of the American Spirit* by Brauna E. Pouns and Donald Wrye (Pocket Books, 1987), based on Wrye's screenplay.

5. Daniel Markovits, *The Meritocracy Trap: How America's Foundational Myth Feeds Inequality, Dismantles the Middle Class, and Devours the Elite* (Penguin, 2019).

6. Michael J. Sandel, *The Tyranny of Merit: What's Become of the Common Good?* (Farrar, Straus and Giroux, 2020).

7. Adrian Wooldridge, *The Aristocracy of Talent: How Meritocracy Made the Modern World* (Skyhorse, 2021).

8. Marianne Cooper, "The False Promise of Meritocracy," *Atlantic*, December 1, 2015, https://www.theatlantic.com/business/archive/2015/12/meritocracy/418074/.

9. Jacobs, "Can Business Ever Run a True Meritocracy?"

INTRODUCTION

1. Throughout this book, the real names of organizations I have studied and their employees have been changed for privacy reasons.

2. A classic article in the literature is Edward Lazear's study illustrating the advantages and potential challenges of incentive plans; see Edward P. Lazear, "Performance Pay and Productivity," *American Economic Review* 90, no. 5 (2000): 1346–61. In his study, Lazear discusses the impact of introducing a pay-for-performance plan to increase the productivity of technicians at Safelite, an Ohio-based provider of vehicle glass repairs and service; the plan went from a guaranteed hourly wage to piece-rate pay. Additionally, Brian Hall, Lazear, and Carleen Madigan wrote a business case that is taught in business schools worldwide to discuss the benefits—in terms of productivity, pay, turnover, and recruitment—of such a change in pay structure; see Brian J. Hall, Edward Lazear, and Carleen Madigan, *Performance Pay at Safelite Auto Glass (A)*, Harvard Business School Case 800–291 (Harvard Business School, 2000).

3. For a review, see Tim Low, "When Unequal Pay Is Actually Fair," *Harvard Business Review*, March 31, 2016; Donald J. Campbell, Kathleen M. Campbell, and Ho-Beng Chia, "Merit Pay, Performance Appraisal, and Individual Motivation: An Analysis and Alternative," *Human Resource Management* 37, no. 2 (1998): 131–46; George Bohlander and Scott Snell, *Managing Human Resources*, 14th ed. (Thomson South-Western, 2007); Robert L. Mathis and John H. Jackson, *Human Resource Management*, 10th ed. (Cengage South-Western, 2003); and Barry Gerhard, "Chapter Three—Incentives and Pay for Performance in the Workplace," *Advances in Motivation Science* 4 (2017): 91–140.

4. Stephen Miller, "Study: Pay for Performance Pays Off," Society for Human Resource Management, September 14, 2011, https://www.shrm.org/topics-tools/news/benefits -compensation/study-pay-performance-pays. These plans also apply to executives. In 2024, for example, 83 percent of the 250 largest S&P firms were estimated to offer some form of executive annual incentive pay or plan that included performance metrics and weights. See Boris Groysberg et al., "Compensation Packages That Actually Drive Performance," *Harvard Business Review*, January–February 2021.

5. See page 22 of Thomas Lemieux, W. Bentley MacLeod, and Daniel Parent, "Performance Pay and Wage Inequality," *Quarterly Journal of Economics* 124, no. 1 (2009): 1–49.

6. "Trends in Global Employee Engagement," Aon Hewitt, 2011, accessed June 2, 2023, https://cdn5.datascope.io/wp-content/uploads/2018/12/Trends_Global_Employee _Engagement_Final1.pdf.

7. See Raymond A. Noe et al., *Human Resource Management: Gaining a Competitive Advantage* (McGraw-Hill, 2017).

8. Connor Harrison, "77 percent of Organizations Offering Variable Pay Plans" (blog post), Salary.com, January 8, 2019, https://www.salary.com/blog/compensation-trends -organizations-embracing-variable-pay/.

9. Payscale, "2023 Compensation Best Practices Report," Payscale. According to the report, when determining pay increases, 60 percent of the surveyed organizations factor in performance ratings, although 17 percent apply them only to variable pay, while 20 percent do not link pay to performance ratings at all. Payscale gathered survey data for nearly five thousand organizations worldwide, with 78 percent head-quartered in North America and 17 percent in Europe, the Middle East, and Africa.

10. See Martin N. Marger, *Social Inequality: Patterns and Processes* (McGraw-Hill, 2008); Robert A. Rothman, *Inequality and Stratification: Race, Class and Gender* (Prentice Hall, 2005); Julia B. Isaacs, Isabel V. Sawhill, and Ron Haskins, *Getting Ahead or Losing Ground: Economic Mobility in America* (Brookings, 2008); Richard T. Longoria, *Meritocracy and Americans' Views on Distributive Justice* (Lexington, 2009); and Marianne Cooper, "The False Promise of Meritocracy," *Atlantic*, December 1, 2015, https://www .theatlantic.com/business/archive/2015/12/meritocracy/418074/.

11. See James R. Kluegel and Eliot R. Smith, *Beliefs About Inequality: Americans' Views of What Is and What Ought to Be*, 3rd ed. (Aldine Transaction, 2009); Everett Carll Ladd, *The American Ideology: An Exploration of the Origins, Meaning and Role of American Political Ideas* (Roper Center for Public Opinion Research, 1994); Everett Carll Ladd and Karlyn H. Bowman, *Attitudes Toward Economic Inequality* (American Enterprise Institute, 1998); Erin A. Cech and Mary Blair-Loy, "Perceiving Glass Ceilings? Meritocratic Versus Structural Explanations of Gender Inequality Among Women in Science and Technology," *Social Problems* 57, no. 3 (2010): 371–97; Marie Duru-Bellat and Elise Tenret, "Meritocracy: A Widespread Ideology Due to School Socialization?," SciencesPo, 2010, https://sciencespo.hal.science/hal-00972712; Marie Duru-Bellat and Elise Tenret, "Who's for Meritocracy? Individual and Contextual Variations in the Faith," *Comparative Education Review* 56, no. 2 (2012): 223–47; Jeremy Reynolds and He Xian, "Perceptions of Meritocracy in the Land of Opportunity," *Research in Social Stratification and Mobility* 36 (2014): 121–37; Jonathan J. B. Mijs, "Visualizing Belief in Meritocracy, 1930–2010," *Socius: Sociological Research for a Dynamic World* 4 (2018); and Jonathan J. B. Mijs and Mike Savage, "Meritocracy, Elitism and Inequality," *Political Quarterly* 91, no. 2 (2020): 397–404.

12. Jonathan J. B. Mijs, "Stratified Failure: Educational Stratification and Students' Attributions of Their Mathematics Performance in 24 Countries," *Sociology of Education* 89, no. 2 (2016): 137–53.

13. Jeremy Reynolds and He Xian, "Perceptions of Meritocracy in the Land of Opportunity," *Research in Social Stratification and Mobility* 36 (2014): 121–37; and Society for Human Resource Management, *The Journey to Equity and Inclusion* (SHRM, Summer 2020), https://www.shrm.org/content/dam/en/shrm/topics-tools/news/inclusion -equity-diversitytfaw-the-journey-to-equity-and-inclusion.pdf.

14. See Maureen A. Scully, "Meritocracy," in *Blackwell Encyclopedic Dictionary of Business Ethics*, ed. R. Edward Freeman and Patricia H. Werhane (Wiley-Blackwell, 1997);

and Emilio J. Castilla, "Gender, Race, and Meritocracy in Organizational Careers," *American Journal of Sociology* 113, no. 6 (2008): 1479–526.

15. See Robert L. Heneman and Jon M. Werner, *Merit Pay: Linking Pay to Performance in a Changing World*, 2nd ed. (Information Age, 2005); Peter Cappelli, *The New Deal at Work: Managing the Market-Driven Workforce* (Harvard Business Review Press, 1999); Peter Cappelli, *Talent on Demand: Managing Talent in an Age of Uncertainty* (Harvard Business Review Press, 2008); and Peter Cappelli et al., *Change at Work* (Oxford University Press, 1997).

16. Emilio J. Castilla and Stephen Benard, "The Paradox of Meritocracy in Organizations," *Administrative Science Quarterly* 55, no. 4 (2010): 543–76.

17. Emilio J. Castilla and Aruna Ranganathan, "The Production of Merit: How Managers Understand and Apply Merit in the Workplace," *Organization Science* 31, no. 4 (2020): 909–35.

1. THE ORIGINS AND EVOLUTION OF MERITOCRACY

The epigraph to this chapter is from Michael Young, *The Rise of the Meritocracy*, 2nd ed. (Transaction, 1994), xi–xiii; originally published by Thames and Hudson in 1958. The French quote is from Napoleon Bonaparte, who used the expression "career is open to talent" in describing his philosophy as a leader.

1. L. Rafael Reif, "Inaugural Address," September 21, 2012, https://reif.mit.edu/speeches-writing/inaugural-address.

2. Ray Dalio, "The Key to Bridgewater's Success: A Real Idea Meritocracy," September 23, 2017, https://swae.io/downloads/Swae_The_Key_to_Bridgewaters_Success-A_Real_Idea_Meritocracy.pdf.

3. "Our Culture," Red Hat, accessed May 10, 2024, https://www.redhat.com/en/about/brand/standards/culture.

4. Jim Whitehurst, "Meritocracy: The Workplace Culture That Breeds Success," *Wired*, accessed May 10, 2024, https://web.archive.org/web/20160901055443/http:/www.wired.com/insights/2014/10/meritocracy.

5. Accenture, "Global Meritocracy," accessed March 5, 2025, https://www.accenture.com/us-en/support/global-meritocracy.

6. Ambereen Choudhury and Amy Bainbridge, "McKinsey Champions Diversity While Rivals Abandon Targets," Bloomberg, February 12, 2025, https://www.msn.com/en-us/money/companies/mckinsey-says-it-will-prioritize-diversity-despite-trump-s-dei-order/ar-AA1ySNb6.

7. The "Cravath system" was introduced in the early twentieth century by Paul Drennan Cravath, a prominent Manhattan lawyer.

8. Candice Lu, "Honoring Differences Through a Culture of Meritocracy," *Forbes*, May 11, 2021, https://www.forbes.com/sites/theyec/2021/05/11/honoring-differences-through-a-culture-of-meritocracy.

9. Sarah Kessler, "Don't Say 'Elite': Corporate Firms' New Pitch Is Meritocracy," *New York Times*, June 10, 2024, https://www.nytimes.com/2024/06/10/business/corporate-firms-meritocracy-elite.html#.

10. Mary Mazzoni, "Should Business Leaders Experiment to Overcome the Shortcomings of Meritocracy?," Triple Pundit, October 2, 2024, https://www.triplepundit.com/story/2024/meritocracy-dei-business/811341.

11. Alexandr Wang, June 13, 2024, "Today we've formalized an important hiring policy at Scale," X, https://x.com/alexandr_wang/status/1801331034916851995.
12. Mazzoni, "Should Business Leaders Experiment to Overcome the Shortcomings of Meritocracy?"
13. Ellesheva Kissing and Anjli Raval, "Accenture Ditches Diversity and Inclusion Goals," *Financial Times*, February 7, 2025, https://www.ft.com/content/0c0c720f-4292-403b-b4e4-f3c83e58596b.
14. I thank Emma Jacobs for her article, which drew our attention to quotes from the leadership of Accenture, ExxonMobil, and Boston Consulting Group. Emma Jacobs, "Can Business Ever Run a True Meritocracy?" *Financial Times*, February 27, 2025, https://www.ft.com/content/87cdf51c-c8e6-439c-aef6-91cb8faed78a.
15. Dominic-Madori Davis and Kyle Wiggers, "Silicon Valley Leaders Are Once Again Declaring 'DEI' Bad and 'Meritocracy' Good—But They're Wrong," TechCrunch Latest, June 23, 2024, https://techcrunch.com/2024/06/23/silicon-valley-leaders-are-once-again-declaring-dei-bad-and-meritocracy-good-but-theyre-wrong/.
16. Indeed.com UK, "Good Place to Learn. Zero Meritocracy. Promotion Based on Loyalty and Brownnosing," February 25, 2021, https://uk.indeed.com/cmp/Ey/reviews/good-place-to-learn-zero-meritocracy-promotion-based-on-loyalty-and-brownnosing?id=c7a98ca9b4e9e37d.
17. Anonymous, "Where Meritocracy Disappears While You Are Treated with Disrespect and Unfairly—Managing Director J.P. Morgan Employee Review," March 29, 2023, https://www.glassdoor.com/Reviews/Employee-Review-J-P-Morgan-E145-RVW75014650.htm.
18. Caroline Simard, "Saying High-Tech Is a Meritocracy Doesn't Make It So," *HuffPost*, September 16, 2010, last modified May 25, 2011, https://www.huffpost.com/entry/saying-hightech-is-a-meri_b_719804.
19. Jennifer Liu, "15 of the Top Companies for Women Working in Tech," *CNBC*, September 28, 2021, https://www.cnbc.com/2021/09/28/anitaborg-womens-representation-in-tech-is-down-during-the-pandemic.html.
20. See Sara Harrison, "Five Years of Tech Diversity Reports—and Little Progress," *Wired*, October 1, 2019, https://www.wired.com/story/five-years-tech-diversity-reports-little-progress/; and Galen Gruman, "The State of Ethnic Minorities in U.S. Tech: 2020," Computerworld, September 21, 2020, https://www.computerworld.com/article/3574917/the-state-of-ethnic-minorities-in-us-tech-2020.html.
21. U.S. Equal Employment Opportunity Commission, "EEOC Research Finds Unequal Opportunity in the High Tech Sector and Workforce," September 11, 2024, https://www.eeoc.gov/newsroom/eeoc-research-finds-unequal-opportunity-high-tech-sector-and-workforce; and Naomi Nix, "Job Rate for Women in Tech Has Hardly Budged Since 2005, EEOC Finds," *Washington Post*, September 11, 2024, https://www.washingtonpost.com/technology/2024/09/11/big-tech-women-minorities-jobs-dei-eeoc/.
22. Cary Funk and Kim Parker, "Women and Men in STEM Often at Odds over Workplace Equity," Pew Research Center, January 9, 2018.
23. See Simard, "Saying High-Tech Is a Meritocracy"; Nigel Nicholson, "The False Theory of Meritocracy," *Harvard Business Review*, June 1, 2010; Marianne Cooper, "The False Promise of Meritocracy," *Atlantic*, December 1, 2015, https://www.theatlantic.com/business/archive/2015/12/meritocracy/418074/; and Barbara B. Adams, "Viewpoint: The Myth of Meritocracy," *HR Magazine*, August 27, 2018, https://www.shrm.org/hr-today/news/hr-magazine/0918/pages/the-myth-of-meritocracy.aspx.

24. Young, *The Rise of the Meritocracy*; see also "About Us," Institute for Community Studies, accessed June 1, 2023, https://icstudies.org.uk/about-us/introducing-institute-community-studies.

25. Young speculated why this friend's prediction was wrong: "The twentieth century had room for the word [meritocracy]. People of power and privilege were readier than ever to believe that modern society (in the language of the book) was ruled 'not so much by the people as by the cleverest people; not an aristocracy of birth, not a plutocracy of wealth, but a true meritocracy of talent'" (Young, *The Rise of the Meritocracy*, xii).

26. Young writes in the introduction to his book: "For years I thought the book was doomed never to appear. I hawked it around from one publisher to another—eleven of them—and was always turned down.... It was only published at all because I happened to meet an old friend, Walter Neurath, on a beach in North Wales. He and his wife, Eva, started a publishing house, Thames & Hudson, which has become highly renowned on both sides of the Atlantic for its books on the arts. Sociology was not among its interests; Neurath published my book out of friendship. Fortunately, his kindness was rewarded this side of the pearly gates. Soon after the book was first published in 1958, it was taken up by Penguin and sold hundreds of thousands of copies, as well as appearing in seven translations" (Young, *The Rise of the Meritocracy*, xi–xii).

27. Adrian Wooldridge, *The Aristocracy of Talent: How Meritocracy Made the Modern World* (Skyhorse, 2021), 72–85.

28. See Ruiping Fan, "Confucian Meritocracy for Contemporary China," in *The East Asia Challenge for Democracy*, ed. Daniel A. Bell and Chenyang Li (Cambridge University Press, 2013).

29. Cited by William N. Brown, in William N. Brown, *Chasing the Chinese Dream: Four Decades of Following China's War on Poverty* (Springer, 2021), 175–81.

30. See Nicholas Lemann, *The Big Test: The Secret History of the American Meritocracy* (Farrar, Straus and Giroux, 1999).

31. See Ross Douthat, "Can the Meritocracy Survive Without the SAT?," *New York Times*, April 29, 2023, https://www.nytimes.com/2023/04/29/opinion/sat-college.html.

32. Nikoletta Bika, "Pre-Employment Testing: A Selection of Popular Tests," Workable.com, September 2023, https://resources.workable.com/tutorial/pre-employment-tests.

33. Society for Human Resource Management, "Screening by Means of Pre-Employment Testing," SHRM, Summer 2023, accessed July 1, 2023, https://www.shrm.org/resources andtools/tools-and-samples/toolkits/pages/screeningbymeansofpreemployment testing.aspx.

34. Daniel A. Bell, *The China Model: Political Meritocracy and the Limits of Democracy* (Princeton University Press, 2015).

35. Alexis de Tocqueville, *Democracy in America* (D. Appleton, 1899).

36. Richard Samuelson, "Thomas Jefferson and John Adams," in *A Companion to Thomas Jefferson*, ed. Francis D. Cogliano (Wiley-Blackwell, 2011).

37. James Truslow Adams, *The Epic of America* (Little, Brown, 1931). Adams specifically described the American dream as "that dream of a land in which life should be better and richer and fuller for everyone, with opportunity for each according to ability or achievement. It is a difficult dream for the European upper classes to interpret adequately, and too many of us ourselves have grown weary and mistrustful of it. It is not a dream of motor cars and high wages merely, but a dream of social order in which each man and each woman shall be able to attain to the fullest stature of which

they are innately capable, and be recognized by others for what they are, regardless of the fortuitous circumstances of birth or position" (415–16).

38. Wooldridge, *The Aristocracy of Talent.*

39. Wooldridge, *The Aristocracy of Talent,* 87.

40. Daniel Bell, *The Coming of Post-Industrial Society: A Venture in Social Forecasting* (Harper, 1973).

41. See Dorian Abbot et al., "In Defense of Merit in Science," *Journal of Controversial Ideas* 3, no. 1 (2023): 1–26. The quotes come from the abstract of this article on page 1.

42. See James R. Kluegel and Eliot R. Smith, *Beliefs About Inequality: Americans' Views of What Is and What Ought to Be,* 3rd ed. (Aldine Transaction, 2009); Everett Carll Ladd, *The American Ideology: An Exploration of the Origins, Meaning and Role of American Political Ideas* (Roper Center for Public Opinion Research, 1994); and Everett Carll Ladd and Karlyn H. Bowman, *Attitudes Toward Economic Inequality* (American Enterprise Institute, 1998).

43. Jeremy Reynolds and He Xian, "Perceptions of Meritocracy in the Land of Opportunity," *Research in Social Stratification and Mobility* 36 (2014): 121–37. In the wake of social movements aimed at addressing systemic racism and inequality, studies have started to highlight significant differences in perception by demographic group; see Emilio J. Castilla and Aruna Ranganathan, "The Production of Merit: How Managers Understand and Apply Merit in the Workplace," *Organization Science* 31, no. 4 (2020): 909–35; Robert W. Livingston, *The Conversation: How Seeking and Speaking the Truth About Racism Can Radically Transform Individuals and Organizations* (Currency, 2021); and Robert W. Livingston, "How to Promote Racial Equity in the Workplace: A Five-Step Plan," *Harvard Business Review* 98, no. 5 (September–October 2020): 64–72. According to a report by the Society for Human Resource Management (SHRM), for instance, 46 percent of Black employees in the United States think their "workplace [is] not doing enough for Black employees in the organization," while only 21 percent of White employees agree with that statement. Furthermore, 68 percent of Black HR professionals reported that their "organization is not doing enough to provide opportunities for Black employees," compared to 35 percent of White HR professionals. See Society for Human Resource Management, *The Journey to Equity and Inclusion* (SHRM, Summer 2020), https://www.shrm.org/content/dam/en/shrm/topics-tools/news/inclusion-equity-diversitytfaw-the-journey-to-equity-and-inclusion.pdf.

44. Vianney Gómez, "As Courts Weigh Affirmative Action, Grades and Test Scores Seem as Top Factors in College Admissions," Pew Research Center, April 26, 2022, https://www.pewresearch.org/fact-tank/2022/04/26/u-s-public-continues-to-view-grades-test-scores-as-top-factors-in-college-admissions.

45. Jason L. Riley, "Meritocracy Is Worth Defending," *Wall Street Journal,* August 17, 2021, https://www.wsj.com/articles/meritocracy-wooldridge-kendi-carlson-admissions-standardized-tests-affirmative-action-cuny-11629237426.

46. Furthermore, for all their challenges, the United States and Canada, according to the 2022 Gallup State of the Global Workplace Report, remain the best regions in the world to be an employee in terms of job and career prospects. See "State of the Global Workplace: 2022 Report," Gallup Workplace, 2022, https://lts-resource-page.s3.us-west-2.amazonaws.com/2022-engagement.pdf.

47. Stefan Ellerbeck, "This Country Has the Highest Number of People Planning to Quit Their Jobs," World Economic Forum, August 11, 2022, https://www.weforum.org/agenda/2022/08/jobs-work-quit-great-resignation.

48. Michael O'Malley, "What the 'Best Companies to Work For' Do Differently," *Harvard Business Review*, December 12, 2019; Lauren O'Donnell, "What Makes a Company a Great Place to Work?," Great Place to Work, July 30, 2021, https://www.greatpla-cetowork.ca/en/articles/what-makes-a-company-a-great-place-to-work; and Jamie Birt, "What Makes a Company a Great Place to Work: 15 Things," Indeed.com, 2022, accessed June 26, 2023, https://www.indeed.com/career-advice/finding-a-job/what-makes-a-company-a-great-place-to-work.

49. See Maureen A. Scully, "Manage Your Own Employability: Meritocracy and the Legitimation of Inequality in Internal Labor Markets and Beyond," in *Relational Wealth: The Advantages of Stability in a Changing Economy*, ed. Carrie R. Leana and Denise M. Rousseau (Oxford University Press, 2000); and Emilio J. Castilla, "Gender, Race, and Meritocracy in Organizational Careers," *American Journal of Sociology* 113, no. 6 (2008): 1479–526.

50. Robert L. Heneman and Jon M. Werner, *Merit Pay: Linking Pay to Performance in a Changing World*, 2nd ed. (Information Age, 2005).

51. See Chris Brewster and Wolfgang Mayrhofer, *Handbook of Research on Compara-tive Human Resource Management* (Edward Elgar, 2012); Mauro F. Guillén, *Models of Management: Work, Authority, and Organization in a Comparative Perspective* (Uni-versity of Chicago Press, 1994); Bruce E. Kaufman, *Managing the Human Factor: The Early Years of Human Resource Management in American Industry* (ILR Press, 2008); and Bruce E. Kaufman, "The Historical Development of American HRM Broadly Viewed," *Human Resource Management Review* 24, no. 3 (2014): 196–218.

52. Kaufman, "The Historical Development."

53. Frank Dobbin, *Inventing Equal Opportunity* (Princeton University Press, 2009).

54. Ralph Linton, *The Study of Man* (Appleton-Century-Crofts, 1936).

55. Thomas Köllen, "Diversity Management: A Critical Review and Agenda for the Future," *Journal of Management Inquiry* 30, no. 3 (2021): 259–72. It is important to acknowledge that at the time of this writing DEI initiatives are facing increasing scrutiny and political backlash, leading some companies to scale back their commit-ments, while others remain dedicated to integrating DEI into long-term strategies for fostering equitable and inclusive workplaces.

56. See Karsten Jonsen, Martha L. Maznevski, and Susan C. Schneider, "Diversity and Its Not So Diverse Literature: An International Perspective," *International Journal of Cross Cultural Management* 11, no. 1 (2011): 35–62; Adam Cobb, "How Firms Shape Income Inequality: Stakeholder Power, Executive Decision Making, and the Structuring of Employment Relationships," *Academy of Management Review* 41, no. 2 (2016): 324–48; Matthew Bidwell et al., "The Employment Relationship and Inequality: How and Why Changes in Employment Practices Are Reshaping Rewards in Organizations," *Acad-emy of Management Annals* 7, no. 1 (2013): 61–121; Tony Dundon and Anthony Raf-ferty, "The (Potential) Demise of HRM?," *Human Resource Management Journal* 28, no. 3 (2018): 377–91; and Michael Grothe-Hammer and Sebastian Kohl, "The Decline of Organizational Sociology? An Empirical Analysis of Research Trends in Leading Journals Across Half a Century," *Current Sociology* 68, no. 4 (2020): 419–42.

57. See Andrew C. Loignon and David J. Woehr, "Social Class in the Organizational Sci-ences: A Conceptual Integration and Meta-Analytic Review," *Journal of Management* 44, no. 1 (2018): 61–88.

58. Paul Daugherty et al., *A New Era of Generative AI for Everyone*, Accenture, 2023, accessed July 7, 2023, https://www.accenture.com/content/dam/accenture/final/accenture -com/document/Accenture-A-New-Era-of-Generative-AI-for-Everyone.pdf.

59. Diane Gherson, "How IBM Is Reinventing HR with AI and People Analytics—Interview with Diane Gherson," interview by David Green (*myHRfuture* Digital HR Leaders podcast), YouTube, accessed April 14, 2023, https://www.youtube.com/watch?v=dG_EocMgM8k.

60. Jake Silberg and James Manyika, "Notes from the AI Frontier: Tracking Bias in AI (and in Humans)," McKinsey Global Institute, June 2019, https://www.mckinsey.com/~/media/mckinsey/featured%20insights/artificial%20intelligence/tackling%20bias%20in%20artificial%20intelligence%20and%20in%20humans/mgi-tackling-bias-in-ai-june-2019.pdf.

61. Haiyan Zhang et al., "The Role of AI in Mitigating Bias to Enhance Diversity and Inclusion," IBM Smarter Workforce Institute, March 2019, https://www.ibm.com/downloads/cas/2DZELQ4O.

62. See Michael Scheiner, "Will AI Bring Fairness in the Workplace?," CRM.org, accessed June 25, 2023, https://crm.org/articles/will-ai-bring-fairness-in-the-workplace; Adam Zewe, "Explained: How to Tell If Artificial Intelligence Is Working the Way We Want It To," *MIT News*, July 22, 2022; and Abhin Shah et al., "Selective Regression Under Fairness Criteria," *Proceedings of the 39th International Conference on Machine Learning, PMLR* 162 (2022): 19598–615, https://proceedings.mlr.press/v162/shah22a.html.

63. Pymetrics, accessed October 30, 2022, https://www.pymetrics.ai/.

64. Ashley Whillans and Jeff Polzer, "Applied: Using Behavioral Science to Debias Hiring," Harvard Business School, September 2021, https://www.hks.harvard.edu/sites/default/files/centers/wappp/921046-PDF-ENG.pdf; see also Khyati Sundaram, "Why We Don't Use AI for Hiring Decisions," Applied, September 16, 2020, https://www.beapplied.com/post/why-we-dont-use-ai-for-hiring-decisions.

65. Thomas Piketty, *Capital in the Twenty–First Century* (Belknap Press of Harvard University Press, 2014), 9. Piketty further writes, "In previous inequality regimes, the poor were not blamed for their own poverty, or at any rate not to the same extent; earlier justificatory narratives stressed instead the functional complementarity of different social groups."

66. See Daniel Markovits, *The Meritocracy Trap: How America's Foundational Myth Feeds Inequality, Dismantles the Middle Class, and Devours the Elite* (Penguin, 2019); and Michael J. Sandel, *The Tyranny of Merit: What's Become of the Common Good?* (Farrar, Straus and Giroux, 2020).

67. See Richard Breen and John H. Goldthorpe, "Class, Mobility and Merit: The Experience of Two British Birth Cohorts," *European Sociological Review* 17, no. 2 (2001): 81–101; and John H. Goldthorpe, "Sociology as Social Science and Cameral Sociology: Some Further Thoughts," *European Sociological Review* 20, no. 2 (2004): 97–105.

68. For a review of research on this topic, see Emilio J. Castilla and Ethan J. Poskanzer, "Through the Front Door: Why Do Organizations (Still) Prefer Legacy Applicants?," *American Sociological Review* 87, no. 5 (2022): 782–826.

69. See Gerhard E. Lenski, *Power and Privilege: A Theory of Social Stratification* (University of North Carolina Press, 1966); Charles Tilly, *Durable Inequality* (University of California Press, 1998); David B. Grusky, *Social Stratification: Class, Race and Gender in Sociological Perspective*, 2nd ed. (Routledge, 2019); and Thomas Piketty, *Capital and Ideology* (Belknap Press of Harvard University Press, 2020).

70. See Victor Ray, "A Theory of Racialized Organizations," *American Sociological Review* 84, no. 1 (2019): 26–53; and Adia Harvey Wingfield, *Gray Areas: How the Way We Work Perpetuates Racism and What We Can Do to Fix It* (HarperCollins, 2023).

71. Markovits, *The Meritocracy Trap*.
72. Sandel, *The Tyranny of Merit*. Wooldridge in *The Aristocracy of Talent*, a defense of restoring meritocracy in today's institutions, notes that some of those who have most benefited from the meritocratic system seem to be the most critical of meritocracy and its virtues. For instance, Daniel Markovits writes in *The Meritocracy Trap* that merit is "nothing more than a sham." Markovits graduated from Yale in 1991, went to the London School of Economics for an MSc in econometrics, received his BPhil and DPhil at the University of Oxford, and finally got his JD at Yale Law School, where he currently teaches on contracts, federal income taxation, and meritocracy and inequality. Another example is Michael Sandel, author of *The Tyranny of Merit*. Sandel went to Balliol College at Oxford to get his doctorate as a Rhodes Scholar. It goes without saying that without a meritocratic system in place, such scholars may perhaps not have had the opportunity to attend these elite institutions—previously reserved for the children of wealthy, high-status individuals—to obtain their impressive credentials. However, we do not have any information about the two scholars' class background: if they are the children of wealthy, high-status parents, they might have gotten there under earlier systems of allocation.
73. Ifeoma Ajunwa, "What to the Black American Is the Meritocracy? Comment on M. Sandel's *The Tyranny of Merit*," *American Journal of Law and Equality* 1 (2021): 39–45.
74. Randall Kennedy, *For Discrimination: Race, Affirmative Action, and the Law* (Vintage, 2013). Kennedy also notes, "I champion sensibly designed racial affirmative action not because I benefited from it personally—though I have. I support it because, on balance, it is conducive to the public good." The public good of a true meritocracy is the leveling of the playing field so that everyone alike has a chance to advance in society and in organizations.
75. See Margalit Fox, "Michael Young, 86, Scholar; Coined, Mocked 'Meritocracy,'" *New York Times*, January 25, 2022, https://www.nytimes.com/2002/01/25/world/michael-young-86-scholar-coined-mocked-meritocracy.html.
76. See Adam Bryant, "How to Hire the Right Person," *New York Times*, accessed June 26, 2023, https://www.nytimes.com/guides/business/how-to-hire-the-right-person. There is an apparent fascination with interviewing corporate leaders to ask them about how they identify and hire the right candidates. There is indeed a demand for that kind of advice, as such interviews promise to help readers learn about strategies "through trial and error to help you go beyond the polished resumes, pre-screened references, and scripted answers, to hire more creative and effective members for your team."
77. See Joanne Sammer, "Reward Top Performers Even in Lean Times," Society for Human Resource Management, accessed June 26, 2023, https://www.shrm.org/hr-today/news/hr-magazine/pages/0914-rewards-performance-based-pay.aspx. In this essay, which is read by over 300,000 HR professionals worldwide, Sammer writes: "Identifying top performers is the most important step in this process, and employers may struggle to determine who is most deserving."
78. Ziad Obermeyer et al., "Dissecting Racial Bias in an Algorithm Used to Manage the Health of Populations," *Science* 366, no. 6464 (2019): 447–53.
79. Jeffrey Dastin, "Insight—Amazon Scraps Secret AI Recruiting Tool That Showed Bias Against Women," *Reuters*, October 10, 2018, https://www.reuters.com/article/idUSKCN1MK0AG.

80. See Chris Brahm, *Tackling AI's Unintended Consequences*, Bain & Company Report, 2018, https://www.bain.com/contentassets/a7ebfd741daf44b6905c597bede52de4/bain_brief_tackling_ais_unintended_consequences.pdf.

81. Hrvoje Smolic, "AI Biases Examples in the Real World," Graphite Note, March 5, 2024, https://graphite-note.com/ai-biases-examples/.

82. See François Candelon, Rodolphe Charme di Carlo, Midas De Bondt, and Theodoros Evgeniou, "AI Regulation Is Coming," *Harvard Business Review*, September–October 2021; and Blair Levin and Larry Downes, "Who Is Going to Regulate AI?," *Harvard Business Review*, May 19, 2023.

83. David Civil and Joseph J. Himsworth, "Introduction: Meritocracy in Perspective. The Rise of the Meritocracy 60 Years On," *Political Quarterly* 91, no. 2 (2020): 376.

84. See, for instance, Wooldridge, *The Aristocracy of Talent*, "Conclusion: Renewing Meritocracy," 367–98; and Benjamin Sachs-Cobbe, "Recent Work on Meritocracy," *Analysis* 83, no. 1 (2023), 171–85.

85. See Markovits, *The Meritocracy Trap*; and Ajunwa, "What to the Black American Is the Meritocracy?" See also Ifeoma Ajunwa, "Race, Labor, and the Future of Work," in *The Oxford Handbook of Race and Law in the United States*, ed. Khiara M. Bridges, Devon Carbado, and Emily Hough (Oxford University Press, 2021).

2. MERITOCRACY IN THEORY

1. See Emilio J. Castilla, "Meritocracy," in *The SAGE Encyclopedia of Political Behavior*, ed. Fathali M. Moghaddam (Sage, 2017). As I explain in the encyclopedic entry, *meritocracy* also frequently refers to an elite group of individuals whose success is based entirely on intelligence, ability, and talent rather than on class, wealth, or family background. In that context, the term is used to refer to leadership that is selected solely on the basis of merit.

2. Castilla, "Meritocracy."

3. See Enguerran Loos, "The Management Consulting Industry: The Free CaseCoach Guide for Candidates," CaseCoach, last modified September 22, 2023, https://casecoach.com/b/the-management-consulting-industry-the-free-casecoach-guide-for-candidates/; and Enguerran Loos, "How the 'Up or Out' Policy Works at McKinsey, BCG and Bain," CaseCoach, last modified June 16, 2023, https://casecoach.com/b/up-or-out-policy-mckinsey-bcg-or-bain/.

4. Castilla, "Meritocracy."

5. Such approaches contributed to the reproduction of power and economic advantage across generations. See Adrian Wooldridge, *The Aristocracy of Talent: How Meritocracy Made the Modern World* (Skyhorse, 2021). According to Wooldridge, meritocracy was part of a "revolutionary idea" (1) opposing the inheritance of privilege and success and instead promoting the importance of "raw intellectual ability" (11) to determine who gets ahead. This idea was "at the heart of the four great revolutions that created the modern world": the French Revolution, the American Revolution, the Industrial Revolution, and the liberal revolution (11).

6. Cary Funk and Kim Parker, "Women and Men in STEM Often at Odds over Workplace Equity," Pew Research Center, 2018.

7. See Trond Petersen, "On the Promise of Game Theory in Sociology," *Contemporary Sociology* 23, no. 4 (1994): 498–502; Trond Petersen, "Discrimination, Measurement in," in *Encyclopedia of Social Measurement*, ed. Kimberly Kempf-Leonard (Elsevier, 2004); Trond Petersen, "Opportunities," in *The Oxford Handbook of Analytical Sociology*, ed. Peter Bearman and Peter Hedström (Oxford University Press, 2009); and Trond Petersen and Ishak Saporta, "The Opportunity Structure for Discrimination," *American Journal of Sociology* 109, no. 4 (2004): 852–901.

8. I will review some studies on the motherhood penalty in chapter 3, as part of a broader discussion on biases and social barriers that hinder the effective functioning of meritocracy in organizations and businesses.

9. Candace West and Don H. Zimmerman, "Doing Gender," *Gender and Society* 1, no. 2 (1987): 125–51; Candace West and Don H. Zimmerman, "Accounting for Doing Gender," *Gender and Society* 23, no. 1 (2009): 112–22; Cecilia L. Ridgeway and Lynn Smith-Lovin, "The Gender System and Interaction," *Annual Review of Sociology* 25 (1999): 191–216; and Cecilia L. Ridgeway and Shelley J. Correll, "Unpacking the Gender System: A Theoretical Perspective on Gender Beliefs and Social Relations," *Gender and Society* 18, no. 4 (2004): 510–31.

10. See Ridgeway and Smith-Lovin, "The Gender System and Interaction"; David G. Wagner and Joseph Berger, "Gender and Interpersonal Task Behaviors: Status Expectation Accounts," *Sociological Perspectives* 40, no. 1 (1997): 1–32; and David G. Wagner and Joseph Berger, "Expectation States Theory: An Evolving Research Program," in *New Directions in Contemporary Sociological Theory*, ed. Joseph Berger and Morris Zelditch Jr. (Rowman and Littlefield, 2002).

11. Emilio J. Castilla and Hye Jin Rho, "The Gendering of Job Postings in the Online Recruitment Process," *Management Science* 69, no. 11 (2023): 6912–39.

12. Shelley J. Correll, "Constraints into Preferences: Gender, Status, and Emerging Career Aspirations," *American Sociological Review* 69, no. 1 (2004): 93–113.

13. Roxana Barbulescu and Matthew Bidwell, "Do Women Choose Different Jobs from Men? Mechanisms of Application Segregation in the Market for Managerial Workers," *Organization Science* 24, no. 3 (2013): 737–56.

14. Elizabeth H. Gorman, "Gender Stereotypes, Same-Gender Preferences, and Organizational Variation in the Hiring of Women: Evidence from Law Firms," *American Sociological Review* 70, no. 4 (2005): 702–28.

15. Michael A. Stoll, Steven Raphael, and Harry J. Holzer, "Black Job Applicants and the Hiring Officer's Race," *ILR Review* 57, no. 2 (2004): 267–87.

16. A few "meritocratic" (often labeled as diversity) attempts by employers have consisted of aiming to target the recruitment of particular demographic groups. This has often been perceived as unfair and indeed caused much of the backlash against some of those initiatives—particularly in higher education when certain diversity initiatives such as affirmative action in the United States have been perceived as favoring certain disadvantaged groups of candidates over others. While such initiatives are meant to correct past demographic injustices, obstacles, and biases against socially disadvantaged groups, they should also ensure that equal opportunity for all is provided, especially once those imbalances are corrected.

17. In the abundant literature on justice and fairness not only in law but also in social psychology, sociology, and management, *procedural justice* concerns the fairness and the transparency of the processes that determine and allocate resources and opportunities. By contrast, *distributive justice* refers to fairness in the distribution of rights

and outcomes. Procedural justice therefore focuses on the decision-making process, with four core principles behind it: all are treated with respect and dignity, all are given a voice, the decision-making process and decision-maker are neutral and guided by transparent reasoning, and the process and decision-maker convey trustworthy motives about those impacted by their decisions (see the entry on procedural justice posted by the Yale Law School, accessed May 27, 2024, https://law.yale.edu/justice-collaboratory/procedural-justice).

18. See Tom R. Tyler, "The Relationship of the Outcome and Procedural Fairness: How Does Knowing the Outcome Influence Judgments About the Procedure?," *Social Justice Research* 9 (1996): 311–25.

19. For a recent and insightful discussion on the history of equity and fairness—from classical Greek and Roman philosophy to America's Founding Fathers and contemporary debates—see Charles McNamara's *Learning to Be Fair: Equity from Classical Philosophy to Contemporary Politics* (Fortress Press, 2024). Other important investigations into the history, philosophy, and contemporary implications of equity, fairness, and justice across different disciplines include John Rawls, *A Theory of Justice* (Harvard University Press, 1971); Michael Sandel, *Justice: What's the Right Thing to Do?* (Farrar, Straus and Giroux, 2009); Amartya Sen, *The Idea of Justice* (Harvard University Press, 2009); Elizabeth Anderson, *The Imperative of Integration* (Princeton University Press, 2010); and Deborah Hellman, *When Is Discrimination Wrong?* (Harvard University Press, 2008).

20. I am obviously not the first one making connections between meritocracy and equity (and other related concepts). For a few important recent reads from many commentators on this topic, see, for example, Rebekah Bastian, "Equity Before Meritocracy: Why We Must Create Opportunities Before Rewarding Accomplishments," *Forbes*, January 29, 2019, https://www.forbes.com/sites/rebekahbastian/2019/01/29/equity-before-meritocracy-why-we-must-create-opportunities-before-rewarding-accomplishments/; Kartikay Kashyap, "Meritocracy and Equity—Striking a Balance for a Wholesome Company Culture," AdvantageClub.ai Blog, October 23, 2024, https://www.advantageclub.ai/blog/meritocracy-and-equity-balance#:~:text=in%20the%20organization.-,The%20Clash%20of%20Ideas,to%20training%20and%20development%20resources; Henry Horace, "Meritocracy and Equity, Not Diversity and Affirmative Action," Thinking Heart Solutions at LinkedIn, November 28, 2024, https://www.linkedin.com/pulse/meritocracy-equity-diversity-affirmative-action-horace-ed-d--009qc/; and Brian Doubles, "Equity and Meritocracy Aren't Necessarily at Odds. How I Had To Figure Out the Big E to Rethink Our Company's Diversity Approach," *Fortune*, April 26, 2023, https://fortune.com/2023/04/26/equity-meritocracy-companys-diversity-brian-doubles/. Also see some interesting academic work on the connection between meritocracy and equity, for instance, Phillip Ashley Wackym et al., "The Intersection Between Meritocracy and Diversity, Equity, and Inclusion," *Otolaryngol Head Neck Surg* 170: 618–20.

21. Friedrich Hayek, *The Constitution of Liberty: The Collected Works of F.A. Hayek*, vol. XVII, *The Constitution of Liberty: The Definite Edition*, ed. Ronald Hamowy (University of Chicago Press, 1960, 2011), 149. As Hayek writes, "Justice does require that those conditions of people's lives that are determined by government be provided equally for all. But equality of those conditions must lead to inequality of results" (163). Interestingly, Hayek starts his essay with a quote from Oliver Wendell Holmes Jr.: "I have no respect for the passion of equality which seems to me merely idealizing envy"(148).

22. Ronald Dworkin, *Sovereign Virtue: The Theory and Practice of Equality* (Harvard University Press, 2000).

23. Amartya Sen, *Inequality Reexamined* (Harvard University Press, 1995).

24. See James N. Baron and David M. Kreps, *Strategic Human Resources: Frameworks for General Managers* (Wiley, 1999).

25. See Roberto M. Fernandez and Mabel Abraham, "Glass Ceilings and Glass Doors? Internal and External Hiring in an Organizational Hierarchy," MIT Sloan Research Paper No. 4895-11, SSRN, January 31, 2011, https://ssrn.com/abstract=1804896; Roberto M. Fernandez and Santiago Campero, "Gender Sorting and the Glass Ceiling in High-Tech Firms," *ILR Review* 70, no. 1 (2017): 73–104; and Roberto M. Fernandez and Brian Rubineau, "Network Recruitment and the Glass Ceiling: Evidence from Two Firms," *RSF: Russell Sage Foundation Journal of the Social Sciences* 5, no. 3 (2019): 88–102.

26. See Jane Hyun, *Breaking the Bamboo Ceiling: Career Strategies for Asians* (Harper Business, 2005); Buck Gee and Denise Peck, "Asian Americans Are the Least Likely Group in the U.S. to Be Promoted to Management," *Harvard Business Review*, May 31, 2018; and Jackson G. Lu et al., "Why East Asians but Not South Asians Are Underrepresented in Leadership Positions in the United States," *Proceedings of the National Academy of Sciences* 117, no. 9 (2020): 4590–600. Also, for the case of socio-economic class, see, Sam Friedman and Daniel Laurison, *The Class Ceiling* (Policy Press, 2019).

27. For our first discussion of these three logics, in the context of college admissions, see Emilio J. Castilla and Ethan J. Poskanzer, "Through the Front Door: Why Do Organizations (Still) Prefer Legacy Applicants?," *American Sociological Review* 87, no. 5 (2022): 782–826.

28. See Maureen A. Scully, "Meritocracy," in *Blackwell Encyclopedic Dictionary of Business Ethics*, ed. R. Edward Freeman and Patricia H. Werhane (Wiley-Blackwell, 1997); and Maureen A. Scully, "Manage Your Own Employability: Meritocracy and the Legitimation of Inequality in Internal Labor Markets and Beyond," in *Relational Wealth: The Advantages of Stability in a Changing Economy*, ed. Carrie R. Leana and Denise M. Rousseau (Oxford University Press, 2000); and Castilla, "Meritocracy."

29. See Roberto M. Fernandez, Emilio J. Castilla, and Paul Moore, "Social Capital at Work: Networks and Employment at a Phone Center," *American Journal of Sociology* 105, no. 5 (2000): 1288–356; Emilio J. Castilla, "Social Networks and Employee Performance in a Call Center," *American Journal of Sociology* 110, no. 5 (2005): 1243–83; Adina D. Sterling, "Friendships and Search Behavior in Labor Markets," *Management Science* 60, no. 9 (2014): 2341–54; and Emilio J. Castilla and Ben A. Rissing, "Best in Class: The Returns on Application Endorsements in Higher Education," *Administrative Science Quarterly* 64, no. 1 (2019): 230–70.

30. Jorge K. De Alva and Andrew Rosen, *Inside the For-Profit Sector in Higher Education*, Forum for the Future of Higher Education, accessed May 11, 2020, https://www.educause.edu/ir/library/pdf/ff1204s.pdf; Joe Pinsker, "The Real Reasons Legacy Preferences Exist," *Atlantic*, April 4, 2019, https://www.theatlantic.com/education/archive/2019/04/legacy-admissions-preferences-ivy/586465; Stephanie Riegg Cellini, "The Alarming Rise in For-Profit College Enrollment," Brookings, November 2, 2020, https://www.brookings.edu/articles/the-alarming-rise-in-for-profit-college-enrollment; and Don Wenner, *Building an Elite Organization: The Blueprint to Scaling a High-Growth, High-Profit Business* (Lioncrest, 2021).

31. See Margaret Y. Padgett and Kathryn A. Morris, "Keeping It 'All in the Family': Does Nepotism in the Hiring Process Really Benefit the Beneficiary?" *Journal of Leadership and Organizational Studies* 11, no. 2 (2005): 34–45; Marianne Bertrand and Antoinette Schoar, "The Role of Family in Family Firms," *Journal of Economic Perspectives* 20, no. 2 (2006): 73–96; Alberto Alesina and Paola Giuliano, "Family Ties," in *Handbook of Economic Growth*, vol. 2, ed. Philippe Aghion and Steven N. Durlauf (Elsevier, 2014); Francis Kramarz and Oskar Nordström Skans, "When Strong Ties Are Strong: Networks and Youth Labour Market Entry," *Review of Economic Studies* 81, no. 3 (2014): 1164–200; and Lauren A. Rivera, *Pedigree: How Elite Students Get Elite Jobs* (Princeton University Press, 2015).

32. See Morten Bennedsen et al., "Inside the Family Firm: The Role of Families in Succession Decisions and Performance," *Quarterly Journal of Economics* 122, no. 2 (2007): 647–91; Emilio J. Castilla, George J. Lan, and Ben A. Rissing, "Social Networks and Employment: Mechanisms (Part 1) and Outcomes (Part 2)," *Sociology Compass* 7, no. 12 (2013): 999–1026; Shing-Yi Wang, "Marriage Networks, Nepotism, and Labor Market Outcomes in China," *American Economic Journal: Applied Economics* 5, no. 3 (2013): 91–112; and Margaret Y. Padgett, Robert J. Padgett, and Kathryn A. Morris, "Reactions to Nepotism in the Hiring Process: The Role of Family Member Qualifications," *Journal of Organizational Psychology* 19, no. 4 (2019): 106–20.

33. See Castilla and Poskanzer, "Through the Front Door"; Thomas J. Espenshade and Alexandria Walton Radford, *No Longer Separate, Not Yet Equal: Race and Class in Elite College Admission and Campus Life* (Princeton University Press, 2010); and Richard D. Kahlenberg, *Affirmative Action for the Rich: Legacy Preferences in College Admissions* (Century Foundation, 2010).

34. This business logic also relates to the material costs and benefits of using organizational resources and processes to screen and select for hiring, advancement, and rewards; some may be more effective than others if only when considering the material aspects of implementing them (but not necessarily whether the processes are fair).

35. See Robin J. Ely and David A. Thomas, "Getting Serious About Diversity: Enough Already with the Business Case," *Harvard Business Review*, November–December 2020; Society for Human Resource Management, "The Business Case for Diversity, Equity and Inclusion," SHRM, August 2020, https://www.shrm.org/resourcesandtools /tools-and-samples/presentations/pages/thebusinesscasefordiversity.aspx; Deloitte, *Only Skin Deep? Re-Examining the Business Case for Diversity*, Deloitte Point of View, September 2011, https://www.ced.org/pdf/Deloitte_-_Only_Skin_Deep.pdf; and Kim Raymond, "The Business Case for a Diverse Workforce," *Forbes*, August 21, 2019, https://www.forbes.com/sites/forbeshumanresourcescouncil/2019/08/21/the -business-case-for-a-diverse-workforce.

36. In the context of higher education, see Thomas J. Espenshade, Chang Y. Chung, and Joan L. Walling, "Admission Preferences for Minority Students, Athletes, and Legacies at Elite Universities," *Social Science Quarterly* 85, no. 5 (2004): 1422–46; and Thomas J. Espenshade and Chang Y. Chung, "The Opportunity Cost of Admission Preferences at Elite Universities," *Social Science Quarterly* 86, no. 2 (2005): 293–305. In a business context, see Marino Mugayar-Baldocchi, Bill Schaninger, and Kartik Sharma, "The Future of the Workforce: Investing in Talent to Prepare for Uncertainty," McKinsey & Company, June 7, 2021, https://www.mckinsey.com/capabilities /people-and-organizational-performance/our-insights/the-organization-blog/the -future-of-work-the-now-the-how-and-the-why; and Kathryn Kuhn et al., "Mining

for Tech-Talent Gold: Seven Ways to Find and Keep Diverse Talent," McKinsey Digital, September 27, 2022, https://www.mckinsey.com/capabilities/mckinsey-digital /our-insights/mining-for-tech-talent-gold-seven-ways-to-find-and-keep-diverse -talent. In a nonprofit context, see Alex Camp et al., "Six 'Power Practices' to Retain Nonprofit Talent," McKinsey & Company, May 22, 2023, https://www.mckinsey .com/capabilities/people-and-organizational-performance/our-insights/the-organization -blog/six-power-practices-to-retain-nonprofit-talent.

37. "Why Is There a Backlash Against DEI?—And How to Fix It," Catalyst, May 21, 2024, https://www.catalyst.org/2024/05/21/dei-backlash-causes/.

38. Erika Bolstad, "Backlash Against DEI Spreads to More States," Stateline, June 14, 2024, https://stateline.org/2024/06/14/backlash-against-dei-spreads-to-more-states.

39. Emma Jacobs, "Can Business Ever Run a True Meritocracy?" *Financial Times*, February 27, 2025, https://www.ft.com/content/87cdf51c-c8e6-439c-aef6-91cb8faed78a.

40. Conor Friedersdorf, "The DEI Industry Needs to Check Its Privilege," *Atlantic*, May 31, 2023, https://www.theatlantic.com/ideas/archive/2023/05/dei-training-initiatives -consultants-companies-skepticism/674237/.

41. See IBM and Netflix as described in Kuhn et al., "Mining for Tech-Talent Gold."

42. *Students for Fair Admissions v. Harvard*, 600 U.S. 181 at 6–40 (U.S. 2023).

43. Mitchell L. Stevens, *Creating a Class: College Admissions and the Education of Elites* (Harvard University Press, 2007), 186.

44. Interestingly, the reported levels of life satisfaction are higher. While 34 percent of workers globally feel that they are "thriving in life," the percentages are 53 in the United States and Canada, 54 in Latin America and the Caribbean, and 60 in Australia and New Zealand. Yet, stress, worry, anger, and sadness are increasing at work, with 41 percent of employees worldwide experiencing a great deal of stress, 10 percentage points higher than in the 2009 report. See "State of the Global Workplace," Gallup Workplace, 2024, https://www.gallup.com/workplace/349484/state-of-the-global -workplace.aspx.

45. See Correll, "Constraints into Preferences"; Gorman, "Gender Stereotypes"; Roberto M. Fernandez and M. Lourdes Sosa, "Gendering the Job: Networks and Recruitment at a Call Center," *American Journal of Sociology* 111, no. 3 (2005): 859–904; Roberto M. Fernandez and Colette Friedrich, "Gender Sorting at the Application Interface," *Industrial Relations* 50, no. 4 (2011): 591–609; Barbulescu and Bidwell, "Do Women Choose Different Jobs from Men?"; and Alison T. Wynn and Shelley J. Correll, "Gendered Perceptions of Cultural and Skill Alignment in Technology Companies," *Social Sciences* 6, no. 2 (2017): 45.

46. See Emilio J. Castilla, "Gender, Race, and Network Advantage in Organizations," *Organization Science* 33, no. 6 (2022): 2364–403; and Castilla and Rho, "The Gendering of Job Postings."

47. Once offers are extended, there is also the important process of candidates accepting the offer. At this stage, organizations should pay attention to whether particular groups of candidates are more or less likely to accept their offers. There may be constraints and challenges that need to be addressed or resources that could be offered to, once again, ensure equal opportunity.

48. See Boris Groysberg, Ashish Nanda, and Nitin Nohria, "The Risky Business of Hiring Stars," *Harvard Business Review*, May 2004, 92–101; Boris Groysberg, "How Star Women Build Portable Skills," *Harvard Business Review*, February 2008, 74; and

Boris Groysberg, *Chasing Stars: The Myth of Talent and the Portability of Performance* (Princeton University Press, 2010).

49. Validity, reliability, and relevance are key standards that should guide hiring and selection processes. *Validity* refers to the extent to which a particular screening and selection measure accurately assesses only the employment *relevant* aspects essential for job performance. *Reliability* ensures that the measure produces consistent results and is therefore free from random error.

50. I do not particularly like the term *underperformer*, but it has become quite popular. (See Amy Gallo, "How to Help an Underperformer," *Harvard Business Review*, June 23, 2014; or Liz Kislik, "Managing an Underperformer Who Thinks They're Doing Great," *Harvard Business Review*, December 2, 2020.) Here I use the term to refer to those individuals who perform at a level that is below average or below expectations.

3. THE ROLE OF BIASES AND SOCIAL PROCESSES

1. I often find that organizations adopt certain solutions simply because they think or assume they have a particular problem, without any data or analysis to support that assumption. Adopting a widely discussed "best practice" can seem easier than investing time and resources to determine *whether*, and *where*, real issues exists. However, identifying the actual problem and its root causes requires commitment and effort from organizations and their leaders. This approach can lead to more effective problem-solving and ensure a better allocation of time and resources, as I discussed extensively in part III.

2. Laura Silver, "More People Globally See Racial, Ethnic Discrimination as a Serious Problem in the U.S. Than in Their Own Society," Pew Research Center, November 2, 2021, https://www.pewresearch.org/short-reads/2021/11/02/more-people-globally -see-racial-ethnic-discrimination-as-a-serious-problem-in-the-u-s-than-in-their -own-society/.

3. Juliana M. Horowitz and Janell Fetterolf, "Worldwide Optimism About Future of Gender Equality, Even as Many See Advantages for Men," Pew Research Center, April 30, 2020, https://www.pewresearch.org/global/2020/04/30/worldwide-optimism-about -future-of-gender-equality-even-as-many-see-advantages-for-men/. Despite seeing some advantages for men, most respondents expressed optimism about prospects of gender equality in their country: a median of 75 percent thought it likely that women in their country would eventually have the same rights as men. Women were less optimistic than men about the future of gender equality in their countries, with gender differences of at least ten percentage points in ten of the countries surveyed (and smaller and significant gender differences in eleven others).

4. As reported in Richard Fry and Carolina Aragao, "Gender Pay Gap in U.S. Has Narrowed Slightly over 2 Decades," Pew Research Center, March 4, 2025, https://www .pewresearch.org/short-reads/2025/03/04/gender-pay-gap-in-us-has-narrowed -slightly-over-2-decades/.

5. U.S. Bureau of Labor Statistics, "Highlights of Women's Earnings in 2023," BLS Reports, August 2024, https://www.bls.gov/opub/reports/womens-earnings/2023/home.htm.

6. See Liana Christin Landivar et al., "Does Part-Time Work Offer Flexibility to Employed Mothers?," *Monthly Labor Review*, February 2022, 1–19.

7. The LEHD program staff includes a diverse group of professionals. Their mission is to provide "new dynamic information on workers, employers, and jobs with state-of-the-art confidentiality protections and no additional data collection burden." For more information, go to https://lehd.ces.census.gov/.

8. I use the word *hypothesis* intentionally, in its most basic definition: "a supposition or proposed explanation made on the basis of limited evidence as a starting point for further investigation" (definition obtained from Oxford Languages in July 2024 after googling definition of hypothesis). While the concept of a hypothesis is often used in academic research, I argue that it is also a helpful starting point for many leaders interested in discovering where their organizations face challenges (and their root causes) to successfully achieve meritocracy.

9. See, for example, Madeline E. Heilman, "The Impact of Situational Factors on Personnel Decisions Concerning Women: Varying the Sex Composition of the Applicant Pool," *Organizational Behavior and Human Performance* 26, no. 3 (1980): 386–95; Barbara F. Reskin and Patricia A. Roos, *Job Queues, Gender Queues: Explaining Women's Inroads into Male Occupations* (Temple University Press, 1990); William T. Bielby, "Minimizing Workplace Gender and Racial Bias," *Contemporary Sociology* 29, no. 1 (2000): 120–29; Julie A. Kmec, "Setting Occupational Sex Segregation in Motion: Demand-Side Explanations of Sex Traditional Employment," *Work and Occupations* 32, no. 3 (2005): 322–54; and Alexandra Kalev, "How You Downsize Is Who You Downsize: Biased Formalization, Accountability and Managerial Diversity," *American Sociological Review* 79, no. 1 (2014): 109–35.

10. See, for example, Shelley J. Correll, "Gender and the Career Choice Process: The Role of Biased Self-Assessments," *American Journal of Sociology* 106, no. 6 (2001): 1691–730; Shelley J. Correll, "Constraints into Preferences: Gender, Status, and Emerging Career Aspirations," *American Sociological Review* 69, no. 1 (2004): 93–113; Roberto M. Fernandez and Colette Friedrich, "Gender Sorting at the Application Interface," *Industrial Relations* 50, no. 4 (2011): 591–609; and Roxana Barbulescu and Matthew Bidwell, "Do Women Choose Different Jobs from Men? Mechanisms of Application Segregation in the Market for Managerial Workers," *Organization Science* 24, no. 3 (2013): 737–56.

11. See James N. Baron and William T. Bielby, "Bringing the Firms Back In: Stratification, Segmentation, and the Organization of Work," *American Sociological Review* 45, no. 5 (1980): 737–65; James N. Baron, "Organizational Perspectives on Stratification," *Annual Review of Sociology* 10 (1984): 37–69; William T. Bielby and James N. Baron, "Men and Women at Work: Sex Segregation and Statistical Discrimination," *American Journal of Sociology* 91, no. 4 (1986): 759–99; Barbara F. Reskin, "Sex Segregation in the Workplace," *Annual Review of Sociology* 19 (1993): 241–70; and Damon J. Philips, "Organization Genealogies and the Persistence of Gender Inequality: The Case of Silicon Valley Law Firms," *Administrative Science Quarterly* 50, no. 3 (2005): 440–72.

12. Trond Petersen and Ishak Saporta, "The Opportunity Structure for Discrimination," *American Journal of Sociology* 109, no. 4 (2004): 852–901.

13. Some classic studies on this topic include Rachel A. Rosenfeld, "Job Mobility and Career Processes," *Annual Review of Sociology* 18 (1992): 39–61; Peter V. Marsden, "The Hiring Process: Recruitment Methods," *American Behavioral Scientist* 37, no. 7 (1994): 979–91; Peter V. Marsden, "Selection Methods in US Establishments," *Acta Sociologica*

37, no. 3 (1994): 287–301; Stephan Baldi and Debra B. McBrier, "Do the Determinants of Promotion Differ for Blacks and Whites? Evidence from the U.S. Labor Market," *Work and Occupations* 24, no. 4 (1997): 478–97; William P. Barnett et al., "Avenues of Attainment: Occupational Demography and Organizational Careers in the California Civil Service," *American Journal of Sociology* 106, no. 1 (2000): 88–144; Trond Petersen et al., "Offering a Job: Meritocracy and Social Networks," *American Journal of Sociology* 106, no. 3 (2000): 763–816; Marta M. Elvira and Christopher D. Zatzick, "Who's Displaced First? The Role of Race in Layoff Decisions," *Industrial Relations: A Journal of Economy and Society* 41, no. 2 (2002): 329–61; Petersen and Saporta, "The Opportunity Structure"; Roberto M. Fernandez and M. Lourdes Sosa, "Gendering the Job: Networks and Recruitment at a Call Center," *American Journal of Sociology* 111, no. 3 (2005): 859–904; and Roberto M. Fernandez and Isabel Fernandez-Mateo, "Networks, Race and Hiring," *American Sociological Review* 71, no. 1 (2006): 42–71.

14. See Paula England, *Comparable Worth: Theories and Evidence* (de Gruyter, 1992); Jerry A. Jacobs, *Revolving Doors: Sex Segregation and Women's Careers* (Stanford University Press, 1989); Jerry A. Jacobs, *Gender Inequality at Work* (Sage, 1995); Donald Tomaskovic-Devey, *Gender and Racial Inequality at Work: The Sources and Consequences of Job Segregation* (ILR Press, 1993); and Trond Petersen and Laurie A. Morgan, "Separate and Unequal: Occupation-Establishment Sex Segregation and the Gender Wage Gap," *American Journal of Sociology* 101, no. 2 (1995): 329–65.

15. See William P. Bridges and Robert L. Nelson, "Markets in Hierarchies: Organizational and Market Influences on Gender Inequality in a State Pay System," *American Journal of Sociology* 95, no. 3 (1989): 616–58; and James N. Baron and Andrew E. Newman, "For What It's Worth: Organizations, Occupations, and the Value of Work Done by Women and Nonwhites," *American Sociological Review* 55, no. 2 (1990): 155–75. For a review, see England, *Comparable Worth*; and Robert L. Nelson and William P. Bridges, *Legalizing Gender Inequality: Courts, Markets and Unequal Pay for Women in America* (Cambridge University Press, 1999).

16. See Madeline E. Heilman, "Description and Prescription: How Gender Stereotypes Prevent Women's Ascent up the Organizational Ladder," *Journal of Social Issues* 57, no. 4 (2001): 657–74; and Peter Cappelli, "Talent Management for the Twenty-First Century," *Harvard Business Review*, March 2008, 74–81.

17. Cecilia L. Ridgeway, "Interaction and the Conservation of Gender Inequality: Considering Employment," *American Sociological Review* 62, no. 2 (1997): 218–35.

18. See Irene V. Blair and Mahzarin R. Banaji, "Automatic and Controlled Processes in Stereotype Priming," *Journal of Personality and Social Psychology* 70, no. 6 (1996): 1142–63; Laurie A. Rudman and Peter Glick, "Feminized Management and Backlash Toward Agentic Women: The Hidden Costs to Women of a Kinder, Gentler Image of Middle Managers," *Journal of Personality and Social Psychology* 77, no. 5 (1999): 1004–10; Laurie A. Rudman and Peter Glick. "Prescriptive Gender Stereotypes and Backlash Toward Agentic Women," *Journal of Social Issues* 57, no. 4 (2001): 743–62; and Ziva Kunda and Steven J. Spencer, "When Do Stereotypes Come to Mind and When Do They Color Judgment? A Goal-Based Theoretical Framework for Stereotype Activation and Application," *Psychological Bulletin* 129, no. 4 (2003): 522–44.

19. Mary Ann Cejka and Alice H. Eagly, "Gender-Stereotypic Images of Occupations Correspond to the Sex Segregation of Employment," *Personality and Social Psychology Bulletin* 25, no. 4 (1999): 413–23.

20. Monica Biernat and Diane Kobrynowicz, "Gender- and Race-Based Standards of Competence: Lower Minimum Standards but Higher Ability Standards for Devalued Groups," *Journal of Personality and Social Psychology* 72, no. 3 (1997): 544–57.

21. Monica Biernat and Jennifer E. Ma, "Stereotypes and the Confirmability of Trait Concepts," *Personality and Social Psychology Bulletin* 31, no. 4 (2005): 483–95.

22. Shelley J. Correll et al., "Getting a Job: Is There a Motherhood Penalty?," *American Journal of Sociology* 112, no. 5 (2007): 1297–338.

23. Michelle J. Budig and Paula England, "The Wage Penalty for Motherhood," *American Sociological Review* 66, no. 2 (2001): 204–25.

24. See "How Big Is the Wage Penalty for Mothers? Huge in Germany, Not So Big in Denmark," *Economist*, January 28, 2019, https://www.economist.com/graphic-detail /2019/01/28/how-big-is-the-wage-penalty-for-mothers; and Kathy Gurchiek, "The Wage Gap Is Wider for Working Mothers," SHRM, October 21, 2019, https://www .shrm.org/resourcesandtools/hr-topics/compensation/pages/wage-gap-is-wider-for -working-mothers.aspx.

25. Stephen Benard et al., "Cognitive Bias and the Motherhood Penalty," *Hastings Law Journal* 59, no. 6 (2008): 1359–87. See also Joan C. Williams, "Hacking Tech's Diversity Problem," *Harvard Business Review* 92, no. 10 (October 2014): 94–100.

26. Choncé Maddox, "The Motherhood Penalty Affects Everything from a Woman's Wages to Hiring and Promotions After Having a Child," *Business Insider*, March 10, 2022, accessed December 15, 2022, https://www.businessinsider.com/personal -finance/motherhood-penalty.

27. This research was first published in Ben A. Rissing and Emilio J. Castilla, "House of Green Cards: Statistical or Preference-Based Inequality in the Employment of Foreign Nationals," *American Sociological Review* 79, no. 6 (2014): 1226–55.

28. See model 5 in table 2 in Rissing and Castilla, "House of Green Cards," 1239–40.

29. Scholars have claimed that Americans and Canadians are considered similarly competent. See Tiane L. Lee and Susan T. Fiske, "Not an Outgroup, Not Yet an Ingroup: Immigrants in the Stereotype Content Model," *International Journal of Intercultural Relations* 30, no. 6 (2006): 751–68.

30. For a review of such work, see International Labour Organization, "Migrants Face 'Significant Discrimination' in Job Markets," *ILO News*, March 8, 2000, https://www .ilo.org/resource/news/migrants-face-significant-discrimination-job-markets; Stephan Kampelmann and François Rycx, "Wage Discrimination Against Immigrants: Measurement with Firm-Level Productivity Data," *IZA Journal of Development and Migration* 5 (2016): 1–24; Gillian Kingston et al., "Discrimination in the Labour Market: Nationality, Ethnicity and the Recession," *Work, Employment and Society* 29, no. 2 (2015): 213–32; Akhlaq Ahmad, "Ethnic Discrimination Against Second-Generation Immigrants in Hiring: Empirical Evidence from a Correspondence Test," *European Societies* 22, no. 5 (2020): 659–81; and Joselyn Andrea Garcia-Quijano, "Workplace Discrimination and Undocumented First-Generation Latinx Immigrants," Crown Family of Social Work, Policy, and Practice, Advocates' Forum, 2020, accessed February 28, 2023, https://crownschool.uchicago.edu /student-life/advocates-forum/workplace-discrimination-and-undocumented-first -generation-latinx.

31. An audit study is typically used to describe a specific type of field experiment in which a researcher randomizes one or more characteristics of individuals (real or hypothetical) and sends them out into the field to observe the impact of those

characteristics on certain outcomes. Historically, audit studies have primarily focused on race, ethnicity, or gender. For race and ethnicity, see William Wentworth Daniel, *Racial Discrimination in England* (Penguin, 1968); and Marianne Bertrand and Sendhil Mullainathan, "Are Emily and Greg More Employable than Lakisha and Jamal? A Field Experiment on Labor Market Discrimination," *American Economic Review* 94, no. 4 (2004): 991–1013. For gender, see Ian Ayres and Peter Siegelman, "Race and Gender Discrimination in Bargaining for a New Car," *American Economic Review* 85, no. 3 (1995): 304–21; and David Neumark et al., "Sex Discrimination in Restaurant Hiring: An Audit Study," *Quarterly Journal of Economics* 111, no. 3 (1996): 915–41. Researchers have expanded the manipulated characteristics to include age, criminal record, disability, educational credentials, immigrant assimilation or generational status, mental health, military service, parental status, physical appearance, religious affiliation, sexual orientation, social class, and unemployment and part-time employment spells, among other characteristics. For reviews, see Stijn Baert and Eddy Omey, "Hiring Discrimination Against Pro-Union Applicants: The Role of Union Density and Firm Size," *De Economist, Netherlands Economic Review* 163 (2015): 263–80; Nick Drydakis, "Sexual Orientation Discrimination in the Labour Market," *Labour Economics* 16, no. 4 (2009): 364–72; Nick Drydakis, "Religious Affiliation and Employment Bias in the Labor Market," *Journal for the Scientific Study of Religion* 49, no. 3 (2010): 477–93; S. Michael Gaddis, "An Introduction to Audit Studies in the Social Sciences," in *Audit Studies: Behind the Scenes with Theory, Method, and Nuance*, ed. S. Michael Gaddis (Springer, 2018); Heather Kugelmass, "'Sorry, I'm Not Accepting New Patients': An Audit Study of Access to Mental Health Care," *Journal of Health and Social Behavior* 57, no. 2 (2016): 168–83; and Doris Weichselbaumer, "Discrimination Against Female Migrants Wearing Headscarves," SSRN, September 2016, https://ssrn.com/abstract=2842960.

32. András Tilcsik, "Pride and Prejudice: Employment Discrimination Against Openly Gay Men in the United States," *American Journal of Sociology* 117, no. 2 (2011): 586–626.

33. See Tilcsik, "Pride and Prejudice," 607. The second main finding of the Tilcsik's study was that employers who stressed the importance of traits stereotypically associated with heterosexual men in their job postings—that is, they described the ideal job candidate as "aggressive or assertive," "decisive," or "ambitious"—were significantly more likely to discriminate against openly gay applicants than employers who did not emphasize the importance of such traits.

34. Barry D. Adam, "Stigma and Employability: Discrimination by Sex and Sexual Orientation in the Ontario Legal Profession," *Canadian Review of Sociology* 18, no. 2 (1981): 216–21.

35. Doris Weichselbaumer, "Sexual Orientation Discrimination in Hiring," *Labour Economics* 10, no. 6 (2003): 629–42.

36. Weichselbaumer, "Sexual Orientation Discrimination in Hiring," 640.

37. Nick Drydakis, "Sexual Orientation Discrimination in the Labour Market," *Labour Economics* 16, no. 4 (2009): 364–72.

38. See M. V. Lee Badgett, *The Economic Case for LGBT Equality. Why Fair and Equal Treatment Benefits Us All* (Beacon, 2020); Nick Drydakis and Klaus F. Zimmermann, "Sexual Orientation, Gender Identity and Labour Market Outcomes: New Patterns and Insights," GLO Discussion Paper No. 627, Global Labor Organization, 2020; Nick Drydakis, "Sexual Orientation and Labor Market Outcomes," IZA World of Labor,

2019, accessed August 10, 2023, https://wol.iza.org/articles/sexual-orientation-and
-labor-market-outcomes/long; Mats Hammarstedt et al., "Sexual Prejudice and
Labor Market Outcomes for Gays and Lesbians: Evidence from Sweden," *Feminist
Economics* 21, no. 1 (2015): 90–109; Sonia Oreffice, "Sexual Orientation and Household Decision Making: Same-Sex Couples' Balance of Power and Labor Supply
Choices," *Labour Economics* 18, no. 2 (2011): 145–58; and Madeline Zavodny, "Is There
a 'Marriage Premium' for Gay Men?," *Review of Economics of the Household* 6, no. 4
(2008): 369–89.

39. Nick Drydakis, "Sexual Orientation and Earnings: A Meta-Analysis 2012–2020," IZA
Discussion Paper No. 14496, IZA Institute of Labor Economics, June 2021, https://
docs.iza.org/dp14496.pdf. The papers analyzed in this meta-analysis covered the
1991–2018 period for studies of data from countries in Europe, North America, and
Australia. A few studies, however, found better earnings records for gay men; see
Christopher S. Carpenter and Samuel T. Eppink, "Does It Get Better? Recent Estimates of Sexual Orientation and Earnings in the United States," *Southern Economic
Journal* 84, no. 2 (2017): 426–41; and Alex Bryson, "Pay Equity After the Equality Act
2010: Does Sexual Orientation Still Matter?," *Work, Employment and Society* 31, no. 3
(2017): 483–500. Using 2013–2015 National Health Interview data, Carpenter and
Eppink reported that both self-identified gay men and lesbians earned more than
comparable heterosexual men and women, a difference of approximately 10 percent
of annual earnings in the case of men.

40. Erin A. Cech and Michelle V. Pham, "Queer in STEM Organizations: Workplace
Disadvantages for LGBT Employees in STEM Related Federal Agencies," *Social Sciences* 6, no. 1 (2017): 12. Cech and Pham compared the workplace experiences of more
than one thousand LGBT employees with those of their non-LGBT colleagues. All
employees were working in six STEM-related agencies (the Department of Energy,
the Environmental Protection Agency, the National Science Foundation, NASA, the
Nuclear Regulatory Commission, and the Department of Transportation). See also
Erin A. Cech and William R. Rothwell, "LGBT Workplace Inequality in the Federal
Workforce: Intersectional Processes, Organizational Contexts, and Turnover Considerations," *ILR Review* 73, no. 1 (2020): 25–60.

41. Daron Acemoglu and Joshua D. Angrist, "Consequences of Employment Protection?
The Case of the Americans with Disabilities Act," *Journal of Political Economy* 109,
no. 5 (2001): 915–57.

42. Acemoglu and Angrist, "Consequences of Employment Protection?," 11–12, 949.
Consistent with this view, the effects of the ADA appear larger in medium-sized
firms, possibly because small firms were exempt from the law. The effects are also
larger in states with more ADA-related discrimination charges.

43. Jean-François Ravaud et al., "Discrimination Towards Disabled People Seeking
Employment," *Social Science and Medicine* 35, no. 8 (1992): 951–58.

44. Stijn Baert, "Wage Subsidies and Hiring Chances for the Disabled: Some Casual Evidence," *European Journal of Health Economics* 17, no. 1 (2016): 71–86.

45. Mason Ameri et al., "The Disability Employment Puzzle: A Field Experiment on
Employer Hiring Behavior," *ILR Review* 71, no. 2 (2018): 329–64.

46. See Baert, "Wage Subsidies"; Ravaud et al., "Discrimination Towards Disabled
People"; Margery A. Turner et al., *Discrimination Against Persons with Disabilities:
Barriers at Every Step* (Urban Institute, 2005); and Pieter-Paul Verhaeghe et al., "Dis-
crimination of Tenants with a Visual Impairment on the Housing Market: Empirical

Evidence from Correspondence Tests," *Disability Health Journal* 9, no. 2 (2016): 234–38.

47. Regarding mental health, see Stijn Baert, "Facebook Profile Picture Appearance Affects Recruiters' First Hiring Decisions," *New Media and Society* 20, no. 3 (2018): 1220–39. Regarding physical appearance, see Francisco B. Galarza and Gustavo Yamada, "Labor Market Discrimination in Lima, Peru: Evidence from a Field Experiment," *World Development* 58 (2014): 83–94; Margaret Maurer-Fazio and Lei Lei, "'As Rare as a Panda': How Facial Attractiveness, Gender, and Occupation Affect Interview Callbacks at Chinese Firms," *International Journal of Manpower* 36, no. 1 (2015): 68–85; Eleonora Patacchini et al., "Do Employers Discriminate Against Physical Appearance and Sexual Preference? A Field Experiment," in *Unexplored Dimensions of Discrimination*, ed. Tito Boeri et al. (Oxford University Press, 2015); and Bradley J. Ruffle and Ze'ev Shtudiner, "Are Good-Looking People More Employable?," *Management Science* 61, no. 8 (2015): 1760–76.

48. Sonia Ghumman et al., "Religious Discrimination in the Workplace: A Review and Examination of Current and Future Trends," *Journal of Business and Psychology* 28, no. 4 (2013): 439–54. A few important audit studies of religious affiliation include Claire L. Adida et al., "Identifying Barriers to Muslim Integration in France," *Proceedings of the National Academy of Sciences of the United States of America* 107, no. 52 (2010): 22384–90; Guillaume Pierné, "Hiring Discrimination Based on National Origin and Religious Closeness: Results from a Field Experiment in the Paris Area," *IZA Journal of Labor Economics* 2 (2013): 1–15; Michael Wallace et al., "Religious Affiliation and Hiring Discrimination in the American South: A Field Experiment," *Social Currents* 1, no. 2 (2014): 189–207; and Bradley R. E. Wright et al., "Religious Affiliation and Hiring Discrimination in New England: A Field Experiment," *Research in Social Stratification and Mobility* 34 (2013): 111–26.

49. Wallace et al., "Religious Affiliation."

50. Nick Drydakis, "Religious Affiliation and Employment Bias in the Labor Market," *Journal for the Scientific Study of Religion* 49, no. 3 (2010): 477–93.

51. Abhijit Banerjee et al., "Labor Market Discrimination in Delhi: Evidence from a Field Experiment," *Journal of Comparative Economics* 37, no. 1 (2009): 14–27.

52. See Alessandro Acquisti and Christina Fong, "An Experiment in Hiring Discrimination via Online Social Networks," *Management Science* 66, no. 3 (2020): 1005–507; Timothy Bartkoski et al., "A Meta-Analysis of Hiring Discrimination Against Muslims and Arabs," *Personnel Assessment and Decisions* 4, no. 2 (2018): Article 1; and Wallace et al., "Religious Affiliation"; and Wright et al., "Religious Affiliation."

53. See Sonia Ghumman and Ann Marie Ryan, "Not Welcome Here: Discrimination Towards Women Who Wear the Muslim Headscarf," *Human Relations* 66, no. 5 (2013): 671–98; and Eden B. King and Afra S. Ahmad, "An Experimental Field Study of Interpersonal Discrimination Toward Muslim Job Applicants," *Personnel Psychology* 63, no. 4 (2010): 881–906.

54. Craig Considine, "The Racialization of Islam in the United States: Islamophobia, Hate Crimes, and Flying While Brown," *Religions* 8, no. 9 (2017): 165–83; and Khyati Y. Joshi, "Racialization of Religion and Global Migration," in *Intersections of Religion and Migration: Issues at the Global Crossroads*, ed. Jennifer Beth Saunders et al. (Palgrave Macmillan, 2016).

55. Rachel C. Schneider et al., "How Religious Discrimination Is Perceived in the Workplace: Expanding the View," *Socius: Sociological Research for a Dynamic World* 8 (2022): 1–14.

56. Acquisti and Fong, "An Experiment."

57. Acquisti and Fong, "An Experiment," 1015. They also manipulated sexual orientation. They found no significant difference in nationwide callback rates between gay and straight candidates. Unlike with the religion manipulation, there were no significant differences in callback rates for gay versus straight candidates across any of the studied geographical areas.

58. Erving Goffman, *Stigma: Notes on the Management of Spoiled Identity* (Prentice-Hall, 1963).

59. See Kenji Yoshino, "The Pressure to Cover," *New York Times Magazine*, January 15, 2006; and Kenji Yoshino and Christie Smith, *Uncovering Talent: A New Model of Inclusion*, Deloitte University, 2019, https://www2.deloitte.com/content/dam/Deloitte /us/Documents/about-deloitte/us-about-deloitte-uncovering-talent-a-new-model-of -inclusion.pdf.

60. Sonia K. Kang et al., "Whitened Résumés: Race and Self-Presentation in the Labor Market," *Administrative Science Quarterly* 61, no. 3 (2016): 469–502.

61. Edward T. Hall is credited with the first use of the now-popular iceberg analogy, which he used to illustrate the workings of culture. Hall suggested that if a society's culture were an iceberg, some aspects would be visible above the water, while a larger portion would remain hidden beneath the surface. This analogy has been extended to other areas, including the concept of identity. See Edward T. Hall, *Beyond Culture* (Anchor/Doubleday, 1976).

62. Mahzarin R. Banaji and Anthony G. Greenwald, *Blindspot: Hidden Biases of Good People* (Delacorte, 2013).

63. In the standard IAT, participants view a series of words and images on a computer screen. They are instructed to press the "I" key for positive words like "happy" or "pleasant" and the "E" key for negative words like "miserable" or "dangerous." For the racial version of the test, participants are asked to press "I" for a Black face and "E" for a White face. Then, they press "I" for a positive word or a Black face and "E" for a negative word or a White face. This process is reversed to pair Black faces with negative words and White faces with positive words. The software records response times and calculates an IAT score at the end of the test. Participants with higher implicit racial bias may, for example, associate a Black face with a negative word faster than with a positive word. See Scott Sleek, "The Bias Beneath: Two Decades of Measuring Implicit Associations," Association for Psychological Science, January 31, 2018, https://www .psychologicalscience.org/observer/the-bias-beneath-two-decades-of-measuring -implicit-associations.

64. See Hart Blanton et al., "Strong Claims and Weak Evidence: Reassessing the Predictive Validity of the IAT," *Journal of Applied Psychology* 94, no. 3 (2009): 567–82; Frank J. Landy, "Stereotypes, Bias, and Personnel Decisions: Strange and Stranger," *Industrial and Organizational Psychology* 1, no. 4 (2008): 379–92; Philip E. Tetlock and Gregory Mitchell, "Implicit Bias and Accountability Systems: What Must Organizations Do to Prevent Discrimination?," *Research in Organizational Behavior* 29 (2009): 3–38; and Amy L. Wax, "Supply Side or Discrimination? Assessing the Role of Unconscious Bias," *Temple Law Review* 83, no. 4 (2011): 877–902.

65. Jo-Anne Kandola, "Workplace Gender Discrimination and the Implicit Association Test" (PhD diss., Aston University, 2015), https://research.aston.ac.uk/en/studentTheses /workplace-gender-discrimination-and-the-implicit-association-test. See page 263 for the quote.

66. For a review, see Frederick L. Oswald et al., "Predicting Ethnic and Racial Discrimination: A Meta-Analysis of IAT Criterion Studies," *Journal of Personality and Social Psychology* 105, no. 2 (2013): 171–92; and Rickard Carlsson and Jens Agestrom, "A Closer Look at the Discrimination Outcomes in the IAT Literature," Linnaeus University Centre for Labour Market and Discrimination Studies, 2015, https://www.diva-portal.org/smash/get/diva2:911362/FULLTEXT01.pdf.
67. For example, see William J. Chopik and Hannah L. Giasson, "Age Differences in Explicit and Implicit Age Attitudes Across the Life Span," supplement, *Gerontologist* 57, no. S2 (2017): S169–S77.
68. See Rodney L. Bassett et al., "One Effort to Measure Implicit Attitudes Toward Spirituality and Religion," *Journal of Psychology and Christianity* 24, no. 3 (2005): 210–18; and Bethany L. Albertson, "Religious Appeals and Implicit Attitudes," *Political Psychology* 32, no. 1 (2011): 109–30.
69. Erin C. Westgate et al., "Implicit Preferences for Straight People over Lesbian Women and Gay Men Weakened from 2006 to 2013," *Collabra* 1, no. 1 (2015): 1–10.
70. Carlee Beth Hawkins and Brian A. Nosek, "Motivated Independence? Implicit Party Identity Predicts Political Judgements Among Self-Proclaimed Independents," *Personality and Social Psychology Bulletin* 38, no. 11 (2012): 1437–52.
71. Steven R. Pruett and Fong Chan, "The Development and Psychometric Validation of the Disability Attitude Implicit Association Test," *Rehabilitation Psychology* 51, no. 3 (2006): 202–13.
72. Jens Agerström and Dan-Olof Rooth, "The Role of Automatic Obesity Stereotypes in Real Hiring Discrimination," *Journal of Applied Psychology* 96, no. 4 (2011): 790–805.
73. For a review, see Emilio J. Castilla and Aruna Ranganathan, "The Production of Merit: How Managers Understand and Apply Merit in the Workplace," *Organization Science* 31, no. 4 (2020): 909–35.
74. See Oswald et al., "Predicting Ethnic and Racial Discrimination"; and Ulrich Schimmack, "The Validation Crisis in Psychology," *Meta-Psychology* 5, no. 3 (2021).
75. For reviews of these theories, see Roberto M. Fernandez and Jason Greenberg, "Race, Network Hiring, and Statistical Discrimination," in *Research in the Sociology of Work*, vol. 24, *Networks, Work and Inequality*, ed. Steve McDonald (Emerald Group, 2013); and Rissing and Castilla, "House of Green Cards."
76. Gary S. Becker, *The Economics of Discrimination*, 2nd ed. (University of Chicago Press, 1971).
77. See Kenneth J. Arrow, "The Theory of Discrimination," in *Discrimination in Labor Markets*, ed. Orley Ashenfelter and Albert Rees (Princeton University Press, 1973); Kenneth J. Arrow, *Information and Economic Behavior* (Federation of Swedish Industries, 1973); Edmund S. Phelps, "The Statistical Theory of Racism and Sexism," *American Economic Review* 62, no. 4 (1972): 659–61; Dennis J. Aigner and Glen G. Cain, "Statistical Theories of Discrimination in Labor Markets," *ILR Review* 30, no. 2 (1977): 175–87; and William T. Bielby and James N. Baron, "Men and Women at Work: Sex Segregation and Statistical Discrimination," *American Journal of Sociology* 91, no. 4 (1986): 759–99.
78. See, for a review, Emilio J. Castilla, "Gender, Race, and Network Advantage in Organizations," *Organization Science* 33, no. 6 (2022): 2368. See also Fernandez and Greenberg, "Race, Network Hiring, and Statistical Discrimination."
79. András Tilcsik, "Statistical Discrimination and the Rationalization of Stereotypes," *American Sociological Review* 86, no. 1 (2021): 93–122.

80. David Autor, "Lecture Note: The Economics of Discrimination Theory," notes from lecture delivered at MIT, November 24, 2003, http://dspace.mit.edu/bitstream /handle/1721.1/115921/14-661-fall-2003-fall-2004/contents/lecture-notes/lecture_8.pdf.

81. Marianne Bertrand and Esther Duflo, "Field Experiments on Discrimination," Working Paper 22014 (National Bureau of Economic Research, 2016), 312.

82. Tilcsik, "Statistical Discrimination."

83. See Jimmy Calanchini et al., "Reducing Implicit Racial Preferences: III. A Process-Level Examination of Changes in Implicit Preferences," *Journal of Personality and Social Psychology* 121, no. 4 (2021): 796–818. Calanchini et al. draw the following conclusion: "One of the primary findings to emerge from the present research is that 9 of 18 interventions influenced associations. Given the primacy that many prominent theoretical perspectives assign to associations in implicit social cognition . . ., the finding that half of interventions tested here do not influence associations is noteworthy" (811). See also Calvin K. Lai et al., "Reducing Implicit Racial Preferences: II. Intervention Effectiveness Across Time," *Journal of Experimental Psychology* 145, no. 8 (2016): 1001–16. In that article, Lai and colleagues summarized their research as follows: "We tested 9 interventions (8 real and one sham) to reduce implicit racial preferences over time. In two studies with a total of 6,321 participants, all 9 interventions immediately reduced implicit preferences. However, none were effective after a delay of several hours to several days. We also found that these interventions did not change explicit racial preferences and were not reliably moderated by motivations to respond without prejudice" (1002).

84. See Janice G. Asare, "I'm a Diversity and Inclusion Expert Who Admits That 'Unconscious Bias' Trainings Don't Really Work. Here are 3 Ways Companies Can Ensure They're Not a Waste of Time," *Business Insider*, July 9, 2020, https://www.businessinsider.com/how-to-improve-your-companys-dei-unconscious-bias-training-2020-7; Abby Tang and Michelle Yan Huang, "Implicit Bias Trainings Are Imperfect, but We Shouldn't Stop Trying," *Business Insider*, February 17, 2021, https://www.businessinsider.com/implicit-bias-trainings-imperfect-should-we-stop-them-2020-7; and Katica Roy, "Implicit Bias Training Doesn't Work. Here's What Does," *MSNBC*, January 31, 2023, https://www.msnbc.com/know-your-value/business-culture/implicit-bias-training-doesn-t-work-here-s-what-does-n1302608.

85. As an example, see Sally Percy, "Six Top Tips for Networking in the New World of Work," *Forbes*, June 23, 2021, https://www.forbes.com/sites/sallypercy/2021/06/23 /six-top-tips-for-networking-in-the-new-world-of-work/.

86. See Bonnie Marcus, "The Networking Advice No One Tells You," *Forbes*, May 22, 2018, updated April 14, 2022, https://www.forbes.com/sites/bonniemarcus/2018/05/22/the-networking-advice-no-one-tells-you/?sh=77bf52ae7772; Heidi Scott Giusto, "It's Not If It's Going to Be Awkward, It's When: A Beginner's Guide to Successful Networking," Career Path Writing Solutions, https://careerpathwritingsolutions.com/its-not-if-its -going-to-be-awkward-its-when-a-beginners-guide-to-successful-networking/; and Hannah Fleishman, "How to Master Non-Awkward, Effective In-Person Networking," HubSpot, November 9, 2022, archived at https://www.studocu.com/row/document /rivers-state-university-port-harcourt/journalism-and-media-studies/howto-master -non-awkward-effective-in-person-networking-211122-163148/90021969.

87. See Marcus, "The Networking Advice"; and Herminia Ibarra and Mark Lee Hunter, "How Leaders Create and Use Networks," *Harvard Business Review* 85, no. 1 (2007).

88. Mark S. Granovetter, "The Strength of Weak Ties," *American Journal of Sociology* 78, no. 6 (1973): 1360–80.

89. See Granovetter, "The Strength of Weak Ties"; Mark S. Granovetter, "Granovetter Replies to Gans," *American Journal of Sociology* 80, no. 2 (1974): 527–29; and Mark S. Granovetter, "Coase Revisited: Business Groups in the Modern Economy," *Industrial and Corporate Change* 4, no. 1 (1995): 93–130.

90. See Nan Lin et al., "Social Resources and Strength of Ties: Structural Factors in Occupational Status Attainment," *American Sociological Review* 46, no. 4 (1981): 393–405; and Ronald S. Burt, *Structural Holes: The Social Structure of Competition* (Harvard University Press, 1992). For a review of such work, see Emilio J. Castilla et al., "Social Networks and Employment: Mechanisms (Part 1) and Outcomes (Part 2)," *Sociology Compass* 7, no. 12 (2013): 999–1026.

91. See Yanjie Bian, "Bringing Strong Ties Back In: Indirect Ties, Network Bridges, and Job Searches in China," *American Sociological Review* 62, no. 3 (1997): 366–85; and Sinan Aral and Marshall Van Alstyne, "The Diversity-Bandwidth Trade-Off," *American Journal of Sociology* 117, no. 1 (2011): 90–171.

92. See Peter V. Marsden and Jeanne S. Hurlbert, "Social Resources and Mobility Outcomes: A Replication and Extension," *Social Forces* 66, no. 4 (1988): 1038–59; and Valery Yakubovich, "Weak Ties, Information, and Influence: How Workers Find Jobs in a Local Russian Labor Market," *American Sociological Review* 70, no. 3 (2005): 408–21.

93. Karthik Rajkumar et al., "A Causal Test of the Strength of Weak Ties," *Science* 377, no. 6612 (2022): 1304–10.

94. See Roberto M. Fernandez and Nancy Weinberg, "Sifting and Sorting: Personal Contacts and Hiring in a Retail Bank," *American Sociological Review* 62, no. 6 (1997): 883–902; Ted Mouw, "Social Capital and Finding a Job: Do Contacts Matter?," *American Sociological Review* 68, no. 6 (2003): 868–98; Elena Obukhova and George Lan, "Do Job-Seekers Benefit from Contacts? A Direct Test with Contemporaneous Searches," *Management Science* 59, no. 10 (2013): 2204–16; and Elena Obukhova, "Motivation vs. Relevance: Using Strong Ties to Find a Job in Urban China," *Social Science Research* 41, no. 3 (2012): 570–80.

95. Peter V. Marsden and Elizabeth H. Gorman, "Social Networks, Job Changes, and Recruitment," in *Sourcebook of Labor Markets: Evolving Structures and Processes*, ed. Ivar Berg and Arne. L. Kalleberg (Springer, 2001).

96. Marsden and Gorman, "Social Networks."

97. Nan Lin, "Building a Network Theory of Social Capital," *Connections* 22, no. 1 (1999): 28–51.

98. Axel Franzen and Dominik Hangartner, "Social Networks and Labour Market Outcomes: The Non-Monetary Benefits of Social Capital," *European Sociological Review* 22, no. 4 (2006): 353–68.

99. See Antoni Calvó-Armengol and Matthew O. Jackson, "The Effects of Social Networks on Employment and Inequality," *American Economic Review* 94, no. 3 (2004): 426–54; and Federico Cingano and Alfonso Rosolia, "People I Know: Job Search and Social Networks," *Journal of Labor Economics* 30, no. 2 (2012): 291–332.

100. See Emilio J. Castilla and Ben A. Rissing, "Best in Class: The Returns on Application Endorsements in Higher Education," *Administrative Science Quarterly* 64, no. 1 (2019): 230–70. By "application endorsement," we refer to the act of sending a brief

targeted message to key recruiters or screeners in support of a particular applicant (from an individual who supports such an applicant).

101. Gary Paul Green et al., "Racial and Ethnic Differences in Job-Search Strategies in Atlanta, Boston, and Los Angeles," *Social Science Quarterly* 80, no. 2 (1999): 263–78; Fernandez and Sosa, "Gendering the Job"; Fernandez and Fernandez-Mateo, "Networks, Race and Hiring"; Steve McDonald et al., "Networks of Opportunity: Gender, Race, and Job Leads," *Social Problems* 56, no. 3 (2009): 385–402; and Steve McDonald, "What's in the 'Old Boys' Network? Accessing Social Capital in Gendered and Racialized Networks," *Social Networks* 33, no. 4 (2011): 317–30.

102. See Jomills H. Braddock and James M. McPartland, "How Minorities Continue to Be Excluded from Equal Employment Opportunities: Research on Labor Market and Institutional Barriers," *Journal of Social Issues* 43, no. 1 (1987): 5–39; James H. Johnson Jr. et al., "An Empirical Assessment of Four Perspectives on the Declining Fortunes of the African-American Male," *Urban Affairs Review* 35, no. 5 (2000): 695–716; Deirdre Royster, *Race and the Invisible Hand: How White Networks Exclude Black Men from Blue-Collar Jobs* (University of California Press, 2003); and William J. Wilson, *When Work Disappears: The World of the New Urban Poor* (Knopf, 1996).

103. See James R. Elliott, "Social Isolation and Labor Market Insulation: Network and Neighborhood Effects on Less-Educated Urban Workers," *Sociological Quarterly* 40, no. 2 (1999): 199–216; James R. Elliott, "Class, Race, and Job Matching in Contemporary Urban Labor Markets," *Social Science Quarterly* 81, no. 4 (2000): 1036–52; and David A. Reingold, "Social Networks and the Employment Problem of the Urban Poor," *Urban Studies* 36, no. 11 (1999): 1907–32.

104. Royster, *Race and the Invisible Hand*.

105. See Fernandez and Fernandez-Mateo, "Networks, Race and Hiring"; Steve McDonald, "Occupation-Specific Work Experience and Job Matching Through Social Networks," *Social Science Research* 40, no. 6 (2011): 1664–75; and Steve McDonald, "What's in the 'Old Boys' Network? Accessing Social Capital in Gendered and Racialized Networks," *Industrial Relations* 50, no. 4 (2011): 591–609. Fernandez and colleagues have investigated the extent to which referrals shape the gender and racial composition of the pool of applicants. See, for example, Katherine Neckerman and Roberto M. Fernandez, "Keeping a Job: Network Hiring and Turnover in a Retail Bank," in *The Governance of Relations in Markets and Organizations*, ed. Vincent Buskens et al. (Elsevier Science, 2003); Fernandez and Sosa, "Gendering the Job"; and Roberto M. Fernandez and Brian Rubineau, "Network Recruitment and the Glass Ceiling: Evidence from Two Firms," *RSF: The Russell Sage Foundation Journal of the Social Sciences* 5, no. 3 (2019): 88–102.

106. See Ronald S. Burt, "Network Disadvantaged Entrepreneurs: Density, Hierarchy, and Success in China and the West," *Entrepreneurship Theory and Practice* 43, no. 1 (2019): 19–50; Herminia Ibarra, "Homophily and Differential Returns: Sex Differences in Network Structure and Access in an Advertising Firm," *Administrative Science Quarterly* 37, no. 3 (1992): 422–47; Ajay Mehra et al., "At the Margins: A Distinctiveness Approach to the Social Identity and Social Networks of Underrepresented Groups," *Academy of Management Journal* 41, no. 4 (1998): 441–52; and Meredith L. Woehler et al., "Whether, How, and Why Networks Influence Men's and Women's Career Success: Review and Research Agenda," *Journal of Management* 47, no. 1 (2021): 207–36.

107. See Yang Yang et al., "A Network's Gender Composition and Communication Pattern Predict Women's Leadership Success," *Proceedings of the National Academy of*

Sciences 116, no. 6 (2019): 2033–38; Edward Bishop Smith et al., "Social Networks and Cognition," *Annual Review of Sociology* 46, no. 1 (2020): 159–74; Tristan L. Botelho and Mabel Abraham, "Pursuing Quality: How Search Costs and Uncertainty Magnify Gender-Based Double Standards in a Multistage Evaluation Process," *Administrative Science Quarterly* 62, no. 4 (2017): 698–730; Mabel Abraham, "Gender-Role Incongruity and Audience-Based Gender Bias: An Examination of Networking Among Entrepreneurs," *Administrative Science Quarterly* 65, no. 1 (2020): 151–80; and Nabil Khattab et al., "Gender and Mobility: Qatar's Highly Skilled Female Migrants in Context," *Migration and Development* 9, no. 3 (2020): 369–89.

108. Castilla, "Gender, Race, and Network Advantage."

109. One related line of research has explored how job seekers' status affects network use. See Edward B. Smith et al., "Status Differences in the Cognitive Activation of Social Networks," *Organization Science* 23, no. 1 (2012): 67–82; Sandra S. Smith, " 'Don't Put My Name on It': Social Capital Activation and Job-Finding Assistance Among the Black Urban Poor," *American Journal of Sociology* 111, no. 1 (2005): 1–57; and Alexandra Marin, "Don't Mention It: Why People Don't Share Job Information, When They Do, and Why It Matters," *Social Networks* 34, no. 2 (2012): 181–92.

110. Royster, *Race and the Invisible Hand*.

111. For a review, see Barbara F. Reskin and Irene Padavic, *Women and Men at Work* (Pine Forge, 1994); Petersen and Morgan, "Separate and Unequal"; Fernandez and Sosa, "Gendering the Job"; Marin, "Don't Mention It"; Brian Rubineau and Roberto M. Fernandez, "Missing Links: Referrer Behavior and Job Segregation," *Management Science* 59, no. 11 (2013): 2470–89; Brian Rubineau and Roberto M. Fernandez, "Tipping Points: The Gender Segregating and Desegregating Effects of Network Recruitment," *Organization Science* 26, no. 6 (2015): 1646–64; and Fernandez and Rubineau, "Network Recruitment and the Glass Ceiling."

112. For a review, see Fernandez and Sosa, "Gendering the Job."

113. See Petersen et al., "Offering a Job"; and Marc-David L. Seidel et al., "Friends in High Places: The Effects of Social Networks on Discrimination in Salary Negotiations," *Administrative Science Quarterly* 45, no. 1 (2000): 1–24.

114. Fernandez and Sosa, "Gendering the Job."

115. See Patricia Drentea, "Consequences of Women's Formal and Informal Job Search Methods for Employment in Female-Dominated Jobs," *Gender and Society* 12, no. 3 (1998): 321–38; F. Carson Mencken and Idee Winfield, "In Search of the 'Right Stuff': The Advantages and Disadvantages of Informal and Formal Recruiting Practices in External Labor Markets," *American Journal of Economics and Sociology* 57, no. 2 (1998): 135–54; and Bruce C. Straits, "Occupational Sex Segregation: The Role of Personal Ties," *Journal of Vocational Behavior* 52, no. 2 (1998): 191–207.

116. James R. Elliott, "Referral Hiring and Ethnically Homogeneous Jobs: How Prevalent Is the Connection and for Whom?," *Social Science Research* 30, no. 3 (2001): 401–25.

117. See Roberto M. Fernandez et al., "Social Capital at Work: Networks and Employment at a Phone Center," *American Journal of Sociology* 105, no. 5 (2000): 1288–356; Emilio J. Castilla, "Social Networks and Employee Performance in a Call Center," *American Journal of Sociology* 110, no. 5 (2005): 1243–83; and Forrest Briscoe and Katherine C. Kellogg, "The Initial Assignment Effect: Local Employer Practices and Positive Career Outcomes for Work-Family Program Users," *American Sociological Review* 76, no. 2 (2011): 291–319.

118. Smith, " 'Don't Put My Name on It.' "

119. See Steve McDonald, "Patterns of Informal Job Matching Across the Life Course: Entry-Level, Reentry-Level, and Elite Non-Searching," *Sociological Inquiry* 75, no. 3 (2005): 403–28; and Steve McDonald and Glen H. Elder Jr., "When Does Social Capital Matter? Non-Searching for Jobs Across the Life Course," *Social Forces* 85, no. 1 (2006): 521–49.

120. See Burt, *Structural Holes*; Ronald S. Burt, "Structural Holes and Good Ideas," *American Journal of Sociology* 110, no. 2 (2004): 349–99; and Ronald S. Burt, *Brokerage and Closure: An Introduction to Social Capital* (Oxford University Press, 2005). See also Scott E. Seibert et al., "A Social Capital Theory of Career Success," *Academy of Management Journal* 44, no. 2 (2001): 219–37; Joel M. Podolny and James N. Baron, "Resources and Relationships: Social Networks and Mobility in the Workplace," *American Sociological Review* 62, no. 5 (1997): 673–93; and Rob Cross and Jonathon N. Cummings, "Tie and Network Correlates of Individual Performance in Knowledge-Intensive Work," *Academy of Management Journal* 47, no. 6 (2004): 928–37.

121. Fernandez et al., "Social Capital at Work."

122. For reviews of such work, see Smith, "'Don't Put My Name on It'"; Sameer B. Srivastava and Eliott B. Sherman, "Agents of Change or Cogs in the Machine? Reexamining the Influence of Female Managers on the Gender Wage Gap." *American Journal of Sociology* 120, no. 6 (2015): 1778–808; or Jason Greenberg and Ethan Mollick, "Activist Choice Homophily and the Crowdfunding of Female Founders," *Administrative Science Quarterly* 62, no. 2 (2017): 341–74.

123. Michael J. Sandel, *The Tyranny of Merit: What's Become of the Common Good?* (Farrar, Straus and Giroux, 2020), 121.

124. Annette Lareau, *Unequal Childhoods: Class, Race, and Family Life* (University of California Press, 2003).

125. Barbara Ehrenreich, *Fear of Falling: The Inner Life of the Middle Class* (Pantheon, 1989).

126. See Margaret Y. Padgett and Kathryn A. Morris, "Keeping It 'All in the Family': Does Nepotism in the Hiring Process Really Benefit the Beneficiary?," *Journal of Leadership and Organizational Studies* 11, no. 2 (2005): 34–45; Marianne Bertrand and Antoinette Schoar, "The Role of Family in Family Firms," *Journal of Economic Perspectives* 20, no. 2 (2006): 73–96; Alberto Alesina and Paola Giuliano, "Family Ties," in *Handbook of Economic Growth*, vol. 2, ed. Philippe Aghion and Steven N. Durlauf (Elsevier, 2014); Francis Kramarz and Oskar Nordström Skans, "When Strong Ties Are Strong: Networks and Youth Labour Market Entry," *Review of Economic Studies* 81, no. 3 (2014): 1164–200; and Lauren A. Rivera, *How Elite Students Get Elite Jobs* (Princeton University Press, 2015).

127. Morten Bennedsen et al., "Inside the Family Firm: The Role of Families in Succession Decisions and Performance," *Quarterly Journal of Economics* 122, no. 2 (2007): 647–91; Castilla et al., "Social Networks and Employment"; Shing-Yi Wang, "Marriage Networks, Nepotism, and Labor Market Outcomes in China," *American Economic Journal: Applied Economics* 5, no. 3 (2013): 91–112; and Margaret Y. Padgett et al., "Reactions to Nepotism in the Hiring Process: The Role of Family Member Qualifications," *Journal of Organizational Psychology* 19, no. 4 (2019): 106–20.

128. See Thomas J. Espenshade and Alexandria Walton Radford, *No Longer Separate, Not Yet Equal: Race and Class in Elite College Admission and Campus Life* (Princeton University Press, 2010; and Richard D. Kahlenberg, *Affirmative Action for the Rich: Legacy Preferences in College Admissions* (Century Foundation, 2010).

129. See Michael Hurwitz, "The Impact of Legacy Status on Undergraduate Admissions at Elite Colleges and Universities," *Economics of Education Review* 30, no. 3 (2011): 480–92; Peter Arcidiacono et al., "Legacy and Athlete Preferences at Harvard," *Journal of Labor Economics* 40, no. 1 (2022): 133–55; and Peter Arcidiacono et al., "Divergent: The Time Path of Legacy and Athlete Admissions at Harvard," *Journal of Human Resources* 59, no. 3 (2024): 653–83.

130. Similar findings are reported in other empirical studies. See Arcidiacono et al., "Legacy and Athlete Preferences at Harvard"; and Camille G. Caldera, "Legacy, Athlete, and Donor Preferences Disproportionately Benefit White Applicants, Per Analysis," *Harvard Crimson*, October 23, 2019, https://www.thecrimson.com/article/2019/10/23/nber-admissions-data.

131. See Michel Anteby, *Manufacturing Morals: The Values of Silence in Business School Education* (University of Chicago Press, 2013); and Lauren A. Rivera and András Tilcsik, "Class Advantage, Commitment Penalty: The Gendered Effect of Social Class Signals in an Elite Labor Market," *American Sociological Review* 81, no. 6 (2016): 1097–131.

132. See Jenny M. Stuber, *Inside the College Gates: How Class and Culture Matter in Higher Education* (Lexington, 2011); Elizabeth A. Armstrong and Laura T. Hamilton, *Paying for the Party: How College Maintains Inequality* (Harvard University Press, 2015); and Elizabeth M. Lee, *Class and Campus Life: Managing and Experiencing Inequality at an Elite College* (Cornell University Press, 2016).

133. See Max Weber, "Class, Status, Party," in *From Max Weber: Essays in Sociology*, ed. Hans Heinrich Gerth and C. Wright Mills (Oxford University Press, 1958); Pierre Bourdieu, "Cultural Reproduction and Social Reproduction," in *Knowledge, Education and Cultural Change*, ed. Richard Brown (Tavistock, 1973); Paul DiMaggio, "Cultural Entrepreneurship in Nineteenth-Century Boston: The Creation of an Organizational Base for High Culture in America," *Media, Culture and Society* 4, no. 1 (1982): 33–50; and Pierre Bourdieu and Jean-Claude Passeron, *Reproduction in Education, Society and Culture* (Sage, 1990).

134. Castilla and Rissing, "Best in Class."

135. See Rivera, *Pedigree*; and Kyla Thomas, "The Labor Market Value of Taste: An Experimental Study of Class Bias in U.S. Employment," *Sociological Science* 5, no. 24 (2018): 562–95.

136. For instance, advantaged parents strive to ensure that their children's natural talents are developed, not only in terms of cognitive ability but also in other relevant attributes like industriousness and perseverance. See Daniel Markovits, *The Meritocracy Trap: How America's Foundational Myth Feeds Inequality, Dismantles the Middle Class, and Devours the Elite* (Penguin, 2019); and Sandel, *The Tyranny of Merit*, 12–13, 177–79.

137. This is one reason, for instance, that legacy preference keeps garnering significant attention due to college admissions scandals and society's growing emphasis on achieving fairness in higher education admissions processes. See Max Larkin and Mayowa Aina, "Legacy Admissions Offer an Advantage—And Not Just at Schools like Harvard," *NPR*, November 4, 2018, https://www.npr.org/2018/11/04/663629750/legacy-admissions-offer-an-advantage-and-not-just-at-schools-like-harvard; Kate Taylor, "Amid Modest Sentences, Prosecutors Bring New Charges in Admissions Scandal," *New York Times*, October 22, 2019, https://www.nytimes.com/2019/10/22/us/lori-loughlin-bribery-charge.html; Natasha Warikoo, "The Easiest Reform for College Admissions," *Atlantic*, January 29, 2020, https://www.theatlantic.com/ideas

/archive/2020/01/least-difficult-reform-college-admissions/605689; and Jayla Whitfield
-Anderson and Christopher Wilson, "SCOTUS Affirmative Action Ruling Renews
Calls to End 'Unlevel Playing Field' of Legacy Admissions," *Yahoo! News*, last modified June 30, 2023, https://news.yahoo.com/scotus-affirmative-action-ruling-renews
-calls-to-end-unlevel-playing-field-of-legacy-admissions-150545713.html.

138. Hurwitz, "The Impact of Legacy Status"; and Romesh Vaitilingam, "College Admissions," Forum for the Kent A. Clark Center for Global Markets, April 30, 2019, https://
www.igmchicago.org/surveys/college-admissions.

139. See Richard D. Kahlenberg, "A New Call to End Legacy Admissions," *Atlantic*, February
14, 2018, https://www.theatlantic.com/education/archive/2018/02/when-affirmative
-action-benefits-the-wealthy/553313; and Arcidiacono et al., "Legacy and Athlete
Preferences at Harvard"; and Caldera, "Legacy, Athlete, and Donor Preferences."

140. See James L. Shulman and William G. Bowen, *The Game of Life: College Sports and
Educational Values* (Princeton University Press, 2001); William G. Bowen and Sarah
A. Levin, *Reclaiming the Game: College Sports and Educational Values* (Princeton Uni-
versity Press, 2003); William G. Bowen et al., *Equity and Excellence in American Higher
Education* (University of Virginia Press, 2005); Thomas J. Espenshade and Chang Y.
Chung, "The Opportunity Cost of Admission Preferences at Elite Universities," *Social
Science Quarterly* 86, no. 2 (2005): 293–305; and Hurwitz, "The Impact of Legacy Status."

4. MERITOCRACY AND ITS PARADOXES IN PRACTICE

1. Lillian Cunningham and Jena McGregor, "Why Big Business Is Falling Out of Love
with the Annual Performance Review," *Washington Post*, August 17, 2015, https://
www.washingtonpost.com/news/on-leadership/wp/2015/08/17/why-big-business
-is-falling-out-of-love-with-annual-performance-reviews/.

2. Peter Cappelli and Anna Tavis, "The Performance Management Revolution," *Harvard Business Review* 94, no. 10 (October 2016): 58–67.

3. Dana Wilkie, "Is the Annual Performance Review Dead?," SHRM, August 19, 2015, https://
www.shrm.org/resourcesandtools/hr-topics/employee-relations/pages/performance
-reviews-are-dead.aspx.

4. Lillian Cunningham, "In Big Move, Accenture Will Get Rid of Annual Performance
Reviews and Rankings," *Washington Post*, July 21, 2015, https://www.washingtonpost
.com/news/on-leadership/wp/2015/07/21/in-big-move-accenture-will-get-rid-of
-annual-performance-reviews-and-rankings.

5. See Marcus Buckingham and Ashley Goodall, "Reinventing Performance Management," *Harvard Business Review* 93, no. 4 (April 2015); and Stacia Garr and Lisa Barry,
"Performance Management Is Broken," Deloitte Insights, March 5, 2014, https://www2
.deloitte.com/us/en/insights/focus/human-capital-trends/2014/hc-trends-2014
-performance-management.html.

6. David Rock, "Performance Management: Are You Ready for Change?," Inside HR,
October 16, 2023, https://web.archive.org/web/20220326072951/https://www.insidehr
.com.au/performance-management-are-you-ready-for-change/.

7. Wilkie, "Is the Annual Performance Review Dead?"

8. Jathan Janove, "Get Rid of Performance Reviews," SHRM, November 9, 2021, https://
www.shrm.org/resourcesandtools/hr-topics/employee-relations/humanity-into-hr
/pages/get-rid-of-performance-reviews.aspx.

9. Katie Evans-Reber, "Here's What Can Happen When Companies Get Rid of Performance Reviews," *Forbes*, February 19, 2020, https://www.forbes.com/sites/forbeshuman resourcescouncil/2020/02/19/heres-what-can-happen-when-companies-get-rid-of -performance-reviews/.

10. Robert Sutton and Ben Wigert, "More Harm than Good: The Truth About Performance Reviews," Gallup Workplace, May 6, 2019, https://www.gallup.com/workplace /249332/harm-good-truth-performance-reviews.aspx.

11. Evans-Reber, "Here's What Can Happen."

12. Sutton and Wigert, "More Harm than Good."

13. See pages 4 and 6 of Ben Wigert and Jim Harter, "Re-Engineering Performance Management," Gallup Workplace, 2017, https://www.gallup.com/workplace/238064/re -engineering-performance-management.aspx?thank-you-report-form=1.

14. See Theresa Agovino, "The Performance Review Problem," *HR Magazine*, March 14, 2023, https://www.shrm.org/hr-today/news/hr-magazine/spring-2023/pages/the -problem-with-performance-reviews.aspx; and Katie Burke, "Performance Reviews Are Broken," *Inc.*, November 28, 2022, https://www.inc.com/katie-burke/create-more -manageable-performance-review-system.html.

15. Cappelli and Tavis, "The Performance Management Revolution."

16. Cunningham and McGregor, "Why Big Business Is Falling Out of Love with the Annual Performance Review."

17. Benham Tabrizi, "Why the Performance Review Is Dying Out—Including at Companies like Apple and Microsoft," FastCompany, August 24, 2023, https://www.fastcompany .com/90943074/why-the-performance-review-is-dying-out-including-at-companies -like-apple-and-microsoft.

18. See Janove, "Get Rid of Performance Reviews."

19. See Frank Dobbin, *Inventing Equal Opportunity* (Princeton University Press, 2009); and Frank Dobbin and Alexandra Kalev, *Getting to Diversity: What Works and What Doesn't* (Harvard University Press, 2022).

20. For a review of such works, see Emilio J. Castilla, "Gender, Race, and Meritocracy in Organizational Careers," *American Journal of Sociology* 113, no. 6 (2008): 1479–526; and Emilio J. Castilla, "Bringing Managers Back In: Managerial Influences on Workplace Inequality," *American Sociological Review* 76, no. 5 (2011): 667–94.

21. Rachel K. Raczka, "How Bonuses Get Employees to Choose Work over Family," HBS Working Knowledge, November 29, 2021, https://hbswk.hbs.edu/item/how-bonuses -get-employees-to-choose-work-over-family.

22. Short-term incentive programs in the WorldatWork reports include annual incentive plans, spot awards, discretionary bonuses, project bonuses, and team or small-group incentives, among many. See WorldatWork and Compensation Advisory Partners, *Incentive Pay Practices*, July 2021, accessed January 2024, https://worldatwork.org /research/incentive-pay-practices. For WorldatWork individual surveys, see *Incentive Pay Practices: Government Organizations*, https://worldatwork.org/media/CDN /dist/CDN2/documents/pdf/resources/research/2021_Incentive%20Pay%20Practices-Government.pdf; *Incentive Pay Practices: Nonprofit Organizations*, https:// worldatwork.org/media/CDN/dist/CDN2/documents/pdf/resources/research/2021 _Incentive%20Pay%20Practices-Nonprofit.pdf; *Incentive Pay Practices: Privately Held Companies*, https://worldatwork.org/media/CDN/dist/CDN2/documents/pdf /resources/research/2021_Incentive%20Pay%20Practices-Privately%20Held.pdf; and *Incentive Pay Practices: Publicly Traded Companies*, https://worldatwork.org/media

/CDN/dist/CDN2/documents/pdf/resources/research/2021_Incentive%20Pay%20 Practices-Publicly%20Traded.pdf.

23. WorldatWork and Compensation Advisory Partners, *Incentive Pay Practices: Publicly Traded Companies.*

24. Jackie Wiles, "The Real Impact on Employees of Removing Performance Ratings," Gartner, August 15, 2019, https://www.gartner.com/smarterwithgartner/corporate-hr -removing-performance-ratings-is-unlikely-to-improve-performance.

25. Michael Stephan et al., *Global Human Capital Trends 2014: Engaging the 21st-Century Workforce* (Deloitte University Press, 2014), https://www2.deloitte.com/content/dam /Deloitte/ar/Documents/human-capital/arg_hc_global-human-capital-trends-2014 _09062014%20(1).pdf.

26. This section relies on the presentation of materials, methods, and other details of the study published in Emilio J. Castilla and Stephen Benard, "The Paradox of Meritoc- racy in Organizations," *Administrative Science Quarterly* 55, no. 4 (2010): 543–76.

27. Session 1 was conducted as an optional in-class exercise for MBA students and included 95 participants (67 male and 26 female). Sessions 2 and 3 were conducted as optional workshops for a group of professionals attending either an MBA program or a similar business degree program. Session 2 included 68 participants (48 male and 20 female). Session 3 included 66 participants (48 male and 18 female). Addi- tional studies are included and described in Castilla and Benard, "The Paradox of Meritocracy."

28. Four percent of respondents had an MBA, while the rest were enrolled in an MBA program. Additionally, 80.4 percent had previous management experience, averag- ing 2.4 years (with a standard deviation of 2.6 years). About 78.3 percent liked super- visory roles, 5.3 percent did not, and 16 percent were unsure.

29. In the end, as our analyses showed, it did not matter whether respondents agreed or disagreed with such statements; simply being exposed to them, we argue, led them to behave differently at the time of distributing their bonuses, on average, to two otherwise identical employees except for their gender.

30. For example, see Castilla, "Gender, Race, and Meritocracy."

31. The profiles included two types of qualitative feedback: praise and criticism. Each profile had three sentences of praise and two sentences of criticism. For one test profile, the praise read, "Michael/Patricia is hardworking and quick to find ways to solve clients' problems. He/She is also generally popular with the clients. Michael /Patricia reliably completes projects on time." The praise for the other test profile read, "Michael/Patricia's proposals are always well thought-out and highly detailed. He/She always does an excellent job of communicating technical aspects of the profiles to clients. Clients respect and enjoy working with Michael/Patricia." The criticism for one test profile read, "While the quality of Michael/Patricia's work is excellent, several projects this year have gone over budget. In the next appraisal cycle, he/she needs to work on keeping costs down." The criticism for the other test profile read, "Michael/Patricia is a valuable team member, but sometimes tries to take on too many projects at once. In the next year, he/she needs to work on staying focused." The qualitative comments were counterbalanced across the two test profiles: each set of comments was randomly assigned to the male test profile for half of the sample and to the female test profile for the other half. This tactic ensured that any differ- ences in evaluations of the qualitative comments were not biased by the employee's gender being associated to specific comments.

32. After submitting their ratings, in the "final reflections" section, participants were asked for their beliefs about the performance evaluation process and ServiceOne as a company, including whether ServiceOne was meritocratic and fair, using 7-point scales. We expected and indeed found evidence that participants significantly rated the company as more meritocratic and fairer in the meritocratic condition than in the non-meritocratic condition. For more details, see Castilla and Benard, "The Paradox of Meritocracy," 554.

33. For a detailed discussion of the study design and the findings, including further data analyses, robustness checks, and additional experiments, see Castilla and Benard, "The Paradox of Meritocracy," 554–66.

34. Eric L. Uhlmann and Geoffrey L. Cohen, "I Think It, Therefore It's True: Effects of Self-Perceived Objectivity on Hiring Discrimination," *Organizational Behavior and Human Decision Processes* 104, no. 2 (2007): 207–23.

35. See Monica Biernat and Diane Kobrynowicz, "Gender- and Race-Based Standards of Competence: Lower Minimum Standards but Higher Ability Standards for Devalued Groups," *Journal of Personality and Social Psychology* 72, no. 3 (1997): 544–57; Peter Glick and Susan T. Fiske, "The Ambivalent Sexism Inventory: Differentiating Hostile and Benevolent Sexism," *Journal of Personality and Social Psychology* 70, no. 3 (1996): 491–512; Laurie A. Rudman, "Self-Promotion as a Risk Factor for Women: The Costs and Benefits of Counterstereotypical Impression Management," *Journal of Personality and Social Psychology* 74, no. 3 (1998): 629–45; Laurie A. Rudman and Peter Glick, "Feminized Management and Backlash Toward Agentic Women: The Hidden Costs to Women of a Kinder, Gentler Image of Middle Managers," *Journal of Personality and Social Psychology* 77, no. 5 (1999): 1004–10; and Jim Sidanius and Felicia Pratto, *Social Dominance: An Intergroup Theory of Social Hierarchy and Oppression* (Cambridge University Press, 1999).

36. See Uzma Khan and Ravi Dhar, "Licensing Effect in Consumer Choice," *Journal of Marketing Research* 43, no. 2 (2006): 259–66; and Benoît Monin and Dale T. Miller, "Moral Credentials and the Expression of Prejudice," *Journal of Personality and Social Psychology* 81, no. 1 (2001): 33–43.

37. Khan and Dhar, "Licensing Effect."

38. See the article abstract of Anna C. Merritt, Daniel A. Effron, and Benoît Monin, "Moral Self-Licensing: When Being Good Frees Us to Be Bad," *Social and Personality Psychology Compass* 4, no. 5 (2010): 344–57.

39. See Jennifer R. Crosby et al., "Where Do We Look During Potentially Offensive Behavior?," *Psychological Science* 19, no. 3 (2008): 226–28; Daniel A. Effron et al., "Endorsing Obama Licenses Favoring Whites," *Journal of Experimental Social Psychology* 45, no. 3 (2009): 590–93; Anna C. Merritt et al., "The Strategic Pursuit of Moral Credentials," *Journal of Experimental Social Psychology* 48, no. 3 (2012): 774–77; and Jennifer R. Crosby and Benoît Monin, "Failure to Warn: How Student Race Affects Warnings of Potential Academic Difficulty," *Journal of Experimental Social Psychology* 43, no. 4 (2007): 663–70.

40. Effron et al., "Endorsing Obama."

41. Benoît Monin and Dale T. Miller, "Moral Credentials and the Expression of Prejudice," *Journal of Personality and Social Psychology* 81, no. 1 (2001): 33–43.

42. See Maryam Kouchaki, "Vicarious Moral Licensing: The Influence of Others' Past Moral Actions on Moral Behavior," *Journal of Personality and Social Psychology* 101, no. 4 (2011): 702–15; Hanna Reimers et al., "Moral-Psychological Mechanisms

of Rebound Effects from a Consumer-Centered Perspective: A Conceptualization and Research Directions," *Frontiers in Psychology* 13 (2022); Yawei Ran et al., "Moral Observer—Licensing in Cyberspace," *Behavioral Sciences* 12, no. 5 (2022): 148; Molly Lewis et al., "The Puzzling Relationship Between Multi-Laboratory Replications and Meta-Analyses of the Published Literature," *Royal Society Open Science* 9, no. 2 (2022); Kang Zhao et al., "Compensatory Belief in Health Behavior Management: A Concept Analysis," *Frontiers in Psychology* 12 (2021): Article 705991; and Jennifer Sheridan et al., "Improving Department Climate Through Bias Literacy: One College's Experience," *Journal of Women and Minorities in Science and Engineering* 27, no. 2 (2021): 87–106.

43. Effron et al., "Endorsing Obama"; Monin and Miller, "Moral Credentials."

44. Jessica Cascio and E. Ashby Plant, "Prospective Moral Licensing: Does Anticipating Doing Good Later Allow You to Be Bad Now?" *Journal of Experimental Social Psychology* 56 (2015): 110–16.

45. Alexandra Maftei et al., "Is Discrimination Against Disabled Job Candidates Increased by Previously Acquired Non-Discriminatory Moral Credentials?," *Romanian Journal of Applied Psychology* 22, no. 2 (2020): 33–41.

46. Once again, this is consistent with prior research indicating that to the extent that individuals hold stereotypic thoughts and beliefs, a state of self-perceived objectivity and fairness may increase the expression of demographic bias and prejudice. See Patricia G. Devine et al., "Prejudice With and Without Compunction," *Journal of Personality and Social Psychology* 60, no. 6 (1991): 817–30.

47. Anatolia Batruch et al., "Belief in School Meritocracy and the Legitimization of Social and Income Inequality," *Social Psychological and Personality Science* 14, no. 5 (2023): 621–35.

48. By *correlational study*, I refer to a type of research that examines relationships between variables without the researcher controlling or manipulating any of them. In contrast, an *experimental study* allows the researcher to manipulate one or more independent variables and measure their impact on a set of dependent variables of interest. Additionally, other variables can be added as controls to account for their potential impact on the dependent variables. While correlational studies identify associations between variables, controlled experiments provide stronger evidence for causal relationships.

49. Virginie Wiederkehr et al., "Belief in School Meritocracy as a System-Justifying Tool for Low Status Students," *Frontiers in Psychology* 6 (2015): Article 1053.

50. See Jonathan J. B. Mijs, "The Paradox of Inequality: Income Inequality and Belief in Meritocracy Go Hand in Hand," *Socio-Economic Review* 19, no. 1 (2021): 7–35.

51. See Ana F. Madeira et al., "Primes and Consequences: A Systematic Review of Meritocracy in Intergroup Relations," *Frontiers in Psychology* 10 (2019); Article 2007.

52. See Joe Pinsker, "The Real Reasons Legacy Preferences Exist," *Atlantic*, April 4, 2019, https://www.theatlantic.com/education/archive/2019/04/legacy-admissions -preferences-ivy/586465/; Brad Polumbo, "'Legacy' College Admissions Are Affirmative Action for Rich White People," *Washington Examiner*, September 23, 2019, https:// www.washingtonexaminer.com/opinion/2141040/legacy-college-admissions-are -affirmative-action-for-rich-white-people/; and Rebecca Ostriker, "Boycott Targets College Admissions Boost Given to Children of Alumni at Harvard, Other Elite Schools," *Boston Globe*, September 25, 2021, https://www.bostonglobe.com/2021/09 /25/metro/boycott-targets-college-admissions-boost-given-children-alumni -harvard-other-elite-schools/?s_campaign=breakingnews:newsletter.

53. Emilio J. Castilla and Ethan J. Poskanzer, "Through the Front Door: Why Do Organizations (Still) Prefer Legacy Applicants?," *American Sociological Review* 87, no. 5 (2022): 782–826.

54. Ben A. Rissing and Emilio J. Castilla, "House of Green Cards: Statistical or Preference-Based Inequality in the Employment of Foreign Nationals," *American Sociological Review* 79, no. 6 (2014): 1226–55.

55. Canadians were our reference category because of all the nations, Canada is the most structurally similar to the United States: it is similar in location and has similar educational and employment national structures to those in the United States.

56. These nationality effects remained significant even after comparing applicants in the same occupation, industry, work, location, and evaluation month. We further examined computer software engineers, the largest occupation in our dataset with 44,441 applications and a 92.3 percent approval rate. Consistent with our overall findings, Latin American immigrants were 25 percent less likely to receive labor certification than Canadian immigrants. No significant differences were found between Asian and Canadian immigrants. See Rissing and Castilla, "House of Green Cards," 1242.

57. Emilio J. Castilla and Ben A. Rissing, "Best in Class: The Returns on Application Endorsements in Higher Education," *Administrative Science Quarterly* 64, no. 1 (2019): 230–70.

58. Castilla and Rissing, "Best in Class," 8.

59. Castilla and Rissing, "Best in Class," 14.

60. iHire, *The State of Online Recruiting 2022*, Employer Resources Report, 2022, last modified May 31, 2023, https://www.ihire.com/resourcecenter/employer/pages/the-state -of-online-recruiting-2022.

61. By contrast, the same study reports that only 6.2 percent of candidates would like employers to provide information on their commitments to DEI. The top three things candidates want employers to do in an ad are (1) specify the salary range for the position (68 percent); (2) provide a timeline for scheduling interviews (47.8 percent); and (3) reduce the time required to complete the application (40.9 percent).

62. Cheryl R. Kaiser et al., "Presumed Fair: Ironic Effects of Organizational Diversity Structures," *Journal of Personality and Social Psychology* 104, no. 3 (2013): 504–19.

63. Sonia K. Kang et al., "Whitened Résumés: Race and Self-Presentation in the Labor Market," *Administrative Science Quarterly* 61, no. 3 (2016): 469–502; see, specifically, their second study.

64. This section relies on the presentation of materials, methods, and other details of the study published in Castilla, "Gender, Race, and Meritocracy."

65. If 10 percent is the increase for Bob, for instance, I estimated that then the increase for Alice, 0.4 percent lower, is 9.96. To compute these numbers, I used the following compound interest (future value) formula: $W_t = W_0 (1+r)^T$, where W_t is the wage at time t, W_0 is the starting wage, T is the unit of time, and r is the rate of wage increase. For more information, see Castilla, "Gender, Race, and Meritocracy," 1503–10.

66. Castilla, "Gender, Race, and Meritocracy," 1493.

67. While the research projects discussed to this point are based on data collection within single organizations, empirical studies have also assessed the extent to which the meritocracy paradox may be generalizable to other organizations, industries, and societies. Mun and Kodama (2022), for instance, collected and analyzed panel data from four hundred large Japanese companies and 400,000 employees over twelve years to study the meritocracy paradox. They found that the gender gap in bonus pay was larger in workplaces with a merit-based system than in workplaces without

one. This paradox of meritocracy effect was found only in bonus pay, not in other aspects of compensation. See Eunmi Mun and Naomi Kodama, "Meritocracy at Work? Merit-Based Reward Systems and Gender Wage Inequality," *Social Forces* 100, no. 4 (2022): 1561–91.

5. IS MERIT IN THE EYE OF THE BEHOLDER?

1. Peg Thoms, *Finding the Best and the Brightest: A Guide to Recruiting, Selecting, and Retaining Effective Leaders* (Greenwood, 2005).
2. Adam Bryant, "How to Hire the Right Person," *New York Times*, February 13, 2017, https://www.getabstract.com/en/summary/how-to-hire-the-right-person/30260.
3. Douglas A. Ready et al., "Building a Game-Changing Talent Strategy," *Harvard Business Review* 92, nos. 1–2 (January–February 2014): 62–68.
4. Rebecca Knight, "When to Take a Chance on an Imperfect Job Candidate," *Harvard Business Review*, March 8, 2021.
5. Bryant, "How to Hire the Right Person."
6. Lauren A. Rivera, "Guess Who Doesn't Fit In at Work," *New York Times*, May 30, 2015, https://www.nytimes.com/2015/05/31/opinion/sunday/guess-who-doesnt-fit-in-at-work.html.
7. This quote was cited in Sue Shellenbarger, "The Dangers of Hiring for Cultural Fit," *Wall Street Journal*, September 23, 2019, https://www.wsj.com/articles/the-dangers-of-hiring-for-cultural-fit-11569231000.
8. James N. Baron and David M. Kreps, *Strategic Human Resources: Frameworks for General Managers* (Wiley, 1999), 351.
9. Rivera, "Guess Who Doesn't Fit In."
10. Smith was quoted in Bryant, "How to Hire the Right Person."
11. See Kurt VandeMotter, "Hiring Is a Dating Process," CareerUSA.org, August 1, 2021, https://www.careerusa.org/tip-of-the-week/1134-hiring-is-a-dating-process.html.
12. The term *talent* originally referred to a unit of weight or value. In ancient Rome and Greece, the talent was a common weight unit for commercial transactions. See Charles Theodore Seltman, *Athens, Its History and Coinage Before the Persian Invasion* (Cambridge University Press, 1924). In Latin, *talentum* means "balance, weight; sum of money." According to Seltman, the use of the word *talent* to mean "gift or skill" in English originated in the late thirteenth century and gradually came to describe traits, abilities, aptitudes, and even dispositions that are "innate," "natural," and "unique."
13. In many such workshops, I have asked participants to reflect on a recent situation in which they "were involved in making a hiring decision . . . or . . . were involved in selecting or evaluating." I then tell them, "I want you to reflect on which factors you thought were the most important ones when deciding who deserved to be hired or who deserved a high-performance evaluation rating and its consequent high reward. I am asking you to think about what affects your decision-making regarding hiring and performance evaluations regardless of the organizational structures in place at your company, or regardless of the values that your organization or your superiors may be emphasizing when making such decisions."
14. Emilio J. Castilla and Aruna Ranganathan, "The Production of Merit: How Managers Understand and Apply Merit in the Workplace," *Organization Science* 31, no. 4 (2020): 909–35.
15. Castilla and Ranganathan, "The Production of Merit."

16. See Uwe Flick, *Managing Quality in Qualitative Research* (Sage, 1998).

17. See James P. Spradley, *The Ethnographic Interview* (Holt, Rinehart and Winston, 1979).

18. Each interview was digitally recorded. In addition to taking notes on the respondents' answers during the interview, at the end of each interview we also wrote down our overall impressions of the interviewees and the location where the interview took place. This contextual information proved to be informative in interpreting interviewee responses. The transcripts of all 56 interviews, along with our interview notes, amounted to more than 1,300 single-spaced pages.

19. See Martha S. Feldman, *Strategies for Interpreting Qualitative Data* (Sage, 1994); Kathy Charmaz, *Constructing Grounded Theory: A Practical Guide Through Qualitative Analysis* (Pine Forge, 2006); Juliet Corbin and Anselm Strauss, *Basics of Qualitative Research: Grounded Theory Procedures and Techniques*, 2nd ed. (Sage, 1990); and Juliet Corbin and Anselm Strauss, *Basics of Qualitative Research: Techniques and Procedures for Developing Grounded Theory*, 3rd ed. (Sage, 2007).

20. See Ferdinand de Saussure, *Course in General Linguistics*, ed. Charles Bally, Albert Sechehaye, and Albert Riedlinger, trans. Wade Baskin (McGraw-Hill, 1966); and Spradley, *The Ethnographic Interview*.

21. A similar methodological approach can be found in, for instance, Catherine J. Turco, "Difficult Decoupling: Employee Resistance to the Commercialization of Personal Settings," *American Journal of Sociology* 118, no. 2 (2012): 380–419.

22. See Iddo Tavory and Ann Swidler, "Condom Semiotics: Meaning and Condom Use in Rural Malawi," *American Sociological Review* 74, no. 2 (2009): 171–89. We began by coding the interviews, first line by line and then paragraph by paragraph. We used the Atlas.ti qualitative software package. For further details about our data analysis, see Castilla and Ranganathan, "The Production of Merit," 5–7.

23. Judy B. Rosener, "Standards of Meritocracy Don't Add Up," *Los Angeles Times*, February 2, 1997.

24. Richard B. Williams, "Objective Stuff Won't Tell All? We Know That," letter to the editor, *Los Angeles Times*, April 6, 1997.

25. Richard Showstack, "Defending the Merits of the 'Meritocracy,'" letter to the editor, *Los Angeles Times*, February 16, 1997, https://www.latimes.com/archives/la-xpm-1997 -02-16-fi-29183-story.html.

26. Jeanette N. Cleveland, Kevin R. Murphy, and Richard E. Williams, "Multiple Uses of Performance Appraisal: Prevalence and Correlates," *Journal of Applied Psychology* 74, no. 1 (1989): 130–35.

27. See Robert G. Eccles and Dwight B. Crane, *Doing Deals: Investment Banks at Work* (Harvard Business School, 1988), 166; and Catherine J. Turco, "Cultural Foundations of Tokenism: Evidence from the Leveraged Buyout Industry," *American Sociological Review* 75, no. 6 (2010): 894–913.

28. Eccles and Crane, *Doing Deals*, 170. See also Louise M. Roth, *Selling Women Short: Gender and Money on Wall Street* (Princeton University Press, 2006); Boris Groysberg, *Chasing Stars: The Myth of Talent and the Portability of Performance* (Princeton University Press, 2012); and Boris Groysberg and Paul M. Healy, *Wall Street Research: Past, Present, and Future* (Stanford University Press, 2013).

29. See Alan Manning and Joanna Swaffield, "The Gender Gap in Early-Career Wage Growth," *Economic Journal* 118, no. 530 (2008): 983–1024; and Emilio J. Castilla, "Bringing Managers Back In: Managerial Influences on Workplace Inequality," *American Sociological Review* 76, no. 5 (2011): 667–94.

30. See Margaret A. Neale, Elizabeth A. Mannix, and Deborah H. Gruenfeld, eds., *Research on Managing Groups and Teams*, vol. 1, *Composition* (JAI, 1998); and Margaret A. Neale, Elizabeth A. Mannix, and Katherine Phillips, eds., *Research on Managing Groups and Teams*, vol. 2, *Diversity and Groups* (Emerald Group, 2008).

31. See John C. Turner, *Social Influence* (Thomson Brooks/Cole, 1991); and Robert B. Cialdini and Brad J. Sagarin, "Principles of Interpersonal Influence," in *Persuasion: Psychological Insights and Perspectives*, ed. Sharon Shavitt and Timothy C. Brock (Allyn and Bacon, 1994).

32. Bengt Holmstrom, "Moral Hazard in Teams," *Bell Journal of Economics* 13, no. 2 (1982): 324–40.

33. This idea of reading into impressions dates back to the work of Erving Goffman. See Erving Goffman, *The Presentation of Self in Everyday Life* (Doubleday, 1959).

34. For a review, see Xiaoquan Zhang and Feng Zhu, "Group Size and Incentives to Contribute: A Natural Experiment at Chinese Wikipedia," *American Economic Review* 101, no. 4 (2011): 1601–15.

35. For reviews of academic work on social networks and employment, see Emilio J. Castilla, George J. Lan, and Ben A. Rissing, "Social Networks and Employment: Mechanisms (Part 1) and Outcomes (Part 2)," *Sociology Compass* 7, no. 12 (2013): 999–1026; Brian Rubineau and Roberto M. Fernandez, "Missing Links: Referrer Behavior and Job Segregation," *Management Science* 59, no. 11 (2013): 2470–89; and Brian Rubineau and Roberto M. Fernandez, "Tipping Points: The Gender Segregating and Desegregating Effects of Network Recruitment," *Organization Science* 26, no. 6 (2015): 1646–64.

36. See Nan Lin, Walter M. Ensel, and John C. Vaughn, "Social Resources and Strength of Ties: Structural Factors in Occupational Status Attainment," *American Sociological Review* 46, no. 4 (1981): 393–405; Nan Lin, "Building a Network Theory of Social Capital," *Connections* 22, no. 1 (1999): 28–51; Nan Lin, "Social Networks and Status Attainment," *Annual Review of Sociology* 25 (1999): 467–87; and Nan Lin, *Social Capital: A Theory of Social Structure and Action* (Cambridge University Press, 2002).

37. Early discussions of these concepts include Kingsley Davis, *Human Society* (MacMillan, 1950); and Talcott Parsons, *The Social System* (Free Press of Glencoe, 1951).

38. Ralph Linton, *The Study of Man* (Appleton-Century-Crofts, 1936).

39. See Peter M. Blau and Otis D. Duncan, *The American Occupational Structure* (Wiley, 1967). Blau and Duncan transformed the sociological study of intergenerational social mobility. Their work allowed for a consideration of achievement (for example, level of education) versus ascription (for example, gender, parents' class) in explaining intergenerational mobility. Since then, there has been a plethora of research on this topic. For useful reviews of that research, see William T. Bielby, "Models of Status Attainment," *Research in Social Stratification and Mobility* 1 (1981): 3–26; and Michael Hout and Thomas A. DiPrete, "What We Have Learned: RC28's Contributions to Knowledge About Social Stratification," *Research in Social Stratification and Mobility* 24, no. 1 (2006): 1–20.

40. See, for instance, Barbara F. Reskin, "Employment Discrimination and Its Remedies," in *Sourcebook of Labor Markets: Evolving Structures and Processes*, ed. Ivar Berg and Arne L. Kalleberg (Springer Science+Business Media, 2001).

41. See Pierre Bourdieu, "Cultural Reproduction and Social Reproduction," in *Knowledge, Education and Cultural Change*, ed. J. Richardson (Greenwood, 1973); Pierre Bourdieu, *Outline of a Theory of Practice*, trans. Richard Nice (Cambridge University

Press, 1977); and Pierre Bourdieu, *La Distinction: Critique Sociale du Jugement* (Éditions de Minuit, 1979).

42. See Parsons, *The Social System*; Leon H. Mayhew, *Law and Equal Opportunity: A Study of the Massachusetts Commission Against Discrimination* (Harvard University Press, 1968); and Theodore D. Kemper, "On the Nature and Purpose of Ascription," *American Sociological Review* 39, no. 6 (1974): 844–53.

43. Individuals prefer, like, and trust similar others, a phenomenon known as *homophily*. See Miller McPherson, Lynn Smith-Lovin, and James M Cook, "Birds of a Feather: Homophily in Social Networks," *Annual Review of Sociology* 27 (2001): 415–44.

44. Reskin, "Employment Discrimination."

45. These are, in fact, common explanations provided in the literature on statistical labor market discrimination. See Edmund S. Phelps, "The Statistical Theory of Racism and Sexism," *American Economic Review* 62, no. 4 (1972): 659–61; Kenneth J. Arrow, "The Theory of Discrimination," in *Discrimination in Labor Markets*, ed. Orley Ashenfelter and Albert Rees (Princeton University Press, 1973); Kenneth J. Arrow, *Information and Economic Behavior* (Federation of Swedish Industries, 1973); Dennis J. Aigner and Glen G. Cain, "Statistical Theories of Discrimination in Labor Markets," *ILR Review* 30, no. 2 (1977): 175–87; and William T. Bielby and James N. Baron, "Men and Women at Work: Sex Segregation and Statistical Discrimination," *American Journal of Sociology* 91, no. 4 (1986): 759–99.

46. See Daniel A. Bell, *The Coming of Post-Industrial Society: A Venture in Social Forecasting* (Harper, 1973).

47. See Richard T. Longoria, *Meritocracy and Americans' Views on Distributive Justice* (Lexington, 2009).

48. Castilla and Ranganathan, "The Production of Merit," 914–15.

49. The study design was similar to the main one used in Emilio J. Castilla and Stephen Benard, "The Paradox of Meritocracy in Organizations," *Administrative Science Quarterly* 55, no. 4 (2010): 543–76, also described in the prior chapter.

50. As in Castilla and Benard, "The Paradox of Meritocracy," it was key that the test profiles were of equivalent performance but not so similar as to raise participants' suspicion that studying gender bias was a goal of the research. To this end, I gave each test profile equal quantitative performance scores and similar but not identical qualitative comments that were counterbalanced across profiles.

51. The process model presented in this section was also described in an earlier version of the Castilla and Ranganathan article "The Production of Merit" presented at the American Sociological Association Annual Meeting in August 2014.

52. There are reasons to suspect that such understandings of merit are formed and shaped well before entering the labor market, while, for instance, individuals are being educated in schools and colleges, as well as while they are being trained by organizations and institutions before joining hiring organizations. However, we were not empirically able to assess those details in our study.

53. See Linda L. Carli and Alice H. Eagly, "Gender, Hierarchy, and Leadership: An Introduction," *Journal of Social Issues* 57, no. 4 (2001): 629–36; and Aruna Ranganathan and Ranjitha Shivaram, "Getting Their Hands Dirty: How Female Managers Motivate Female Worker Productivity Through Subordinate Scut Work," *Management Science* 67, no. 5 (2021): 2657–3320.

54. See Bernard M. Bass, "From Transactional to Transformational Leadership: Learning to Share the Vision," *Organizational Dynamics* 18, no. 3 (1990): 19–31; and Sonia

Ospina and Erica Foldy, "A Critical Review of Race and Ethnicity in the Leadership Literature: Surfacing Context, Power and the Collective Dimensions of Leadership," *Leadership Quarterly* 20, no. 6 (2009): 876–96.

55. See Alice H. Eagly and Blair T. Johnson, "Gender and Leadership Style: A Meta-Analysis," *Psychological Bulletin* 108, no. 2 (1990): 233–56; and Alice H. Eagly, Mary C. Johannesen-Schmidt, and Marloes L. van Engen, "Transformational, Transactional, and Laissez-Faire Leadership Styles: A Meta-Analysis Comparing Women and Men," *Psychological Bulletin* 129, no. 4 (2003): 569–91.

56. Fremont Shull and William P. Anthony, "Do Black and White Supervisory Problem Solving Styles Differ?," *Personnel Psychology* 31, no. 4 (1978): 761–82.

57. See Bernard M. Bass, "From Transactional to Transformational Leadership"; and Bernard M. Bass, *The Bass Handbook of Leadership: Theory, Research, and Managerial Applications*, 4th ed. (Free Press, 2008).

58. For a review, see Emilio J. Castilla, "Gender, Race, and Meritocracy in Organizational Careers," *American Journal of Sociology* 113, no. 6 (2008): 1479–526; John C. Dencker, "Relative Bargaining Power, Corporate Restructuring, and Managerial Incentives," *Administrative Science Quarterly* 54, no. 3 (2009): 453–85; Trond Petersen and Ishak Saporta, "The Opportunity Structure for Discrimination," *American Journal of Sociology* 109, no. 4 (2004): 852–901; Julie A. Kmec, "Setting Occupational Sex Segregation in Motion: Demand-Side Explanations of Sex Traditional Employment," *Work and Occupations* 32, no. 3 (2005): 322–54; Eva Skuratowicz and Larry W. Hunter, "Where Do Women's Jobs Come From? Job Resegregation in an American Bank," *Work and Occupations* 31, no. 1 (2004): 73–110; and Curtis K. Chan and Michel Anteby, "Task Segregation as a Mechanism for Within-Job Inequality: Women and Men of the Transportation Security Administration," *Administrative Science Quarterly* 61, no. 2 (2016): 184–216.

59. The two examples described in the main text were used in an earlier version of Castilla and Ranganathan, "The Production of Merit."

6. A DATA-DRIVEN APPROACH TO ACHIEVING MERITOCRACY

1. The risk behind such adoption patterns is what La'Wana Harris calls "D&I lip service," a widespread practice that symbolizes the "superficial expression of support for a diverse and inclusive culture without any corresponding action or sincere intent to effect meaningful change [that] can hinder companies' talent acquisition, retention, and—perhaps above all—bottom lines." La'Wana Harris, *Diversity Beyond Lip Service: A Coaching Guide for Challenging Bias* (Berrett-Koehler, 2019), xi.

2. "Focusing on What Works for Workplace Diversity," McKinsey & Company, April 7, 2017, https://www.mckinsey.com/featured-insights/gender-equality/focusing-on-what-works-for-workplace-diversity.

3. Zulekha Nathoo, "Why Ineffective Diversity Training Won't Go Away," *BBC Worklife*, June 16, 2021, https://www.bbc.com/worklife/article/20210614-why-ineffective-diversity-training-wont-go-away.

4. Frank Dobbin and Alexandra Kalev, "Why Diversity Programs Fail," *Harvard Business Review*, July–August 2016, 14.

5. Frank Dobbin and Alexandra Kalev, "Frank Dobbin and Alexandra Kalev Explain Why Diversity Training Does Not Work," *Economist*, May 21, 2021, https://www

.economist.com/by-invitation/2021/05/21/frank-dobbin-and-alexandra-kalev-explain -why-diversity-training-does-not-work.

6. Dobbin and Kalev, "Why Diversity Programs Fail," 55.

7. See Carol T. Kulik et al., "Ironic Evaluation Processes: Effects of Thought Suppression on Evaluations of Older Job Applicants," *Journal of Organizational Behavior* 26, no. 6 (2000): 689–711; and Neil Macrae et al., "Out of Mind but Back in Sight: Stereotypes on the Rebound," *Journal of Personality and Social Psychology* 67, no. 5 (1994): 808–17.

8. See Erin Cooley et al., "Complex Intersections of Race and Class: Among Social Liberals, Learning About White Privilege Reduces Sympathy, Increases Blame, and Decreases External Attributions for White People Struggling with Poverty," *Journal of Experimental Psychology: General* 148, no. 12 (2019): 2218–28; Madeline Heilman and Brian Welle, "Disadvantaged by Diversity? The Effects of Diversity Goals on Competence Perceptions," *Journal of Applied Social Psychology* 36, no. 5 (2006): 1291–319; Kulick et al., "Ironic Evaluation Processes"; Macrae et al., "Out of Mind"; Victoria Plaut et al., "Is Multiculturalism or Color Blindness Better for Minorities?," *Psychological Science* 20, no. 4 (2009): 444–46; and Leigh Wilton et al., "Valuing Differences and Reinforcing Them: Multiculturalism Increases Race Essentialism," *Social Psychological and Personality Science* 10, no. 5 (2019): 681–89.

9. Dobbin and Kalev, "Why Diversity Programs Fail," 55.

10. Frank Dobbin and Alexandra Kalev, *Getting to Diversity: What Works and What Doesn't* (Harvard University Press, 2022).

11. Sara Rynes and Benson Rosen, "A Field Survey of Factors Affecting the Adoption and Perceived Success of Diversity Training," *Personnel Psychology* 48, no. 2 (1995): 247–70.

12. Edward H. Chang et al., "The Mixed Effects of Online Diversity Training," *PNAS* 116, no. 16 (2019): 7778–83.

13. Chang et al., "The Mixed Effects," 7778. They also reported no significant differences in employees' willingness to speak to a female or male new hire when they compared the treatment and control conditions (percent willing to talk to female: 42.3 percent versus 39.1 percent; percent willing to talk to male: 34.8 percent versus 35.1 percent).

14. Chang et al., "The Mixed Effects," 7778.

15. See Dobbin and Kalev, "Why Diversity Programs Fail"; Robert W. Livingston, "How to Promote Racial Equity in the Workplace: A Five-Step Plan," *Harvard Business Review* 98, no. 5 (2020): 64–72; Jesse Singal, "What If Diversity Training Is Doing More Harm than Good?," *New York Times*, January 17, 2023, https://www.nytimes .com/2023/01/17/opinion/dei-trainings-effective.html; and Hoa P. Nguyen, "Diversity Training Doesn't Work. And Don't Bother Fixing It," Medium, October 6, 2020, https:// medium.com/swlh/diversity-training-doesnt-work-and-don-t-bother-fixing-it.

16. See Sarah M. Jackson et al., "Using Implicit Bias Training to Improve Attitudes Toward Women in STEM," *Social Psychology of Education* 17 (2014): 419–38; Molly Carnes et al., "The Effect of an Intervention to Break the Gender Bias Habit for Faculty at One Institution: A Cluster Randomized, Controlled Trial," *Academic Medicine* 90, no. 2 (2015): 221–30; and Corinne A. Moss-Racusin et al., "Scientific Diversity Interventions," *Science* 343, no. 6171 (2014): 615–16.

17. The blog post is by Jordan Axt and can be found at https://implicit.harvard.edu /implicit/user/jaxt/blogposts/piblogposto20.html. Project Implicit is a 501(c)(3) nonprofit organization and international collaborative of researchers interested in

implicit social cognition. Its mission is "to educate the public about bias and to provide a 'virtual laboratory' for collecting data on the internet. Project Implicit scientists produce high-impact research that forms the basis of our scientific knowledge about bias and disparities" (the quote is from https://implicit.harvard.edu/implicit /aboutus.html).

18. Chloë FitzGerald et al., "Interventions Designed to Reduce Implicit Prejudices and Implicit Stereotypes in Real World Contexts: A Systematic Review," *BMC Psychology* 7, no. 1 (2019): Article 29.

19. For example, see Ulrich Schimmack, "What Multi-Method Data Tell Us About Construct Validity," *European Journal of Personality* 24 (3) (2010): 241–57; Frederick L. Oswald et al., "Predicting Ethnic and Racial Discrimination: A Meta-Analysis of IAT Criterion Studies," *Journal of Personality and Social Psychology* 105, no. 2 (2013): 171–92; Ulrich Schimmack, "Invalid Claims About the Validity of Implicit Association Tests by Prisoners of the Implicit Social-Cognition Paradigm," *Perspectives on Psychological Science* 16, no. 2 (2021): 435–42; and Ulrich Schimmack, "The Validation Crisis in Psychology," *Meta-Psychology* 5, no. 3 (2021). Go to https://replicationindex .com/2019/02/06/raceiat-predictive-validity/ (accessed April 21, 2023) to find some serious accusations: "Greenwald and colleagues had 20 years and ample funding to conduct such validation studies, but they failed to do so. In contrast, their articles consistently confuse measures and constructs and give the impression that the IAT measures unconscious processes that are hidden from introspection."

20. As Greenwald and colleagues reported in Anthony G. Greenwald et al., "The Implicit Association Test at Age 20: What Is Known and What Is Not Known About Implicit Bias," PsyArXiv Preprints, April 6, 2020.

21. For example, see FitzGerald et al., "Interventions Designed to Reduce Implicit Prejudices."

22. See Alexandra Kalev et al., "Best Practices or Best Guesses? Assessing the Efficacy of Corporate Affirmative Action and Diversity Policies," *American Sociological Review* 71, no. 4 (2006): 589–617; and Alexandra Kalev et al., "Diversity Management in Corporate America," *Contexts* 6, no. 4 (2007): 21–27.

23. FitzGerald et al., "Interventions Designed to Reduce Implicit Prejudices."

24. Meredith Lepore, "The Top 10 Words Men Use on Resumes Versus Women Are Shockingly Different," Ladders, June 28, 2018, https://www.theladders.com/career-advice /the-top-10-words-men-use-on-resumes-versus-women-are-shockingly-different.

25. Claudia Goldin and Cecilia Rouse, "Orchestrating Impartiality: The Impact of 'Blind' Auditions on Female Musicians," *American Economic Review* 90, no. 4 (2000): 717.

26. Marianne Bertrand and Sendhil Mullainathan, "Are Emily and Greg More Employable than Lakisha and Jamal? A Field Experiment on Labor Market Discrimination," *American Economic Review* 94, no. 4 (2004): 991–1013.

27. Patrick M. Kline et al., "Systemic Discrimination Among Large U.S. Employers," *Quarterly Journal of Economics* 137, no. 4 (2022): 1963–2036.

28. From Pinpoint's official website (https://www.pinpointhq.com/) as accessed on April 19, 2023.

29. James N. Baron and David M. Kreps, *Strategic Human Resources: Frameworks for General Managers* (Wiley, 1999), 351.

30. See Frank L. Schmidt and John E. Hunter, "The Validity and Utility of Selection Methods in Personnel Psychology: Practical and Theoretical Implications of 85 Years of Research Findings," *Psychological Bulletin* 124 (2) (1998): 262–74.

31. For a review of such studies, see Baron and Kreps, *Strategic Human Resources*; and Tomas Chamorro-Premuzic, *The Talent Delusion: Why Data, Not Intuition, Is the Key to Unlocking Human Potential* (Little, Brown, 2017).

32. See Ramakrishnan Vivek, "Is Blind Recruitment an Effective Recruitment Method?," *International Journal of Applied Research in Business and Management* 3, no. 3 (2022): 56–72; and John Feldmann, "The Benefits and Shortcomings of Blind Hiring in the Recruitment Process," *Forbes*, April 3, 2018, https://www.forbes.com/sites/forbes humanresourcescouncil/2018/04/03/the-benefits-and-shortcomings-of-blind-hiring -in-the-recruitment-process/.

33. For example, see Luc Behaghel et al., "Unintended Effects of Anonymous Résumés," *American Economic Journal: Applied Economics* 7, no. 3 (2015): 1–27.

34. Michael J. Hiscox et al., *Going Blind to See More Clearly: Unconscious Bias in Australian Public Service Shortlisting Processes*, Commonwealth of Australia, Department of the Prime Minister and Cabinet, June 2017, https://behaviouraleconomics.pmc.gov .au/sites/default/files/projects/unconscious-bias.pdf.

35. Goldin and Rouse, "Orchestrating Impartiality," 715.

36. See Sandra L. Bem and Daryl J. Bem, "Does Sex-Biased Job Advertising 'Aid and Abet' Sex Discrimination?," *Journal of Applied Social Psychology* 3, no. 1 (1973): 6–18; Elizabeth H. Gorman, "Gender Stereotypes, Same-Gender Preferences, and Organizational Variation in the Hiring of Women: Evidence from Law Firms," *American Sociological Review* 70, no. 4 (2005): 702–28; and Nicholas Pedriana and Amanda Abraham, "Now You See Them, Now You Don't: The Legal Field and Newspaper Desegregation of Sex-Segregated Help Wanted Ads 1965–75," *Law and Social Inquiry* 31, no. 4 (2006): 905–38.

37. See Danielle Gaucher et al., "Evidence That Gendered Wording in Job Advertisements Exists and Sustains Gender Inequality," *Journal of Personality and Social Psychology* 101, no. 1 (2011): 109–28.

38. Emilio J. Castilla and Hye Jin Rho, "The Gendering of Job Postings in the Online Recruitment Process," *Management Science* 69, no. 11 (2023): 6912–39.

39. Gaucher et al., "Evidence That Gendered Wording."

40. For example, Bem and Bem, "Does Sex-Biased Job Advertising 'Aid and Abet' Sex Discrimination?"; and Nicholas Pedriana, "Help Wanted NOW: Legal Resources, the Women's Movement, and the Battle over Sex-Segregated Job Advertisements," *Social Problems* 51, no. 2 (2004): 182–201.

41. Jeffrey Dastin, "Insight—Amazon Scraps Secret AI Recruiting Tool That Showed Bias Against Women," Reuters, October 10, 2018, https://www.reuters.com/article /idUSKCN1MK0AG/.

42. Paul Daugherty et al., *A New Era of Generative AI for Everyone*, Accenture, 2023, accessed July 7, 2023, https://www.accenture.com/content/dam/accenture/final/accenture-com /document/Accenture-A-New-Era-of-Generative-AI-for-Everyone.pdf#zoom=40.

43. For example, see Nicole Lewis, "Technology Can Be Used to Achieve Pay Equity," SHRM, June 19, 2023, https://www.shrm.org/resourcesandtools/hr-topics/technology /pages/technology-can-be-used-achieve-pay-equity.aspx.

44. See Chris Brahm, *Tackling AI's Unintended Consequences*, Bain & Company, 2023, https://www.bain.com/contentassets/a7ebfd741daf44b6905c597bede52de4/bain _brief_tackling_ais_unintended_consequences.pdf.

45. See Zoe Larkin, "AI Bias—What Is It and How to Avoid It?," Levity, September 30, 2024, https://levity.ai/blog/ai-bias-how-to-avoid; and Ethan Mollick and Lilach Mollick,

"Assigning AI: Seven Approaches for Students, with Prompts," arXiv:2306.10052, June 13, 2023, https://arxiv.org/abs/2306.10052.

46. See, for example, Thomas A. Kochan, et al., "Bringing Worker Voice into Generative AI," MIT Open Publishing, 2024, https://doi.org/10.21428/e4baedd9.0d255ab6; David Autor, et al., *The Work of the Future: Building Better Jobs in an Age of Intelligent Machines* (MIT Press, 2021); Timothy F. Bresnahan, et al., "Technology, Organization, and the Demand for Skilled Labor," in *The New Relationship: Human Capital in the American Corporation*, ed. Margaret M. Blair and Thomas A. Kochan (Brookings Institution Press, 2000), 145–84; Adam Litwin, "Technological Change at Work: The Impact of Employee Involvement on the Effectiveness of Health Information Technology," *ILR Review* 64, no. 5 (2011): 863–68; and John Paul MacDuffie and John F. Krafcik, "Integrating Technology and Human Resources for High-Performance Manufacturing: Evidence from the International Auto Industry," in *Transforming Organizations*, ed. Thomas A. Kochan and Michael Useem (New York: Oxford University Press, 1992), 213–24.

47. See Kelsey Butler, "Big Tech Layoffs Are Hitting Diversity and Inclusion Jobs Hard," *Bloomberg News*, January 24, 2023, https://www.bloomberg.com/news/articles/2023-01-24/tech-layoffs-are-hitting-diversity-and-inclusion-jobs-hard; and Eira May, "The People Most Affected by the Tech Layoffs," The Stack Overflow Blog, April 2, 2023, https://stackoverflow.blog/2023/04/02/the-people-most-affected-by-the-tech-layoffs/.

48. See John C. Dencker, "Corporate Restructuring and Sex Differences in Managerial Promotion," *American Sociological Review* 73, no. 3 (2008): 455–76; and Alexandra Kalev, "How You Downsize Is Who You Downsize: Biased Formalization, Accountability and Managerial Diversity," *American Sociological Review* 79, no. 1 (2014): 109–35.

49. Daniel Wiessner, "Latest Twitter Lawsuit Says Company Targeted Women for Layoffs," Reuters, December 8, 2022, https://www.reuters.com/legal/latest-twitter-lawsuit-says-company-targeted-women-layoffs-2022-12-08/.

50. For a review of such work, see N. Derek Brown and Drew S. Jacoby-Senghor, "Majority Members Misperceive Even 'Win-Win' Diversity Policies as Unbeneficial to Them," *Journal of Personality and Social Psychology* 122, no. 6 (2022): 1075–97.

51. By qualitative data, I refer to information collected through questionnaires, interviews, focus groups, or observation. As with the analysis of quantitative data, the analysis of qualitative data allows researchers to better understand people-related processes, criteria, and outcomes in organizations. To develop such insights, you will need to collect qualitative data that are comprehensive, rich, and of high quality, allowing themes and patterns to emerge through careful investigation. (For an example of such an approach, see Emilio J. Castilla and Aruna Ranganathan, "The Production of Merit: How Managers Understand and Apply Merit in the Workplace," *Organization Science* 31, no. 4 (2020): 909–35.)

52. See "Diversity, Equity, and Inclusion Analytics," HireRoad, February 27, 2023, https://hireroad.com/resources/diversity-equity-and-inclusion-analytics; Sundiatu Dixon-Fyle et al., "Diversity Wins: How Inclusion Matters," McKinsey & Company, May 19, 2020, https://www.mckinsey.com/featured-insights/diversity-and-inclusion/diversity-wins-how-inclusion-matters; and Workday Staff Writers, "Best Practices: Optimizing Analytics for Diversity, Equity, Inclusion, and Belonging" (blog post), Workday, January 14, 2022, https://blog.workday.com/en-us/2022/best-practices-optimizing-analytics-diversity-equity-inclusion-belonging.html.

53. For example, see Joseph B. Fuller Manjari Raman, *Dismissed by Degrees*, Accenture Grads of Life and Harvard Business School Report, 2017, https://www.hbs.edu/ris /Publication%20Files/dismissed-by-degrees_707b3f0e-a772-40b7-8f77-aed4a16016cc .pdf; and Rachel M. Cohen, "Stop Requiring College Degrees for Jobs That Don't Need Them," Vox, March 19, 2023, https://www.vox.com/policy/23628627/degree-inflation -college-bacheors-stars-labor-worker-paper-ceiling.

54. For more information about employers that are proactively advancing and developing workers, visit the American Opportunity Index at https://americanopportunity index.org/ (accessed July 28, 2024).

55. For example, see Lewis, "Technology Can Be Used."

56. Yolanda Slan, "Viewpoint: A Reflection on Juneteenth, Transparency in Diversity Reporting," SHRM, June 16, 2023, https://www.shrm.org/resourcesandtools/hr-topics /behavioral-competencies/global-and-cultural-effectiveness/pages/viewpoint-the -relationship-between-juneteenth-and-transparency-in-diversity-reporting.aspx.

57. Some employees seem to feel comfortable sharing their demographic information in certain companies and organizations worldwide. As of December of 2024, for instance, Salesforce has committed to DEI and regularly releases data on its workforce demographics, encouraging employees to disclose their race, ethnicity, gender, and other demographic details. Similarly, Airbnb has implemented "Project Lighthouse" to collect data on discrimination and bias experienced by its users while also collecting demographic information from employees to inform its DEI initiatives. Microsoft and Target follow similar practices, encouraging employees to share demographic data. Target encourages employees to share their demographic information to help inform its diversity and inclusion initiatives and to track progress over time. However, as workplace policies, privacy concerns, and legal regulations continue to evolve worldwide, companies may continue to adapt their approaches to demographic data collection and DEI transparency.

58. For example, see Lily Zheng, "How to Effectively—and Legally—Use Racial Data for DEI," *Harvard Business Review*, July 24, 2023.

59. See Dawit Habtemariam, "3 Must-Dos for Collecting Employee Demographic Data Beyond Race and Gender," Senior Executive, April 21, 2022, accessed April 15, 2023, https://seniorexecutive.com/collecting-employee-demographic-data-beyond-race -gender/; Bobby Melloy, "What Demographic Question Should You Ask in Surveys?," CultureAmp, March 27, 2023, https://www.cultureamp.com/blog/demographic-questions -surveys; or Kimberly Magoon et al., "Best Practice for Demographic Data Collection & Reporting: Evaluator's Guide," Public Consulting Group, August 2022, https:// www.publicconsultinggroup.com/media/4124/demographic-data-collection-and -reporting_brief.pdf.

60. Payscale, "Gender Pay Gap Report," 2024, 5, https://www.payscale.com/content/report /2024-gender-pay-gap-report.pdf.

61. Google offers a similar example. As reported on its Re:Work site (https://rework .withgoogle.com), the company identified a gender disparity in one of its promotion cycles: junior female software engineers were being promoted at a lower rate than their male peers. Google's People Analytics team discovered that the issue was rooted in differing self-nomination rates. Since engineers at Google can self-nominate for promotion when they feel ready, the data revealed that men were doing so more frequently than equally qualified women. To address this problem, a senior leader shared these findings with employees and encouraged all engineers to self-nominate

when they felt prepared. After this simple intervention, Google reported that the gender gap in promotion rates was eliminated.

62. Emilio J. Castilla, "Gender, Race, and Meritocracy in Organizational Careers," *American Journal of Sociology* 113, no. 6 (2008): 1479–526.

63. To test whether demographics influenced the size of the merit-based bonus, I estimated various regression models like the one specified in equation (1) below:

$$\ln (b_{i,t}) = \alpha + \beta_1 {}^{'}P_{i,t\text{-}1} + \beta_2 {}^{'}X_{i,t\text{-}1} + \beta_3 {}^{'}Z_{i,t\text{-}1} + \varepsilon_{i,t} \tag{1}$$

where the dependent variable is the natural logarithm of annual bonus pay at time t. As predictors of bonus pay, I included three vectors: (1) $P_{i,t}$ includes a set of dummy variables for 4 of the 5 possible annual employee performance ratings (the omitted category is 3, when "performance consistently meets established expectations for the job"); (2) $X_{i,t}$ includes demographic variables, specifically dummy variables for female, Black, Asian, Hispanic, and non-US-born employees (the omitted category is US-born White male) and for marital status (married, divorced, and widowed; single is the omitted category); (3) $Z_{i,t\text{-}1}$ includes a set of dummy variables for level of education (where the omitted category is a bachelor's degree), age, job tenure, and part-time status; it also includes dummy variables for job title, work unit, and manager. Adding all these variables to the equation allowed me to examine the impact of performance evaluations on merit-based pay decisions while controlling for key work-level variables. For more details, see Castilla, "Gender, Race, and Meritocracy."

7. DEBIASING TALENT MANAGEMENT PROCESSES IN THE WORKPLACE

1. For example, see Richard Mulgan, "'Accountability': An Ever-Expanding Concept?," *Public Administration* 78, no. 3 (2000): 555–73; Mark Bovens, "Analyzing and Assessing Accountability: A Conceptual Framework," *European Law Journal* 13, no. 4 (2007): 447–68; and Harald Bergsteiner, *Accountability Theory Meets Accountability Practice* (Emerald Group, 2012).

2. For a review, see Daniel Lederman et al., "Accountability and Corruption: Political Institutions Matter," *Economics and Politics* 17, no. 1 (2005): 1–35.

3. Michael F. Weigold and Barry R. Schlenker, "Accountability and Risk Taking," *Personality and Social Psychology Bulletin* 17, no. 1 (1991): 25–29.

4. Philip E. Tetlock, "The Impact of Accountability on Judgment and Choice: Toward a Social Contingency Model," in *Advances in Experimental Social Psychology*, ed. Mark P. Zanna (Academic, 1992), 25:331.

5. Jennifer S. Lerner and Philip E. Tetlock, "Accounting for the Effects of Accountability," *Psychological Bulletin* 125, no. 2 (1999): 255–75.

6. Philip E. Tetlock, "Accountability: A Social Check on the Fundamental Attribution Error," *Social Psychology Quarterly* 48, no. 3 (1985): 227–36.

7. See Lerner and Tetlock, "Accounting for the Effects"; and Tetlock, "Accountability." See also Sheldon Adelberg and C. Daniel Batson, "Accountability and Helping: When Needs Exceed Resources," *Journal of Personality and Social Psychology* 36, no. 4 (1978): 343–50; and Philip E. Tetlock et al., "Social and Cognitive Strategies for Coping with Accountability: Conformity, Complexity, and Bolstering," *Journal of Personality and Social Psychology* 57, no. 4 (1989): 632–40.

8. Lerner and Tetlock, "Accounting for the Effects."

9. For a review of such studies, see Bergsteiner, *Accountability Theory Meets Accountability Practice*.

10. Philip E. Tetlock and Gregory Mitchell, "Implicit Bias and Accountability Systems: What Must Organizations Do to Prevent Discrimination?," *Research in Organizational Behavior* 29 (2009): 3–38.

11. Tetlock and Mitchell, "Implicit Bias and Accountability Systems," 17.

12. For a review, see Alexandra Kalev et al., "Best Practices or Best Guesses? Assessing the Efficacy of Corporate Affirmative Action and Diversity Policies," *American Sociological Review* 71, no. 4 (2006): 589–617; and Sharon R. Bird, "Unsettling Universities' Incongruous, Gendered Bureaucratic Structures: A Case-Study Approach," *Gender, Work and Organization* 18, no. 2 (2011): 202–30.

13. Frank Dobbin, *Inventing Equal Opportunity* (Princeton University Press, 2009).

14. See Lauren B. Edelman, "Legal Environments and Organizational Governance: The Expansion of Due Process in the American Workplace," *American Journal of Sociology* 95, no. 6 (1990): 1401–40.

15. See Samuel L. Bradley et al., *Equity at the Workplace: A Moment in Time and Place* (Boston College School of Social Work and United Way & Center for Social Innovation, 2021), https://www.bc.edu/content/dam/bc1/schools/sw/csi/Final-WorkEquity-10-5.19.22.pdf; and Ragan Decker et al., "The Key to Improving Equity in the Workplace: An Analytical Aptitude," SHRM, March 16, 2023, https://www.shrm.org/resources andtools/hr-topics/behavioral-competencies/pages/improve-equity-analytical-aptitude.aspx.

16. Bradley et al., *Equity at the Workplace.*

17. Decker et al., "The Key to Improving Equity."

18. "Gartner HR Research Reveals 82 Percent of Employees Report Working Environment Lacks Fairness," Gartner Press Release, November 8, 2021, https://www.gartner.com/en/newsroom/press-releases/2021-08-11-gartner-hr-research-reveals-eighty-two-percent-of-employees-report-working-environment-lacks-fairness.

19. For an exception, see Bird, "Unsettling Universities' Incongruous, Gendered Bureaucratic Structures."

20. For example, see Lederman et al., "Accountability and Corruption."

21. For example, see Ana Bellver and Daniel Kaufmann, "Transparenting Transparency: Initial Empirics and Policy Applications," working paper, National Bureau of Economic Research, 2005, http://dx.doi.org/10.2139/ssrn.808664.

22. See Ivar Kolstad and Arne Wiig, "Is Transparency the Key to Reducing Corruption in Resource-Rich Countries?," *World Development* 37, no. 3 (2009): 521–32; and Sandeep A. Patel and George S. Dallas, "Transparency and Disclosure: Overview of Methodology and Study Results—United States," Standard & Poor's (available via SSRN), October 16, 2002, https://ssrn.com/abstract=422800.

23. For a review, see Ethan S. Bernstein, "The Transparency Paradox: A Role for Privacy in Organizational Learning and Operational Control," *Administrative Science Quarterly* 57, no. 2 (2012): 181–216.

24. See Melissa J. Anderson, "Firms Must Employ Transparency to Eliminate Hidden Bias Against Female Leaders," The glasshammer, April 27, 2011, http://www.theglass hammer.com/news/2011/04/27/firms-must-employ-transparency-to-eliminate-hidden-bias-against-female-leaders/; Melissa J. Anderson, "6 Ways Transparency Can Boost Women in Leadership in the Financial Services," The glasshammer, March 31, 2011, http://www.theglasshammer.com/news/2011/03/31/6-ways-transparency-can-boost

-women-in-leadership-in-the-financial-services/; Daniel Indiviglio, "The Case for Making Wages Public: Better Pay, Better Workers," *Atlantic*, July 20, 2011, http://www.theatlantic.com/business/archive/2011/07/the-case-for-making-wages-public-better-pay-better-workers/242238/; Tanya K. Hernandez, *Racial Subordination in Latin America: The Role of the State, Customary Law, and the New Civil Rights Response* (Cambridge University Press, 2012); and Tanya K. Hernandez, "Legally Mandate Wage Transparency," *New York Times*, March 31, 2013, http://www.nytimes.com/roomfordebate/2013/03/31/why-has-salary-parity-still-not-happened/legally-mandate-wage-transparency.

25. Anderson, "Firms Must Employ Transparency."

26. See Michael Baker et al., "Pay Transparency and the Gender Gap," *American Economic Journal: Applied Economics* 15, no. 2 (2023): 157–83; William Heisler, "Increasing Pay Transparency: A Guide for Change," *Business Horizons* 64, no. 1 (2021): 73–81; and Morten Bennedsen et al., "Do Firms Respond to Gender Pay Gap Transparency?," *Journal of Finance* 77, no. 4 (2022): 2051–91.

27. Richard G. Trotter et al., "The New Age of Pay Transparency," *Business Horizons* 60, no. 4 (2017): 529–39.

28. Shelly Marasi and Rebecca J. Bennett, "Pay Communication: Where Do We Go from Here?," *Human Resource Management Review* 26, no. 1 (2016): 50–58.

29. Sally Percy, "What's So Great About Pay Transparency?," *Forbes*, December 2, 2022, https://www.forbes.com/sites/sallypercy/2022/12/02/whats-so-great-about-pay-transparency/?sh=4d2e7b6f35ce.

30. David N. Avdul et al., "Pay Transparency: Why It Is Important to Be Thoughtful and Strategic," *Compensation and Benefits Review* 56, no. 2 (2023): 1.

31. Examples include Louise H. Kidder et al., "Secret Ambitions and Public Performances: The Effects of Anonymity on Reward Allocations Made by Men and Women," *Journal of Experimental Social Psychology* 13, no. 1 (1977): 70–80; Edward E. Lawler III, *Pay and Organizational Effectiveness: A Psychological View* (McGraw-Hill, 1971); and Edward E. Lawler III, *Pay and Organization Development* (Addison-Wesley, 1981). For a review of additional research, see Kathryn M. Bartol and David C. Martin, "Effects of Dependence, Dependency Threats, and Pay Secrecy on Managerial Pay Allocations," *Journal of Applied Psychology* 74, no. 1 (1989): 105–13; Adrienne Colella et al., "Exposing Pay Secrecy," *Academy of Management Review* 32, no. 1 (2007): 55–71; and Peter Bamberger and Elena Belogolovsky, "The Impact of Pay Secrecy on Individual Task Performance," *Personnel Psychology* 63, no. 4 (2010): 965–96. Additionally, see, Peter Bamberger, *Exposing Pay: Pay Transparency and What It Means for Employees, Employers, and Public Policy* (Oxford University Press, 2023).

32. See Jeffrey Pfeffer, *Power in Organizations* (Pitman, 1981); and Trond Petersen and Ishak Saporta, "The Opportunity Structure for Discrimination," *American Journal of Sociology* 109, no. 4 (2004): 852–901.

33. See Faye J. Crosby, *Relative Deprivation and Working Women* (Oxford University Press, 1982); Faye J. Crosby, "Relative Deprivation in Organizational Settings," *Research in Organizational Behavior* 6 (1984): 51–93; and Brenda Major et al., "Perceiving Personal Discrimination: The Role of Group Status and Legitimizing Ideology," *Journal of Personality and Social Psychology* 82, no. 3 (2002): 269–82.

34. Faye J. Crosby et al., "Cognitive Biases in the Perception of Discrimination: The Importance of Format," *Sex Roles* 14 (1986): 637–46.

35. Research shows that decision-makers tend to allocate pay more equally with pay transparency than with pay secrecy. See Gerald S. Leventhal, "The Distribution of Rewards and Resources in Groups and Organizations," in *Advances in Experimental Social Psychology*, vol. 9, ed. Leonard Berkowitz and Elaine Walster (Academic, 1976); Gerald S. Leventhal et al., "Beyond Fairness: A Theory of Allocation Preferences," in *Justice and Social Interaction: Experimental and Theoretical Contributions from Psychological Research*, ed. Gerold Mikula (Springer-Verlag, 1980); and Brenda Major and Jeffrey B. Adams, "Role of Gender, Interpersonal Orientation, and Self-Presentation in Distributive-Justice Behavior," *Journal of Personality and Social Psychology* 45, no. 3 (1983): 598–608.

36. See William T. Bielby and James N. Baron, "Men and Women at Work: Sex Segregation and Statistical Discrimination," *American Journal of Sociology* 91, no. 4 (1986): 759–99; and Bird, "Unsettling Universities' Incongruous, Gendered Bureaucratic Structures."

37. See, for example, Emilio J. Castilla, "Gender, Race, and Meritocracy in Organizational Careers," *American Journal of Sociology* 113, no. 6 (2008): 1479–526.

38. This finding was consistent with the results of other field studies; see, for example, Petersen and Saporta, "The Opportunity Structure for Discrimination."

39. Castilla, "Gender, Race, and Meritocracy."

40. Gowri Ramachandran, "Pay Transparency," *Penn State Law Review* 116, no. 4 (2012): 1043–80.

41. See Marta M. Elvira and Ishak Saporta, "How Does Collective Bargaining Affect the Gender Pay Gap?," *Work and Occupations* 28, no. 4 (2001): 469–90.

42. Uwe Jirjahn and Gesine Stephan, "Gender, Piece Rates and Wages: Evidence from Matched Employer-Employee Data," *Cambridge Journal of Economics* 28, no. 5 (2004): 683–704. Similarly, advocates of national pay fairness legislation argue that in companies where pay scales are public and collective bargaining is allowed, women and men tend to receive more equal pay. See Heidi Hartmann, "Pass the Paycheck Fairness Act," *New York Times*, March 31, 2013, http://www.nytimes.com/roomfordebate/2013/03/31/why-has-salary-parity-still-not-happened/pass-the-paycheck-fairness-act; and Hernandez, "Legally Mandate Wage Transparency."

43. See Brian Nordli, "Pay Transparency: What It Is and How to Do It Right," Built In, June 28, 2022, https://builtin.com/people-management/pay-transparency; "Unlock the Benefits of Salary Transparency: A Strategic Guide for HR Leaders," Wellhub, January 28, 2025, https://wellhub.com/en-us/blog/talent-acquisition-and-retention/salary-transparency/; Hailley Griffis, "2022 Pay Analysis: Our Unadjusted Gender Pay Gap Is Below 1%," Buffer, March 15, 2022, https://buffer.com/resources/2022-pay-analysis/; and Alexandra Arnold et al., "Variable Pay Transparency in Organizations: When Are Organizations More Likely to Open Up About Pay?," *Compensation and Benefits Review* 56, no. 1 (2024): 16–36.

44. For instance, in December 2021, the New York City Council passed a bill requiring employers to post the salary range for all job openings, promotions, and transfers. By mid-2023, at least fourteen US states had passed laws that prohibit employers from asking job candidates their salary history. See Jennifer Liu, " 'It's About Fairness and Respect': California May Get a New Salary Transparency Law Soon," CNBC Make It, August 31, 2022, https://www.cnbc.com/2022/08/31/california-may-get-new-salary-transparency-law-soon.html; Jennifer Liu, "Here Are All the New Salary Transparency Laws Going into Effect in 2023," CNBC Make It, December 29, 2022, https://www.cnbc.com/2022/12/29/new-salary-transparency-laws-going-into-effect-in-2023

.html; Genni Burkhart, "What You Need to Know About Pay Transparency Laws Going into Effect in 2023," DOCS Education, January 6, 2023, https://www.docseducation .com/blog/what-you-need-know-about-pay-transparency-laws-going-effect-2023; and Caitlin Harrington, "Pay Transparency Is Sweeping Across the US," Wired, September 10, 2023, https://www.wired.com/story/pay-transparency-is-sweeping-across-us/.

45. European Commission, "Commission Recommendation of 7 March 2014 on Strengthening the Principle of Equal Pay Between Men and Women Through Transparency," EUR-Lex, March 8, 2014, https://eur-lex.europa.eu/legal-content/EN/TXT /?uri=CELEX%3A32014H0124&qid=1721051805240; European Parliament, "Directive (EU) 2023/970 of the European Parliament and of the Council of 10 May 2023 to Strengthen the Application of the Principle of Equal Pay for Equal Work or Work of Equal Value Between Men and Women Through Pay Transparency and Enforcement Mechanisms," EUR-Lex, May 17, 2023, https://eur-lex.europa.eu/legal-content/EN /TXT/?uri=CELEX%3A32023L0970&qid=1721051805240; and Council of the European Union, "Pay Transparency in the EU," last modified March 21, 2024, https:// www.consilium.europa.eu/en/policies/pay-transparency/.

46. Martha Ceballos et al., "Pay Transparency Across Countries and Legal Systems," CESifo Forum 23, no. 2 (2022): 3–11. Legal measures enacted in the EU include requirements for employers, such as mandatory gender pay reports by job position, gender pay audits, and equal pay certification. Employers are also prohibited from asking job seekers about their salary history. Other measures include granting options or rights to job seekers and employees—such as access to pay ranges for a position, the right to request pay information, and the ability to include gender pay gap discussions in collective bargaining.

47. For example, see Tim Herrera, "The Benefits of Sharing Your Salary," New York Times, November 18, 2018, https://www.nytimes.com/2018/11/18/smarter-living/the -benefits-of-sharing-your-salary.html; Kristin Wong, "Want to Close the Pay Gap? Pay Transparency Will Help," New York Times, January 20, 2019, https://www.nytimes .com/2019/01/20/smarter-living/pay-wage-gap-salary-secrecy-transparency .html; and Lynne M. Finn, "How to Introduce Pay Transparency to Help Close the Gender Pay Gap," Forbes, February 2, 2023, https://www.forbes.com/sites/forbes humanresourcescouncil/2023/02/02/how-to-introduce-pay-transparency-to-help -close-the-gender-pay-gap/.

48. See Morela Hernandez et al., "Bargaining While Black: The Role of Race in Salary Negotiations," Journal of Applied Psychology 104, no. 4 (2019): 581–92; and Michael Baker et al., "Pay Transparency and the Gender Gap," American Economic Journal: Applied Economics 15, no. 2 (2023): 157–83.

49. A note of caution here. The effects of pay transparency are suggested to be much more complicated than what we have anticipated. See Peter Bamberger and Elena Belogolovsky, "The Dark Side of Transparency: How and When Pay Administration Practices Affect Employee Helping," Journal of Applied Psychology 102, no. 4 (2017): 658–671; Tomasz Obloj and Todd R. Zenger, "Research: The Complicated Effects of Pay Transparency," Harvard Business Review, February 8, 2023; Tomasz Obloj and Todd R. Zenger, "The Influence of Pay Transparency on (Gender) Inequity, Inequality, and the Performance Basis of Pay," Nature Human Behavior 6 (2022): 646–55; and Avdul et al., "Pay Transparency." Some scholars have cautioned that certain types of pay transparency could have unintended consequences, such as by compressing or reducing overall pay (see Leon Lam et al., "Research: The Unintended Consequences

of Pay Transparency," *Harvard Business Review*, August 12, 2022). In their study of pay transparency among employees in the United States, the UK, and China, Lam et al. further report that when pay transparency led to compressed pay ranges, employees requested less visible personalized rewards and managers were more likely to grant such requests to motivate them. Similarly, Obloj and Zenger, after analyzing demographic and salary data for nearly 100,000 US academics from 1997 to 2017, reported that pay transparency resulted in "significant and sizeable reductions in the link between pay and individual measured performance" (see Obloj and Zenger, "The Influence of Pay Transparency.")

50. "Does Pay Transparency Close the Gender Gap? Pay Equity for Men and Women," Payscale, 2019, accessed June 19, 2023, https://www.payscale.com/content/whitepaper/Pay-Transparency-Closing-Gender-Wage-Gap.pdf.

51. This example was first discussed in Emilio J. Castilla, "Accounting for the Gap: A Firm Study Manipulating Organizational Accountability and Transparency in Pay Decisions," *Organization Science* 26, no. 2 (2015): 311–33.

52. Regarding the definition of pay transparency, two distinct concepts are often confounded: visibility and formalization of pay criteria and processes. However, the presence of one does not imply the presence of the other. For example, while the criteria and procedures regarding pay may be formalized, they can still be kept secret (invisible) or unavailable to certain audiences inside the organization.

53. This example of a performance-reward system was used in Emilio J. Castilla, "Achieving Meritocracy in the Workplace," *MIT Sloan Management Review*, June 13, 2016, https://sloanreview.mit.edu/article/achieving-meritocracy-in-the-workplace/.

54. See Indeed Employer Content Team, "Chief Diversity Officers: Who They Are and When You Need One," Indeed.com, last updated December 3, 2024, https://www.indeed.com/hire/c/info/chief-diversity-officers; d&i Leaders, "What Does a Chief Diversity, Equity and Inclusion Officer/Leader Do?," https://dileaders.com/what-does-a-diversity-equity-and-inclusion-professional-do/; and The OR Briefings: People & Organisational Research, "Chief Diversity Officer (CDO) – Definition and Explanation," https://oxford-review.com/the-oxford-review-dei-diversity-equity-and-inclusion-dictionary/chief-diversity-officer-cdo-definition-and-explanation/.

55. See page 3 of George B. Cunningham, *Diversity, Equity, and Inclusion at Work* (Taylor and Francis, 2023); and Sheree R. Curry, "'I Represent Their Voices': As Corporate America Embraces Diversity, This Is How Some DEI Officers See Their Work," *USA Today*, February 28, 2023, https://www.usatoday.com/story/money/2023/02/28/diversity-officers-role-corporate-america/11150087002/.

56. See Drew Goldstein et al., "Unlocking the Potential of Chief Diversity Officers," McKinsey & Company, November 18, 2022, https://www.mckinsey.com/capabilities/people-and-organizational-performance/our-insights/unlocking-the-potential-of-chief-diversity-officers.

57. Sundiatu Dixon-Fyle et al., "Diversity Wins: How Inclusion Matters," McKinsey & Company, May 19, 2020, https://www.mckinsey.com/featured-insights/diversity-and-inclusion/diversity-wins-how-inclusion-matters.

58. See Anand Janefalkar, "Diversity Isn't Just the Right Thing to Do; It's Also Good Business," *Forbes*, March 26, 2020, https://www.forbes.com/councils/forbestechcouncil/2020/03/26/diversity-isnt-just-the-right-thing-to-do-its-also-good-business/; Alex Edmans, "Is There Really a Business Case for Diversity?," Medium, October 30, 2021,

https://medium.com/@alex.edmans/is-there-really-a-business-case-for-diversity
-c58ef67ebffa; Dixon-Fyle et al., "Diversity Wins"; and Denise Pirrotti Hummel, "The
Business Case for Diversity and Inclusion," Lead Inclusively, https://leadinclusively
.com/wp-content/uploads/2020/01/The-Business-Case-for-Diversity-and-Inclusion
.pdf.

59. Robin J. Ely and David A. Thomas, "Getting Serious About Diversity: Enough Already
with the Business Case," *Harvard Business Review*, 2020, https://hbr.org/2020/11
/getting-serious-about-diversity-enough-already-with-the-business-case.

60. See, for instance, Sarah Kessler, "D.E.I. Goes Quiet," *New York Times*, January 13,
2024, https://www.nytimes.com/2024/01/13/business/dealbook/dei-goes-quiet.html;
Matt Gonzales, "Why Are DEI Roles Disappearing?," SHRM, March 15, 2023, https://www
.shrm.org/topics-tools/news/inclusion-diversity/dei-roles-disappearing; and George
Anders, "Who's Vaulting into the C-Suite? Trends Changed Fast in 2022," LinkedIn Workforce Insights, February 1, 2023, https://www.linkedin.com/pulse/whos
-vaulting-c-suite-trends-changed-fast-2022-george-anders/. Additionally, see Emma
Goldberg, Aaron Krolik, and Lily Boyce, "How Corporate America Is Retreating
From D.E.I." *New York Times*, March 13, 2025, https://www.nytimes.com/interactive
/2025/03/13/business/corporate-america-dei-policy-shifts.html.

61. *Students for Fair Admissions v. Harvard*, 600 US 181 at 6–40 (US 2023).

62. For examples, see Rahem D. Hamid, "Ivy League, Other Peer Schools Pledge to
Uphold Diversity While Complying with Supreme Court Ruling," *Harvard Crimson*,
July 3, 2023, https://www.thecrimson.com/article/2023/7/3/peer-universities-scotus/;
and Colleen Flaherty, "Presidents Break with Supreme Court on Affirmative Action,"
Inside Higher Ed, October 17, 2023, https://www.insidehighered.com/news/diversity
/socioeconomics/2023/10/17/survey-two-three-college-presidents-oppose-affirmative.

63. Supreme Court of the United States, *Students for Fair Admissions, Inc. v. President
and Fellows of Harvard College*, October Term, 2022, https://www.supremecourt.gov
/opinions/22pdf/20-1199_hgdj.pdf: 39.

64. See Paige McGlauflin and Trey Williams, "Microsoft, Salesforce, and Other Fortune
500 Companies React to Supreme Court Striking Down Affirmative Action: 'Our
Commitment to Equality Doesn't Waver,'" *Fortune*, June 30, 2023, https://fortune
.com/2023/06/30/major-companies-ceos-react-supreme-court-affrmative-action
-decision-microsoft-salesforce-gm-hp/; Paige McGlauflin, "HR Leaders Say They're
Still Committed to DEI in 2024 Despite the 'Anti-woke' Backlash," *Fortune*, January 2,
2024, https://fortune.com/2024/01/02/hr-leaders-committed-to-diversity-initiatives
-dei-programs-in-2024/; and Paige McGlauflin and Emma Burleigh, "The Vast
Majority of C-Suite Leaders Say They're doubling Down on DEI, but They're Still
Fighting an Uphill Battle," *Fortune*, June 3, 2024, https://fortune.com/2024/06/03
/majority-of-c-suite-leaders-say-theyre-doubling-down-on-dei-still-fighting-uphill
-battle/.

65. See Shaun Harper, "Why Business Leaders Are Pulling the Plug on DEI," *Forbes*, July
18, 2023, https://www.forbes.com/sites/shaunharper/2023/07/18/why-corporate-execs
-are-pulling-the-plug-on-dei/.

66. For example, see Tina Opie and Ella F. Washington, "Why Companies Can—and
Should—Recommit to DEI in the Wake of the SCOTUS Decision," *Harvard Busi-
ness Review*, July 27, 2023; and Kenji Yoshino and David Glasgow, "What SCOTUS's
Affirmative Action Decision Means for Corporate DEI," *Harvard Business Review*,
July 12, 2023.

67. See page 1 of Lily Zheng, "How to Effectively—and Legally—Use Racial Data for DEI," *Harvard Business Review*, July 24, 2023.
68. See Matt Gonzales, "The Evolving Meaning of 'Woke' in Corporate America," SHRM, July 29, 2023, https://www.shrm.org/topics-tools/news/all-things-work/the-meaning -of--woke-; Taylor Telford, "Deere Dials Back DEI Presence, Cuts 'Socially Moti- vated Messages,'" *Washington Post*, July 17, 2024, https://www.washingtonpost.com /business/2024/07/17/deere-dei-tractor-supply/; and Nathaniel Meyersohn, "Harley-Davidson Is Dropping Diversity Initiatives After Right-Wing Anti-DEI Campaign," *CNN*, August 19, 2024, https://www.cnn.com/2024/08/19/business/harley -davidson-dei-john-deere-tractor-supply/index.html. At the time I am finishing this book, in the United States, many important corporations appear to be cutting several of their DEI programs in response to pressures from conservative activists and a new administration. See, for example, Conor Murray and Molly Bohannon, "Citigroup Rolls Back Diversity Initiatives—Here Are All the Companies Cutting DEI Programs," *Forbes*, February 21, 2025, https://www.forbes.com/sites/conormurray/2025/02/21 /pepsi-rolling-back-diversity-initiatives-here-are-all-the-companies-cutting-dei -programs/; and Lian Kit Wee et al., "A List of Companies that Have Pulled Back on DEI, including Amazon, Google, Walmart, and Meta," *Business Insider*, February 21, 2025, https://www.businessinsider.com/companies-cutting-dei-activist-backlash -harley-davidson-deere-tractor-supply-2024-8.
69. The concern is also that movements emphasizing merit and meritocracy may too yield unintended negative consequences for organizations and their employees if they are not carefully designed and implemented by leaders. In this regard, the research discussed in chapter 4—particularly my article with Steve Benard on the paradox of meritocracy—remains highly relevant today. As you may recall, our primary finding is that when an organization and its leaders explicitly promote meritocratic values, managers tend to favor male employees over equally performing female employ- ees, awarding them higher merit-based rewards even when both genders achieve identical performance levels. This outcome underscores the unintended drawbacks of an overemphasis on meritocracy in the workplace. See, for example, Jack Kelly, "President Trump Shifts To 'Merit, Excellence And Intelligence' In The Work- place And Away From DEI," *Forbes*, February 1, 2025, https://www.forbes.com/sites /jackkelly/2025/02/01/president-trump-shifts-to-merit-excellence-and-intelligence -in-the-workplace-and-away-from-dei/; and Paige McGauflin, "Elon Musk and other DEI critics are latching on to 'MEI,' a new hiring catchphrase that experts say misses the point," *Fortune*, June 25, 2024, "https://fortune.com/2024/06/24/mei -elon-musk-alexandr-wang-anti-dei-hiring-merit-excellence-intelligence/.
70. Carl Van Horn et al., *A Workplace Divided: A National Survey Exploring Workers' Per- ceptions of Discrimination and Unfair Treatment at Work and How Government and Employers Can Help Advance More Equitable Workplaces*, Heldrich Center for Work- force Development, June 2023, https://heldrich.rutgers.edu/sites/default/files/2023 -06/Workplace_Divided_%20Executive_Summary.pdf.
71. For example, experimental studies have shown that decision-makers are less likely to make gender or racial judgments when given clear and specific standards for assess- ing ability and competency; see David G. Wagner et al., "Can Gender Inequalities Be Reduced?," *American Sociological Review* 51, no. 1 (1986): 47–61. Similarly, when standards for ability assessments are made very explicit and performance informa- tion is public and clear, biased judgments are less likely to occur; see Margaret Foddy

and Michael Smithson, "Can Gender Inequalities Be Eliminated?," *Social Psychology Quarterly* 62, no. 4 (1999): 311.

72. See Tetlock et al., "Social and Cognitive Strategies"; and Lerner and Tetlock, "Accounting for the Effects."

73. This quote can also be found on page 38 in Castilla, "Achieving Meritocracy in the Workplace."

CONCLUSION

1. I stress the word *relevant* because we are entering an exceptional moment in history regarding data collection and analysis using AI and many related emerging technologies. Unfortunately, I see more and more evidence of organizations collecting data that are neither relevant for the improvement of people-related processes nor collected according to any reasonable and acceptable research protocol aimed at protecting the individuals and processes involved. I further worry about privacy, surveillance, additional biases, and ethical, moral, and political issues relating to some employer efforts to collect data pertaining to their personnel if such efforts are not designed carefully. Similar concerns are being expressed in current discussions about the use of AI and other technologies in the workplace. See, for example, Roy Maurer, "SHRM Research: AI Use on the Rise, Ethics Questions Remain," SHRM, April 24, 2022, https://www .shrm.org/resourcesandtools/hr-topics/technology/pages/shrm-research-ai-use-rise -ethics-questions-remain.aspx; Roy Maurer, "HR Must Be Vigilant About the Ethical Use of AI Technology," SHRM, September 26, 2022, https://www.shrm.org/topics -tools/news/technology/hr-must-vigilant-ethical-use-ai-technology; Ben Dattner et al., "The Legal and Ethical Implications of Using AI in Hiring," *Harvard Business Review*, April 25, 2019; Christina Pazzanese, "Great Promise but Potential for Peril," *Harvard Gazette*, October 26, 2020, https://news.harvard.edu/gazette/story/2020/10/ethical -concerns-mount-as-ai-takes-bigger-decision-making-role/; and Alex Edquist et al., "Data Ethics: What It Means and What It Takes," McKinsey Digital, September 23, 2022, https://www.mckinsey.com/capabilities/mckinsey-digital/our-insights/data-ethics -what-it-means-and-what-it-takes.

REFERENCES

Abbot, Dorian, et al. "In Defense of Merit in Science." *Journal of Controversial Ideas* 3, no. 1 (2023): 1–26.

Abraham, Mabel. "Gender-Role Incongruity and Audience-Based Gender Bias: An Examination of Networking Among Entrepreneurs." *Administrative Science Quarterly* 65, no. 1 (2020): 151–80.

Acemoglu, Daron, and Joshua D. Angrist. "Consequences of Employment Protection? The Case of the Americans with Disabilities Act." *Journal of Political Economy* 109, no. 5 (2001): 915–57.

Acquisti, Alessandro, and Christina Fong. "An Experiment in Hiring Discrimination via Online Social Networks." *Management Science* 66, no. 3 (2020): 1005–507.

Adam, Barry D. "Stigma and Employability: Discrimination by Sex and Sexual Orientation in the Ontario Legal Profession." *Canadian Review of Sociology* 18, no. 2 (1981): 216–21.

Adams, Barbara B. "Viewpoint: The Myth of Meritocracy." *HR Magazine*, August 27, 2018. https://www.shrm.org/hr-today/news/hr-magazine/0918/pages/the-myth-of-meritocracy.aspx.

Adams, James Truslow. *The Epic of America*. Little, Brown, 1931.

Adelberg, Sheldon, and C. Daniel Batson. "Accountability and Helping: When Needs Exceed Resources." *Journal of Personality and Social Psychology* 36, no. 4 (1978): 343–50.

Adida, Claire L., David Laitin, and Marie-Anne Valfort. "Identifying Barriers to Muslim Integration in France." *Proceedings of the National Academy of Sciences of the United States of America* 107, no. 52 (2010): 22384–90.

Agerström, Jens, and Dan-Olof Rooth. "The Role of Automatic Obesity Stereotypes in Real Hiring Discrimination." *Journal of Applied Psychology* 96, no. 4 (2011): 790–805.

Agovino, Theresa. "The Performance Review Problem." *HR Magazine*, March 14, 2023. https://www.shrm.org/hr-today/news/hr-magazine/spring-2023/pages/the-problem-with-performance-reviews.aspx.

Ahmad, Akhlaq. "Ethnic Discrimination Against Second-Generation Immigrants in Hiring: Empirical Evidence from a Correspondence Test." *European Societies* 22, no. 5 (2020): 659–81.

Aigner, Dennis J., and Glen G. Cain. "Statistical Theories of Discrimination in Labor Markets." *ILR Review* 30, no. 2 (1977): 175–87.

Ajunwa, Ifeoma. "An Auditing Imperative for Automated Hiring Systems." *Harvard Journal of Law and Technology* 34, no. 2 (2021): 621–85.

Ajunwa, Ifeoma. "Race, Labor, and the Future of Work." In *The Oxford Handbook of Race and Law in the United States*, ed. Khiara M. Bridges, Devon Carbado, and Emily Hough. Oxford University Press, 2021.

Ajunwa, Ifeoma. "What to the Black American Is the Meritocracy? Comment on M. Sandel's *The Tyranny of Merit*." *American Journal of Law and Equality* 1 (2021): 39–45.

Albertson, Bethany L. "Religious Appeals and Implicit Attitudes." *Political Psychology* 32, no. 1 (2011): 109–30.

Alesina, Alberto, and Paola Giuliano. "Culture and Institutions." *Journal of Economic Literature* 53, no. 4 (2015): 898–944.

Alesina, Alberto, and Paola Giuliano. "Culture and Institutions." Working paper 19750, National Bureau of Economic Research, 2015.

Alesina, Alberto, and Paola Giuliano. "Family Ties." In *Handbook of Economic Growth*, vol. 2, ed. Philippe Aghion and Steven N. Durlauf. Elsevier, 2014.

Ali, Muhammad, et al. "Discrimination Through Optimization: How Facebook's Ad Delivery Can Lead to Skewed Outcomes." *Proceedings of the ACM on Human-Computer Interaction* 3, no. CSCW (2019): Article 199.

Alon, Sigal, and Marta Tienda. "Diversity, Opportunity, and the Shifting Meritocracy in Higher Education." *American Sociological Review* 72, no. 4 (2007): 487–511.

Ameri, Mason, Lisa Schur, Meera Adya, Scott Bentley, Patrick McKay, and Douglas Kruse. "The Disability Employment Puzzle: A Field Experiment on Employer Hiring Behavior." *ILR Review* 71, no. 2 (2018): 329–64.

Anders, George. "Who's Vaulting into the C-Suite? Trends Changed Fast in 2022." LinkedIn, February 1, 2023. https://www.linkedin.com/pulse/whos-vaulting-c-suite -trends-changed-fast-2022-george-anders/.

Anderson, Elizabeth. *The Imperative of Integration*. Princeton University Press, 2010.

Anderson, Melissa J. "Firms Must Employ Transparency to Eliminate Hidden Bias Against Female Leaders." The glasshammer, April 27, 2011. http://www.theglasshammer.com /news/2011/04/27/firms-must-employ-transparency-to-eliminate-hidden-bias-against -female-leaders/.

Anderson, Melissa J. "6 Ways Transparency Can Boost Women in Leadership in the Financial Services." The glasshammer, March 31, 2011. https://theglasshammer.com/2011 /03/6-ways-transparency-can-boost-women-in-leadership-in-the-financial-services/.

Anteby, Michel. *Manufacturing Morals: The Values of Silence in Business School Education*. University of Chicago Press, 2013.

Aral, Sinan, and Marshall Van Alstyne. "The Diversity-Bandwidth Trade-Off." *American Journal of Sociology* 117, no. 1 (2011): 90–171.

Arcidiacono, Peter, Josh Kinsler, and Tyler Ransom. "Divergent: The Time Path of Legacy and Athlete Admissions at Harvard." *Journal of Human Resources* 59, no. 3 (2024): 653–83.

Arcidiacono, Peter, Josh Kinsler, and Tyler Ransom. "Legacy and Athlete Preferences at Harvard." *Journal of Labor Economics* 40, no. 1 (2022): 133–55.

Armstrong, Elizabeth A., and Laura T. Hamilton. *Paying for The Party: How College Maintains Inequality.* Harvard University Press, 2015.

Arnold, Alexandra, Anna Sender, and David Allen. "Variable Pay Transparency in Organizations: When Are Organizations More Likely to Open Up About Pay?" *Compensation and Benefits Review* 56, no. 1 (2024): 16–36.

Arrow, Kenneth J. "Higher Education as a Filter." *Journal of Public Economics* 2, no. 3 (1973): 193–216.

Arrow, Kenneth J. *Information and Economic Behavior.* Federation of Swedish Industries, 1973.

Arrow, Kenneth J. "Social Responsibility and Economic Efficiency." *Public Policy* 21 (1973): 303–17.

Arrow, Kenneth J. "The Theory of Discrimination." In *Discrimination in Labor Markets,* ed. Orley Ashenfelter and Albert Rees. Princeton University Press, 1973.

Asare, Janice G. "I'm a Diversity and Inclusion Expert Who Admits That 'Unconscious Bias' Trainings Don't Really Work. Here Are 3 Ways Companies Can Ensure They're Not a Waste of Time." *Business Insider,* July 9, 2020. https://www.businessinsider.com/how-to-improve-your-companys-dei-unconscious-bias-training-2020-7.

Autor, David. "Lecture Note: The Economics of Discrimination Theory." Notes from lecture delivered at MIT, November 24, 2003. http://dspace.mit.edu/bitstream/handle/1721.1/115921/14-661-fall-2003-fall-2004/contents/lecture-notes/lecture_8.pdf.

Autor, David, and David Dorn. "This Job Is 'Getting Old': Measuring Changes in Job Opportunities Using Occupational Age Structure." *American Economic Review* 99, no. 2 (2009): 45–51.

Autor, David, David A. Mindell, and Elisabeth B. Reynolds. *The Work of the Future: Building Better Jobs in an Age of Intelligent Machines.* MIT Press, 2021.

Autor, David, David A. Mindell, and Elisabeth B. Reynolds. *The Work of the Future: Shaping Technology and Institutions.* Massachusetts Institute of Technology (MIT) and the MIT Work of the Future Initiative, 2019. https://workofthefuture.mit.edu/wp-content/uploads/2020/08/WorkoftheFuture_Report_Shaping_Technology_and_Institutions.pdf.

Avdul, David N., William Marty Martin, and Yvette P. Lopez. "Pay Transparency: Why It Is Important to Be Thoughtful and Strategic." *Compensation and Benefits Review* 56, no. 2 (2023): 1–14.

Axt, Jordan. "Tracking the Use of Project Implicit Data." *Project Implicit.* Accessed March 7, 2025. https://implicit.harvard.edu/implicit/user/jaxt/blogposts/piblogpost020.html.

Ayres, Ian, and Peter Siegelman. "Race and Gender Discrimination in Bargaining for a New Car." *American Economic Review* 85, no. 3 (1995): 304–21.

Badgett, M. V. Lee. *The Economic Case for LGBT Equality. Why Fair and Equal Treatment Benefits Us All.* Beacon, 2020.

Baert, Stijn. "Facebook Profile Picture Appearance Affects Recruiters' First Hiring Decisions." *New Media and Society* 20, no. 3 (2018): 1220–39.

Baert, Stijn. "Wage Subsidies and Hiring Chances for the Disabled: Some Casual Evidence." *European Journal of Health Economics* 17, no. 1 (2016): 71–86.

Baert, Stijn, and Eddy Omey. "Hiring Discrimination Against Pro-Union Applicants: The Role of Union Density and Firm Size." *De Economist, Netherlands Economic Review* 163 (2015): 263–80.

Bailey, Catherine, and Adrian Madden. "What Makes Work Meaningful—or Meaningless." *MIT Sloan Management Review*, June 1, 2016. https://sloanreview.mit.edu/article/what-makes-work-meaningful-or-meaningless/.

Baker, Michael, Yosh Halberstam, Kory Kroft, Alexandre Mas, and Derek Messacar. "Pay Transparency and the Gender Gap." *American Economic Journal: Applied Economics* 15, no. 2 (2023): 157–83.

Baldi, Stephane, and Debra B. McBrier. "Do the Determinants of Promotion Differ for Blacks and Whites? Evidence from the U.S. Labor Market." *Work and Occupations* 24, no. 4 (1997): 478–97.

Bamberger, Peter. *Exposing Pay: Pay Transparency and What It Means for Employees, Employers, and Public Policy*. Oxford University Press, 2023.

Bamberger, Peter, and Elena Belogolovsky. "The Dark Side of Transparency: How and When Pay Administration Practices Affect Employee Helping." *Journal of Applied Psychology* 102, no. 4 (2017): 658–71.

Bamberger, Peter, and Elena Belogolovsky. "The Impact of Pay Secrecy on Individual Task Performance." *Personnel Psychology* 63, no. 4 (2010): 965–96.

Banaji, Mahzarin R., and Anthony G. Greenwald. *Blindspot: Hidden Biases of Good People*. Delacorte, 2013.

Banerjee, Abhijit, Marianne Bertrand, Saugato Datta, and Sendhil Mullainathan. "Labor Market Discrimination in Delhi: Evidence from a Field Experiment." *Journal of Comparative Economics* 37, no. 1 (2009): 14–27.

Barbulescu, Roxana, and Matthew Bidwell. "Do Women Choose Different Jobs from Men? Mechanisms of Application Segregation in the Market for Managerial Workers." *Organization Science* 24, no. 3 (2013): 737–56.

Barley, Stephen R. "Semiotics and the Study of Occupational and Organizational Cultures." *Administrative Science Quarterly* 28, no. 3 (1983): 393–413.

Barnett, William P., James N. Baron, and Toby E. Stuart. "Avenues of Attainment: Occupational Demography and Organizational Careers in the California Civil Service." *American Journal of Sociology* 106, no. 1 (2000): 88–144.

Baron, James N. "Organizational Perspectives on Stratification." *Annual Review of Sociology* 10 (1984): 37–69.

Baron, James N., and William T. Bielby. "Bringing the Firms Back In: Stratification, Segmentation, and the Organization of Work." *American Sociological Review* 45, no. 5 (1980): 737–65.

Baron, James N., and William T. Bielby. "The Organization of Work in a Segmented Economy." *American Sociological Review* 49, no. 4 (1984): 454–73.

Baron, James N., and David M. Kreps. *Strategic Human Resources: Frameworks for General Managers*. Wiley, 1999.

Baron, James N., and Andrew E. Newman. "For What It's Worth: Organizations, Occupations, and the Value of Work Done by Women and Nonwhites." *American Sociological Review* 55, no. 2 (1990): 155–75.

Bartkoski, Timothy, Ellen Lynch, Chelsea Witt, and Cort Rudolph. "A Meta-Analysis of Hiring Discrimination Against Muslims and Arabs." *Personnel Assessment and Decisions* 4, no. 2 (2018): Article 1.

Bartol, Kathryn M., and David C. Martin. "Effects of Dependence, Dependency Threats, and Pay Secrecy on Managerial Pay Allocations." *Journal of Applied Psychology* 74, no. 1 (1989): 105–13.

Bass, Bernard M. *The Bass Handbook of Leadership: Theory, Research and Managerial Applications*. 4th ed. Free Press, 2008.

Bass, Bernard M. "From Transactional to Transformational Leadership: Learning to Share the Vision." *Organizational Dynamics* 18, no. 3 (1990): 19–31.

Bassett, Rodney L., A. Smith, J. Thrower, et al. "One Effort to Measure Implicit Attitudes Toward Spirituality and Religion." *Journal of Psychology and Christianity* 24, no. 3 (2005): 210–18.

Bastian, Rebekah. "Equity Before Meritocracy: Why We Must Create Opportunities Before Rewarding Accomplishments," *Forbes*, January 29, 2019. https://www.forbes .com/sites/rebekahbastian/2019/01/29/equity-before-meritocracy-why-we-must-create -opportunities-before-rewarding-accomplishments/.

Basu, Lex. "What Is a Chief Diversity Officer and What Do They Do?" Indeed.com, April 20, 2023. https://www.indeed.com/career-advice/finding-a-job/what-is-chief -diversity-officer.

Batruch, Anatolia, Jolanda Jetten, Herman Van de Werfhorst, Céline Darnon, and Fabrizio Butera. "Belief in School Meritocracy and the Legitimization of Social and Income Inequality." *Social Psychological and Personality Science* 14, no. 5 (2023): 621–35.

BBC. " 'Half of Women' Sexually Harassed at Work, Says BBC Survey." *BBC News*, October 25, 2017. https://www.bbc.com/news/uk-41741615.

Becker, Gary S. *The Economics of Discrimination*. 2nd ed. University of Chicago Press, 1971.

Behaghel, Luc, Bruno Crépon, and Thomas Le Barbanchon. "Unintended Effects of Anonymous Résumés." *American Economic Journal: Applied Economics* 7, no. 3 (2015): 1–27.

Bell, Daniel A. *The China Model: Political Meritocracy and the Limits of Democracy*. Princeton University Press, 2015.

Bell, Daniel A. *The Coming of Post-Industrial Society: A Venture in Social Forecasting*. Harper, 1973.

Bellver, Ana, and Daniel Kaufmann. "Transparenting Transparency: Initial Empirics and Policy Applications." Working paper, National Bureau of Economic Research, 2005. http://dx.doi.org/10.2139/ssrn.808664.

Bem, Sandra L., and Daryl J. Bem. "Does Sex-Biased Job Advertising 'Aid and Abet' Sex Discrimination?" *Journal of Applied Social Psychology* 3, no. 1 (1973): 6–18.

Benard, Stephen, In Paik, and Shelley J. Correll. "Cognitive Bias and the Motherhood Penalty." *Hastings Law Journal* 59, no. 6 (2008): 1359–87.

Benko, Cathy, Robin Erickson, John Hagel, and Jungle Wong. *Global Human Capital Trends 2014: Engaging the 21st-Century Workforce*. Deloitte University Press, 2014. https://www2.deloitte.com/content/dam/Deloitte/ar/Documents/human-capital/arg _hc_global-human-capital-trends-2014_09062014%20(1).pdf.

Morten Bennedsen, Kasper Meisner Nielsen, Francisco Perez-Gonzalez, and Daniel Wolfenzon. "Inside the Family Firm: The Role of Families in Succession Decisions and Performance." *Quarterly Journal of Economics* 122, no. 2 (2007): 647–91.

Bennedsen, Morten, Elena Simintzi, Margarita Tsoutsoura, and Daniel Wolfenson. "Do Firms Respond to Gender Pay Gap Transparency?" *Journal of Finance* 77, no. 4 (2022): 2051–91.

Berdahl, Jennifer L., and Celia Moore. "Workplace Harassment: Double Jeopardy for Minority Women." *Journal of Applied Psychology* 91, no. 2 (2006): 426–36.

Bergsteiner, Harald. *Accountability Theory Meets Accountability Practice*. Emerald Group, 2012.

Bernstein, Ethan S. "The Transparency Paradox: A Role for Privacy in Organizational Learning and Operational Control." *Administrative Science Quarterly* 57, no. 2 (2012): 181–216.

Bertrand, Marianne, and Esther Duflo. "Field Experiments on Discrimination." Working Paper 22014. National Bureau of Economic Research, 2016.

Bertrand, Marianne, and Sendhil Mullainathan. "Are Emily and Greg More Employable than Lakisha and Jamal? A Field Experiment on Labor Market Discrimination." *American Economic Review* 94, no. 4 (2004): 991–1013.

Bertrand, Marianne, and Antoinette Schoar. "Managing with Style: The Effect of Managers on Firm Policies." *Quarterly Journal of Economics* 118, no. 4 (2003): 1169–208.

Bertrand, Marianne, and Antoinette Schoar. "The Role of Family in Family Firms." *Journal of Economic Perspectives* 20, no. 2 (2006): 73–96.

Bian, Yanjie. "Bringing Strong Ties Back In: Indirect Ties, Network Bridges, and Job Searches in China." *American Sociological Review* 62, no. 3 (1997): 366–85.

Bidwell, Matthew, Forrest Briscoe, Isabel Fernandez-Mateo, and Adina Sterling. "The Employment Relationship and Inequality: How and Why Changes in Employment Practices Are Reshaping Rewards in Organizations." *Academy of Management Annals* 7, no. 1 (2013): 61–121.

Bielby, William T. "Minimizing Workplace Gender and Racial Bias." *Contemporary Sociology* 29, no. 1 (2000): 120–29.

Bielby, William T. "Models of Status Attainment." *Research in Social Stratification and Mobility* 1 (1981): 3–26.

Bielby, William T., and James N. Baron. "Men and Women at Work: Sex Segregation and Statistical Discrimination." *American Journal of Sociology* 91, no. 4 (1986): 759–99.

Biernat, Monica, and Diane Kobrynowicz. "Gender- and Race-Based Standards of Competence: Lower Minimum Standards but Higher Ability Standards for Devalued Groups." *Journal of Personality and Social Psychology* 72, no. 3 (1997): 544–57.

Biernat, Monica, and Jennifer E. Ma. "Stereotypes and the Confirmability of Trait Concepts." *Personality and Social Psychology Bulletin* 31, no. 4 (2005): 483–95.

Biernat, Monica, and Theresa K. Vescio. "Values and Prejudice." In *Social Psychology of Prejudice: Historical and Contemporary Issues*, ed. Christian S. Crandall and Mark Schaller. Lewinian, 2005.

Bika, Nikoletta. "Pre-Employment Testing: A Selection of Popular Tests." Workable.com, September 2023. https://resources.workable.com/tutorial/pre-employment-tests.

Bird, Sharon R. "Unsettling Universities' Incongruous, Gendered Bureaucratic Structures: A Case-Study Approach." *Gender, Work and Organization* 18, no. 2 (2011): 202–30.

Birt, Jamie. "What Makes a Company a Great Place to Work: 15 Things." Indeed, 2022. Accessed June 26, 2023. https://www.indeed.com/career-advice/finding-a-job/what-makes-a-company-a-great-place-to-work.

Blair, Irene V., and Mahzarin R. Banaji. "Automatic and Controlled Processes in Stereotype Priming." *Journal of Personality and Social Psychology* 70, no. 6 (1996): 1142–63.

Blanton, Hart, James Jaccard, Jonathan Klick, Barbara Mellers, Gregory Mitchell, and Philip E. Tetlock. "Strong Claims and Weak Evidence: Reassessing the Predictive Validity of the IAT." *Journal of Applied Psychology* 94, no. 3 (2009): 567–82.

Blau, Peter M., and Otis D. Duncan. *The American Occupational Structure*. Wiley, 1967.

Bohlander, George, and Scott Snell. *Managing Human Resources*. 14th ed. Thomson South-Western, 2007.

Bolstad, Erika. "Backlash Against DEI Spreads to More States." Stateline, June 14, 2024. https://stateline.org/2024/06/14/backlash-against-dei-spreads-to-more-states.

Botelho, Tristan L., and Mabel Abraham. "Pursuing Quality: How Search Costs and Uncertainty Magnify Gender-Based Double Standards in a Multistage Evaluation Process." *Administrative Science Quarterly* 62, no. 4 (2017): 698–730.

Bourdieu, Pierre. "Cultural Reproduction and Social Reproduction." In *Knowledge, Education and Cultural Change*, ed. J. Richardson. Greenwood, 1973.

Bourdieu, Pierre. *La distinction: critique sociale du jugement.* Minuit, 1979.

Bourdieu, Pierre. *Outline of a Theory of Practice*, trans. Richard Nice. Cambridge University Press, 1977.

Bourdieu, Pierre, and Jean-Claude Passeron. *Reproduction in Education, Society and Culture.* Sage, 1990.

Bourke, Juliet, and Bernadette Dillon. "The Diversity and Inclusion Revolution. Eight Powerful Truths." *Deloitte Review*, January 22, 2018, 82–99.

Bovens, Mark. "Analyzing and Assessing Accountability: A Conceptual Framework." *European Law Journal* 13, no. 4 (2007): 447–68.

Bowen, William G., Martin A. Kurzweil, and Eugene M. Tobin. *Equity and Excellence in American Higher Education.* University of Virginia Press, 2005.

Bowen, William G., and Sarah A. Levin. *Reclaiming the Game: College Sports and Educational Values.* Princeton University Press, 2003.

Braddock, Jomills H., and James M. McPartland. "How Minorities Continue to Be Excluded from Equal Employment Opportunities: Research on Labor Market and Institutional Barriers." *Journal of Social Issues* 43, no. 1 (1987): 5–39.

Bradley, Samuel L., Kathleen Christensen, Marcie-Pitt-Catsouphes, and Tay McNamara. *Equity at the Workplace: A Moment in Time and Place.* Boston College School of Social Work and United Way & Center for Social Innovation, 2021. https://www.bc.edu /content/dam/bc1/schools/sw/csi/Final-WorkEquity-10-5.19.22.pdf.

Brahm, Chris. *Tackling AI's Unintended Consequences.* Bain & Company, 2023. https://www .bain.com/contentassets/a7ebfd741daf44b6905c597bede52de4/bain_brief_tackling _ais_unintended_consequences.pdf.

Breen, Richard, and John H. Goldthorpe. "Class, Mobility and Merit: The Experience of Two British Birth Cohorts." *European Sociological Review* 17, no. 2 (2001): 81–101.

Bresnahan, Timothy F., Erik Brynjolfsson, and Lorin M. Hitt. "Technology, Organization, and the Demand for Skilled Labor." In *The New Relationship: Human Capital in the American Corporation*, ed. Margaret M. Blair and Thomas A. Kochan (Washington, DC: Brookings Institution Press, 2000), 145–84.

Brewster, Chris, and Wolfgang Mayrhofer. *Handbook of Research on Comparative Human Resource Management.* Edward Elgar, 2012.

Bridges, William P., and Robert L. Nelson. "Markets in Hierarchies: Organizational and Market Influences on Gender Inequality in a State Pay System." *American Journal of Sociology* 95, no. 3 (1989): 616–58.

Brigham, Carl C. "Intelligence Tests of Immigrant Groups." *Psychological Review* 37, no. 2 (1930): 158–65.

Briscoe, Forrest, and Katherine C. Kellogg. "The Initial Assignment Effect: Local Employer Practices and Positive Career Outcomes for Work-Family Program Users." *American Sociological Review* 76, no. 2 (2011): 291–319.

Brown, Anna. "More than Twice as Many Americans Support than Oppose the #MeToo Movement." Pew Research Center, September 29, 2022. https://www.pewresearch.org /social-trends/2022/09/29/more-than-twice-as-many-americans-support-than-oppose -the-metoo-movement/.

Brown, N. Derek, and Drew S. Jacoby-Senghor. "Majority Members Misperceive Even 'Win-Win' Diversity Policies as Unbeneficial to Them." *Journal of Personality and Social Psychology* 122, no. 6 (2022): 1075–97.

Brown, William N. *Chasing the Chinese Dream: Four Decades of Following China's War on Poverty.* Springer, 2021.

Bryant, Adam. "How to Hire the Right Person." *New York Times,* February 13, 2017. Accessed June 26, 2023. https://www.nytimes.com/guides/business/how-to-hire-the -right-person.

Bryson, Alex. "Pay Equity After the Equality Act 2010: Does Sexual Orientation Still Matter?" *Work, Employment and Society* 31, no. 3 (2017): 483–500.

Buckingham, Marcus, and Ashley Goodall. "Reinventing Performance Management." *Harvard Business Review,* April 2015. https://hbr.org/2015/04/reinventing-performance -management.

Budig, Michelle J., and Paula England. "The Wage Penalty for Motherhood." *American Sociological Review* 66, no. 2 (2001): 204–25.

Burke, Elizabeth. "2005 Reward Programs and Incentive Compensation: Survey Report. A Study by the Society for Human Resource Management." SHRM Research Department, 2005.

Burke, Katie. "Performance Reviews Are Broken." Inc, November 28, 2022. https://www .inc.com/katie-burke/create-more-manageable-performance-review-system.html.

Burkhart, Genni. "What You Need to Know About Pay Transparency Laws Going into Effect in 2023." DOCS Education, January 6, 2023. https://www.docseducation.com /blog/what-you-need-know-about-pay-transparency-laws-going-effect-2023.

Burt, Ronald S. *Brokerage and Closure: An Introduction to Social Capital.* Oxford University Press, 2005.

Burt, Ronald S. "Network Disadvantaged Entrepreneurs: Density, Hierarchy, and Success in China and the West." *Entrepreneurship Theory and Practice* 43, no. 1 (2019): 19–50.

Burt, Ronald S. "The Networks and Success of Female Entrepreneurs in China." *Social Networks* 58 (2019): 37–49.

Burt, Ronald S. "Structural Holes and Good Ideas." *American Journal of Sociology* 110, no. 2 (2004): 349–99.

Burt, Ronald S. *Structural Holes: The Social Structure of Competition.* Harvard University Press, 1992.

Butler, Kelsey. "Big Tech Layoffs Are Hitting Diversity and Inclusion Jobs Hard." *Bloomberg News,* January 24, 2023. https://www.bloomberg.com/news/articles/2023-01-24 /tech-layoffs-are-hitting-diversity-and-inclusion-jobs-hard.

Butler, Kelsey, and Patricia Hurtado. "Affirmative Action End Will Crush the Diversity Talent Pipeline." *Bloomberg Law,* October 30, 2022. https://news.bloomberglaw.com /us-law-week/affirmative-action-end-will-crush-the-diversity-talent-pipeline.

Calanchini, Jimmy, Calvin K. Lai, and Karl Christoph Klauer. "Reducing Implicit Racial Preferences: III. A Process-Level Examination of Changes in Implicit Preferences." *Journal of Personality and Social Psychology* 121, no. 4 (2021): 796–818.

Caldera, Camille G. "Legacy, Athlete, and Donor Preferences Disproportionately Benefit White Applicants, per Analysis." *Harvard Crimson,* October 23, 2019. https://www .thecrimson.com/article/2019/10/23/nber-admissions-data.

Callahan, Cloey. "Supreme Court's Affirmative Action Ruling—What It Means for Employers." Worklife, June 29, 2023. https://www.worklife.news/dei/affirmative-action -business/.

Calvó-Armengol, Antoni, and Matthew O. Jackson. "The Effects of Social Networks on Employment and Inequality." *American Economic Review* 94, no. 3 (2004): 426–54.

Camp, Alex, Mackenzie Cramblit, Maryellen Kwasie, and Pawel Poplawski. "Six 'Power Practices' to Retain Nonprofit Talent." McKinsey & Company, May 22, 2023. https://www.mckinsey.com/capabilities/people-and-organizational-performance/our-insights/the-organization-blog/six-power-practices-to-retain-nonprofit-talent.

Campbell, Donald J., Kathleen M. Campbell, and Ho-Beng Chia. "Merit Pay, Performance Appraisal, and Individual Motivation: An Analysis and Alternative." *Human Resource Management* 37, no. 2 (1998): 131–46.

Candelon, François, Rodolphe Charme di Carlo, Midas De Bondt, and Theodoros Evgeniou. "AI Regulation Is Coming." *Harvard Business Review*, September–October 2021. https://hbr.org/2021/09/ai-regulation-is-coming.

Cappelli, Peter, ed. *Employment Relationships: New Models of White-Collar Work.* Cambridge University Press, 2008.

Cappelli, Peter. *The New Deal at Work: Managing the Market-Driven Workforce.* Harvard Business Review Press, 1999.

Cappelli, Peter. "Talent Management for the Twenty-First Century." *Harvard Business Review*, March 2008, 74–81. https://hbr.org/2008/03/talent-management-for-the-twenty-first-century.

Cappelli, Peter. *Talent on Demand: Managing Talent in an Age of Uncertainty.* Harvard Business Review Press, 2008.

Cappelli, Peter, Laurie Bassi, Harry Katz, David Knoke, Paul Osterman, and Michael Useem. *Change at Work.* Oxford University Press, 1997.

Cappelli, Peter, and Anna Tavis. "The Performance Management Revolution." *Harvard Business Review*, October 2016. https://hbr.org/2016/10/the-performance-management-revolution.

Carli, Linda L., and Alice H. Eagly. "Gender, Hierarchy, and Leadership: An Introduction." *Journal of Social Issues* 57, no. 4 (2001): 629–36.

Carlsson, Rickard, and Jens Agestrom. "A Closer Look at the Discrimination Outcomes in the IAT Literature." Linnaeus University Centre for Labour Market and Discrimination Studies, 2015. https://www.diva-portal.org/smash/get/diva2:911362/FULLTEXT01.pdf.

Carnes, Molly, Patricia G. Devine, L. B. Manwell, et al. "The Effect of an Intervention to Break the Gender Bias Habit for Faculty at One Institution: A Cluster Randomized, Controlled Trial." *Academic Medicine* 90, no. 2 (2015): 221–30.

Carpenter, Christopher S., and Samuel T. Eppink. "Does It Get Better? Recent Estimates of Sexual Orientation and Earnings in the United States." *Southern Economic Journal* 84, no. 2 (2017): 426–41.

Casciaro, Tiziana, Francesca Gino, and Maryam Kouchaki. "The Contaminating Effects of Building Instrumental Ties: How Networking Can Make Us Feel Dirty." *Administrative Science Quarterly* 59, no. 4 (2014): 705–35.

Cascio, Jessica, and E. Ashby Plant. "Prospective Moral Licensing: Does Anticipating Doing Good Later Allow You to Be Bad Now?" *Journal of Experimental Social Psychology* 56 (2015): 110–16.

Cassirer, Naomi, and Barbara Reskin. "High Hopes: Organizational Position, Employment Experiences, and Women's and Men's Promotion Aspirations." *Work and Occupations* 27, no. 4 (2000): 438–63.

Castilla, Emilio J. "Accounting for the Gap: A Firm Study Manipulating Organizational Accountability and Transparency in Pay Decisions." *Organization Science* 26, no. 2 (2015): 311–33.

Castilla, Emilio J. "Book Review: La Profesión de Economista: El Auge de Economistas, Ejecutivos y Empresarios en España by Mauro F. Guillen," *REIS* 59 (July-September, 1992), 379–95.

Castilla, Emilio J. "Bringing Managers Back In: Managerial Influences on Workplace Inequality." *American Sociological Review* 76, no. 5 (2011): 667–94.

Castilla, Emilio J. "Gender, Race, and Meritocracy in Organizational Careers." *American Journal of Sociology* 113, no. 6 (2008): 1479–526.

Castilla, Emilio J. "Gender, Race, and Network Advantage in Organizations." *Organization Science* 33, no. 6 (2022): 2364–403.

Castilla, Emilio J. "Meritocracy." In *The SAGE Encyclopedia of Political Behavior*, ed. Fathali M. Moghaddam. Sage, 2017.

Castilla, Emilio J. "Social Networks and Employee Performance in a Call Center." *American Journal of Sociology* 110, no. 5 (2005): 1243–83.

Castilla, Emilio J., and Stephen Benard. "The Paradox of Meritocracy in Organizations." *Administrative Science Quarterly* 55, no. 4 (2010): 543–76.

Castilla, Emilio J., George J. Lan, and Ben A. Rissing. "Social Networks and Employment: Mechanisms (Part 1) and Outcomes (Part 2)." *Sociology Compass* 7, no. 12 (2013): 999–1026.

Castilla, Emilio J., and Ethan J. Poskanzer. "Through the Front Door: Why Do Organizations (Still) Prefer Legacy Applicants?" *American Sociological Review* 87, no. 5 (2022): 782–826.

Castilla, Emilio J., and Aruna Ranganathan. "The Production of Merit: How Managers Understand and Apply Merit in the Workplace." *Organization Science* 31, no. 4 (2020): 909–35.

Castilla, Emilio J., and Hye Jin Rho. "The Gendering of Job Postings in the Online Recruitment Process." *Management Science* 69, no. 11 (2023): 6912–39.

Castilla, Emilio J., and Ben A. Rissing. "Best in Class: The Returns on Application Endorsements in Higher Education." *Administrative Science Quarterly* 64, no. 1 (2019): 230–70.

Ceballos, Martha, Annick Masselot, and Richard Watt. "Pay Transparency Across Countries and Legal Systems." *CESifo Forum* 23, no. 2 (2022): 3–11.

Cech, Erin A., and Mary Blair-Loy. "Perceiving Glass Ceilings? Meritocratic Versus Structural Explanations of Gender Inequality Among Women in Science and Technology." *Social Problems* 57, no. 3 (2010): 371–97.

Cech, Erin A., and Michelle V. Pham. "Queer in STEM Organizations: Workplace Disadvantages for LGBT Employees in STEM Related Federal Agencies." *Social Sciences* 6, no. 1 (2017): 12.

Cech, Erin A., and William R. Rothwell. "LGBT Workplace Inequality in the Federal Workforce: Intersectional Processes, Organizational Contexts, and Turnover Considerations." *ILR Review* 73, no. 1 (2020): 25–60.

Cejka, Mary Ann, and Alice H. Eagly. "Gender-Stereotypic Images of Occupations Correspond to the Sex Segregation of Employment." *Personality and Social Psychology Bulletin* 25, no. 4 (1999): 413–23.

Cellini, Stephanie Riegg. "The Alarming Rise in For-Profit College Enrollment." *Brown Center Chalkboard*, November 2, 2020. https://www.brookings.edu/blog/brown-center-chalkboard/2020/11/02/the-alarming-rise-in-for-profit-college-enrollment/.

Chamorro-Premuzic, Tomas. *The Talent Delusion: Why Data, Not Intuition, Is the Key to Unlocking Human Potential*. Little, Brown, 2017.

Chamorro-Premuzic, Tomas, Frida Polli, and Ben Dattner. "Building Ethical AI for Talent Management." *Harvard Business Review*, November 21, 2019. https://hbr.org/2019/11 /building-ethical-ai-for-talent-management.

Chan, Curtis K., and Michel Anteby. "Task Segregation as a Mechanism for Within-Job Inequality: Women and Men of the Transportation Security Administration." *Administrative Science Quarterly* 61, no. 2 (2016): 184–216.

Chang, Edward H., Katherine L. Milkman, Dena M. Gromet, et al. "The Mixed Effects of Online Diversity Training." *PNAS* 116, no. 16 (2019): 7778–83.

Charmaz, Kathy. *Constructing Grounded Theory: A Practical Guide Through Qualitative Analysis*. Pine Forge, 2006.

Chopik, William J., and Hannah L. Giasson. "Age Differences in Explicit and Implicit Age Attitudes Across the Life Span." Supplement, *Gerontologist* 57, no. S2 (2017): S169–S77.

Choudhury, Ambereen and Amy Bainbridge. "McKinsey Champions Diversity While Rivals Abandon Targets," *Bloomberg*, February 12, 2025. https://www.msn.com/en-us/money /companies/mckinsey-says-it-will-prioritize-diversity-despite-trump-s-dei-order/ar -AA1ySNb6.

Cialdini, Robert B., and Brad J. Sagarin. "Principles of Interpersonal Influence." In *Persuasion: Psychological Insights and Perspectives*, ed. Sharon Shavitt and Timothy C. Brock. Allyn and Bacon, 1994.

Cingano, Federico, and Alfonso Rosolia. "People I Know: Job Search and Social Networks." *Journal of Labor Economics* 30, no. 2 (2012): 291–332.

Civil, David, and Joseph J. Himsworth. "Introduction: Meritocracy in Perspective. The Rise of the Meritocracy 60 Years On." *Political Quarterly* 91, no. 2 (2020): 373–78.

Cleveland, Jeanette N., Kevin R. Murphy, and Richard E. Williams. "Multiple Uses of Performance Appraisal: Prevalence and Correlates." *Journal of Applied Psychology* 74, no. 1 (1989): 130–35.

Cobb, Adam. "How Firms Shape Income Inequality: Stakeholder Power, Executive Decision Making, and the Structuring of Employment Relationships." *Academy of Management Review* 41, no. 2 (2016): 324–48.

Cohen, Rachel M. "Stop Requiring College Degrees for Jobs That Don't Need Them." *Vox*, March 19, 2023. https://www.vox.com/policy/23628627/degree-inflation-college-bacheors -stars-labor-worker-paper-ceiling.

Colella, Adrienne, Ramona L. Paetzold, Asghar Zardkoohi, and Michael J. Wesson. "Exposing Pay Secrecy." *Academy of Management Review* 32, no. 1 (2007): 55–71.

Considine, Craig. "The Racialization of Islam in the United States: Islamophobia, Hate Crimes, and Flying While Brown." *Religions* 8, no. 9 (2017): 165–83.

Considine, Craig. "Young Pakistani Men and Irish Identity: Religion, Race and Ethnicity in Post-Celtic Tiger Ireland." *Sociology* 52, no. 4 (2018): 655–70.

Considine, Jennifer R., Jennifer E. Mihalick, Yoko R. Mogi-Hein, Marguerite W. Penick-Parks, and Paul M. Van Auken. "How Do You Achieve Inclusive Excellence in the Classroom?" *Teaching and Learning* 2017, no. 151 (2017): 171–87.

Cooper, Marianne. "The False Promise of Meritocracy." *Atlantic*, December 1, 2015. https://www.theatlantic.com/business/archive/2015/12/meritocracy/418074/.

Corbin, Juliet, and Anselm Strauss. *Basics of Qualitative Research: Grounded Theory Procedures and Techniques*. 2nd ed. Sage, 1990.

Corbin, Juliet, and Anselm Strauss. *Basics of Qualitative Research: Techniques and Procedures for Developing Grounded Theory*. 3rd ed. Sage, 2007.

Cornell, Stephen, and Douglas Hartmann. *Ethnicity and Race: Making Identities in a Changing World*. 2nd ed. Pine Forge, 2007.

Correll, Shelley J. "Constraints into Preferences: Gender, Status, and Emerging Career Aspirations." *American Sociological Review* 69, no. 1 (2004): 93–113.

Correll, Shelley J. "Gender and the Career Choice Process: The Role of Biased Self-Assessments." *American Journal of Sociology* 106, no. 6 (2001): 1691–730.

Correll, Shelley J., Stephen Benard, and In Paik. "Getting a Job: Is There a Motherhood Penalty?" *American Journal of Sociology* 112, no. 5 (2007): 1297–338.

Cortina, Lilia M., and Jennifer L. Berdahl. "Sexual Harassment in Organizations: A Decade of Research in Review." In *The SAGE Handbook of Organizational Behavior*, ed. Julian Barling and Cary L. Cooper. Sage, 2008.

Council of the European Union. "Pay Transparency in the EU." Last modified March 21, 2024. https://www.consilium.europa.eu/en/policies/pay-transparency/.

Crosby, Faye J. "Relative Deprivation in Organizational Settings." *Research in Organizational Behavior* 6 (1984): 51–93.

Crosby, Faye J. *Relative Deprivation and Working Women*. Oxford University Press, 1982.

Crosby, Faye J., Susan Clayton, Olaf Alksnis, and Kathryn Hemker. "Cognitive Biases in the Perception of Discrimination: The Importance of Format." *Sex Roles* 14 (1986): 637–46.

Crosby, Jennifer R., and Benoît Monin. "Failure to Warn: How Student Race Affects Warnings of Potential Academic Difficulty." *Journal of Experimental Social Psychology* 43, no. 4 (2007): 663–70.

Crosby, Jennifer R., and Benoît Monin. "How the Opinions of Racial Minorities Influence Judgments of Discrimination." *Basic and Applied Social Psychology* 35, no. 4 (2013): 334–45.

Crosby, Jennifer R., Benoît Monin, and Daniel Richardson. "Where Do We Look During Potentially Offensive Behavior?" *Psychological Science* 19, no. 3 (2008): 226–28.

Cross, Rob, and Jonathon N. Cummings. "Tie and Network Correlates of Individual Performance in Knowledge-Intensive Work." *Academy of Management Journal* 47, no. 6 (2004): 928–37.

Cunningham, George B. *Diversity, Equity, and Inclusion at Work*. Taylor and Francis, 2023.

Cunningham, Lillian. "In Big Move, Accenture Will Get Rid of Annual Performance Reviews and Rankings." *Washington Post*, July 21, 2015. https://www.washingtonpost.com/news/on-leadership/wp/2015/07/21/in-big-move-accenture-will-get-rid-of-annual-performance-reviews-and-rankings/.

Cunningham, Lillian, and Jena McGregor. "Why Big Business Is Falling Out of Love with the Annual Performance Review." *Washington Post*, August 17, 2015. https://www.washingtonpost.com/news/on-leadership/wp/2015/08/17/why-big-business-is-falling-out-of-love-with-annual-performance-reviews/.

Curry, Sheree R. " 'I Represent Their Voices': As Corporate America Embraces Diversity, This Is How Some DEI Officers See Their Work." *USA Today*, February 28, 2023. https://www.usatoday.com/story/money/2023/02/28/diversity-officers-role-corporate-america/11150087002/.

Dalio, Ray. "The Key to Bridgewater's Success: A Real Idea Meritocracy, September 23, 2017. https://swae.io/downloads/Swae_The_Key_to_Bridgewaters_Success-A_Real_Idea_Meritocracy.pdf.

Daniel, William Wentworth. *Racial Discrimination in England*. Penguin, 1969.

Dastin, Jeffrey. "Insight—Amazon Scraps Secret AI Recruiting Tool That Showed Bias Against Women." Reuters, October 10, 2018. https://www.reuters.com/article /idUSKCN1MK0AG/.

Dattner, Ben, Tomas Chamorro-Premuzic, Richard Buchband, and Lucinda Schettler. "The Legal and Ethical Implications of Using AI in Hiring." *Harvard Business Review*, April 25, 2019. https://hbr.org/2019/04/the-legal-and-ethical-implications-of-using-ai-in-hiring.

Daugherty, Paul, Bhaskar Ghosh, Karthick Narain, Lan Guan, and Jim Wilson. *A New Era of Generative AI for Everyone*. Accenture, 2023. Accessed July 7, 2023. https://www .accenture.com/content/dam/accenture/final/accenture-com/document/Accenture -A-New-Era-of-Generative-AI-for-Everyone.pdf#zoom=40.

Davis, Dominic-Madori, and Kyle Wiggers. "Silicon Valley Leaders Are Once Again Declaring 'DEI' Bad and 'Meritocracy' Good—but They're Wrong," *TechCrunch Latest*, June 23, 2024. https://techcrunch.com/2024/06/23/silicon-valley-leaders-are-once -again-declaring-dei-bad-and-meritocracy-good-but-theyre-wrong/.

Davis, Kingsley. *Human Society*. MacMillan, 1950.

De Alva, Jorge K., and Andrew Rosen. *Inside the For-Profit Sector in Higher Education*. Forum for the Future of Higher Education. Accessed May 11, 2020. https://www .educause.edu/ir/library/pdf/ff1204s.pdf.

De Smet, Aaron, Bonnie Dowling, Bryan Hancock, and Bill Schaninger. "The Great Attrition Is Making Hiring Harder. Are You Searching the Right Talent Pools?" *McKinsey Quarterly*, July 13, 2022. https://www.mckinsey.com/capabilities/people-and -organizational-performance/our-insights/the-great-attrition-is-making-hiring -harder-are-you-searching-the-right-talent-pools.

Decker, Ragan, Kerri Nelson, and Kirsteen Anderson. "The Key to Improving Equity in the Workplace: An Analytical Aptitude." SHRM, March 16, 2023. https://www.shrm .org/resourcesandtools/hr-topics/behavioral-competencies/pages/improve-equity -analytical-aptitude.aspx.

Deloitte. *Missing Pieces Report: The 2018 Board Diversity Census of Women and Minorities on Fortune 500 Boards*. Deloitte and the Alliance for Board Diversity, 2018. https://www2 .deloitte.com/content/dam/Deloitte/us/Documents/center-for-board-effectiveness /us-cbe-missing-pieces-report-2018-board-diversity-census.pdf.

Deloitte. *Only Skin Deep? Re-Examining the Business Case for Diversity*. Deloitte Point of View, September 2011. https://www.ced.org/pdf/Deloitte_-_Only_Skin_Deep.pdf.

Dencker, John C. "Corporate Restructuring and Sex Differences in Managerial Promotion." *American Sociological Review* 73, no. 3 (2008): 455–76.

Dencker, John C. "Relative Bargaining Power, Corporate Restructuring, and Managerial Incentives." *Administrative Science Quarterly* 54, no. 3 (2009): 453–85.

Devine, Patricia G., and Sara M. Baker. "Measurement of Racial Stereotype Subtyping." *Personality and Social Psychology Bulletin* 17, no. 1 (1991): 44–50.

Devine, Patricia G., Margo J. Monteith, J. R. Zuwerink, and A. J. Elliot. "Prejudice With and Without Compunction." *Journal of Personality and Social Psychology* 60, no. 6 (1991): 817–30.

DiMaggio, Paul. "Cultural Entrepreneurship in Nineteenth-Century Boston: The Creation of an Organizational Base for High Culture in America." *Media, Culture and Society* 4, no. 1 (1982): 33–50.

"Diversity, Equity, and Inclusion Analytics." HireRoad, February 27, 2023. https://hireroad .com/resources/diversity-equity-and-inclusion-analytics.

Dixon-Fyle, Sundiatu, Kevin Dolan, Dame Vivian Hunt, and Sata Prince. "Diversity Wins: How Inclusion Matters." McKinsey & Company, May 19, 2020. https://www.mckinsey.com/featured-insights/diversity-and-inclusion/diversity-wins-how-inclusion-matters.

Dobbin, Frank. *Inventing Equal Opportunity*. Princeton University Press, 2009.

Dobbin, Frank, and Alexandra Kalev. "The Civil Rights Revolution at Work: What Went Wrong." *Annual Review of Sociology* 47 (2021): 281–303.

Dobbin, Frank, and Alexandra Kalev. "Frank Dobbin and Alexandra Kalev Explain Why Diversity Training Does Not Work." *Economist*, May 21, 2021. https://www.economist.com/by-invitation/2021/05/21/frank-dobbin-and-alexandra-kalev-explain-why-diversity-training-does-not-work.

Dobbin, Frank, and Alexandra Kalev. *Getting to Diversity: What Works and What Doesn't*. Harvard University Press, 2022.

Dobbin, Frank, and Alexandra Kalev. "The Origins and Effects of Corporate Diversity Programs." In *The Oxford Handbook of Diversity and Work*, ed. Quinetta M. Roberson. Oxford University Press, 2013.

Dobbin, Frank, and Alexandra Kalev. "Why Diversity Programs Fail." *Harvard Business Review*, 2016, 14. https://hbr.org/2016/07/why-diversity-programs-fail.

Dobbin, Frank, and Alexandra Kalev. "Why Firms Need Diversity Managers and Task Forces." In *How Global Migration Changes the Workforce Diversity Equation*, ed. Massimo Pilati, Hina Sheikh, and Chris Tilly. Cambridge Scholars, 2015.

Dobbin, Frank, Daniel Schrage, and Alexandra Kalev. "Rage Against the Iron Cage: The Varied Effects of Bureaucratic Personnel Reforms on Diversity." *American Sociological Review* 80, no. 5 (2015): 1014–44.

Doubles, Brian. "Equity and Meritocracy Aren't Necessarily at Odds. How I Had to Figure out the Big E to Rethink Our Company's Diversity Approach." *Fortune*, April 26, 2023. https://fortune.com/2023/04/26/equity-meritocracy-companys-diversity-brian-doubles/.

Douthat, Ross. "Can the Meritocracy Survive Without the SAT?" *New York Times*, April 29, 2023. https://www.nytimes.com/2023/04/29/opinion/sat-college.html.

Drentea, Patricia. "Consequences of Women's Formal and Informal Job Search Methods for Employment in Female-Dominated Jobs." *Gender and Society* 12, no. 3 (1998): 321–38.

Drydakis, Nick. "Ethnic Differences in Housing Opportunities in Athens." *Urban Studies* 47, no. 12 (2010): 2573–96.

Drydakis, Nick. "Health Impairments and Labour Market Outcomes." *European Journal of Health Economics* 11, no. 5 (2010): 457–69.

Drydakis, Nick. "Religious Affiliation and Employment Bias in the Labor Market." *Journal for the Scientific Study of Religion* 49, no. 3 (2010): 477–93.

Drydakis, Nick. "Sexual Orientation and Earnings: A Meta-Analysis 2012–2020." IZA Discussion Paper No. 14496. IZA Institute of Labor Economics, June 2021. https://docs.iza.org/dp14496.pdf.

Drydakis, Nick. "Sexual Orientation and Labor Market Outcomes." IZA World of Labor, 2019. Accessed August 10, 2023. https://wol.iza.org/articles/sexual-orientation-and-labor-market-outcomes/long.

Drydakis, Nick. "Sexual Orientation Discrimination in the Labour Market." *Labour Economics* 16, no. 4 (2009): 364–72.

Drydakis, Nick, and Klaus F. Zimmermann. "Sexual Orientation, Gender Identity and Labour Market Outcomes: New Patterns and Insights." GLO Discussion Paper No. 627. Global Labor Organization, 2020.

Dundon, Tony, and Anthony Rafferty. "The (Potential) Demise of HRM?" *Human Resource Management Journal* 28, no. 3 (2018): 377–91.

Duru-Bellat, Marie, and Elise Tenret. "Meritocracy: A Widespread Ideology Due to School Socialization?" SciencesPo, 2010. https://sciencespo.hal.science/hal-00972712.

Duru-Bellat, Marie, and Elise Tenret. "Who's for Meritocracy? Individual and Contextual Variations in the Faith." *Comparative Education Review* 56, no. 2 (2012): 223–47.

Dworkin, Ronald. *Sovereign Virtue: The Theory and Practice of Equality.* Harvard University Press, 2000.

Eagly, Alice H., Mary C. Johannesen-Schmidt, and Marloes L. van Engen. "Transformational, Transactional, and Laissez-Faire Leadership Styles: A Meta-Analysis Comparing Women and Men." *Psychological Bulletin* 129, no. 4 (2003): 569–91.

Eagly, Alice H., and Blair T. Johnson. "Gender and Leadership Style: A Meta-Analysis." *Psychological Bulletin* 108, no. 2 (1990): 233–56.

Eccles, Robert G., and Dwight B. Crane. *Doing Deals: Investment Banks at Work.* Harvard Business School Press, 1988.

Edelman, Lauren B. "Legal Environments and Organizational Governance: The Expansion of Due Process in the American Workplace." *American Journal of Sociology* 95, no. 6 (1990): 1401–40.

Edmans, Alex. "Is There Really a Business Case for Diversity?" Medium, October 30, 2021. https://medium.com/@alex.edmans/is-there-really-a-business-case-for-diversity-c58ef67ebffa.

Edquist, Alex, Liz Grennan, Sian Griffiths, and Kayvaun Rowshankish. "Data Ethics: What It Means and What It Takes." McKinsey Digital, September 23, 2022. https://www.mckinsey.com/capabilities/mckinsey-digital/our-insights/data-ethics-what-it-means-and-what-it-takes.

Effron, Daniel A., Jessica S. Cameron, and Benoît Monin. "Endorsing Obama Licenses Favoring Whites." *Journal of Experimental Social Psychology* 45, no. 3 (2009): 590–93.

Ehrenreich, Barbara. *Fear of Falling: The Inner Life of the Middle Class.* Pantheon, 1989.

Ellerbeck, Stefan. "This Country Has the Highest Number of People Planning to Quit Their Jobs." World Economic Forum, August 11, 2022. https://www.weforum.org/agenda/2022/08/jobs-work-quit-great-resignation.

Elliott, James R. "Class, Race, and Job Matching in Contemporary Urban Labor Markets." *Social Science Quarterly* 81, no. 4 (2000): 1036–52.

Elliott, James R. "Referral Hiring and Ethnically Homogeneous Jobs: How Prevalent Is the Connection and for Whom?" *Social Science Research* 30, no. 3 (2001): 401–25.

Elliott, James R. "Social Isolation and Labor Market Insulation: Network and Neighborhood Effects on Less-Educated Urban Workers." *Sociological Quarterly* 40, no. 2 (1999): 199–216.

Elvira, Marta M., and Ishak Saporta. "How Does Collective Bargaining Affect the Gender Pay Gap?" *Work and Occupations* 28, no. 4 (2001): 469–90.

Elvira, Marta M., and Christopher D. Zatzick. "Who's Displaced First? The Role of Race in Layoff Decisions." *Industrial Relations: A Journal of Economy and Society* 41, no. 2 (2002): 329–61.

Ely, Robin J., and David A. Thomas. "Getting Serious About Diversity: Enough Already with the Business Case." *Harvard Business Review*, 2020. https://hbr.org/2020/11/getting-serious-about-diversity-enough-already-with-the-business-case.

England, Paula. *Comparable Worth: Theories and Evidence.* Aldine de Gruyter, 1992.

Espenshade, Thomas J., and Chang Y. Chung. "The Opportunity Cost of Admission Preferences at Elite Universities." *Social Science Quarterly* 86, no. 2 (2005): 293–305.

Espenshade, Thomas J., Chang Y. Chung, and Joan L. Walling. "Admission Preferences for Minority Students, Athletes, and Legacies at Elite Universities." *Social Science Quarterly* 85, no. 5 (2004): 1422–46.

Espenshade, Thomas J., Lauren E. Hale, and Chang Y. Chung. "The Frog Pond Revisited: High School Academic Context, Class Rank, and Elite College Admission." *Sociology of Education* 78, no. 4 (2005): 269–93.

Espenshade, Thomas J., and Alexandria Walton Radford. *No Longer Separate, Not Yet Equal: Race and Class in Elite College Admission and Campus Life.* Princeton University Press, 2010.

European Commission. "Commission Recommendation of 7 March 2014 on Strengthening the Principle of Equal Pay Between Men and Women Through Transparency." *EUR-Lex*, March 8, 2014. https://eur-lex.europa.eu/legal-content/EN/TXT/?uri=CEL EX%3A32014H0124&qid=1721051805240.

European Parliament. "Directive (EU) 2023/970 of the European Parliament and of the Council of 10 May 2023 to Strengthen the Application of the Principle of Equal Pay for Equal Work or Work of Equal Value Between Men and Women Through Pay Transparency and Enforcement Mechanisms." *EUR-Lex*, May 17, 2023. https://eur-lex. europa.eu/legal-content/EN/TXT/?uri=CELEX%3A32023L0970&qid=1721051805240.

Evans-Reber, Katie. "Here's What Can Happen When Companies Get Rid of Performance Reviews." *Forbes*, February 19, 2020. https://www.forbes.com/sites/forbeshuman resourcescouncil/2020/02/19/heres-what-can-happen-when-companies-get-rid-of -performance-reviews/.

Fan, Ruiping. "Confucian Meritocracy for Contemporary China." In *The East Asia Challenge for Democracy*, ed. Daniel A. Bell and Chenyang Li. Cambridge University Press, 2013.

Fatemi, Ali, Martin Glaum, and Stefanie Kaiser. "ESG Performance and Firm Value: The Moderating Role of Disclosure." *Global Finance Journal* 38 (2018): 45–64.

Fazio, Russel H., and Tamara Towles-Schwen. "The MODE Model of Attitude-Behavior Processes." In *Dual-Process Theories in Social Psychology*, ed. Shelly Chaiken and Yaacov Trope. Guilford, 1999.

Feldman, Martha S. *Strategies for Interpreting Qualitative Data.* Sage, 1994.

Feldmann, John. "The Benefits and Shortcomings of Blind Hiring in the Recruitment Process." *Forbes*, April 3, 2018. https://www.forbes.com/sites/forbeshumanresources council/2018/04/03/the-benefits-and-shortcomings-of-blind-hiring-in-the-recruitment -process/.

Fernandez, Roberto M., Emilio J. Castilla, and Paul Moore. "Social Capital at Work: Networks and Employment at a Phone Center." *American Journal of Sociology* 105, no. 5 (2000): 1288–356.

Fernandez, Roberto M., and Isabel Fernandez-Mateo. "Networks, Race and Hiring." *American Sociological Review* 71, no. 1 (2006): 42–71.

Fernandez, Roberto M., and Colette Friedrich. "Gender Sorting at the Application Interface." *Industrial Relations* 50, no. 4 (2011): 591–609.

Fernandez, Roberto M., and Roman V. Galperin. "The Causal Status of Social Capital in Labor Markets." In *Contemporary Perspectives on Organizational Social Networks*, ed. Daniel Brass, Giuseppe Labianca, Ajay Mehra, Daniel Halgin, and Stephen P. Borgatti. Emerald Group, 2014.

Fernandez, Roberto M., and Jason Greenberg. "Race, Network Hiring, and Statistical Discrimination." In *Research in the Sociology of Work*, vol. 24, *Networks, Work and Inequality*, ed. Steve McDonald. Emerald Group, 2013.

Fernandez, Roberto M., and Brian Rubineau. "Network Recruitment and the Glass Ceiling: Evidence from Two Firms." *RSF: Russell Sage Foundation Journal of the Social Sciences* 5, no. 3 (2019): 88–102.

Fernandez, Roberto M., and M. Lourdes Sosa. "Gendering the Job: Networks and Recruitment at a Call Center." *American Journal of Sociology* 111, no. 3 (2005): 859–904.

Fernandez, Roberto M., and Celina Su. "Space in the Study of Labor Markets." *Annual Review of Sociology* 30 (2004): 545–69.

Fernandez, Roberto M., and Nancy Weinberg. "Sifting and Sorting: Personal Contacts and Hiring in a Retail Bank." *American Sociological Review* 62, no. 6 (1997): 883–902.

Finn, Lynne M. "How to Introduce Pay Transparency to Help Close the Gender Pay Gap." *Forbes*, February 2, 2023. https://www.forbes.com/sites/forbeshumanresources-council/2023/02/02/how-to-introduce-pay-transparency-to-help-close-the-gender-pay-gap/.

FitzGerald, Chloë, Angela Martin, Delphine Berner, and Samia Hurst. "Interventions Designed to Reduce Implicit Prejudices and Implicit Stereotypes in Real World Contexts: A Systematic Review." *BMC Psychology* 7, no. 1 (2019): Article 29.

Flaherty, Colleen. "Presidents Break with Supreme Court on Affirmative Action." Inside Higher Ed, October 17, 2023. https://www.insidehighered.com/news/diversity/socioeconomics/2023/10/17/survey-two-three-college-presidents-oppose-affirmative.

Fleishman, Hannah. "How to Master Non-Awkward, Effective In-Person Networking." HubSpot, November 9, 2022. https://blog.hubspot.com/sales/effective-in-person-networking.

Flick, Uwe. *Managing Quality in Qualitative Research*. Sage, 1998.

Foddy, Margaret, and Michael Smithson. "Can Gender Inequalities Be Eliminated?" *Social Psychology Quarterly* 62, no. 4 (1999): 307–324.

Fox, Margalit. "Michael Young, 86, Scholar; Coined, Mocked 'Meritocracy.'" *New York Times*, January 25, 2022. https://www.nytimes.com/2002/01/25/world/michael-young-86-scholar-coined-mocked-meritocracy.html.

Francis, Ali. "Gen Z: The Workers Who Want It All." *BBC Worklife*, June 14, 2022. https://www.bbc.com/worklife/article/20220613-gen-z-the-workers-who-want-it-all.

Franzen, Axel, and Dominik Hangartner. "Social Networks and Labour Market Outcomes: The Non-Monetary Benefits of Social Capital." *European Sociological Review* 22, no. 4 (2006): 353–68.

Friedersdorf, Conor. "The DEI Industry Needs to Check Its Privilege." *Atlantic*, May 31, 2023. https://www.theatlantic.com/ideas/archive/2023/05/dei-training-initiatives-consultants-companies-skepticism/674237/.

Frum, David. "The Trump Crew's Incompetence Lasted to the End." *Atlantic*, February 12, 2021. https://www.theatlantic.com/ideas/archive/2021/02/the-trump-crews-incompetence-lasted-to-the-very-end/618022/.

Fry, Richard and Carolina Aragao. "Gender Pay Gap in U.S. Has Narrowed Slightly over 2 Decades." Pew Research Center, March 4, 2025, https://www.pewresearch.org/short-reads/2025/03/04/gender-pay-gap-in-us-has-narrowed-slightly-over-2-decades/.

Fuller, Joseph B., and Manjari Raman. *Dismissed by Degrees*. Accenture Grads of Life and Harvard Business School Report, 2017. https://www.hbs.edu/ris/Publication%20Files/dismissed-by-degrees_707b3f0e-a772-40b7-8f77-aed4a16016cc.pdf.

Funk, Cary, and Kim Parker. "Women and Men in STEM Often at Odds over Workplace Equity." Pew Research Center, 2018.

Gaddis, S. Michael. "An Introduction to Audit Studies in the Social Sciences." In *Audit Studies: Behind the Scenes with Theory, Method, and Nuance*, ed. S. Michael Gaddis. Springer, 2018.

Gaddis, S. Michael. "Social Capital in the Creation of Cultural Capital, Habitus, and Achievement: Access vs. Mobilization for Low-Income and Racial Minority Adolescents." Working paper, National Bureau of Economic Research, 2018.

Galarza, Francisco B., and Gustavo Yamada. "Labor Market Discrimination in Lima, Peru: Evidence from a Field Experiment." *World Development* 58 (2014): 83–94.

Gallo, Amy. "How to Help an Underperformer." *Harvard Business Review*, June 23, 2014. https://hbr.org/2014/06/how-to-help-an-underperformer.

Gallup. "State of the Global Workplace: 2023 Report." Gallup Workplace, 2023. Accessed September 1, 2023. https://www.gallup.com/workplace/349484/state-of-the-global -workplace.aspx.

Gallup. "Transform Performance Management." Gallup Workplace. Accessed August 12, 2023. https://www.gallup.com/workplace/215927/performance-management.aspx.

Garcia-Quijano, Joselyn Andrea. "Workplace Discrimination and Undocumented First-Generation Latinx Immigrants." Crown Family of Social Work, Policy, and Practice, Advocates' Forum, 2020. Accessed February 28, 2023. https://crownschool.uchicago .edu/student-life/advocates-forum/workplace-discrimination-and-undocumented -first-generation-latinx.

Garr, Stacia, and Lisa Barry. "Performance Management Is Broken." Deloitte Insights, March 5, 2014. https://www2.deloitte.com/us/en/insights/focus/human-capital-trends /2014/hc-trends-2014-performance-management.html.

Gartner. "Gartner HR Research Reveals 82 Percent of Employees Report Working Environment Lacks Fairness." Gartner press release, November 8, 2021. https://www.gartner .com/en/newsroom/press-releases/2021-08-11-gartner-hr-research-reveals-eighty -two-percent-of-employees-report-working-environment-lacks-fairness.

Gaucher, Danielle, Justin Friesen, and Aaron C. Kay. "Evidence That Gendered Wording in Job Advertisements Exists and Sustains Gender Inequality." *Journal of Personality and Social Psychology* 101, no. 1 (2011): 109–28.

Gay, Claudine. "A Message from President Claudine Gay." Video, Harvard University, June 29, 2023. https://www.harvard.edu/admissionscase/2023/06/29/a-message-from -president-elect-claudine-gay/.

Gee, Buck, and Denise Peck. "Asian Americans Are the Least Likely Group in the U.S. to Be Promoted to Management." *Harvard Business Review*, May 31, 2018. https://hbr.org/2018/05 /asian-americans-are-the-least-likely-group-in-the-u-s-to-be-promoted-to-management.

Gerhard, Barry. "Chapter Three—Incentives and Pay for Performance in the Workplace." *Advances in Motivation Science* 4 (2017): 91–140.

Ghumman, Sonia, and Ann Marie Ryan. "Not Welcome Here: Discrimination Towards Women Who Wear the Muslim Headscarf." *Human Relations* 66, no. 5 (2013): 671–98.

Ghumman, Sonia, Ann Marie Ryan, Lizabeth A. Barclay, and Karen S. Markel. "Religious Discrimination in the Workplace: A Review and Examination of Current and Future Trends." *Journal of Business and Psychology* 28, no. 4 (2013): 439–54.

Glick, Peter, and Susan T. Fiske. "The Ambivalent Sexism Inventory: Differentiating Hostile and Benevolent Sexism." *Journal of Personality and Social Psychology* 70, no. 3 (1996): 491–512.

Goffman, Erving. "Embarrassment and Social Organization." *American Journal of Sociology* 62 (1956): 264–71.

Goffman, Erving. *The Presentation of Self in Everyday Life*. Anchor, Doubleday, 1959.

Goffman, Erving. *Stigma. Notes on the Management of Spoiled Identity*. Prentice-Hall, 1963.

Goldberg, Emma, Aaron Krolik, and Lily Boyce. "How Corporate America Is Retreating From D.E.I." *New York Times*, March 13, 2025, https://www.nytimes.com/interactive/2025/03/13/business/corporate-america-dei-policy-shifts.html.

Goldin, Claudia, and Cecilia Rouse. "Orchestrating Impartiality: The Impact of 'Blind' Auditions on Female Musicians." *American Economic Review* 90, no. 4 (2000): 715–41.

Goldstein, Drew, Manveer Greval, Ruth Imose, and Monne Williams. "Unlocking the Potential of Chief Diversity Officers." McKinsey & Company, November 18, 2022. https://www.mckinsey.com/capabilities/people-and-organizational-performance/our-insights/unlocking-the-potential-of-chief-diversity-officers.

Goldthorpe, John H. "Sociology as Social Science and Cameral Sociology: Some Further Thoughts." *European Sociological Review* 20, no. 2 (2004): 97–105.

Goldthorpe, John H., and Michelle Jackson. "Education-Based Meritocracy: The Barriers to Its Realization." *Stato e Mercato* 1 (2008): 31–60.

Gomez, Karianne, Tiffany Mawhinney, and Kimberly Betts. *Welcome to Generation Z*. Network of Executive Women, Deloitte, 2018. https://www2.deloitte.com/content/dam/Deloitte/us/Documents/consumer-business/welcome-to-gen-z.pdf.

Gómez, Vianney. "As Courts Weigh Affirmative Action, Grades and Test Scores Seen as Top Factors in College Admissions." Pew Research Center, April 26, 2022. https://www.pewresearch.org/fact-tank/2022/04/26/u-s-public-continues-to-view-grades-test-scores-as-top-factors-in-college-admissions/.

Gonzales, Matt. "The Meaning of 'Woke.'" SHRM. Accessed August 11, 2023. https://www.shrm.org/topics-tools/news/all-things-work/the-meaning-of--woke.

Gonzales, Matt. "Why Are DEI Roles Disappearing?" SHRM, March 15, 2023. https://www.shrm.org/topics-tools/news/inclusion-diversity/dei-roles-disappearing.

Google. *2022 Diversity Annual Report*. Accessed August 12, 2022. https://about.google/belonging/diversity-annual-report/2022/.

Gorman, Elizabeth H. "Gender Stereotypes, Same-Gender Preferences, and Organizational Variation in the Hiring of Women: Evidence from Law Firms." *American Sociological Review* 70, no. 4 (2005): 702–28.

Granovetter, Mark S. "Coase Revisited: Business Groups in the Modern Economy." *Industrial and Corporate Change* 4, no. 1 (1995): 93–130.

Granovetter, Mark S. "Granovetter Replies to Gans." *American Journal of Sociology* 80, no. 2 (1974): 527–29.

Granovetter, Mark S. "The Strength of Weak Ties." *American Journal of Sociology* 78, no. 6 (1973): 1360–80.

Green, Gary Paul, Leann M. Tigges, and Daniel Diaz. "Racial and Ethnic Differences in Job-Search Strategies in Atlanta, Boston, and Los Angeles." *Social Science Quarterly* 80, no. 2 (1999): 263–78.

Greenberg, Jason, and Ethan Mollick. "Activist Choice Homophily and the Crowdfunding of Female Founders." *Administrative Science Quarterly* 62, no. 2 (2017): 341–74.

Greenwald, Anthony G., Mahzarin R. Banaji, and Brian A. Nosek. "Statistically Small Effects of the Implicit Association Test Can Have Societally Large Effects." *Journal of Personality and Social Psychology* 108, no. 4 (2015): 553–61.

Greenwald, Anthony G., Miguel Brendl, Huajian Cai, et al., "Best Research Practices for Using the Implicit Association Test." *Behavioral Research Methods* 54, no. 3 (2022): 1161–80.

Greenwald, Anthony G., Miguel Brendl, Huajian Cal, et al. "The Implicit Association Test at Age 20: What Is Known and What Is Not Known About Implicit Bias." PsyArXiv Preprints, April 7, 2020.

Griffis, Hailley. "2022 Pay Analysis: Our Unadjusted Gender Pay Gap Is Below 1 Percent." Buffer, March 15, 2022. https://buffer.com/resources/2022-pay-analysis/.

Grothe-Hammer, Michael, and Sebastian Kohl. "The Decline of Organizational Sociology? An Empirical Analysis of Research Trends in Leading Journals Across Half a Century." *Current Sociology* 68, no. 4 (2020): 419–42.

Groysberg, Boris. *Chasing Stars: The Myth of Talent and the Portability of Performance.* Princeton University Press, 2010.

Groysberg, Boris. "How Star Women Build Portable Skills." *Harvard Business Review,* February 2008. https://hbr.org/2008/02/how-star-women-build-portable-skills.

Groysberg, Boris, and Paul M. Healy. *Wall Street Research: Past, Present, and Future.* Stanford University Press, 2013.

Groysberg, Boris, Ashish Nanda, and Nitin Nohria. "The Risky Business of Hiring Stars." *Harvard Business Review,* May 2004. https://hbr.org/2004/05/the-risky-business-of -hiring-stars.

Groysberg, Boris, Sarah Abbott, Michael R. Morino, and Metin Aksoy. "Compensation Packages That Actually Drive Performance." *Harvard Business Review,* January–February 2021. https://hbr.org/2021/01/compensation-packages-that-actually-drive-performance.

Gruman, Galen. "The State of Ethnic Minorities in U.S. Tech: 2020." Computerworld, September 21, 2020. https://www.computerworld.com/article/3574917/the-state-of-ethnic -minorities-in-us-tech-2020.html.

Grusky, David B. *Social Stratification: Class, Race and Gender in Sociological Perspective.* 2nd ed. Routledge, 2019.

Guillén, Mauro F. *Models of Management: Work, Authority, and Organization in a Comparative Perspective.* University of Chicago Press, 1994.

Guillen, Mauro F. *La Profesión de Economista: El Auge de Economistas, Ejecutivos y Empresarios en España.* Ariel, 1989.

Gurchiek, Kathy. "Employers Don't Understand the Work People with Disabilities Can Do, SHRM Research Finds." SHRM, October 29, 2019. https://www.shrm.org/resources andtools/hr-topics/behavioral-competencies/global-and-cultural-effectiveness/pages /shrm-foundation-report-employees-with-disabilities.aspx.

Gurchiek, Kathy. "The Wage Gap Is Wider for Working Mothers." SHRM, October 21, 2019. https://www.shrm.org/resourcesandtools/hr-topics/compensation/pages/wage-gap -is-wider-for-working-mothers.aspx.

Habtemariam, Dawit. "3 Must-Dos for Collecting Employee Demographic Data Beyond Race and Gender." Senior Executive, April 21, 2022. Accessed April 15, 2023. https:// seniorexecutive.com/collecting-employee-demographic-data-beyond-race-gender/.

Hall, Brian J., Edward Lazear, and Carleen Madigan. *Performance Pay at Safelite Auto Glass (A).* Harvard Business School Case 800–291. Harvard Business School, 2000.

Hall, Edward T. *Beyond Culture.* Anchor, Doubleday, 1976.

Hall, Francine S., and Douglas T. Hall. "Effects of Job Incumbents' Race and Sex on Evaluations of Managerial Performance." *Academy of Management Journal* 19, no. 3 (1976): 476–81.

Hamid, Rahem D. "Ivy League, Other Peer Schools Pledge to Uphold Diversity While Complying with Supreme Court Ruling." *Harvard Crimson*, July 3, 2023. https://www .thecrimson.com/article/2023/7/3/peer-universities-scotus/.

Hammarstedt, Mats, Ali M. Ahmed, and Lina Andersson. "Sexual Prejudice and Labor Market Outcomes for Gays and Lesbians: Evidence from Sweden." *Feminist Economics* 21, no. 1 (2015): 90–109.

Hao, Karen. "Facebook's Ad-Serving Algorithm Discriminates by Gender and Race." *MIT Technology Review*, April 5, 2019. https://www.technologyreview.com/2019/04/05/1175 /facebook-algorithm-discriminates-ai-bias/.

Harper, Shaun. "Why Business Leaders Are Pulling the Plug on DEI." *Forbes*, July 18, 2023. https://www.forbes.com/sites/shaunharper/2023/07/18/why-corporate-execs-are -pulling-the-plug-on-dei/.

Harrington, Caitlin. "Pay Transparency Is Sweeping Across the US." Wired, September 10, 2023. https://www.wired.com/story/pay-transparency-is-sweeping-across-us/.

Harris, La'Wana. *Diversity Beyond Lip Service: A Coaching Guide for Challenging Bias.* Berrett-Koehler, 2019.

Harrison, Connor. "77 percent of Organizations Offering Variable Pay Plans" (blog post). Salary.com, January 8, 2019. https://www.salary.com/blog/compensation-trends -organizations-embracing-variable-pay/.

Harrison, Sara. "Five Years of Tech Diversity Reports—and Little Progress." Wired, October 1, 2019. https://www.wired.com/story/five-years-tech-diversity-reports-little -progress.

Harter, Jim. "Is Quiet Quitting Real?" Gallup Workplace, September 6, 2022. Last modified May 17, 2023. https://www.gallup.com/workplace/398306/quiet-quitting-real.aspx.

Hartmann, Heidi. "Pass the Paycheck Fairness Act." *New York Times*, March 31, 2013. http://www.nytimes.com/roomfordebate/2013/03/31/why-has-salary-parity-still-not -happened/pass-the-paycheck-fairness-act.

Hawkins, Carlee Beth, and Brian A. Nosek. "Motivated Independence? Implicit Party Identity Predicts Political Judgements Among Self-Proclaimed Independents." *Personality and Social Psychology Bulletin* 38, no. 11 (2012): 1437–52.

Hayek, Friedrich. *The Constitution of Liberty*, vol. 17. University of Chicago Press, 1960.

Heilman, Madeline E. "Description and Prescription: How Gender Stereotypes Prevent Women's Ascent up the Organizational Ladder." *Journal of Social Issues* 57, no. 4 (2001): 657–74.

Heilman, Madeline E. "The Impact of Situational Factors on Personnel Decisions Concerning Women: Varying the Sex Composition of the Applicant Pool." *Organizational Behavior and Human Performance* 26, no. 3 (1980): 386–95.

Heilman, Madeline, and Brian Welle. "Disadvantaged by Diversity? The Effects of Diversity Goals on Competence Perceptions." *Journal of Applied Social Psychology* 36, no. 5 (2006): 1291–319.

Heisler, William. "Increasing Pay Transparency: A Guide for Change." *Business Horizons* 64, no. 1 (2021): 73–81.

Hellman, Deborah. *When Is Discrimination Wrong?* Harvard University Press, 2008.

Heneman, Robert L., and Jon M. Werner. *Merit Pay: Linking Pay to Performance in a Changing World.* 2nd ed. Information Age, 2005.

Hernandez, Morela, Sabrina D. Volpone, Derek R. Avery, and Cheryl R. Kaiser. "Bargaining While Black: The Role of Race in Salary Negotiations." *Journal of Applied Psychology* 104, no. 4 (2019): 581–92.

Hernandez, Tanya K. "Legally Mandate Wage Transparency." *New York Times*, March 31, 2013. http://www.nytimes.com/roomfordebate/2013/03/31/why-has-salary-parity-still -not-happened/legally-mandate-wage-transparency.

Hernandez, Tanya K. *Racial Subordination in Latin America: The Role of the State, Customary Law, and the New Civil Rights Response*. Cambridge University Press, 2012.

Herrera, Tim. "The Benefits of Sharing Your Salary." *New York Times*, November 18, 2018. https://www.nytimes.com/2018/11/18/smarter-living/the-benefits-of-sharing-your -salary.html.

Herrnstein, Richard J. *I.Q. in the Meritocracy*. Little, Brown, 1973.

Hewitt. "Trends in Global Employee Engagement." Aon Hewitt, 2011. https://cdn5.data-scope.io/wp-content/uploads/2018/12/Trends_Global_Employee_Engagement_Final1 .pdf?x32440.

Hiatt, Fred. "Yes, Trump Is Incompetent. But He's Becoming Alarmingly Good at Corrupting the Government." *Washington Post*, August 9, 2020. https://www.washingtonpost .com/opinions/trump-is-learning-to-bend-the-bureaucracy-to-his-will/2020/08/09 /f9b48ab0-d8dd-11ea-aff6-220dd3a14741_story.html.

Hiscox, Michael J., Tara Oliver, Michael Ridgway, Lilia Arcos-Holzinger, Alastair Warren, and Andrea Willis. *Going Blind to See More Clearly: Unconscious Bias in Australian Public Service Shortlisting Processes*. Commonwealth of Australia, Department of the Prime Minister and Cabinet, June 2017. https://behaviouraleconomics.pmc.gov.au/sites /default/files/projects/unconscious-bias.pdf.

Holmstrom, Bengt. "Moral Hazard in Teams." *Bell Journal of Economics* 13, no. 2 (1982): 324–40.

Horace, Henry. "Meritocracy and Equity, Not Diversity and Affirmative Action." *Thinking Heart Solutions at LinkedIn*, November 28, 2024. https://www.linkedin.com/pulse /meritocracy-equity-diversity-affirmative-action-horace-ed-d--oo9qc/.

Horowitz, Juliana M., and Janell Fetterolf. "Worldwide Optimism About Future of Gender Equality, Even as Many See Advantages for Men." Pew Research Center, April 30, 2020. https://www.pewresearch.org/global/2020/04/30/worldwide-optimism-about-future -of-gender-equality-even-as-many-see-advantages-for-men/.

Hout, Michael, and Thomas A. DiPrete. "What We Have Learned: RC28's Contributions to Knowledge About Social Stratification." *Research in Social Stratification and Mobility* 24, no. 1 (2006): 1–20.

"How Big Is the Wage Penalty for Mothers? Huge in Germany, Not So Big in Denmark." *Economist*, January 28, 2019. https://www.economist.com/graphic-detail/2019/01/28 /how-big-is-the-wage-penalty-for-mothers.

Hummel, Denise Pirrotti. "The Business Case for Diversity and Inclusion." Lead Inclusively. https://leadinclusively.com/wp-content/uploads/2020/01/The-Business-Case-for -Diversity-and-Inclusion.pdf.

Hurwitz, Michael. "The Impact of Legacy Status on Undergraduate Admissions at Elite Colleges and Universities." *Economics of Education Review* 30, no. 3 (2011): 480–92.

Hyun, Jane. *Breaking the Bamboo Ceiling: Career Strategies for Asians*. Harper Business, 2005.

Ibarra, Herminia. "Homophily and Differential Returns: Sex Differences in Network Structure and Access in an Advertising Firm." *Administrative Science Quarterly* 37, no. 3 (1992): 422–47.

Ibarra, Herminia, and Mark Lee Hunter. "How Leaders Create and Use Networks." *Harvard Business Review* 85, no. 1 (2007). https://hbr.org/2007/01/how-leaders-create-and-use-networks.

iHire. *The State of Online Recruiting 2022.* Employer Resources Report, 2022. Last modified May 31, 2023. https://www.ihire.com/resourcecenter/employer/pages/the-state-of-online-recruiting-2022.

Indiviglio, Daniel. "The Case for Making Wages Public: Better Pay, Better Workers." *Atlantic,* July 20, 2011. http://www.theatlantic.com/business/archive/2011/07/the-case-for-making-wages-public-better-pay-better-workers/242238/.

International Labour Organization. "Migrants Face 'Significant Discrimination' in Job Markets." *ILO News,* March 8, 2000. https://www.ilo.org/resource/news/migrants-face-significant-discrimination-job-markets.

Isaacs, Julia B., Isabel V. Sawhill, and Ron Haskins. *Getting Ahead or Losing Ground: Economic Mobility in America.* Brookings, 2008.

Jackson, Michelle. "How Far Merit Selection? Social Stratification and the Labour Market." *British Journal of Sociology* 58, no. 3 (2007): 367–90.

Jackson, Michelle. "Non-Meritocratic Job Requirements and the Reproduction of Class Inequality: An Investigation." *Work, Employment and Society* 15, no. 3 (2001): 619–30.

Jackson, Sarah M., Amy L. Hillard, and Tamera R. Schneider. "Using Implicit Bias Training to Improve Attitudes Toward Women in STEM." *Social Psychology of Education* 17 (2014): 419–38.

Jacobs, Emma. "Can Business Ever Run a True Meritocracy?" *Financial Times,* February 27, 2025. https://www.ft.com/content/87cdf51c-c8e6-439c-aef6-91cb8faed78a.

Jacobs, Jerry A. *Gender Inequality at Work.* Sage, 1995.

Jacobs, Jerry A. *Revolving Doors: Sex Segregation and Women's Careers.* Stanford University Press, 1989.

Janefalkar, Anand. "Diversity Isn't Just the Right Thing to Do; It's Also Good Business." *Forbes,* March 26, 2020. https://www.forbes.com/councils/forbestechcouncil/2020/03/26/diversity-isnt-just-the-right-thing-to-do-its-also-good-business/.

Janove, Jathan. "Get Rid of Performance Reviews." SHRM, November 9, 2021. https://www.shrm.org/resourcesandtools/hr-topics/employee-relations/humanity-into-hr/pages/get-rid-of-performance-reviews.aspx.

Jee, Charlotte. "Facebook Is Going to Stop Letting Advertisers Target by Race, Gender, or Age." *MIT Technology Review,* March 20, 2019. https://www.technologyreview.com/2019/03/20/1225/facebook-is-going-to-stop-letting-advertisers-target-by-race-gender-or-age/.

Jillson, Cal. *Pursuing the American Dream: Opportunity and Exclusion over Four Centuries.* University Press of Kansas, 2004.

Jirjahn, Uwe, and Gesine Stephan. "Gender, Piece Rates and Wages: Evidence from Matched Employer-Employee Data." *Cambridge Journal of Economics* 28, no. 5 (2004): 683–704.

Johnson, Blair T., and Alice H. Eagly. "Involvement and Persuasion: Types, Traditions, and the Evidence." *Psychological Bulletin* 107, no. 3 (1990): 375–84.

Johnson, James H., Jr., Walter C. Farrell Jr., and Jennifer A. Stoloff. "An Empirical Assessment of Four Perspectives on the Declining Fortunes of the African-American Male." *Urban Affairs Review* 35, no. 5 (2000): 695–716.

Jonsen, Karsten, Martha L. Maznevski, and Susan C. Schneider. "Diversity and Its Not So Diverse Literature: An International Perspective." *International Journal of Cross Cultural Management* 11, no. 1 (2011): 35–62.

Joshi, Khyati Y. "Racialization of Religion and Global Migration." In *Intersections of Religion and Migration: Issues at the Global Crossroads,* ed. Jennifer B. Saunders, Elena Fiddian-Qasmiyeh, and Susanna Snyder. Palgrave Macmillan, 2016.

Kahlenberg, Richard D. "Letter to Congress: College Legacy Preferences Must Go." Century Foundation, February 27, 2018. https://tcf.org/content/commentary/letter -congress-college-legacy-preferences-must-go/#easy-footnote-bottom-3.

Kahlenberg, Richard D. *Affirmative Action for the Rich: Legacy Preferences in College Admissions*. Century Foundation, 2010.

Kahlenberg, Richard D. "A New Call to End Legacy Admissions." *Atlantic*, February 14, 2018. https://www.theatlantic.com/education/archive/2018/02/when-affirmative-action -benefits-the-wealthy/553313.

Kaiser, Cheryl R., Brenda Major, Ines Jurcevic, Tessa L. Dover, Laura M. Brady, and Jenessa R. Shapiro. "Presumed Fair: Ironic Effects of Organizational Diversity Structures." *Journal of Personality and Social Psychology* 104, no. 3 (2013): 504–19.

Kalev, Alexandra. "Cracking the Glass Cages? Restructuring and Ascriptive Inequality at Work." *American Journal of Sociology* 114, no. 6 (2009): 1591–643.

Kalev, Alexandra. "How You Downsize Is Who You Downsize: Biased Formalization, Accountability and Managerial Diversity." *American Sociological Review* 79, no. 1 (2014): 109–35.

Kalev, Alexandra, Frank Dobbin, and Erin Kelly. "Best Practices or Best Guesses? Assessing the Efficacy of Corporate Affirmative Action and Diversity Policies." *American Sociological Review* 71, no. 4 (2006): 589–617.

Kalev, Alexandra, Frank Dobbin, and Erin Kelly. "Diversity Management in Corporate America." *Contexts* 6, no. 4 (2007): 21–27.

Kampelmann, Stephan, and François Rycx. "Wage Discrimination Against Immigrants: Measurement with Firm-Level Productivity Data." *IZA Journal of Development and Migration* 5 (2016): 1–24.

Kandola, Jo-Anne. "Workplace Gender Discrimination and the Implicit Association Test." PhD diss., Aston University, 2015.

Kang, Sonia K., Katherine A. DeCelles, András Tilcsik, and Sora Jun. "Whitened Résumés: Race and Self-Presentation in the Labor Market." *Administrative Science Quarterly* 61, no. 3 (2016): 469–502.

Kashyap, Kartikay. "Meritocracy and Equity – Striking a Balance for a Wholesome Company Culture." AdvantageClub.ai Blog, October 23, 2024. https://www.advantageclub .ai/blog/meritocracy-and-equity-balance.

Kaufman, Bruce E. "The Historical Development of American HRM Broadly Viewed." *Human Resource Management Review* 24, no. 3 (2014): 196–218.

Kaufman, Bruce E. *Managing the Human Factor: The Early Years of Human Resource Management in American Industry*. ILR Press, 2008.

Kelly, Jack. "President Trump Shifts To 'Merit, Excellence And Intelligence' In The Workplace And Away From DEI." *Forbes*, February 1, 2025. https://www.forbes.com/sites /jackkelly/2025/02/01/president-trump-shifts-to-merit-excellence-and-intelligence -in-the-workplace-and-away-from-dei/.

Kemper, Theodore D. "On the Nature and Purpose of Ascription." *American Sociological Review* 39, no. 6 (1974): 844–53.

Kennedy, Randall. *For Discrimination: Race, Affirmative Action, and the Law*. Vintage, 2013.

Kessler, Sarah. "D.E.I. Goes Quiet." *New York Times*, January 13, 2024. https://www .nytimes.com/2024/01/13/business/dealbook/dei-goes-quiet.html.

Kessler, Sarah. "Don't Say 'Elite': Corporate Firms' New Pitch Is Meritocracy." *New York Times*, June 10, 2024. https://www.nytimes.com/2024/06/10/business/corporate-firms -meritocracy-elite.html#.

Khan, Shamus Rahman. *Privilege: The Making of an Adolescent Elite at St. Paul's School.* Princeton University Press, 2011.

Khan, Uzma, and Ravi Dhar. "Licensing Effect in Consumer Choice." *Journal of Marketing Research* 43, no. 2 (2006): 259–66.

Khattab, Nabil, Zahra Babar, Michael Ewers, and Miriam Shaath. "Gender and Mobility: Qatar's Highly Skilled Female Migrants in Context." *Migration and Development* 9, no. 3 (2020): 369–89.

Kidder, Louise H., Gerald Bellettirie, and Ellen S. Cohn. "Secret Ambitions and Public Performances: The Effects of Anonymity on Reward Allocations Made by Men and Women." *Journal of Experimental Social Psychology* 13, no. 1 (1977): 70–80.

King, Eden B., and Afra S. Ahmad. "An Experimental Field Study of Interpersonal Discrimination Toward Muslim Job Applicants." *Personnel Psychology* 63, no. 4 (2010): 881–906.

Kingston, Gillian, Frances McGinnity, and Philip J. O'Connell. "Discrimination in the Labour Market: Nationality, Ethnicity and the Recession." *Work, Employment and Society* 29, no. 2 (2015): 213–32.

Kislik, Liz. "Managing an Underperformer Who Thinks They're Doing Great." *Harvard Business Review*, December 2, 2020. https://hbr.org/2020/12/managing-an-underperformer-who-thinks-theyre-doing-great.

Kissing, Ellesheva, and Anjli Raval. "Accenture Ditches Diversity and Inclusion Goals," *Financial Times*, February 7, 2025. https://www.ft.com/content/0c0c720f-4292-403b-b4e4-f3c83e58596b.

Kline, Patrick M., Evan K. Rose, and Christopher R. Walters. "Systemic Discrimination Among Large U.S. Employers." *Quarterly Journal of Economics* 137, no. 4 (2022): 1963–2036.

Kluegel, James R., and Eliot R. Smith. *Beliefs About Inequality: Americans' Views of What Is and What Ought to Be.* 3rd ed. Aldine Transaction, 2009.

Kmec, Julie A. "Setting Occupational Sex Segregation in Motion: Demand-Side Explanations of Sex Traditional Employment." *Work and Occupations* 32, no. 3 (2005): 322–54.

Knight, Rebecca. "When to Take a Chance on an Imperfect Job Candidate." *Harvard Business Review*, March 8, 2021. https://hbr.org/2021/03/when-to-take-a-chance-on-an-imperfect-job-candidate.

Kochan, Thomas A., Ben Armstrong, Julie Shah, Emilio J. Castilla, Ben Likis, and Martha E. Mangelsdorf. "Bringing Worker Voice into Generative AI." MIT, 2024. https://doi.org/10.21428/e4baedd9.0d255ab6.

Kochan, Thomas A., Lee Dyer, Joel Cutcher-Gershenfeld, and Alexander Kowalski. "Negotiating a New Social Contract for Work: An Online, Distributed Approach." *Negotiation Journal* 34, no. 2 (2018): 187–206.

Kochan, Thomas A., Janice R. Fine, Kate Bronfenbrenner, et al. *U.S. Workers' Organizing Efforts and Collective Actions: A Review of the Current Landscape.* Worker Empowerment Research Network (WERN), 2022.

Kochan, Thomas A., Russell D. Landsbury, and John Paul MacDuffie. *After Lean Production: Evolving Employment Practices in the World Auto Industry.* Cornell University Press, 2018.

Köllen, Thomas. "Diversity Management: A Critical Review and Agenda for the Future." *Journal of Management Inquiry* 30, no. 3 (2021): 259–72.

Kolstad, Ivar, and Arne Wiig. "Is Transparency the Key to Reducing Corruption in Resource-Rich Countries?" *World Development* 37, no. 3 (2009): 521–32.

Kornbluth, Sally. "Thoughts on Yesterday's Supreme Court Ruling." MIT Organization Chart, June 30, 2023. https://orgchart.mit.edu/letters/thoughts-yesterdays-supreme-court -ruling.

Kouchaki, Maryam. "Vicarious Moral Licensing: The Influence of Others' Past Moral Actions on Moral Behavior." *Journal of Personality and Social Psychology* 101, no. 4 (2011): 702–15.

Kramarz, Francis, and Oskar Nordström Skans. "When Strong Ties Are Strong: Networks and Youth Labour Market Entry." *Review of Economic Studies* 81, no. 3 (2014): 1164–200.

Kugelmass, Heather. " 'Sorry, I'm Not Accepting New Patients': An Audit Study of Access to Mental Health Care." *Journal of Health and Social Behavior* 57, no. 2 (2016): 168–83.

Kuhn, Kathryn, Eric Lamarre, Chris Perkins, and Suman Thareja. "Mining for Tech-Talent Gold: Seven Ways to Find and Keep Diverse Talent." McKinsey Digital, September 27, 2022. https://www.mckinsey.com/capabilities/mckinsey-digital/our-insights/mining -for-tech-talent-gold-seven-ways-to-find-and-keep-diverse-talent.

Kulick, Carol, Elissa Perry, and Anne Bourhis. "Ironic Evaluation Processes: Effects of Thought Suppression on Evaluations of Older Job Applicants." *Journal of Organizational Behaviour* 21, no. 6 (2000): 689–711.

Kunda, Ziva, and Steven J. Spencer. "When Do Stereotypes Come to Mind and When Do They Color Judgment? A Goal-Based Theoretical Framework for Stereotype Activation and Application." *Psychological Bulletin* 129, no. 4 (2003): 522–44.

Kunovich, Sheri L., and Kazimierz M. Slomczynski. "Systems of Distribution and a Sense of Equity: A Multilevel Analysis of Meritocratic Attitudes in Post-Industrial Societies." *European Sociological Review* 23, no. 5 (2007): 649–63.

Kurdi, Benedek, et al. "Relationship Between the Implicit Association Test and Intergroup Behavior: A Meta-Analysis." *American Psychologist* 74, no. 5 (2019): 569–86.

Ladd, Everett Carll. *The American Ideology: An Exploration of the Origins, Meaning and Role of American Political Ideas.* Roper Center for Public Opinion Research, 1994.

Ladd, Everett Carll, and Karlyn H. Bowman. *Attitudes Toward Economic Inequality.* American Enterprise Institute, 1998.

Lai, Calvin K., Allison L. Skinner, Erin Cooley, et al. "Reducing Implicit Racial Preferences: II. Intervention Effectiveness Across Time." *Journal of Experimental Psychology* 145, no. 8 (2016): 1001–16.

Lam, Leon, Bonnie Hayden Cheng, Peter Bamberger, and Man-Nok Wong. "Research: The Unintended Consequences of Pay Transparency." *Harvard Business Review,* August 12, 2022. https://hbr.org/2022/08/research-the-unintended-consequences-of -pay-transparency.

Lamont, Michèle. *How Professors Think: Inside the Curious World of Academic Judgment.* Harvard University Press, 2010.

Landivar, Liana Christin, Rose A. Woods, and Gretchen M. Livingston. "Does Part-Time Work Offer Flexibility to Employed Mothers?" *Monthly Labor Review,* February 2022, 1–19.

Landy, Frank J. "Stereotypes, Bias, and Personnel Decisions: Strange and Stranger." *Industrial and Organizational Psychology* 1, no. 4 (2008): 379–92.

Lareau, Annette. *Unequal Childhoods: Class, Race, and Family Life.* University of California Press, 2003.

Larkin, Max, and Mayowa Aina. "Legacy Admissions Offer an Advantage—and Not Just at Schools like Harvard." *NPR,* November 4, 2018. https://www.npr.org/2018/11/04 /663629750/legacy-admissions-offer-an-advantage-and-not-just-at-schools-like -harvard.

Larkin, Zoe. "AI Bias—What Is It and How to Avoid It?" Levity, September 30, 2024. https://levity.ai/blog/ai-bias-how-to-avoid.

Lawler, Edward E., III. *Pay and Organization Development*. Addison-Wesley, 1981.

Lawler, Edward E., III. *Pay and Organizational Effectiveness: A Psychological View*. McGraw-Hill, 1971.

Lazear, Edward P. "Performance Pay and Productivity." *American Economic Review* 90, no. 5 (2000): 1346–61.

Lederman, Daniel, Norman V. Loayza, and Rodrigo R. Soares. "Accountability and Corruption: Political Institutions Matter." *Economics and Politics* 17, no. 1 (2005): 1–35.

Lee, Elizabeth M. *Class and Campus Life: Managing and Experiencing Inequality at an Elite College*. Cornell University Press, 2016.

Lee, Tiane L., and Susan T. Fiske. "Not an Outgroup, Not Yet an Ingroup: Immigrants in the Stereotype Content Model." *International Journal of Intercultural Relations* 30, no. 6 (2006): 751–68.

Legault, Lisa, Jennifer N. Gutsell, and Michael Inzlicht. "Ironic Effects of Antiprejudice Messages: How Motivational Interventions Can Reduce (but Also Increase) Prejudice." *Psychological Science* 22, no. 12 (2011): 1472–77.

Lemieux, Thomas, W. Bentley MacLeod, and Daniel Parent. "Performance Pay and Wage Inequality." *Quarterly Journal of Economics* 124, no. 1 (2009): 1–49.

Lenski, Gerhard E. *Power and Privilege: A Theory of Social Stratification*. University of North Carolina Press, 1966.

Lepore, Meredith. "The Top 10 Words Men Use on Resumes Versus Women Are Shockingly Different." Ladders, June 28, 2018. https://www.theladders.com/career-advice/the-top-10-words-men-use-on-resumes-versus-women-are-shockingly-different.

Lerner, Jennifer S., and Philip E. Tetlock. "Accounting for the Effects of Accountability." *Psychological Bulletin* 125, no. 2 (1999): 255–75.

Leventhal, Gerald S. "The Distribution of Rewards and Resources in Groups and Organizations." In *Advances in Experimental Social Psychology*, vol. 9, ed. Leonard Berkowitz and Elaine Walster. Academic, 1976.

Leventhal, Gerald S., Jurgis Karuza Jr., and William R. Fry. "Beyond Fairness: A Theory of Allocation Preferences." In *Justice and Social Interaction: Experimental and Theoretical Contributions from Psychological Research*, ed. Gerold Mikula. Springer-Verlag, 1980.

Leventhal, Gerald S., James W. Michaels, and Charles Sanford. "Inequity and Interpersonal Conflict: Reward Allocation and Secrecy About Reward as Methods of Preventing Conflict." *Journal of Personality and Social Psychology* 23, no. 1 (1972): 88–102.

Levin, Blair, and Larry Downes. "Who Is Going to Regulate AI?" *Harvard Business Review*, May 19, 2023. https://hbr.org/2023/05/who-is-going-to-regulate-ai?

Lewis, Molly, Maya B. Mathur, Tyler J. VanderWheel, and Michael C. Frank. "The Puzzling Relationship Between Multi-Laboratory Replications and Meta-Analyses of the Published Literature." *Royal Society Open Science* 9, no. 2 (2022).

Lewis, Nicole. "Technology Can Be Used to Achieve Pay Equity." SHRM, June 19, 2023. https://www.shrm.org/resourcesandtools/hr-topics/technology/pages/technology-can-be-used-achieve-pay-equity.aspx.

Lin, Nan. "Building a Network Theory of Social Capital." *Connections* 22, no. 1 (1999): 28–51.

Lin, Nan. *Social Capital: A Theory of Social Structure and Action*. Cambridge University Press, 2002.

Lin, Nan. "Social Networks and Status Attainment." *Annual Review of Sociology* 25 (1999): 467–87.

Lin, Nan, Walter M. Ensel, and John C. Vaughn. "Social Resources and Strength of Ties: Structural Factors in Occupational Status Attainment." *American Sociological Review* 46, no. 4 (1981): 393–405.

Linton, Ralph. *The Study of Man.* Appleton-Century-Crofts, 1936.

Lipset, Seymour M. *Continental Divide: The Values and Institutions of the United States and Canada.* Routledge, 1990.

Litwin, Adam. "Technological Change at Work: The Impact of Employee Involvement on the Effectiveness of Health Information Technology." *ILR Review* 64, no. 5 (2011): 863–68.

Liu, Jennifer. "15 of the Top Companies for Women Working in Tech." *CNBC*, September 28, 2021. https://www.cnbc.com/2021/09/28/anitaborg-womens-representation-in-tech-is -down-during-the-pandemic.html.

Liu, Jennifer. "Here Are All the New Salary Transparency Laws Going into Effect in 2023." CNBC Make It, December 29, 2022. https://www.cnbc.com/2022/12/29/new-salary -transparency-laws-going-into-effect-in-2023.html.

Liu, Jennifer. " 'It's About Fairness and Respect': California May Get a New Salary Trans-parency Law Soon." CNBC Make It, August 31, 2022. https://www.cnbc.com/2022/08/31 /california-may-get-new-salary-transparency-law-soon.html.

Livingston, Robert W. *The Conversation: How Seeking and Speaking the Truth About Rac-ism Can Radically Transform Individuals and Organizations.* Currency, 2021.

Livingston, Robert W. "How to Promote Racial Equity in the Workplace: A Five-Step Plan." *Harvard Business Review* 98, no. 5 (2020): 64–72. https://hbr.org/2020/09 /how-to-promote-racial-equity-in-the-workplace.

Livingston, Robert W., and Ashleigh S. Rosette. "Stigmatization, Subordination, or Mar-ginalization? The Complexity of Social Disadvantage Across Gender and Race." In *Inclusive Leadership: Transforming Diverse Lives, Organizations, and Societies*, ed. Ber-nardo M. Ferdman, Jeanine Prime, and Ronald E. Riggio. Routledge, 2020.

Loignon, Andrew C., and David J. Woehr. "Social Class in the Organizational Sciences: A Conceptual Integration and Meta-Analytic Review." *Journal of Management* 44, no. 1 (2018): 61–88.

Longoria, Richard T. *Meritocracy and Americans' Views on Distributive Justice.* Lexington, 2009.

Loos, Enguerran. "How the 'Up or Out' Policy Works at McKinsey, BCG and Bain." CaseCoach. Last modified June 16, 2023. https://casecoach.com/b/up-or-out-policy -mckinsey-bcg-or-bain/.

Loos, Enguerran. "The Management Consulting Industry: The Free CaseCoach Guide for Candidates." CaseCoach. Last modified September 22, 2023. https://casecoach.com/b /the-management-consulting-industry-the-free-casecoach-guide-for-candidates/.

Low, Tim. "When Unequal Pay Is Actually Fair." *Harvard Business Review*, March 31, 2016. https://hbr.org/2016/03/when-unequal-pay-is-actually-fair.

Lu, Candice. "Honoring Differences Through a Culture of Meritocracy." *Forbes*, May 11, 2021. https://www.forbes.com/sites/theyec/2021/05/11/honoring-differences-through-a -culture-of-meritocracy/?sh=61fb45fa5a18.

Lu, Jackson G., Richard E. Nisbett, and Michael W. Morris. "Why East Asians but Not South Asians Are Underrepresented in Leadership Positions in the United States." *Proceedings of the National Academy of Sciences* 117, no. 9 (2020): 4590–600.

MacDuffie, John Paul, and John F. Krafcik. "Integrating Technology and Human Resources for High-Performance Manufacturing: Evidence from the International

Auto Industry." In *Transforming Organizations*, ed. Thomas A. Kochan and Michael Useem. Oxford University Press, 1992.

Macrae, C. Neil, Galen V. Bodenhausen, Alan B. Milne, and Jolanda Jetten. "Out of Mind but Back in Sight: Stereotypes on the Rebound." *Journal of Personality and Social Psychology* 67, no. 5 (1994): 808–17.

Maddox, Choncé, "The Motherhood Penalty Affects Everything from a Woman's Wages to Hiring and Promotions After Having a Child." *Business Insider*, March 10, 2022. Accessed December 15, 2022. https://www.businessinsider.com/personal-finance/motherhood -penalty.

Madeira, Ana F., Rui Costa-Lopes, John F. Dovidio, Goncalo Freitas, and Mafalda F. Mascarenhas. "Primes and Consequences: A Systematic Review of Meritocracy in Intergroup Relations." *Frontiers in Psychology* 10 (2019): Article 2007.

Maftei, Alexandra, Andrei C. Holman, and Diana A. Oancea-Matei. "Is Discrimination Against Disabled Job Candidates Increased by Previously Acquired Non-Discriminatory Moral Credentials?" *Romanian Journal of Applied Psychology* 22, no. 2 (2020): 33–41.

Magoon, Kimberly, Mary-Jo Robinson, Alexandra Kissling, and Victory Ozeua. "Best Practice for Demographic Data Collection and Reporting: Evaluator's Guide." Public Consulting Group, August 2022. https://www.publicconsultinggroup.com/media /4124/demographic-data-collection-and-reporting_brief.pdf.

Major, Brenda, and Jeffrey B. Adams. "Role of Gender, Interpersonal Orientation, and Self-Presentation in Distributive-Justice Behavior." *Journal of Personality and Social Psychology* 45, no. 3 (1983): 598–608.

Major, Brenda, Richard H. Gramzow, Shannon K. McCoy, Shana Levin, Toni Schmader, and Jim Sedanius. "Perceiving Personal Discrimination: The Role of Group Status and Legitimizing Ideology." *Journal of Personality and Social Psychology* 82, no. 3 (2002): 269–82.

Mandler, Peter. *The Crisis of the Meritocracy: Britain's Transition to Mass Education Since the Second World War*. Oxford University Press, 2020.

Manning, Alan, and Joanna Swaffield. "The Gender Gap in Early-Career Wage Growth." *Economic Journal* 118, no. 530 (2008): 983–1024.

Manyika, James, Jake Silberg, and Brittany Presten. "What Do We Do About the Biases in AI?" *Harvard Business Review*, October 25, 2019. https://hbr.org/2019/10/what-do -we-do-about-the-biases-in-ai.

Marasi, Shelly, and Rebecca J. Bennett. "Pay Communication: Where Do We Go from Here?" *Human Resource Management Review* 26, no. 1 (2016): 50–58.

Marcus, Bonnie. "The Networking Advice No One Tells You." *Forbes*, May 22, 2018. https://www.forbes.com/sites/bonniemarcus/2018/05/22/the-networking-advice -no-one-tells-you/?sh=77bf52ae7772.

Marger, Martin N. *Social Inequality: Patterns and Processes*. McGraw-Hill, 2008.

Marin, Alexandra. "Don't Mention It: Why People Don't Share Job Information, When They Do, and Why It Matters." *Social Networks* 34, no. 2 (2012): 181–92.

Markovits, Daniel. *The Meritocracy Trap: How America's Foundational Myth Feeds Inequality, Dismantles the Middle Class, and Devours the Elite*. Penguin, 2019.

Marks, Rachel. "Educational Triage and Ability-Grouping in Primary Mathematics: A Case-Study of the Impacts on Low-Attaining Pupils." *Research in Mathematics Education* 16, no. 1 (2014): 38–53.

Marsden, Peter V. "The Hiring Process: Recruitment Methods." *American Behavioral Scientist* 37, no. 7 (1994): 979–91.

Marsden, Peter V. "Selection Methods in US Establishments." *Acta Sociologica* 37, no. 3 (1994): 287–301.

Marsden, Peter V., and Elizabeth H. Gorman. "Social Networks, Job Changes, and Recruitment." In *Sourcebook of Labor Markets: Evolving Structures and Processes*, ed. Ivar Berg and Arne. L. Kalleberg. Springer, 2001.

Marsden, Peter V., and Jeanne S. Hurlbert. "Social Resources and Mobility Outcomes: A Replication and Extension." *Social Forces* 66, no. 4 (1988): 1038–59.

Mathis, Robert L., and John H. Jackson. *Human Resource Management*. 10th ed. Cengage South-Western, 2003.

Maurer, Roy. "HR Must Be Vigilant About the Ethical Use of AI Technology." SHRM, September 26, 2022. https://www.shrm.org/topics-tools/news/technology/hr-must -vigilant-ethical-use-ai-technology.

Maurer, Roy. "SHRM Research: AI Use on the Rise, Ethics Questions Remain." SHRM, April 24, 2022. https://www.shrm.org/resourcesandtools/hr-topics/technology/pages /shrm-research-ai-use-rise-ethics-questions-remain.aspx.

Maurer-Fazio, Margaret, and Lei Lei. "'As Rare as a Panda': How Facial Attractiveness, Gender, and Occupation Affect Interview Callbacks at Chinese Firms." *International Journal of Manpower* 36, no. 1 (2015): 68–85.

May, Eira. "The People Most Affected by the Tech Layoffs." *The Stack Overflow Blog*, April 2, 2023. https://stackoverflow.blog/2023/04/02/the-people-most-affected-by-the -tech-layoffs/.

Mayhew, Leon H. *Law and Equal Opportunity: A Study of the Massachusetts Commission Against Discrimination*. Harvard University Press, 1968.

Mayorga-Gallo, Sarah. *Behind the White Picket Fence: Power and Privilege in a Multiethnic Neighborhood*. University of North Carolina Press, 2014.

Mazzoni, Mary. "Should Business Leaders Experiment to Overcome the Shortcomings of Meritocracy?" Triple Pundit, October 2, 2024. https://www.triplepundit.com/story /2024/meritocracy-dei-business/811341.

McDonald, Steve. "Patterns of Informal Job Matching Across the Life Course: Entry-Level, Reentry-Level, and Elite Non-Searching." *Sociological Inquiry* 75, no. 3 (2005): 403–28.

McDonald, Steve. "What You Know or Who You Know? Occupation-Specific Work Experience and Job Matching Through Social Networks." *Social Science Research* 40, no. 6 (2011): 1664–75.

McDonald, Steve. "What's in the 'Old Boys' Network? Accessing Social Capital in Gendered and Racialized Networks." *Social Networks* 33, no. 4 (2011): 317–30.

McDonald, Steve, and Glen H. Elder Jr. "When Does Social Capital Matter? Non-Searching for Jobs Across the Life Course." *Social Forces* 85, no. 1 (2006): 521–49.

McDonald, Steve, Nan Lin, and Dan Ao. "Networks of Opportunity: Gender, Race, and Job Leads." *Social Problems* 56, no. 3 (2009): 385–402.

McGauflin, Paige. "Elon Musk and Other DEI Critics Are Latching on to 'MEI,' a New Hiring Catchphrase That Experts Say Misses the Point." *Fortune*, June 25, 2024. https://fortune.com/2024/06/24/mei-elon-musk-alexandr-wang-anti-dei-hiring -merit-excellence-intelligence/.

McGlauflin, Paige. "HR Leaders Say They're Still Committed to DEI in 2024 Despite the 'Anti-Woke' Backlash." *Fortune*, January 2, 2024. https://fortune.com/2024/01/02 /hr-leaders-committed-to-diversity-initiatives-dei-programs-in-2024/.

McGlauflin, Paige, and Emma Burleigh. "The Vast Majority of C-Suite Leaders Say They're Doubling Down on DEI, but They're Still Fighting an Uphill Battle." *Fortune*,

June 3, 2024. https://fortune.com/2024/06/03/majority-of-c-suite-leaders-say-theyre-doubling-down-on-dei-still-fighting-uphill-battle/.

McGlauflin, Paige, and Trey Williams. "Microsoft, Salesforce, and Other Fortune 500 Companies React to Supreme Court Striking Down Affirmative Action: 'Our Commitment to Equality Doesn't Waver.'" *Fortune*, June 30, 2023. https://fortune.com/2023/06/30/major-companies-ceos-react-supreme-court-affrmative-action-decision-microsoft-salesforce-gm-hp/.

McKay, Patrick F., and Michael A. McDaniel. "A Reexamination of Black-White Mean Differences in Work Performance: More Data, More Moderators." *Journal of Applied Psychology* 91, no. 3 (2006): 538–54.

McNamara, Charles. *Learning to Be Fair: Equity from Classical Philosophy to Contemporary Politics*. Fortress, 2024.

McPherson, Miller, Lynn Smith-Lovin, and James M Cook. "Birds of a Feather: Homophily in Social Networks." *Annual Review of Sociology* 27 (2001): 415–44.

Mehra, Ajay, Martin Kilduff, and Daniel J. Brass. "At the Margins: A Distinctiveness Approach to the Social Identity and Social Networks of Underrepresented Groups." *Academy of Management Journal* 41, no. 4 (1998): 441–52.

Melloy, Bobby. "What Demographic Questions Should You Ask in Surveys?" CultureAmp, March 27, 2023. https://www.cultureamp.com/blog/demographic-questions-surveys.

Mencken, F. Carson, and Idee Winfield. "In Search of the 'Right Stuff': The Advantages and Disadvantages of Informal and Formal Recruiting Practices in External Labor Markets." *American Journal of Economics and Sociology* 57, no. 2 (1998): 135–54.

Merritt, Anna C., Daniel A. Effron, Steven Fein, Kenneth K. Savitsky, Daniel M. Tuller, and Benoît Monin. "The Strategic Pursuit of Moral Credentials." *Journal of Experimental Social Psychology* 48, no. 3 (2012): 774–77.

Merritt, Anna C., Daniel A. Effron, and Benoît Monin. "Moral Self-Licensing: When Being Good Frees Us to Be Bad." *Social and Personality Psychology Compass* 4, no. 5 (2010): 344–57.

Meyershohn, Nathaniel. "Harley-Davidson Is Dropping Diversity Initiatives After Right-Wing Anti-DEI Campaign." *CNN*, August 19, 2024. https://www.cnn.com/2024/08/19/business/harley-davidson-dei-john-deere-tractor-supply/index.html.

Mijs, Jonathan J. B. "Inequality Is a Problem of Inference: How People Solve the Social Puzzle of Unequal Outcomes." *Societies* 8, no. 3 (2018): 64.

Mijs, Jonathan J. B. "The Paradox of Inequality: Income Inequality and Belief in Meritocracy Go Hand in Hand." *Socio-Economic Review* 19, no. 1 (2021): 7–35.

Mijs, Jonathan J. B. "Stratified Failure: Educational Stratification and Students' Attributions of Their Mathematics Performance in 24 Countries." *Sociology of Education* 89, no. 2 (2016): 137–53.

Mijs, Jonathan J. B. "The Unfulfillable Promise of Meritocracy: Three Lessons and Their Implications for Justice in Education." *Social Justice Research* 29, no. 1 (2016): 14–34.

Mijs, Jonathan J. B. "Visualizing Belief in Meritocracy, 1930–2010." *Socius: Sociological Research for a Dynamic World* 4 (2018).

Mijs, Jonathan J. B., and Mike Savage. "Meritocracy, Elitism and Inequality." *Political Quarterly* 91, no. 2 (2020): 397–404.

Miller, Stephen. "Study: Pay for Performance Pays Off." SHRM, September 14, 2011. https://www.shrm.org/topics-tools/news/benefits-compensation/study-pay-performance-pays.

Mollick, Ethan, and Lilach Mollick. "Assigning AI: Seven Approaches for Students, with Prompts." arXiv:2306.10052, June 13, 2023. https://arxiv.org/abs/2306.10052.

Monin, Benoît, and Dale T. Miller. "Moral Credentials and the Expression of Prejudice." *Journal of Personality and Social Psychology* 81, no. 1 (2001): 33–43.

Moss-Racusin, Corinne A., Jojanneke van der Toorn, John F. Dovidio, Victoria L. Brescoll, Mark J. Graham, and Jo Handelsman. "Scientific Diversity Interventions." *Science* 343, no. 6171 (2014): 615–16.

Mouw, Ted. "Social Capital and Finding a Job: Do Contacts Matter?" *American Sociological Review* 68, no. 6 (2003): 868–98.

Mugayar-Baldocchi, Marino, Bill Schaninger, and Kartik Sharma. "The Future of the Workforce: Investing in Talent to Prepare for Uncertainty." McKinsey & Company, June 7, 2021. https://www.mckinsey.com/capabilities/people-and-organizational-performance /our-insights/the-organization-blog/the-future-of-work-the-now-the-how-and-the-why.

Mulgan, Richard. "'Accountability': An Ever-Expanding Concept?" *Public Administration* 78, no. 3 (2000): 555–73.

Mun, Eunmi, and Naomi Kodama. "Meritocracy at Work? Merit-Based Reward Systems and Gender Wage Inequality." *Social Forces* 100, no. 4 (2022): 1561–91.

Murphy-Hill, Emerson, Ciera Jaspan, Carolyn Egelman, and Lan Cheng. "The Pushback Effects of Race, Ethnicity, Gender, and Age in Code Review." *Communications of the ACM* 65, no. 3 (2022): 52–57.

Nathoo, Zulekha. "Why Ineffective Diversity Training Won't Go Away." *BBC Worklife*, June 16, 2021. https://www.bbc.com/worklife/article/20210614-why-ineffective-diversity -training-wont-go-away.

National Center for Science and Engineering. "Women, Minorities, and Persons with Disabilities in Science and Engineering." Assorted data tables, National Center for Science and Engineering Statistics, 2020. https://ncses.nsf.gov/pubs/nsf21321 /table/5-1.

National Labor Relations Board. "Election Petitions Up 53%, Board Continues to Reduce Case Processing Time in FY22." National Labor Relations Board, October 6, 2022. https://www.nlrb.gov/news-outreach/news-story/election-petitions-up-53-board -continues-to-reduce-case-processing-time-in.

Neale, Margaret A., Elizabeth A. Mannix, and Deborah H. Gruenfeld, eds. *Research on Managing Groups and Teams.* Vol. 1, *Composition.* JAI, 1998.

Neale, Margaret A., Elizabeth A. Mannix, and Katherine Phillips, eds. *Research on Managing Groups and Teams.* Vol. 11, *Diversity and Groups.* Emerald Group, 2008.

Neckerman, Katherine, and Roberto M. Fernandez. "Keeping a Job: Network Hiring and Turnover in a Retail Bank." In *The Governance of Relations in Markets and Organizations,* ed. Chris Snijders, Vincent Willem Buskens, and Werner Raub. Elsevier Science, 2003.

Nelson, Robert L., and William P. Bridges. *Legalizing Gender Inequality: Courts, Markets and Unequal Pay for Women in America.* Cambridge University Press, 1999.

Neumark, David, Roy J. Bank, and Kyle D. Van Nort. "Sex Discrimination in Restaurant Hiring: An Audit Study." *Quarterly Journal of Economics* 111, no. 3 (1996): 915–41.

Newman, Katherine S. *Falling from Grace: The Experience of Downward Mobility in the American Middle Class.* Free Press, 1988.

Nguyen, Hoa P. "Diversity Training Doesn't Work. And Don't Bother Fixing It." Medium, October 6, 2020. https://medium.com/swlh/diversity-training-doesnt-work-and-don -t-bother-fixing-it.

Nicholson, Nigel. "The False Theory of Meritocracy." *Harvard Business Review,* June 1, 2010. https://hbr.org/2010/06/the-false-theory-of-meritocrac.

Nix, Naomi. "Job Rate for Women in Tech Has Hardly Budged Since 2005, EEOC Finds." *Washington Post*, September 11, 2024. https://www.washingtonpost.com/technology /2024/09/11/big-tech-women-minorities-jobs-dei-eeoc/.

Noe, Raymond A., John R. Hollenbeck, Barry Gerhart, and Patrick M. Wright. *Human Resource Management: Gaining a Competitive Advantage.* McGraw-Hill, 2017.

Nordli, Brian. "Pay Transparency: What It Is and How to Do It Right." Built In, June 28, 2022. https://builtin.com/people-management/pay-transparency.

Obermeyer, Ziad, Brian Powers, Christine Vogeli, and Sendhil Mullainathan. "Dissecting Racial Bias in an Algorithm Used to Manage the Health of Populations." *Science* 366, no. 6464 (2019): 447–53.

Obloj, Tomasz, and Todd R. Zenger. "The Influence of Pay Transparency on (Gender) Inequity, Inequality, and the Performance Basis of Pay." *Nature Human Behavior* 6 (2022): 646–55.

Obloj, Tomasz, and Todd R. Zenger. "Research: The Complicated Effects of Pay Transparency." *Harvard Business Review*, February 8, 2023. https://hbr.org/2023/02/research -the-complicated-effects-of-pay-transparency.

Obukhova, Elena. "Motivation vs. Relevance: Using Strong Ties to Find a Job in Urban China." *Social Science Research* 41, no. 3 (2012): 570–80.

Obukhova, Elena, and George Lan. "Do Job-Seekers Benefit from Contacts? A Direct Test with Contemporaneous Searches." *Management Science* 59, no. 10 (2013): 2204–16.

O'Donnell, Lauren. "What Makes a Company a Great Place to Work?" Great Place to Work, July 30, 2021. https://www.greatplacetowork.ca/en/articles/what-makes-a-company -a-great-place-to-work.

OECD. *A Broken Social Elevator? How to Promote Social Mobility.* OECD iLibrary, June 15, 2018. https://doi.org/10.1787/9789264301085-en.

OECD. *Does Inequality Matter? How People Perceive Economic Disparities and Social Mobility.* OECD iLibrary, November 18, 2021. https://www.oecd-ilibrary.org/sites/3023ed40 -en/index.html?itemId=/content/publication/3023ed40-en.

O'Malley, Michael. "What the 'Best Companies to Work For' Do Differently." *Harvard Business Review*, December 12, 2019. https://hbr.org/2019/12/what-the-best-companies -to-work-for-do-differently.

Opie, Tina, and Ella F. Washington. "Why Companies Can—and Should—Recommit to DEI in the Wake of the SCOTUS Decision." *Harvard Business Review*, July 27, 2023. https://hbr.org/2023/07/why-companies-can-and-should-recommit-to-dei-in-the -wake-of-the-scotus-decision.

Oreffice, Sonia. "Sexual Orientation and Household Decision Making: Same-Sex Couples' Balance of Power and Labor Supply Choices." *Labour Economics* 18, no. 2 (2011): 145–58.

Ospina, Sonia, and Erica Foldy. "A Critical Review of Race and Ethnicity in the Leadership Literature: Surfacing Context, Power and the Collective Dimensions of Leadership." *Leadership Quarterly* 20, no. 6 (2009): 876–96.

Ostriker, Rebecca. "Boycott Targets College Admissions Boost Given to Children of Alumni at Harvard, Other Elite Schools." *Boston Globe*, September 25, 2021. https://www .bostonglobe.com/2021/09/25/metro/boycott-targets-college-admissions-boost-given -children-alumni-harvard-other-elite-schools/?s_campaign=breakingnews:newsletter.

Oswald, Frederick L., Gregory Mitchell, Hart Blanton, James Jaccard, and Philip E. Tetlock. "Predicting Ethnic and Racial Discrimination: A Meta-Analysis of IAT Criterion Studies." *Journal of Personality and Social Psychology* 105, no. 2 (2013): 171–92.

Padgett, Margaret Y., and Kathryn A. Morris. "Keeping It 'All in the Family': Does Nepotism in the Hiring Process Really Benefit the Beneficiary?" *Journal of Leadership and Organizational Studies* 11, no. 2 (2005): 34–45.

Padgett, Margaret Y., Robert J. Padgett, and Kathryn A. Morris. "Reactions to Nepotism in the Hiring Process: The Role of Family Member Qualifications." *Journal of Organizational Psychology* 19, no. 4 (2019): 106–20.

Paluck, Elizabeth Levy. "Diversity Training and Intergroup Contact: A Call to Action Research." *Journal of Social Issues* 62, no. 3 (2006): 577–95.

Paluck, Elizabeth Levy, and Donald P. Green. "Prejudice Reduction: What Works? A Review and Assessment of Research and Practice." *Annual Review of Psychology* 60 (2009): 339–67.

Parsons, Talcott. *The Social System*. Free Press of Glencoe, 1951.

Patacchini, Eleonora, Giuseppe Ragusa, and Yves Zenou. "Discrimination and Labor Market Outcomes: Theoretical Mechanisms and Existing Empirical Studies." In *Unexplored Dimensions of Discrimination*, ed. Tito Boeri, Eleonora Patacchini, and Giovanni Peri. Oxford University Press, 2015.

Patacchini, Eleonora, Giuseppe Ragusa, and Yves Zenou. "Do Employers Discriminate Against Physical Appearance and Sexual Preference? A Field Experiment." In Boeri et al., *Unexplored Dimensions of Discrimination*.

Patacchini, Eleonora, Giuseppe Ragusa, and Yves Zenou. "Other Dimensions of Discrimination." In Boeri et al., *Unexplored Dimensions of Discrimination*.

Patacchini, Eleonora, Giuseppe Ragusa, and Yves Zenou. "Unexplored Dimensions of Discrimination in Europe: Homosexuality and Physical Appearance." *Journal of Population Economics* 28, no. 4 (2015): 1045–73.

Patel, Sandeep A., and George S. Dallas. "Transparency and Disclosure: Overview of Methodology and Study Results—United States." Standard & Poor's (available via SSRN), October 16, 2002. https://ssrn.com/abstract=422800.

Paycale. "Does Pay Transparency Close the Gender Gap? Pay Equity for Men and Women." PayScale, 2019. Accessed June 19, 2023. https://www.payscale.com/content/whitepaper/Pay-Transparency-Closing-Gender-Wage-Gap.pdf.

Payscale. "2023 Compensation Best Practices Report." 2023. Hard copy available with author.

Pazzanese, Christina. "Great Promise but Potential for Peril." *Harvard Gazette*, October 26, 2020. https://news.harvard.edu/gazette/story/2020/10/ethical-concerns-mount-as-ai-takes-bigger-decision-making-role/.

Pedriana, Nicholas. "Help Wanted NOW: Legal Resources, the Women's Movement, and the Battle over Sex-Segregated Job Advertisements." *Social Problems* 51, no. 2 (2004): 182–201.

Pedriana, Nicholas, and Amanda Abraham. "Now You See Them, Now You Don't: The Legal Field and Newspaper Desegregation of Sex-Segregated Help Wanted Ads 1965–75." *Law and Social Inquiry* 31, no. 4 (2006): 905–38.

Percy, Sally. "Six Top Tips for Networking in the New World of Work." *Forbes*, June 23, 2021. https://www.forbes.com/sites/sallypercy/2021/06/23/six-top-tips-for-networking-in-the-new-world-of-work/.

Percy, Sally. "What's So Great About Pay Transparency?" *Forbes*, December 2, 2022. https://www.forbes.com/sites/sallypercy/2022/12/02/whats-so-great-about-pay-transparency/?sh=4d2e7b6f35ce.

Petersen, Trond. "Aage Bøttger Sørensen's Contributions to Quantitative Sociology: From Studying Processes to Studying Structure." *Research in Social Stratification and Mobility* 21 (2004): 27–44. (Special issue, ed. Arne L. Kalleberg et al., entitled *Inequality: Structures, Dynamics and Mechanisms: Essays in Honor of Aage B. Sørensen*).

Petersen, Trond. "Discrimination, Measurement in." In *Encyclopedia of Social Measurement*, ed. Kimberly Kempf-Leonard. Academic, 2004.

Petersen, Trond. "On the Promise of Game Theory in Sociology." *Contemporary Sociology* 23, no. 4 (1994): 498–502.

Petersen, Trond. "Opportunities." In *The Oxford Handbook of Analytical Sociology*, ed. Peter Bearman and Peter Hedström. Oxford University Press, 2009.

Petersen, Trond, and Laurie A. Morgan. "Separate and Unequal: Occupation-Establishment Sex Segregation and the Gender Wage Gap." *American Journal of Sociology* 101, no. 2 (1995): 329–65.

Petersen, Trond, and Ishak Saporta. "The Opportunity Structure for Discrimination." *American Journal of Sociology* 109, no. 4 (2004): 852–901.

Pfeffer, Jeffrey. *Power in Organizations*. Pitman, 1981.

Phelps, Edmund S. "The Statistical Theory of Racism and Sexism." *American Economic Review* 62, no. 4 (1972): 659–61.

Philips, Damon J. "Organization Genealogies and the Persistence of Gender Inequality: The Case of Silicon Valley Law Firms." *Administrative Science Quarterly* 50, no. 3 (2005): 440–72.

Pierné, Guillaume. "Hiring Discrimination Based on National Origin and Religious Closeness: Results from a Field Experiment in the Paris Area." *IZA Journal of Labor Economics* 2 (2013): Article 4.

Piketty, Thomas. *Capital and Ideology*. Belknap, 2020.

Piketty, Thomas. *Capital in the Twenty–First Century*. Belknap Press of Harvard University Press, 2014.

Piketty, Thomas. "Capital in the Twenty-First Century: A Multidimensional Approach to the History of Capital and Social Classes." *British Journal of Sociology* 65, no. 4 (2014): 736–47.

Piketty, Thomas, and Emmanuel Saez. "Inequality in the Long Run." *Science* 344, no. 6186 (2014): 838–43.

Piketty, Thomas, and Emmanuel Saez. "Top Incomes and the Great Recession: Recent Evolutions and Policy Implications." *IMF Economic Review* 61, no. 3 (2013): 456–78.

Piketty, Thomas, and Gabriel Zucman. "Capital Is Back: Wealth-Income Ratios in Rich Countries 1700–2010." *Quarterly Journal of Economics* 129, no. 3 (2014): 1255–310.

Pinsker, Joe. "The Real Reasons Legacy Preferences Exist." *Atlantic*, April 4, 2019. https://www.theatlantic.com/education/archive/2019/04/legacy-admissions-preferences-ivy/586465/.

Plaut, Victoria, Kecia M. Thomas, and Matt J. Goren. "Is Multiculturalism or Color Blindness Better for Minorities?" *Psychological Science* 20, no. 4 (2009): 444–46.

Podolny, Joel M., and James N. Baron. "Resources and Relationships: Social Networks and Mobility in the Workplace." *American Sociological Review* 62, no. 5 (1997): 673–93.

Polumbo, Brad. "'Legacy' College Admissions Are Affirmative Action for Rich White People." *Washington Examiner*, September 23, 2019. https://www.washingtonexaminer.com/opinion/2141040/legacy-college-admissions-are-affirmative-action-for-rich-white-people/.

Pruett, Steven R., and Fong Chan. "The Development and Psychometric Validation of the Disability Attitude Implicit Association Test." *Rehabilitation Psychology* 51, no. 3 (2006): 202–13.

Pulakos, Elaine D., Leonard A. White, Scott H. Oppler, and Walter C. Borman. "Examination of Race and Sex Effects on Performance Ratings." *Journal of Applied Psychology* 74, no. 5 (1989): 770–80.

Raczka, Rachel K. "How Bonuses Get Employees to Choose Work over Family." HBS Working Knowledge, November 29, 2021. https://hbswk.hbs.edu/item/how-bonuses -get-employees-to-choose-work-over-family.

Rajkumar, Karthik, Guillaume Saint-Jacques, Iavor Bojinov, Erik Brynjolfsson, and Sinan Aral. "A Causal Test of the Strength of Weak Ties." *Science* 377, no. 6612 (2022): 1304–10.

Ramachandran, Gowri. "Pay Transparency." *Penn State Law Review* 116, no. 4 (2012): 1043–80.

Ran, Yawei, Yubo Hou, Zhiwen Dong, and Qi Wang. "Moral Observer—Licensing in Cyberspace." *Behavioral Sciences* 12, no. 5 (2022): 148.

Ranganathan, Aruna, and Ranjitha Shivaram. "Getting Their Hands Dirty: How Female Managers Motivate Female Worker Productivity Through Subordinate Scut Work." *Management Science* 67, no. 5 (2021): 2657–3320.

Ravaud, Jean-François, Béatrice Madiot, and Isabelle Ville. "Discrimination Towards Disabled People Seeking Employment." *Social Science and Medicine* 35, no. 8 (1992): 951–58.

Rawls, John. *A Theory of Justice.* Harvard University Press, 1971.

Raymond, Adam K., and Matt Stieb. "Trump Hired Them, Then He Called Them Incompetent." *New York Magazine—Intelligencer*, February 13, 2020. https://nymag.com /intelligencer/2020/02/dumb-as-a-rock-9-times-trump-insulted-people-he-appointed .html.

Raymond, Kim. "The Business Case for a Diverse Workforce." *Forbes*, August 21, 2019. https://www.forbes.com/sites/forbeshumanresourcescouncil/2019/08/21/the-business -case-for-a-diverse-workforce/?sh=2de433c64d4a.

Ready, Douglas A., Linda A. Hill, and Robert J. Thomas. "Building a Game-Changing Talent Strategy." *Harvard Business Review* 92, nos. 1–2 (January–February 2014): 62–68. https://hbr.org/2014/01/building-a-game-changing-talent-strategy.

Reif, L. Rafael. MIT Inaugural Address, September 21, 2013. https://reif.mit.edu/speeches -writing/inaugural-address.

Reimers, Hanna, Wassili Lasarov, and Stefan Hoffmann. "Moral-Psychological Mechanisms of Rebound Effects from a Consumer-Centered Perspective: A Conceptualization and Research Directions." *Frontiers in Psychology* 13 (2022).

Reingold, David A. "Social Networks and the Employment Problem of the Urban Poor." *Urban Studies* 36, no. 11 (1999): 1907–32.

Reskin, Barbara F. "Employment Discrimination and Its Remedies." In *Sourcebook of Labor Markets: Evolving Structures and Processes*, ed. Ivar Berg and Arne L. Kalleberg. Springer, 2001.

Reskin, Barbara F. "Getting It Right: Sex and Race Inequality in Work Organizations." *Annual Review of Sociology* 26 (2000): 707–9.

Reskin, Barbara F. "Labor Markets as Queues: A Structural Approach to Changing Occupational Sex Composition." In *Macro-Micro Linkages in Sociology*, ed. Joan Huber. Sage, 1991.

Reskin, Barbara F. "The Proximate Causes of Employment Discrimination." *Contemporary Sociology* 29, no. 2 (2000): 319–28.

Reskin, Barbara F. "Sex Segregation in the Workplace." *Annual Review of Sociology* 19 (1993): 241–70.

Reskin, Barbara F., and Debra B. McBrier. "Why Not Ascription? Organizations' Employment of Male and Female Managers." *American Sociological Review* 65, no. 2 (2000): 210–33.

Reskin, Barbara F., and Irene Padavic. *Women and Men at Work.* Pine Forge, 1994.

Reskin, Barbara F., and Patricia A. Roos. *Job Queues, Gender Queues: Explaining Women's Inroads into Male Occupations.* Temple University Press, 1990.

Reynolds, Jeremy, and He Xian. "Perceptions of Meritocracy in the Land of Opportunity." *Research in Social Stratification and Mobility* 36 (2014): 121–37.

Ridgeway, Cecilia L. "Interaction and the Conservation of Gender Inequality: Considering Employment." *American Sociological Review* 62, no. 2 (1997): 218–35.

Ridgeway, Cecilia L., and Shelley J. Correll. "Unpacking the Gender System: A Theoretical Perspective on Gender Beliefs and Social Relations." *Gender and Society* 18, no. 4 (2004): 51031.

Ridgeway, Cecilia L., and Lynn Smith-Lovin. "The Gender System and Interaction." *Annual Review of Sociology* 25 (1999): 191–216.

Riley, Jason L. "Meritocracy Is Worth Defending." *Wall Street Journal*, August 17, 2021. https://www.wsj.com/articles/meritocracy-wooldridge-kendi-carlson-admissions -standardized-tests-affirmative-action-cuny-11629237426.

Rissing, Ben A., and Emilio J. Castilla. "House of Green Cards: Statistical or Preference-Based Inequality in the Employment of Foreign Nationals." *American Sociological Review* 79, no. 6 (2014): 1226–55.

Rivera, Lauren A. "Guess Who Doesn't Fit In at Work." *New York Times*, May 30, 2015. https://www.nytimes.com/2015/05/31/opinion/sunday/guess-who-doesnt-fit-in-at-work.html.

Rivera, Lauren A. "Hiring as Cultural Matching: The Case of Elite Professional Service Firms." *American Sociological Review* 77, no. 6 (2012): 999–1022.

Rivera, Lauren A. *Pedigree: How Elite Students Get Elite Jobs.* Princeton University Press, 2015.

Rivera, Lauren A., and András Tilcsik. "Class Advantage, Commitment Penalty: The Gendered Effect of Social Class Signals in an Elite Labor Market." *American Sociological Review* 81, no. 6 (2016): 1097–131.

Rivera, Lauren A., and András Tilcsik. "How Subtle Class Cues Can Backfire on Your Resume." *Harvard Business Review*, December 21, 2016. https://hbr.org/2016/12 /research-how-subtle-class-cues-can-backfire-on-your-resume.

Rock, David. "Performance Management: Are You Ready for Change?" Inside HR, October 16, 2023. https://web.archive.org/web/20220326072951/https://www.insidehr.com .au/performance-management-are-you-ready-for-change/.

Rosener, Judy B. "Standards of Meritocracy Don't Add Up." *Los Angeles Times*, February 2, 1997.

Rosenfeld, Rachel A. "Job Mobility and Career Processes." *Annual Review of Sociology* 18 (1992): 39–61.

Roth, Louise M. *Selling Women Short: Gender and Money on Wall Street.* Princeton University Press, 2006.

Rothman, Robert A. *Inequality and Stratification: Race, Class and Gender.* Prentice Hall, 2005.

Roy, Katica. "Implicit Bias Training Doesn't Work. Here's What Does." *MSNBC*, January 31, 2023. https://www.msnbc.com/know-your-value/business-culture/implicit-bias-training -doesn-t-work-here-s-what-does-n1302608.

Royster, Deirdre. *Race and the Invisible Hand: How White Networks Exclude Black Men from Blue-Collar Jobs*. University of California Press, 2003.

Rubineau, Brian, and Roberto M. Fernandez. "Missing Links: Referrer Behavior and Job Segregation." *Management Science* 59, no. 11 (2013): 2470–89.

Rubineau, Brian, and Roberto M. Fernandez. "Tipping Points: The Gender Segregating and Desegregating Effects of Network Recruitment." *Organization Science* 26, no. 6 (2015): 1646–64.

Rudman, Laurie A. "Self-Promotion as a Risk Factor for Women: The Costs and Benefits of Counterstereotypical Impression Management." *Journal of Personality and Social Psychology* 74, no. 3 (1998): 629–45.

Rudman, Laurie A., and Peter Glick. "Feminized Management and Backlash Toward Agentic Women: The Hidden Costs to Women of a Kinder, Gentler Image of Middle Managers." *Journal of Personality and Social Psychology* 77, no. 5 (1999): 1004–10.

Rudman, Laurie A., and Peter Glick. "Prescriptive Gender Stereotypes and Backlash Toward Agentic Women." *Journal of Social Issues* 57, no. 4 (2001): 743–62.

Ruffle, Bradley J., and Ze'ev Shtudiner. "Are Good-Looking People More Employable?" *Management Science* 61, no. 8 (2015): 1760–76.

Rynes, Sara, and Benson Rosen. "A Field Survey of Factors Affecting the Adoption and Perceived Success of Diversity Training." *Personnel Psychology* 48, no. 2 (1995): 247–70.

Sachs-Cobbe, Benjamin. "Recent Work on Meritocracy." *Analysis* 83, no. 1 (2023): 171–85.

Sammer, Joanne. "Reward Top Performers Even in Lean Times." SHRM. Accessed June 26, 2023. https://www.shrm.org/hr-today/news/hr-magazine/pages/0914-rewards-performance-based-pay.aspx.

Sandel, Michael J. "Disdain for the Less Educated Is the Last Acceptable Prejudice." *New York Times*, September 2, 2020.

Sandel, Michael. *Justice: What's the Right Thing to Do?* Farrar, Straus and Giroux, 2009.

Sandel, Michael J. *The Tyranny of Merit: What's Become of the Common Good?* Farrar, Straus and Giroux, 2020.

Saussure, Ferdinand de. *Course in General Linguistics*, trans. and ed. Charles Bally and Albert Sechehaye. McGraw-Hill, 1916.

Scheiber, Noam. "Affirmative Action Ruling May Upend Hiring Policies, Too." *New York Times*, June 30, 2023. https://www.nytimes.com/2023/06/30/business/economy/hiring-affirmative-action.html.

Scheiner, Michael. "Will AI Bring Fairness in the Workplace?" CRM.org. Accessed June 25, 2023. https://crm.org/articles/will-ai-bring-fairness-in-the-workplace.

Schimmack, Ulrich. "Invalid Claims About the Validity of Implicit Association Tests by Prisoners of the Implicit Social-Cognition Paradigm." *Perspectives on Psychological Science* 16, no. 2 (2021): 435–42.

Schimmack, Ulrich. "The Validation Crisis in Psychology." *Meta-Psychology* 5, no. 3 (2021).

Schimmack, Ulrich. "What Multi-Method Data Tell Us About Construct Validity." *European Journal of Personality* 24, no. 3 (2010): 241–57.

Schmidt, Frank L., and John E. Hunter. "The Validity and Utility of Selection Methods in Personnel Psychology: Practical and Theoretical Implications of 85 Years of Research Findings." *Psychological Bulletin* 124, no. 2 (1998): 262–74.

Schneider, Rachel C., Diedra Carroll Coleman, Elaine Howard Eklund, and Denise Daniels. "How Religious Discrimination Is Perceived in the Workplace: Expanding the View." *Socius: Sociological Research for a Dynamic World* 8 (2022): 1–14.

Scully, Maureen A. "Manage Your Own Employability: Meritocracy and the Legitimation of Inequality in Internal Labor Markets and Beyond." In *Relational Wealth: The Advantages of Stability in a Changing Economy*, ed. Carrie R. Leana and Denise M. Rousseau. Oxford University Press, 2000.

Scully, Maureen A. "Meritocracy." In *Blackwell Encyclopedic Dictionary of Business Ethics*, ed. R. Edward Freeman and Patricia H. Werhane. Wiley-Blackwell, 1997.

Seibert, Scott E., Maria L. Kraimer, and Robert C. Liden. "A Social Capital Theory of Career Success." *Academy of Management Journal* 44, no. 2 (2001): 219–37.

Seidel, Marc-David L., Jeffrey T. Polzer, and Katherine J. Stewart. "Friends in High Places: The Effects of Social Networks on Discrimination in Salary Negotiations." *Administrative Science Quarterly* 45, no. 1 (2000): 1–24.

Seltman, Charles Theodore. *Athens, Its History and Coinage Before the Persian Invasion*. Cambridge University Press, 1924.

Sen, Amartya. *Development as Freedom*. Oxford University Press, 1999.

Sen, Amartya. *The Idea of Justice*. Harvard University Press, 2009.

Sen, Amartya. *Inequality Reexamined*. Harvard University Press, 1995.

Shah, Abhin, Yuheng Bu, Joshua K. Lee, et al. "Selective Regression Under Fairness Criteria." *Proceedings of the 39th International Conference on Machine Learning*, PMLR 162 (2022): 19598–615. https://proceedings.mlr.press/v162/shah22a.html.

Shellenbarger, Sue. "The Dangers of Hiring for Cultural Fit." *Wall Street Journal*, September 23, 2019. https://www.wsj.com/articles/the-dangers-of-hiring-for-cultural-fit-11569231000.

Sheridan, Jennifer, Eve Fine, Manuela Romero, et al. "Improving Department Climate Through Bias Literacy: One College's Experience." *Journal of Women and Minorities in Science and Engineering* 27, no. 2 (2021): 87–106.

Shull, Fremont, and William P. Anthony. "Do Black and White Supervisory Problem Solving Styles Differ?" *Personnel Psychology* 31, no. 4 (1978): 761–82.

Shulman, James L., and William G. Bowen. *The Game of Life: College Sports and Educational Values*. Princeton University Press, 2001.

Sidanius, Jim, and Felicia Pratto. *Social Dominance: An Intergroup Theory of Social Hierarchy and Oppression*. Cambridge University Press, 1999.

Sienkewicz, Thomas J., ed. *Encyclopedia of the Ancient World*. Salem, 2003.

Silberg, Jake, and James Manyika. "Notes from the AI Frontier: Tracking Bias in AI (and in Humans)." McKinsey Global Institute, June 2019. https://www.mckinsey.com/~/media/mckinsey/featured%20insights/artificial%20intelligence/tackling%20bias%20in%20artificial%20intelligence%20and%20in%20humans/mgi-tackling-bias-in-ai-june-2019.pdf.

Silver, Laura. "More People Globally See Racial, Ethnic Discrimination as a Serious Problem in the U.S. than in Their Own Society." Pew Research Center, November 2, 2021. https://www.pewresearch.org/fact-tank/2021/11/02/more-people-globally-see-racial-ethnic-discrimination-as-a-serious-problem-in-the-u-s-than-in-their-own-society/.

Simard, Caroline. "Saying High-Tech Is a Meritocracy Doesn't Make It So." *HuffPost*, September 16, 2010. Last modified May 25, 2011. https://www.huffpost.com/entry/saying-hightech-is-a-meri_b_719804.

Singal, Jesse. "What If Diversity Training Is Doing More Harm than Good?" *New York Times*, January 17, 2023. https://www.nytimes.com/2023/01/17/opinion/dei-trainings-effective.html.

Skuratowicz, Eva, and Larry W. Hunter. "Where Do Women's Jobs Come From? Job Resegregation in an American Bank." *Work and Occupations* 31, no. 1 (2004): 73–110.

Slan, Yolanda. "Viewpoint: A Reflection on Juneteenth, Transparency in Diversity Reporting." SHRM, June 16, 2023. https://www.shrm.org/resourcesandtools/hr-topics /behavioral-competencies/global-and-cultural-effectiveness/pages/viewpoint-the -relationship-between-juneteenth-and-transparency-in-diversity-reporting.aspx.

Sleek, Scott. "The Bias Beneath: Two Decades of Measuring Implicit Associations." Association for Psychological Science, January 31, 2018. https://www.psychologicalscience .org/observer/the-bias-beneath-two-decades-of-measuring-implicit-associations.

Smith, Edward B., Raina A. Brands, Matthew E. Brashears, and Adam M. Kleinbaum. "Social Networks and Cognition." *Annual Review of Sociology* 46, no. 1 (2020): 159–74.

Smith, Edward B., Tanya Menon, and Leigh Thompson. "Status Differences in the Cognitive Activation of Social Networks." *Organization Science* 23, no. 1 (2012): 67–82.

Smith, Sandra S. "'Don't Put My Name on It': Social Capital Activation and Job-Finding Assistance Among the Black Urban Poor." *American Journal of Sociology* 111, no. 1 (2005): 1–57.

Smolic, Hrvoje. "AI Biases Examples in the Real World." Graphite Note, March 5, 2024. Accessed July 27, 2024. https://graphite-note.com/ai-biases-examples/.

Soares, Joseph A. *The Decline of Privilege: The Modernization of Oxford University*. Stanford University Press, 1999.

Soares, Joseph A. *The Power of Privilege: Yale and America's Elite Colleges*. Stanford University Press, 2007.

Society for Human Resource Management. *The Business Case for Diversity, Equity and Inclusion*. SHRM, August 2020. https://www.shrm.org/resourcesandtools/tools-and -samples/presentations/pages/thebusinesscasefordiversity.aspx.

Society for Human Resource Management. *The Journey to Equity and Inclusion*. SHRM, Summer 2020. https://www.shrm.org/content/dam/en/shrm/topics-tools/news/inclusion -equity-diversitytfaw-the-journey-to-equity-and-inclusion.pdf.

Society for Human Resource Management. "Screening by Means of Pre-Employment Testing." SHRM, Summer 2023. Accessed July 1, 2023. https://www.shrm.org/resources andtools/tools-and-samples/toolkits/pages/screeningbymeansofpreemploymenttesting .aspx.

Spradley, James P. *The Ethnographic Interview*. Holt, Rinehart and Winston, 1979.

Srivastava, Sameer B., and Eliott B. Sherman. "Agents of Change or Cogs in the Machine? Reexamining the Influence of Female Managers on the Gender Wage Gap." *American Journal of Sociology* 120, no. 6 (2015): 1778–808.

Sterling, Adina D. "Friendships and Search Behavior in Labor Markets." *Management Science* 60, no. 9 (2014): 2341–54.

Stevens, Mitchell L. *Creating a Class: College Admissions and the Education of Elites*. Harvard University Press, 2007.

Stoll, Michael A., Steven Raphael, and Harry J. Holzer. "Black Job Applicants and the Hiring Officer's Race." *ILR Review* 57, no. 2 (2004): 267–87.

Stop Street Harassment and RALIANCE. *The Facts Behind the #MeToo Movement: A National Study on Sexual Harassment and Assault*. Stop Street Harassment and RALIANCE, February 2018. https://www.stopstreetharassment.org/wp-content/uploads/2018/01 /Survey-Questions-2018-National-Study-on-Sexual-Harassment-and-Assault.pdf.

Straits, Bruce C. "Occupational Sex Segregation: The Role of Personal Ties." *Journal of Vocational Behavior* 52, no. 2 (1998): 191–207.

Stryker, Robin, Taylor Danielson, and Zachary Schrank. "Equal Employment Opportunity, Affirmative Action and the Social Construction of Merit in the United States."

Paper presentation, SASE Annual Conference, November 25, 2011, Autonomous University of Madrid.

Stuber, Jenny M. *Inside the College Gates: How Class and Culture Matter in Higher Education.* Lexington, 2011.

Sundaram, Khyati. "Why We Don't Use AI for Hiring Decisions." Applied, September 16, 2020. https://www.beapplied.com/post/why-we-dont-use-ai-for-hiring-decisions.

Supreme Court of the United States. *Students for Fair Admissions, Inc. v. President and Fellows of Harvard College.* October Term, 2022. https://www.supremecourt.gov/opinions/22pdf/20-1199_hgdj.pdf.

Sutton, Robert, and Ben Wigert. "More Harm than Good: The Truth About Performance Reviews." Gallup Workplace, May 6, 2019. https://www.gallup.com/workplace/249332/harm-good-truth-performance-reviews.aspx.

Tabrizi, Benham. "Why the Performance Review Is Dying Out Including at Companies like Apple and Microsoft." FastCompany, August 24, 2023. https://www.fastcompany.com/90943074/why-the-performance-review-is-dying-out-including-at-companies-like-apple-and-microsoft.

Tang, Abby, and Michelle Yan Huang. "Implicit Bias Trainings Are Imperfect, but We Shouldn't Stop Trying." *Business Insider*, February 17, 2021. https://www.businessinsider.com/implicit-bias-trainings-imperfect-should-we-stop-them-2020-7.

Tavory, Iddo, and Ann Swidler. "Condom Semiotics: Meaning and Condom Use in Rural Malawi." *American Sociological Review* 74, no. 2 (2009): 171–89.

Taylor, Kate. "Amid Modest Sentences, Prosecutors Bring New Charges in Admissions Scandal." *New York Times*, October 22, 2019. https://www.nytimes.com/2019/10/22/us/lori-loughlin-bribery-charge.html.

Telford, Taylor. "Deere Dials Back DEI Presence, Cuts 'Socially Motivated Messages.'" *Washington Post*, July 17, 2024. https://www.washingtonpost.com/business/2024/07/17/deere-dei-tractor-supply/.

Terrell, Josh, et al. "Gender Differences and Bias in Open Source: Pull Request Acceptance of Women Versus Men." *PeerJ Computer Science* 3 (2017): e111.

Tetlock, Philip E. "Accountability and Complexity of Thought." *Journal of Personality and Social Psychology* 45, no. 1 (1983): 74–83.

Tetlock, Philip E. "Accountability and the Perseverance of First Impressions." *Social Psychology Quarterly* 46, no. 4 (1983): 285–92.

Tetlock, Philip E. "Accountability: A Social Check on the Fundamental Attribution Error." *Social Psychology Quarterly* 48, no. 3 (1985): 227–36.

Tetlock, Philip E. "The Impact of Accountability on Judgment and Choice: Toward a Social Contingency Model." In *Advances in Experimental Social Psychology*, ed. Mark P. Zanna. Vol. 25. Academic, 1992.

Tetlock, Philip E., and Jae Il Kim. "Accountability and Judgment Processes in a Personality Prediction Task." *Journal of Personality and Social Psychology* 52, no. 4 (1987): 700–9.

Tetlock, Philip E., and Gregory Mitchell. "Implicit Bias and Accountability Systems: What Must Organizations Do to Prevent Discrimination?" *Research in Organizational Behavior* 29 (2009): 3–38.

Tetlock, Philip E., Linda Skitka, and Richard Boettger. "Social and Cognitive Strategies for Coping with Accountability: Conformity, Complexity, and Bolstering." *Journal of Personality and Social Psychology* 57, no. 4 (1989): 632–40.

Thomas, Kyla. "The Labor Market Value of Taste: An Experimental Study of Class Bias in U.S. Employment." *Sociological Science* 5, no. 24 (2018): 562–95.

Thoms, Peg. *Finding the Best and the Brightest: A Guide to Recruiting, Selecting, and Retaining Effective Leaders.* Praeger, 2005.

Tienda, Marta. "Hispanics and US Schools: Problems, Puzzles, and Possibilities." In *Frontiers in Sociology of Education,* ed. Maureen T. Hallinan. Springer Netherlands, 2011.

Tilcsik, András. "Pride and Prejudice: Employment Discrimination against Openly Gay Men in the United States." *American Journal of Sociology* 117, no. 2 (2011): 586–626.

Tilcsik, András. "Statistical Discrimination and the Rationalization of Stereotypes." *American Sociological Review* 86, no. 1 (2021): 93–122.

Tilly, Charles. *Durable Inequality.* University of California Press, 1998.

Tocqueville, Alexis de. *Democracy in America.* D. Appleton, 1899.

Tomaskovic-Devey, Donald. *Gender and Racial Inequality at Work: The Sources and Consequences of Job Segregation.* ILR Press, 1993.

Ton, Zeynep. *The Case for Good Jobs: How Great Companies Bring Dignity, Pay, and Meaning to Everyone's Work.* Harvard Business Review Press, 2023.

Ton, Zeynep. *The Good Jobs Strategy: How the Smartest Companies Invest in Employees to Lower Costs and Boost Profits.* New Harvest, 2014.

Townsend, Peter. "The Meaning of Poverty." *British Journal of Sociology* 13, no. 3 (1962): 210–27.

Trix, Frances, and Carolyn Psenka. "Exploring the Color of Glass: Letters of Recommendation for Female and Male Medical Faculty." *Discourse and Society* 14, no. 2 (2003): 191–220.

Trotter, Richard G., Susan R. Zacur and Lisa T. Stickney. "The New Age of Pay Transparency." *Business Horizons* 60, no. 4 (2017): 529–39.

Tsui, Anne S., and Barbara A. Gutek. "A Role Set Analysis of Gender Differences in Performance, Affective Relationships, and Career Success of Industrial Middle Managers." *Academy of Management Journal* 27, no. 3 (1984): 619–35.

Turco, Catherine J. "Cultural Foundations of Tokenism: Evidence from the Leveraged Buyout Industry." *American Sociological Review* 75, no. 6 (2010): 894–913.

Turco, Catherine J. "Difficult Decoupling: Employee Resistance to the Commercialization of Personal Settings." *American Journal of Sociology* 118, no. 2 (2012): 380–419.

Turner, John C. *Social Influence.* Thomson Brooks/Cole, 1991.

Turner, Margery A., Carla Herbig, Deborah Kaye, Julie Fenderson, and Diane Levy. *Discrimination Against Persons with Disabilities: Barriers at Every Step.* Urban Institute, 2005.

Uhlmann, Eric L., and Geoffrey L. Cohen. "I Think It, Therefore It's True: Effects of Self-Perceived Objectivity on Hiring Discrimination." *Organizational Behavior and Human Decision Processes* 104, no. 2 (2007): 207–23.

U.S. Bureau of Labor Statistics. "Highlights of Women's Earnings in 2023". U.S. Bureau of Labor Statistics Report, August 2024. https://www.bls.gov/opub/reports/womens-earnings/2023/home.htm.

U.S. Equal Employment Opportunity Commission. "EEOC Research Finds Unequal Opportunity in the High Tech Sector and Workforce." Press Release, September 11, 2024.

Vaitilingam, Romesh. "College Admissions." Forum for the Kent A. Clark Center for Global Markets, April 30, 2019. https://www.igmchicago.org/surveys/college-admissions.

Van Horn, Carl, Ronald Quincy, Jessica Starace, and Anton House. *A Workplace Divided: A National Survey Exploring Workers' Perceptions of Discrimination and Unfair Treatment at Work and How Government and Employers Can Help Advance More Equitable*

Workplaces. Heldrich Center for Workforce Development, June 2023. https://heldrich
.rutgers.edu/sites/default/files/2023-06/Workplace_Divided_%20Executive
_Summary.pdf.

VandeMotter, Kurt. "Hiring Is a Dating Process." CareerUSA.org, August 1, 2021. https://
www.careerusa.org/tip-of-the-week/1134-hiring-is-a-dating-process.html.

Verhaeghe, Pieter-Paul, Koen Van der Bracht, and Bart Van de Putte. "Discrimination of
Tenants with a Visual Impairment on the Housing Market: Empirical Evidence from
Correspondence Tests." *Disability Health Journal* 9, no. 2 (2016): 234–38.

Visier. "The Age of Employees Is Here." Visier Workplace Trends, 2022. Accessed August
12, 2023. https://www.visier.com/workplace-trends-2022/.

Vivek, Ramakrishnan. "Is Blind Recruitment an Effective Recruitment Method?" *International Journal of Applied Research in Business and Management* 3, no. 3 (2022):
56–72.

Wackym, Phillip Ashley, Elizabeth Hui Yee Toh, Stephanie Ann Moody-Antonio, and
Troy Donovan Woodard. "The Intersection Between Meritocracy and Diversity,
Equity, and Inclusion,"*Otolaryngoly Head Neck Surgery* 170, no. 2 (2024): 618–20.

Wagner, David G., and Joseph Berger. "Expectation States Theory: An Evolving Research
Program." In *New Directions in Contemporary Sociological Theory*, ed. Joseph Berger
and Morris Zelditch Jr. Rowman and Littlefield, 2002.

Wagner, David G., and Joseph Berger. "Gender and Interpersonal Task Behaviors: Status
Expectation Accounts." *Sociological Perspectives* 40, no. 1 (1997): 1–32.

Wagner, David G., Rebecca S. Ford, and Thomas W. Ford. "Can Gender Inequalities Be
Reduced?" *American Sociological Review* 51, no. 1 (1986): 47–61.

Wallace, Michael, Bradley R. E. Wright, and Allen Hyde. "Religious Affiliation and Hiring
Discrimination in the American South: A Field Experiment." *Social Currents* 1, no. 2
(2014): 189–207.

Wang, Shing-Yi. "Marriage Networks, Nepotism, and Labor Market Outcomes in China."
American Economic Journal: Applied Economics 5, no. 3 (2013): 91–112.

Warikoo, Natasha. "The Easiest Reform for College Admissions." *Atlantic*, January 29, 2020.
https://www.theatlantic.com/ideas/archive/2020/01/least-difficult-reform-college
-admissions/605689/.

Wax, Amy L. "Supply Side or Discrimination? Assessing the Role of Unconscious Bias."
Temple Law Review 83, no. 4 (2011): 877–902.

Weber, Max. "Class, Status, Party." In *From Max Weber: Essays in Sociology*, ed. H. H.
Gerth and C. Wright Mills. Oxford University Press, 1958.

Weichselbaumer, Doris. "Discrimination Against Female Migrants Wearing Headscarves." SSRN, September 2016. https://ssrn.com/abstract=2842960.

Weichselbaumer, Doris. "Sexual Orientation Discrimination in Hiring." *Labour Economics* 10, no. 6 (2003): 629–42.

Weigold, Michael F., and Barry R. Schlenker. "Accountability and Risk Taking." *Personality and Social Psychology Bulletin* 17, no. 1 (1991): 25–29.

Wellhub Editorial Team. "Start Talking: The Right Way to Do Salary Transparency."
Wellhub, December 20, 2022. https://wellhub.com/en-us/blog/talent-acquisition-and
-retention/salary-transparency/.

Wenner, Don. *Building an Elite Organization: The Blueprint to Scaling a High-Growth,
High-Profit Business*. Lioncrest, 2021.

Werner, Steve, and David B. Balkin. "Strategic Benefits: How Employee Benefits Can Create a Sustainable Competitive Edge." *Journal of Total Rewards* 30, no. 1 (2021): 8–22.

West, Candace, and Don H. Zimmerman. "Accounting for Doing Gender." *Gender and Society* 23, no. 1 (2009): 112–22.

West, Candace, and Don H. Zimmerman. "Doing Gender." *Gender and Society* 1, no. 2 (1987): 125–51.

Westgate, Erin C., Rachel G. Riskind, and Brian A. Nosek. "Implicit Preferences for Straight People over Lesbian Women and Gay Men Weakened from 2006 to 2013." *Collabra* 1, no. 1 (2015): 1–10.

Whillans, Ashley, and Jeff Polzer. "Applied: Using Behavioral Science to Debias Hiring." Harvard Business School, September 7, 2021. https://www.hks.harvard.edu/sites/default/files/centers/wappp/921046-PDF-ENG.pdf.

Whitehurst, Jim. "Meritocracy: The Workplace Culture That Breeds Success." Wired. Accessed June 25, 2023. https://web.archive.org/web/20160901055443/http:/www.wired.com/insights/2014/10/meritocracy.

Whitfield-Anderson, Jayla, and Christopher Wilson. "SCOTUS Affirmative Action Ruling Renews Calls to End 'Unlevel Playing Field' of Legacy Admissions." *Yahoo! News*. Last modified June 30, 2023. https://news.yahoo.com/scotus-affirmative-action-ruling-renews-calls-to-end-unlevel-playing-field-of-legacy-admissions-150545713.html.

"Why Is There a Backlash Against DEI?—and How to Fix It." Catalyst, May 21, 2024. https://www.catalyst.org/2024/05/21/dei-backlash-causes/.

Wiederkehr, Virginie, Verginie Bonnot, Silvia Krauth-Gruber, and Céline Darnon. "Belief in School Meritocracy as a System-Justifying Tool for Low Status Students." *Frontiers in Psychology* 6 (2015): Article 1053.

Wiederkehr, Virginie, Céline Darnon, Sébastien Chazal, Serge Guimond, and Delphine Martinot. "From Social Class to Self-Efficacy: Internalization of Low Social Status Pupils' School Performance." *Social Psychology of Education* 18, no. 4 (2015): 769–84.

Wiessner, Daniel. "Latest Twitter Lawsuit Says Company Targeted Women for Layoffs." Reuters, December 8, 2022. https://www.reuters.com/legal/latest-twitter-lawsuit-says-company-targeted-women-layoffs-2022-12-08/.

Wigert, Ben, and Jim Harter. "Re-Engineering Performance Management." Gallup Workplace, 2017. https://www.gallup.com/workplace/238064/re-engineering-performance-management.aspx?thank-you-report-form=1.

Wiles, Jackie. "The Real Impact on Employees of Removing Performance Ratings." Gartner, August 15, 2019. https://www.gartner.com/smarterwithgartner/corporate-hr-removing-performance-ratings-is-unlikely-to-improve-performance.

Wilkie, Dana. "Is the Annual Performance Review Dead?" SHRM, August 19, 2015. https://www.shrm.org/resourcesandtools/hr-topics/employee-relations/pages/performance-reviews-are-dead.aspx.

Williams, Joan C. "Hacking Tech's Diversity Problem." *Harvard Business Review* 92, no. 10 (2014): 94–100. https://hbr.org/2014/10/hacking-techs-diversity-problem.

Williamson, Sue, and Linda Colley. "Gender in the Australian Public Service: Doing, Undoing, Redoing or Done?" *Australian Journal of Public Administration* 77, no. 4 (2018): 583–96.

Williamson, Sue, and Linda Colley. "Research Shows 'Merit' Is Highly Subjective and Changes with Our Values." *The Conversation*, August 21, 2018. https://theconversation.com/research-shows-merit-is-highly-subjective-and-changes-with-our-values-101441.

Wilson, William J. *When Work Disappears: The World of the New Urban Poor*. Knopf, 1996.

Wilton, Leigh, Evan Apfelbaum, and Jessica Good. "Valuing Differences and Reinforcing Them: Multiculturalism Increases Race Essentialism." *Social Psychological and Personality Science* 10, no. 5 (2019): 681–89.

Woehler, Meredith L., Kristin L. Cullen-Lester, Caitlin M. Porter, and Katherine A. Frear. "Whether, How, and Why Networks Influence Men's and Women's Career Success: Review and Research Agenda." *Journal of Management* 47, no. 1 (2021): 207–36.

Wong, Kristin. "Want to Close the Pay Gap? Pay Transparency Will Help." *New York Times*, January 20, 2019. https://www.nytimes.com/2019/01/20/smarter-living/pay-wage-gap-salary-secrecy-transparency.html.

Wooldridge, Adrian. *The Aristocracy of Talent: How Meritocracy Made the Modern World.* Skyhorse, 2021.

Workday Staff Writers. "Best Practices: Optimizing Analytics for Diversity, Equity, Inclusion, and Belonging" (blog post). Workday, January 14, 2022. https://blog.workday.com/en-us/best-practices-optimizing-analytics-diversity-equity-inclusion-belonging.html.

Workopolis. "How GE Replaced a 40-Year-Old Performance Review System." Workopolis, December 22, 2016. Accessed May 6, 2021. https://web.archive.org/web/20201112013520/https://hiring.workopolis.com/article/ge-replaced-40-year-old-performance-review-system/.

WorldatWork and Compensation Advisory Partners. *Incentive Pay Practices: Government Organizations*, July 2021. https://worldatwork.org/media/CDN/dist/CDN2/documents/pdf/resources/research/2021_Incentive%20Pay%20Practices-Government.pdf.

WorldatWork and Compensation Advisory Partners. *Incentive Pay Practices: Nonprofit Organizations*, July 2021. https://worldatwork.org/media/CDN/dist/CDN2/documents/pdf/resources/research/2021_Incentive%20Pay%20Practices-Nonprofit.pdf.

WorldatWork and Compensation Advisory Partners. *Incentive Pay Practices: Privately Held Companies*, July 2021. https://worldatwork.org/media/CDN/dist/CDN2/documents/pdf/resources/research/2021_Incentive%20Pay%20Practices-Privately%20Held.pdf.

WorldatWork and Compensation Advisory Partners. *Incentive Pay Practices: Publicly Traded Companies*, July 2021. https://worldatwork.org/media/CDN/dist/CDN2/documents/pdf/resources/research/2021_Incentive%20Pay%20Practices-Publicly%20Traded.pdf.

Wren, Kathy. "Q&A: Stuart Schmill on MIT's Decision to Reinstate the SAT/ACT Requirement." Interview, *MIT News*, March 28, 2022. https://news.mit.edu/2022/stuart-schmill-sat-act-requirement-0328.

Wright, Bradley R. E., Michael Wallace, John Bailey, and Allen Hyde. "Religious Affiliation and Hiring Discrimination in New England: A Field Experiment." *Research in Social Stratification and Mobility* 34 (2013): 111–26.

Wynn, Alison T., and Shelley J. Correll. "Gendered Perceptions of Cultural and Skill Alignment in Technology Companies." *Social Sciences* 6, no. 2 (2017): 45.

Yakubovich, Valery. "Weak Ties, Information, and Influence: How Workers Find Jobs in a Local Russian Labor Market." *American Sociological Review* 70, no. 3 (2005): 408–21.

Yang, Yang, Nitesh V. Chawla, and Brian Uzzi. "A Network's Gender Composition and Communication Pattern Predict Women's Leadership Success." *Proceedings of the National Academy of Sciences* 116, no. 6 (2019): 2033–38.

Yoshino, Kenji. "The Pressure to Cover." *New York Times Magazine*, January 15, 2006.

Yoshino, Kenji, and David Glasgow. "What SCOTUS's Affirmative Action Decision Means for Corporate DEI." *Harvard Business Review*, July 12, 2023. https://hbr.org/2023/07/what-scotuss-affirmative-action-decision-means-for-corporate-dei.

Yoshino, Kenji, and Christie Smith. *Uncovering Talent: A New Model of Inclusion.* Deloitte University, 2019. https://www2.deloitte.com/content/dam/Deloitte/us/Documents/about-deloitte/us-about-deloitte-uncovering-talent-a-new-model-of-inclusion.pdf.

Young, Michael. "Down with Meritocracy." *The Guardian*, June 28, 2001. https://www.theguardian.com/politics/2001/jun/29/comment.

Young, Michael. *The Rise of the Meritocracy.* Transaction, 1994.

Zavodny, Madeline. "Is There a 'Marriage Premium' for Gay Men?" *Review of Economics of the Household* 6, no. 4 (2008): 369–89.

Zewe, Adam. "AI That Can Learn the Patterns of Human Language." *MIT News*, August 30, 2022.

Zewe, Adam. "Explained: How to Tell If Artificial Intelligence Is Working the Way We Want It To." *MIT News*, July 22, 2022.

Zhang, Haiyan, Sheri Feinzi, Louise Raisbec, et al. "The Role of AI in Mitigating Bias to Enhance Diversity and Inclusion." IBM Smarter Workforce Institute, March 2019. https://www.ibm.com/downloads/cas/2DZELQ4O.

Zhang, Xiaoquan, and Feng Zhu. "Group Size and Incentives to Contribute: A Natural Experiment at Chinese Wikipedia." *American Economic Review* 101, no. 4 (2011): 1601–15.

Zhao, Kang, Xinyi Xu, Hanfei Zhu, and Qin Xu. "Compensatory Belief in Health Behavior Management: A Concept Analysis." *Frontiers in Psychology* 12 (2021): 705991.

Zheng, Lily. "How to Effectively—and Legally—Use Racial Data for DEI." *Harvard Business Review*, July 24, 2023. https://hbr.org/2023/07/how-to-effectively-and-legally-use-racial-data-for-dei.

Zhou, Xiang. "Equalization or Selection? Reassessing the 'Meritocratic Power' of a College Degree in Intergenerational Income Mobility." *American Sociological Review* 84, no. 3 (2019): 459–85.

INDEX

Page numbers in *italics* refer to figures or tables.

ABOUT THE AUTHOR

Emilio J. Castilla is the *NTU Professor of Management* and a Professor of Work and Organization Studies at the MIT Sloan School of Management, where he is also co-director of the MIT Institute for Work and Employment Research (IWER). Castilla's research focuses on how social and organizational factors shape key employment processes and outcomes over time, with particular emphasis on improving talent management practices such as recruitment, screening and hiring, pay and rewards, training and development, and career progression within organizations. His work has explored the role of merit and merit-based work practices in shaping employees' careers, as well as the impact of biases and social factors on organizational practices and outcomes.

Castilla joined MIT in 2005, after being a faculty member in the Management Department at the Wharton School, University of Pennsylvania. He was head of the MIT Sloan's Work and Organization Studies Group. He is a member of the Economic Sociology group at Sloan, a research fellow at the Center for Human Resources at Wharton, and the elected chair of the Organization and Management Theory (OMT) Division of the Academy of Management—a division that advances scholarship on organizations, organizing, and management, while fostering an inclusive community of researchers, educators, and practitioners. Castilla received his PhD in Sociology from Stanford University.

Castilla's research has been widely published in leading academic journals, including *Administrative Science Quarterly, Management Science, Organization*

Science, ILR Review, American Journal of Sociology, and *American Sociological Review.* He received the W. Richard Scott Award for Distinguished Scholarship in 2001, the Outstanding Publication in Organizational Behavior Award in 2011, and the *MIT Sloan Management Review*'s Richard Beckhard Memorial Prize in 2017. He has written a book on longitudinal methods in social science research, titled *Dynamic Analysis in the Social Sciences* (published by Academic Press/Elsevier). Castilla has also served on the editorial boards of the *American Journal of Sociology, American Sociological Review, Work and Occupations,* and *Administrative Science Quarterly,* and was associate editor of *Management Science* and the *ILR Review.*

In addition to his academic work, Castilla has taught in various degree programs at MIT Sloan, the Wharton School, and several other international universities and institutions. He regularly teaches executive education courses and professional workshops on topics relating to leading people at work and improving talent management in organizations and businesses. His teaching interests include strategic human resource management, strategies for people analytics, leading effective organizations, and building successful careers and organizations.

GPSR Authorized Representative: Easy Access System Europe, Mustamäe tee 50, 10621 Tallinn, Estonia, gpsr.requests@easproject.com